MONOCHROME

ILLUSIONS

II

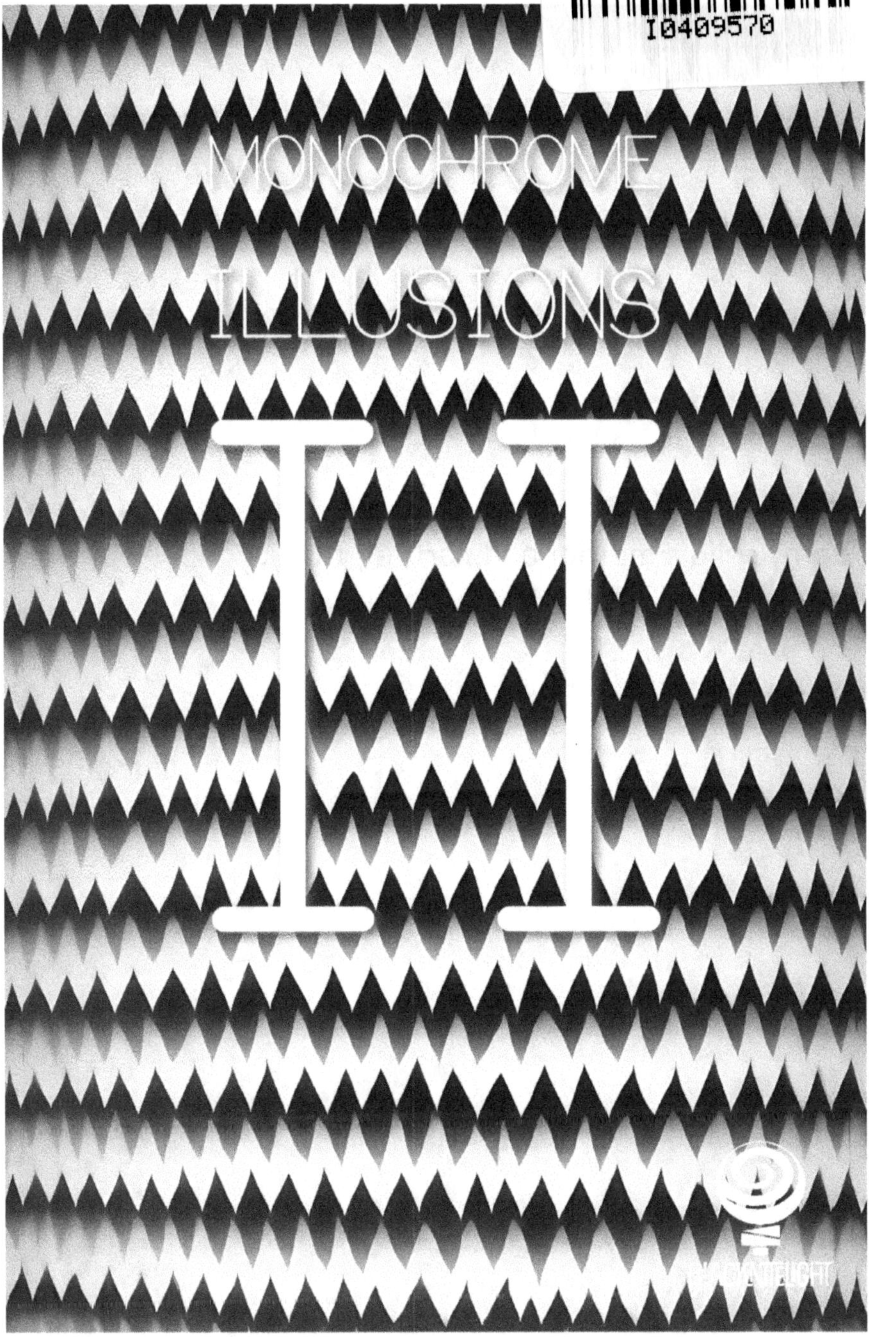

For my child's mother and partner, thank you for putting up with me and ALL this. I love you.

In the realm of perception, where reality and imagination converge, lies a captivating journey through the enigmatic world of black-and-white illusions. These mesmerizing phenomena challenge the foundation of our visual understanding, inviting us to question the nature of reality. As we embark on this exploration, we'll unveil the intricate interplay of light and shadow, contrast and context, and the astonishing ways our minds can be deceived by the simplest grayscale arrangements.

In the following pages, we will delve deep into the captivating realm of visual trickery, where the ordinary transforms into the extraordinary, and the familiar morphs into the fantastical. Our eyes, the windows to our souls, serve as witnesses and accomplices to the captivating dance between perception and deception. Each chapter will unravel the science and artistry behind these mind-bending spectacles, from the peculiar Hermann Grid to the confounding Checker Shadow illusion and so many more.

As we journey through the corridors of perception, we'll encounter the fascinating phenomenon of simultaneous contrast, where neighboring shades conspire to reshape our understanding of reality. We'll decipher the riddle of the Café Wall illusion, where lines and edges conspire to create a world that defies gravity and reason. And with each revelation, we'll realize that the line between reality and illusion is more tenuous than we ever imagined.

But these illusions are more than mere trickery. They offer a glimpse into the inner workings of our cognitive machinery, exposing the subtle nuances of how our brains interpret the world around us. Through the lens of black-and-white illusions, we'll explore the intricate dance of neural connections, the delicate balance of context and expectation, and the profound ways in which culture and experience shape our perception.

With every page turned, we'll venture deeper into the heart of these visual mysteries, guided by curiosity and the relentless pursuit of understanding. Together, we'll unravel the threads that connect art and science, psychology and aesthetics, and the timeless dance between light and darkness.

So, dear viewer, prepare to be astonished, perplexed, and captivated. Let us journey through the shadows, where lines bend, squares morph, and reality shatters in the astonishing world of black-and-white illusions.

-Ross Jaynes
BlackNiteLight 2023

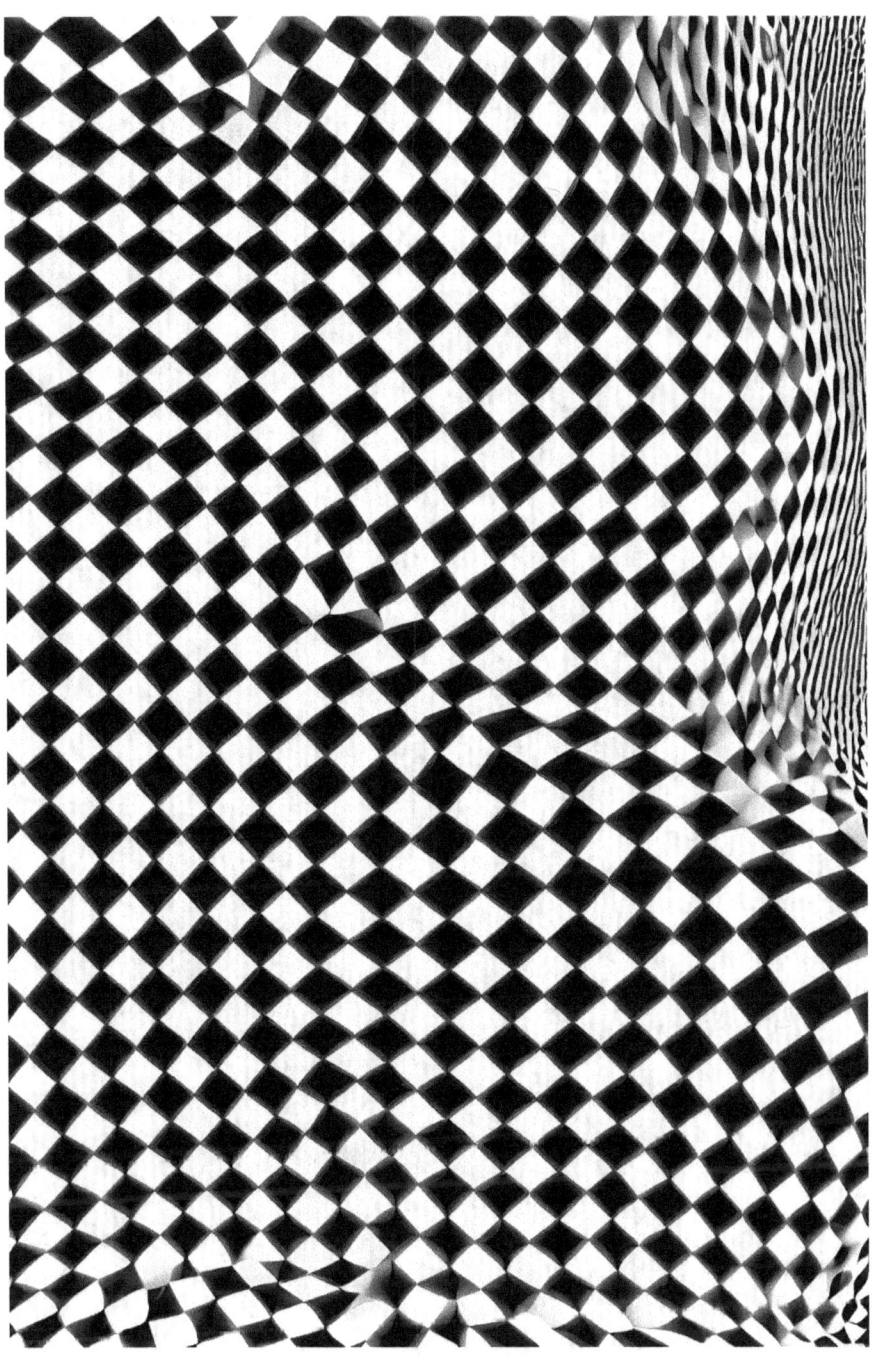

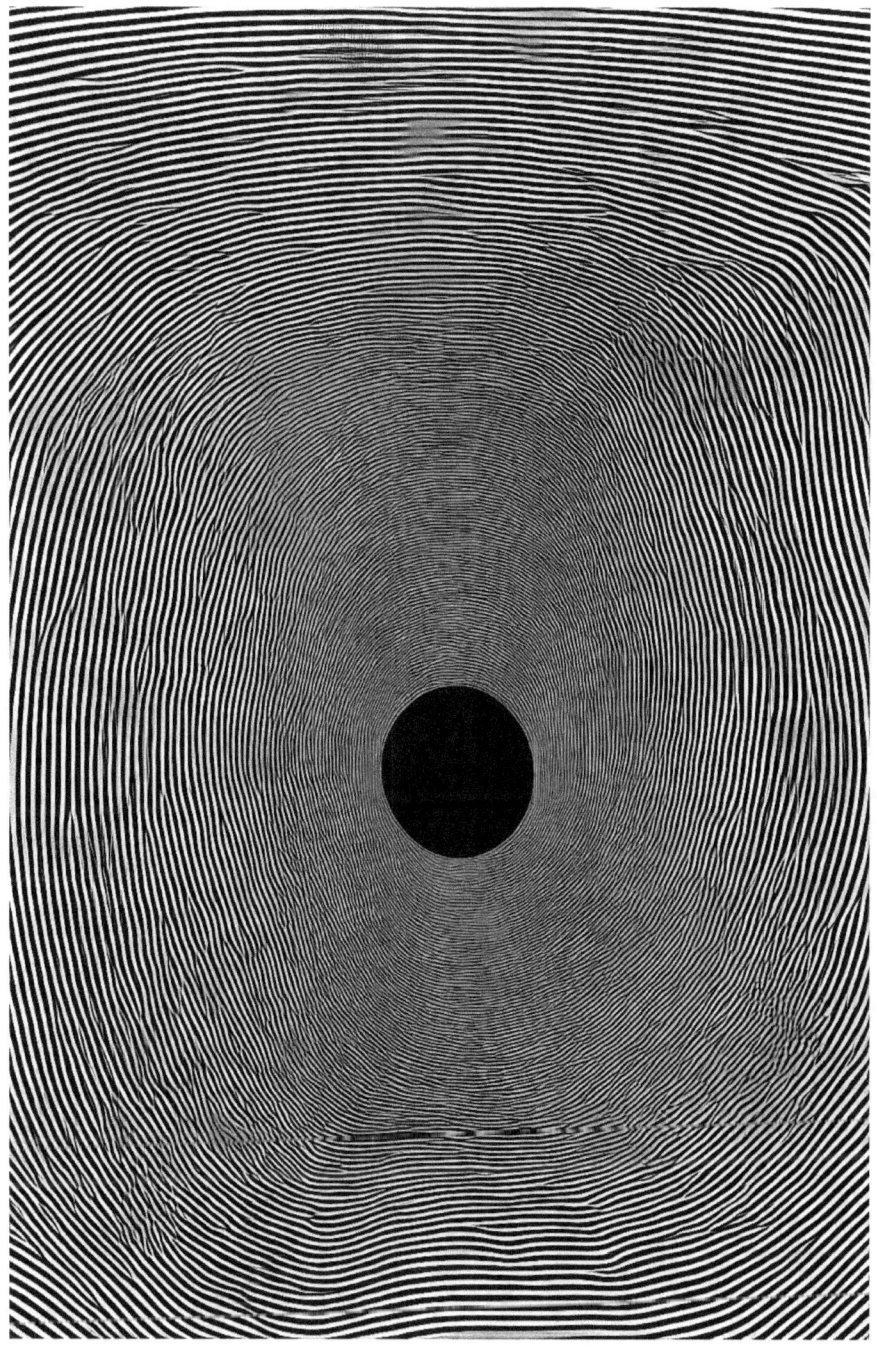

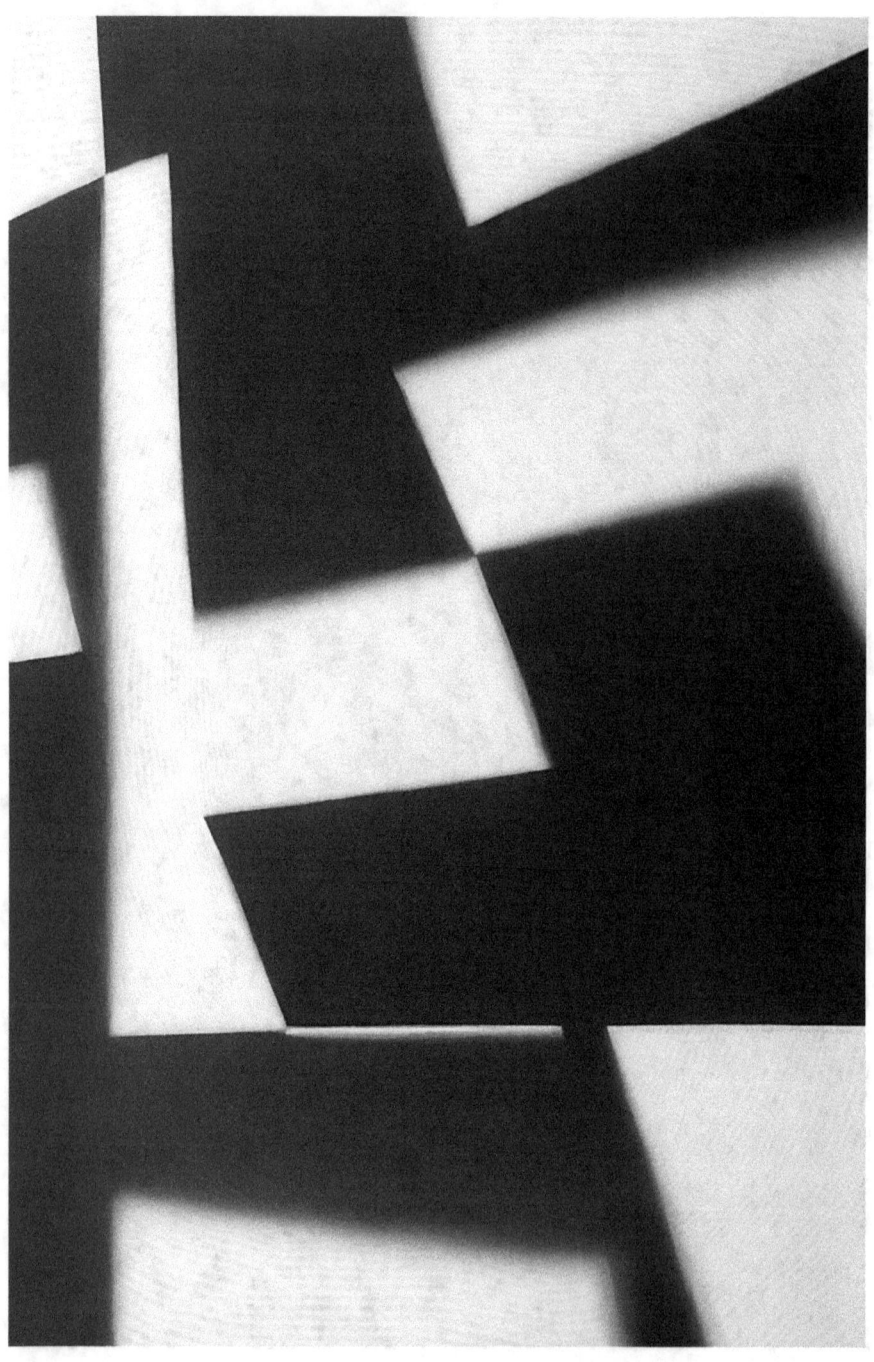

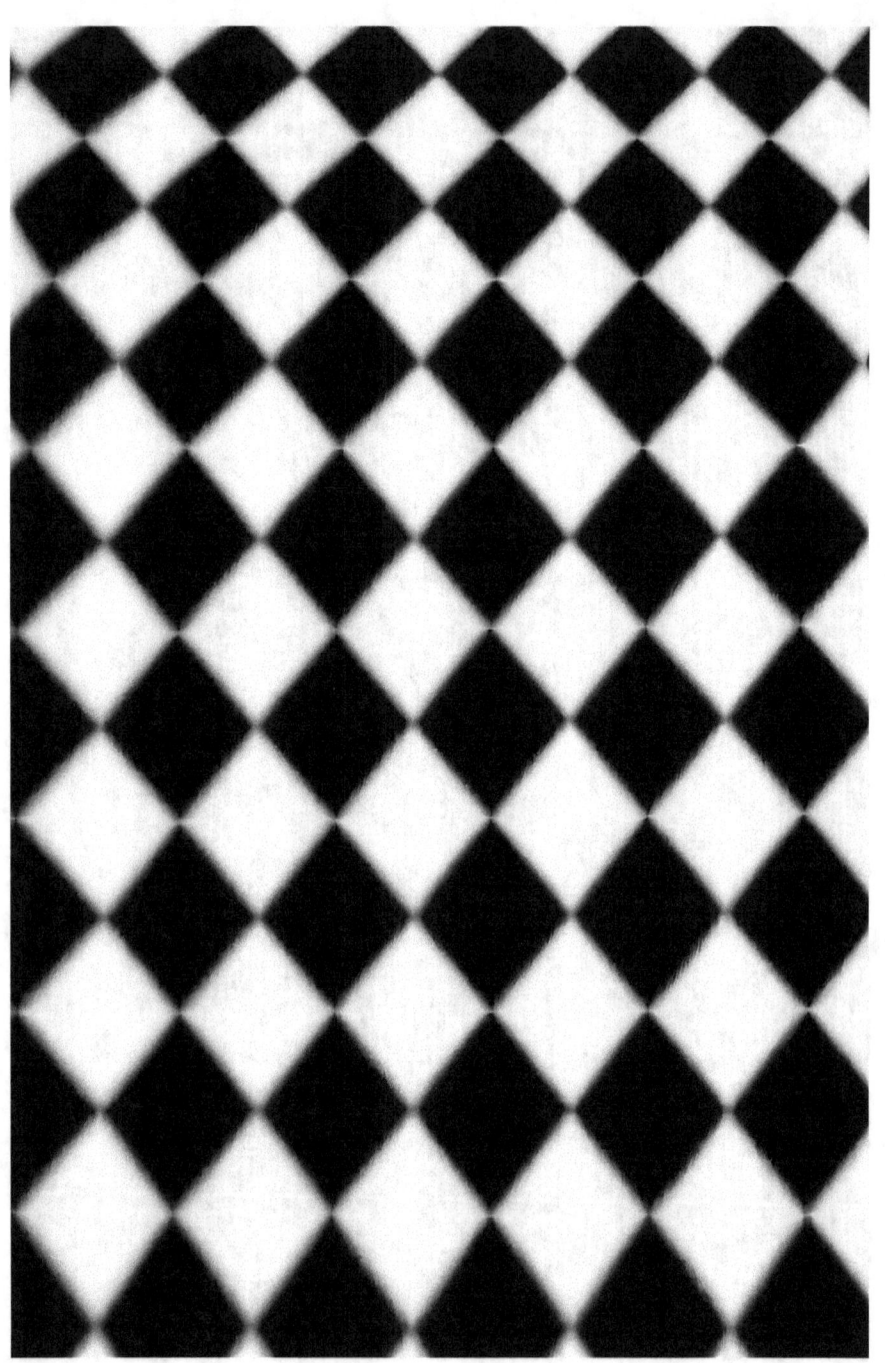

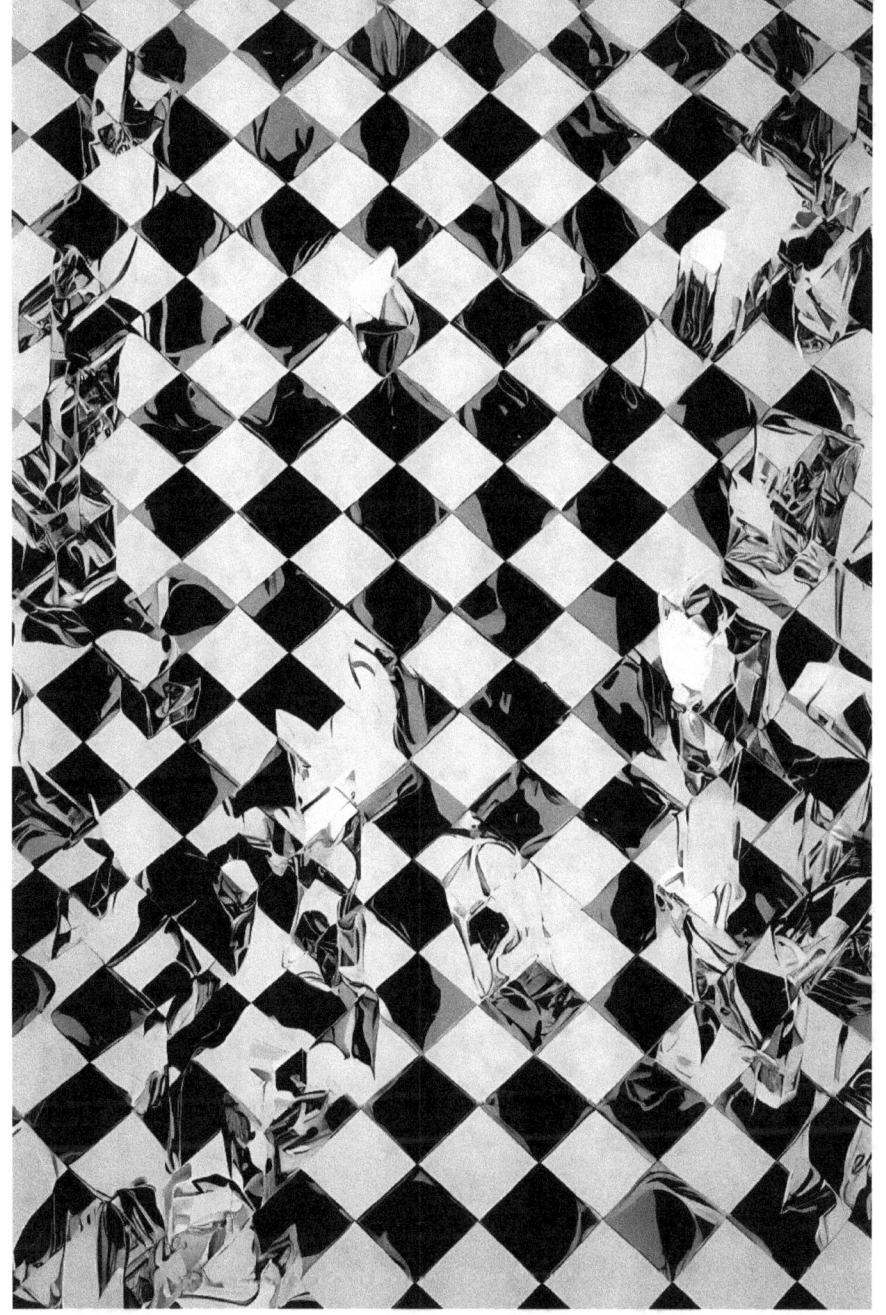

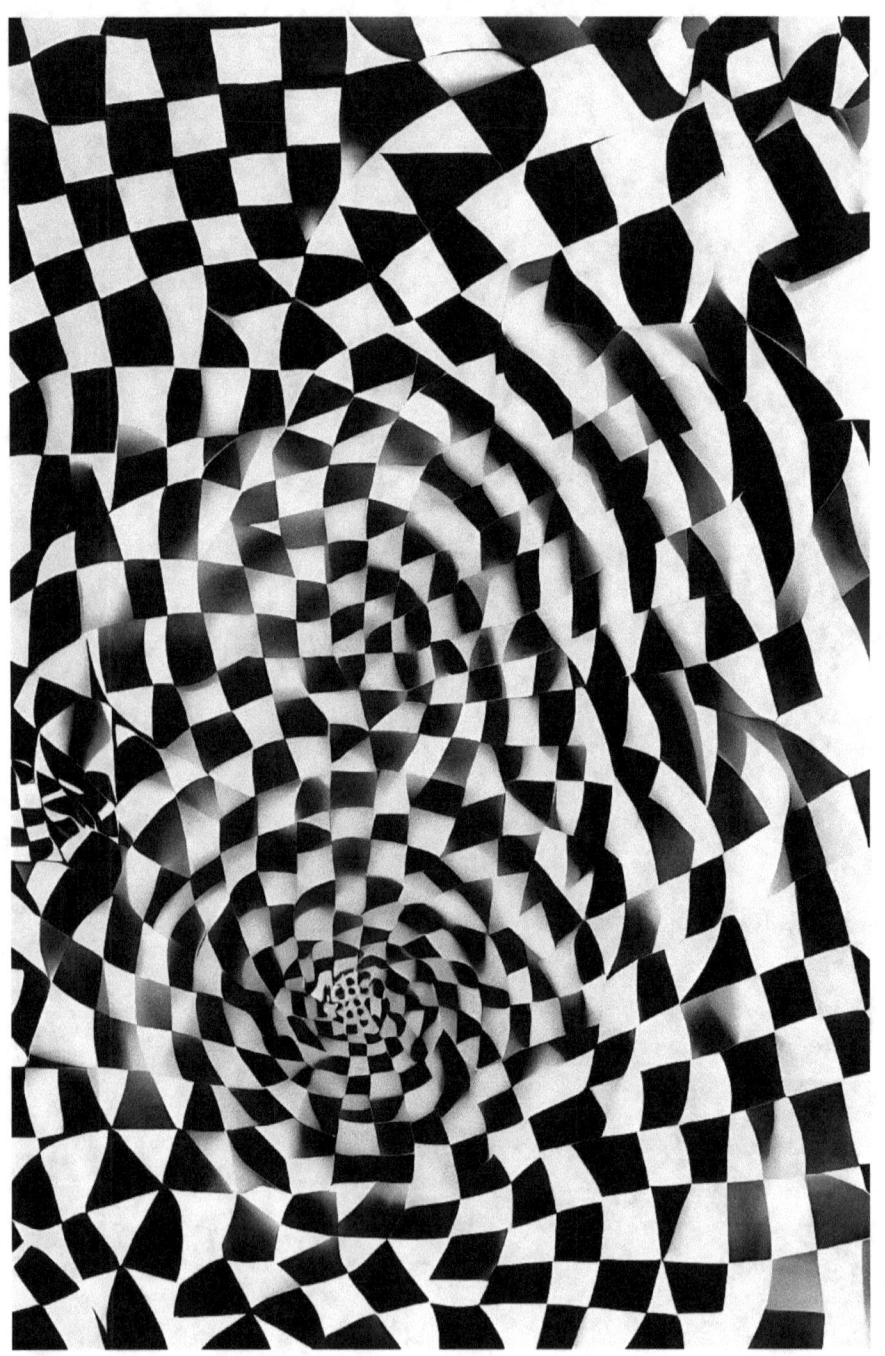

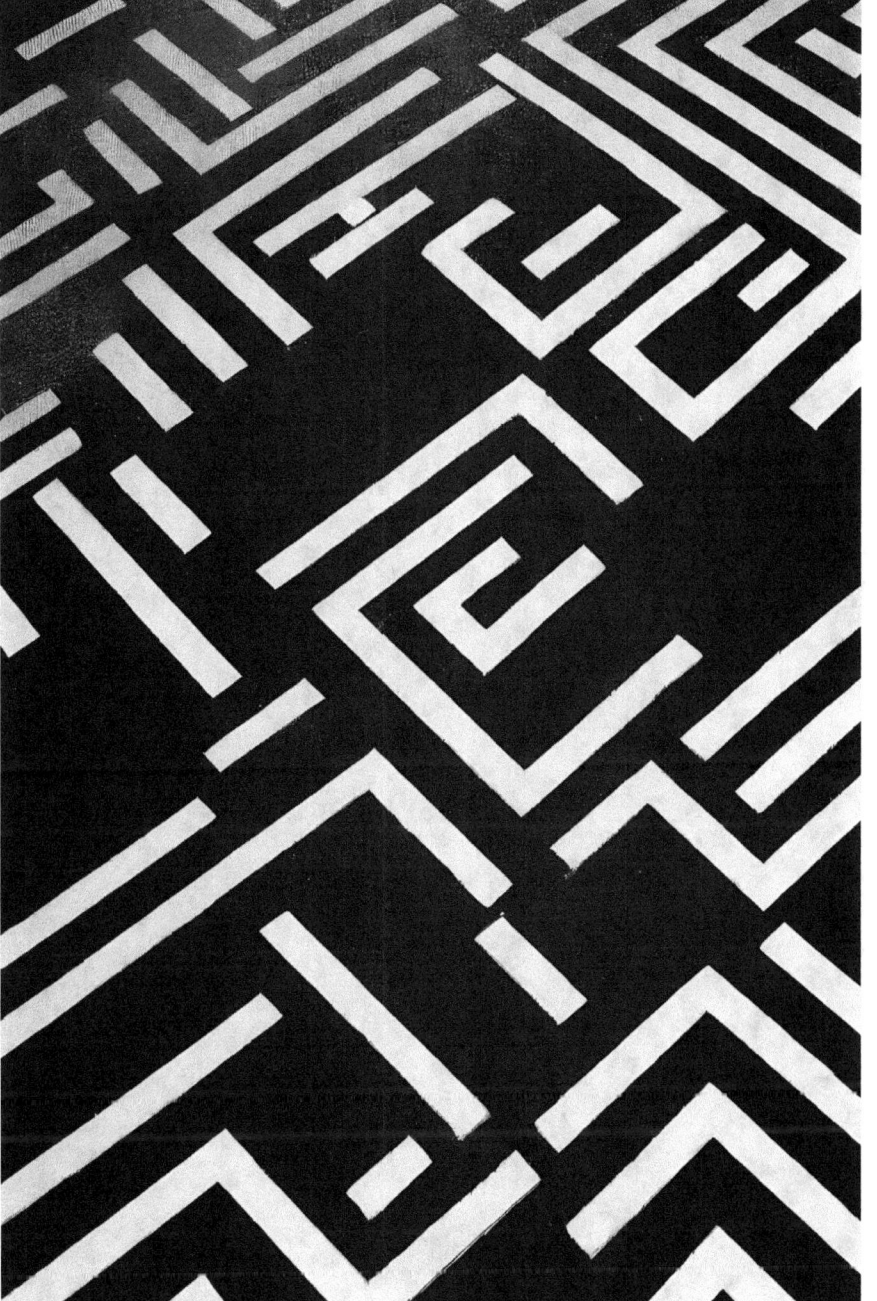

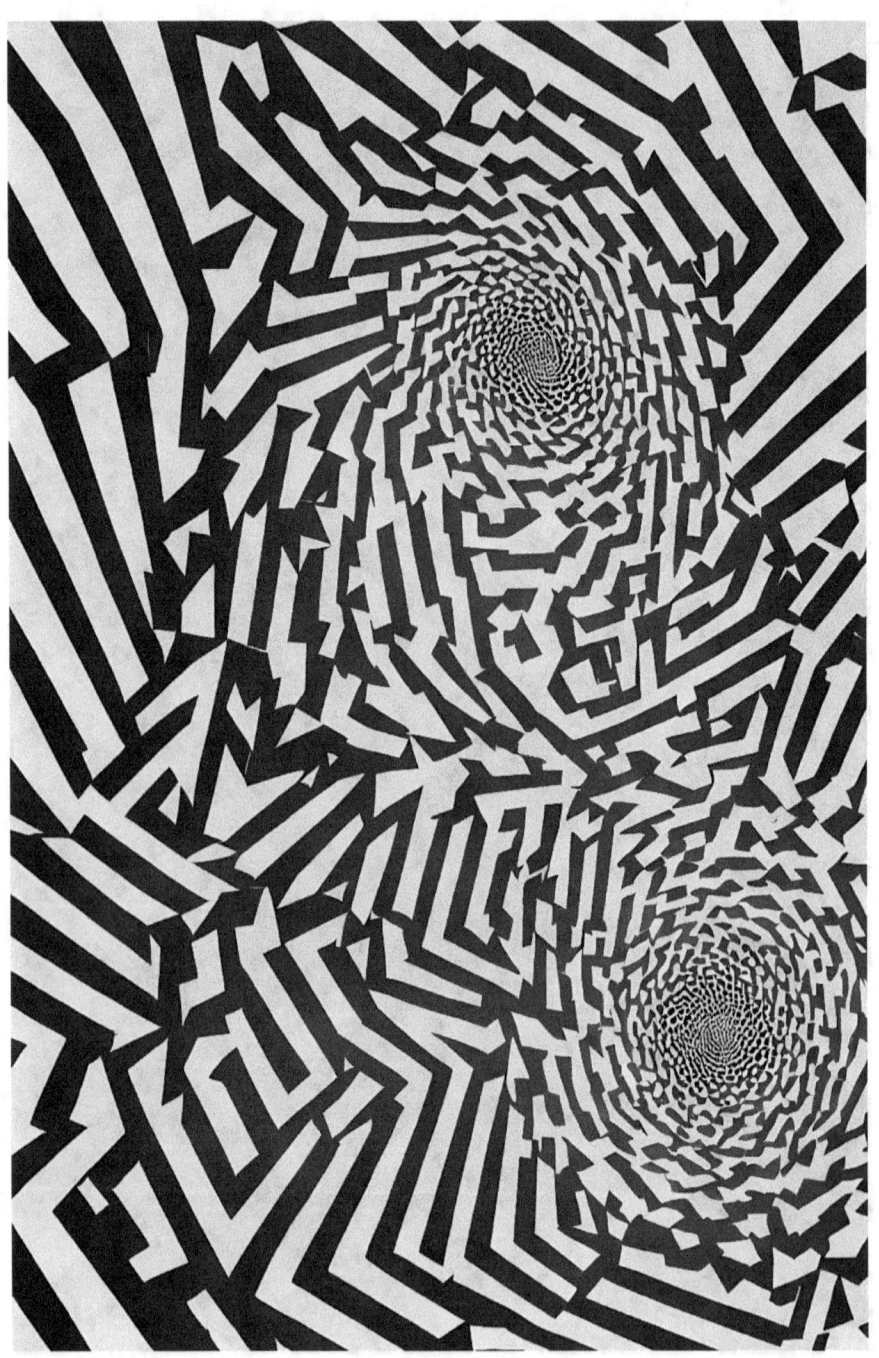

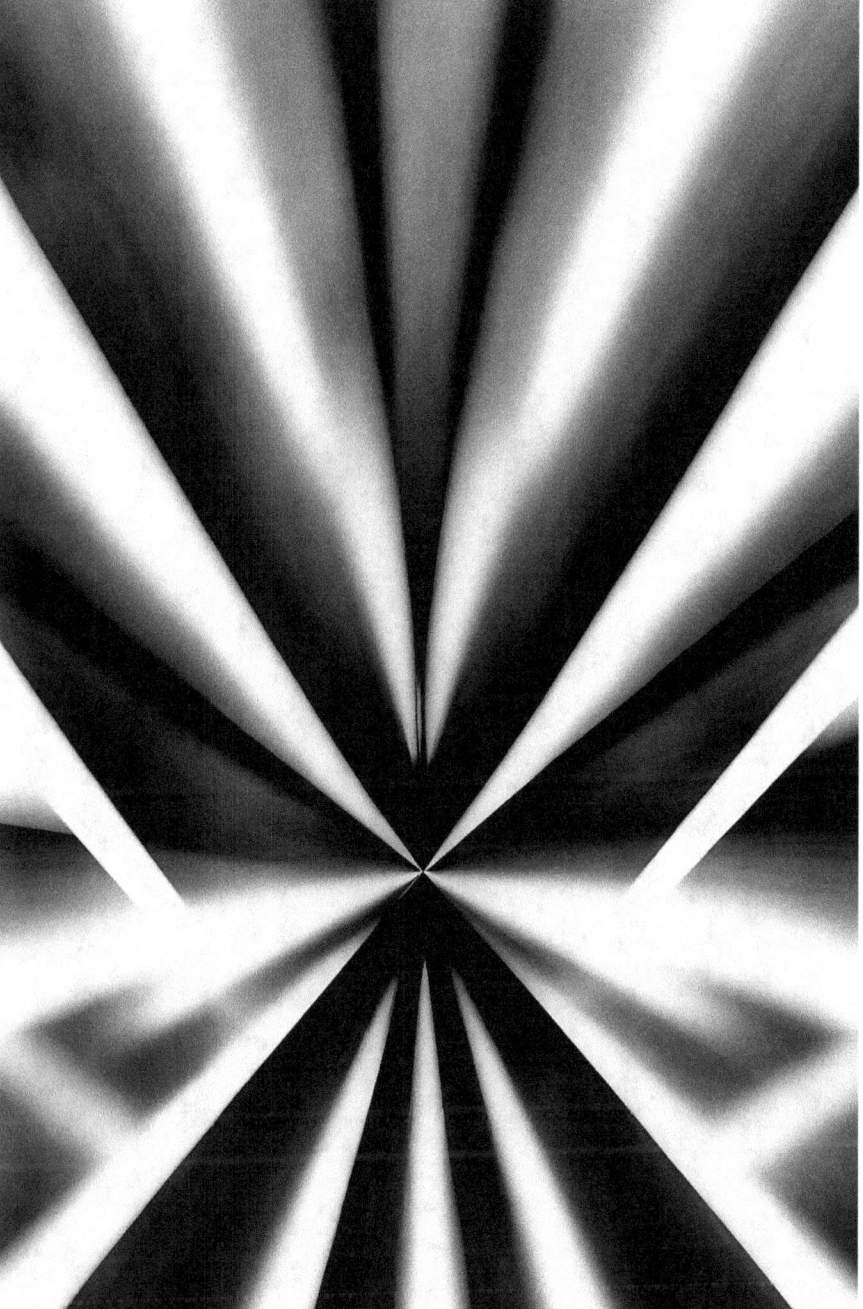

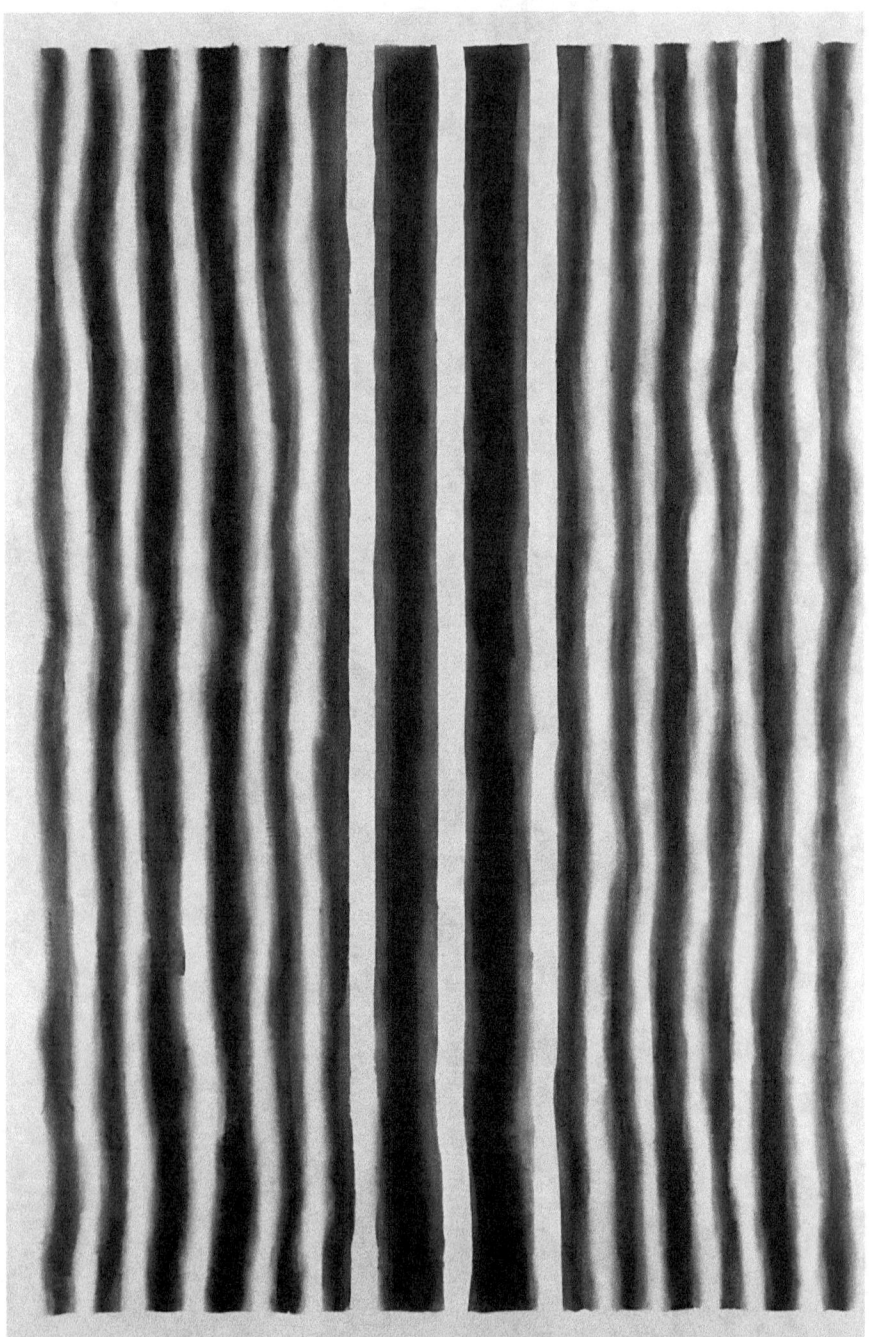

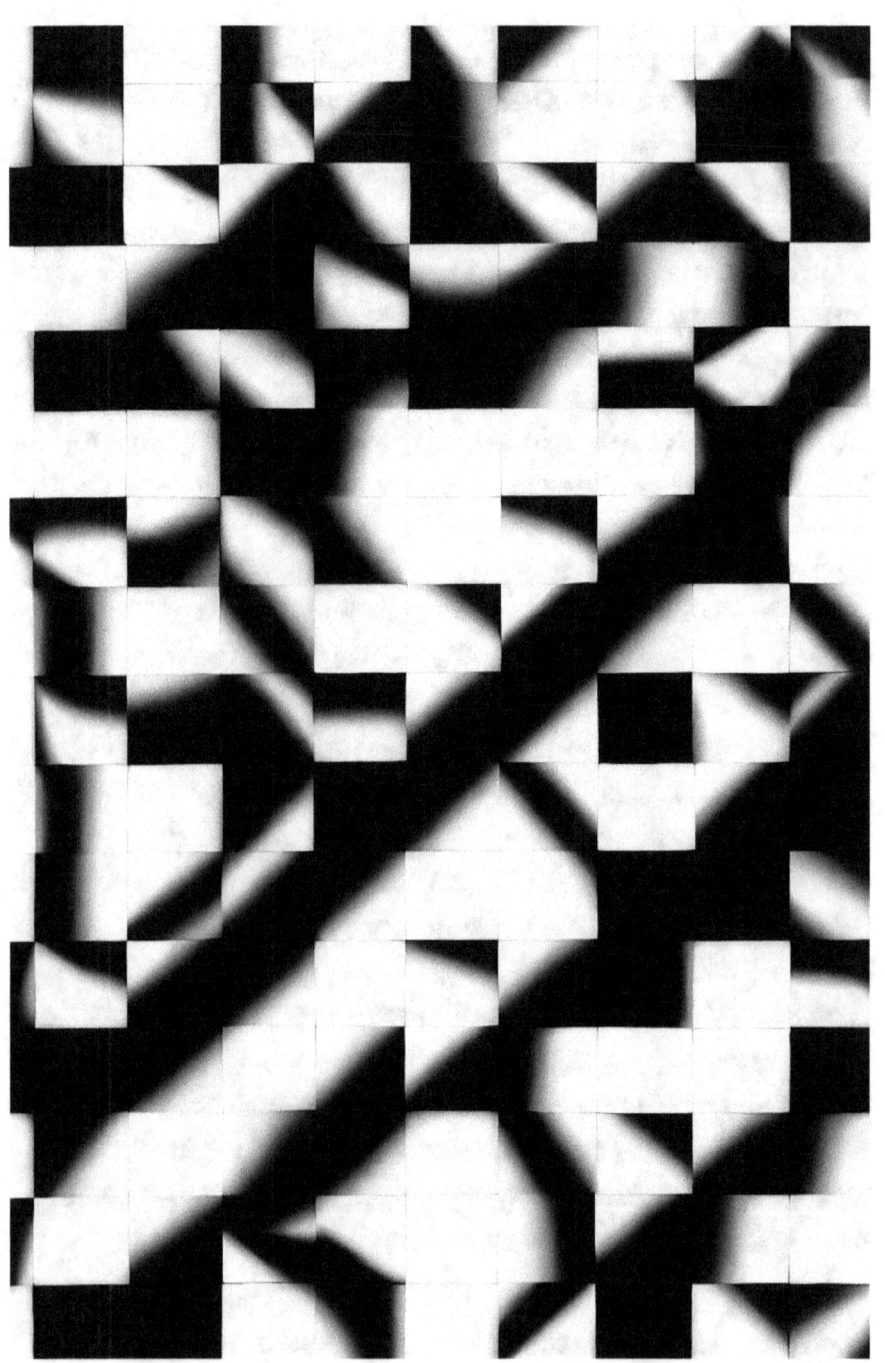

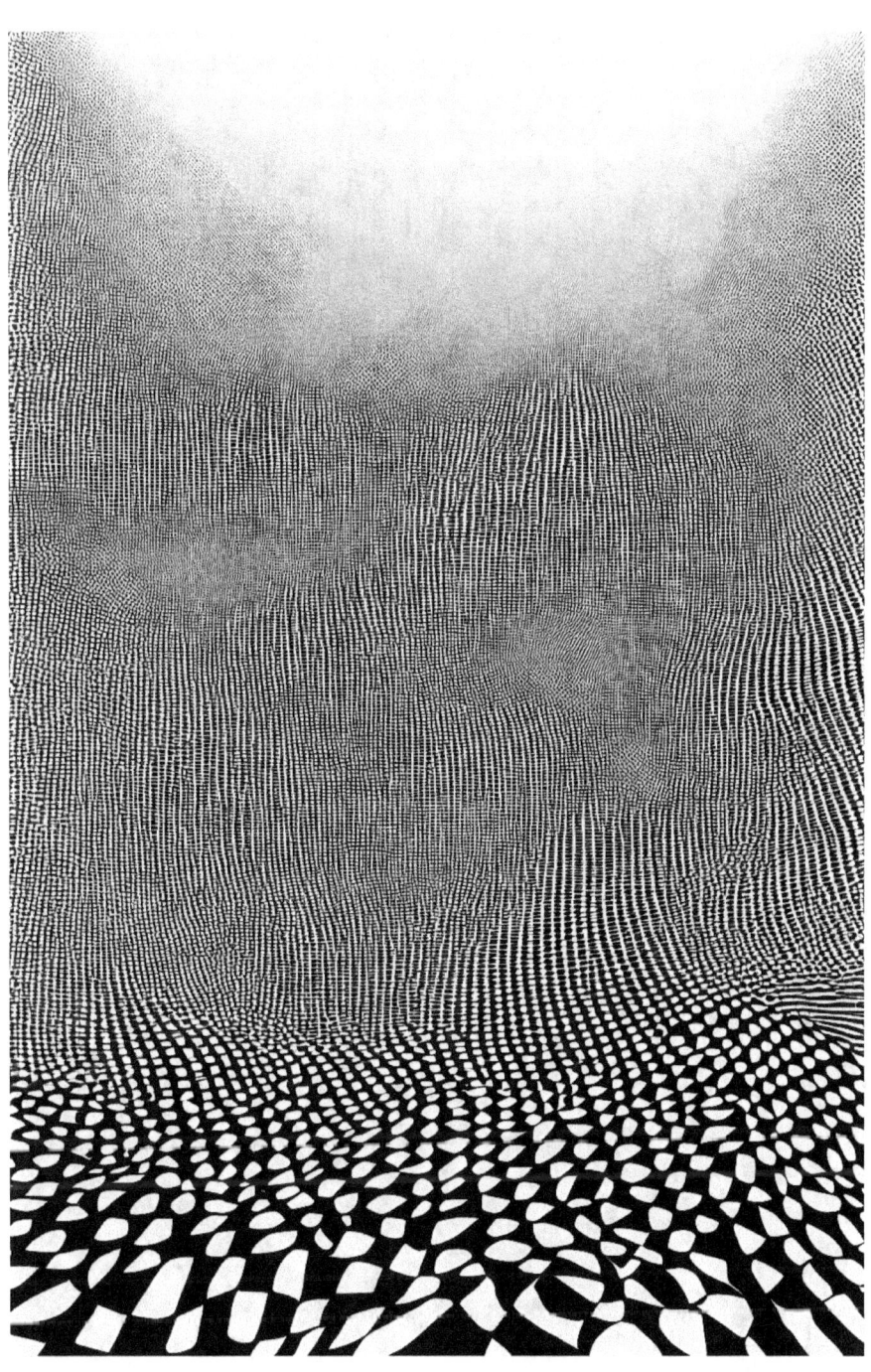

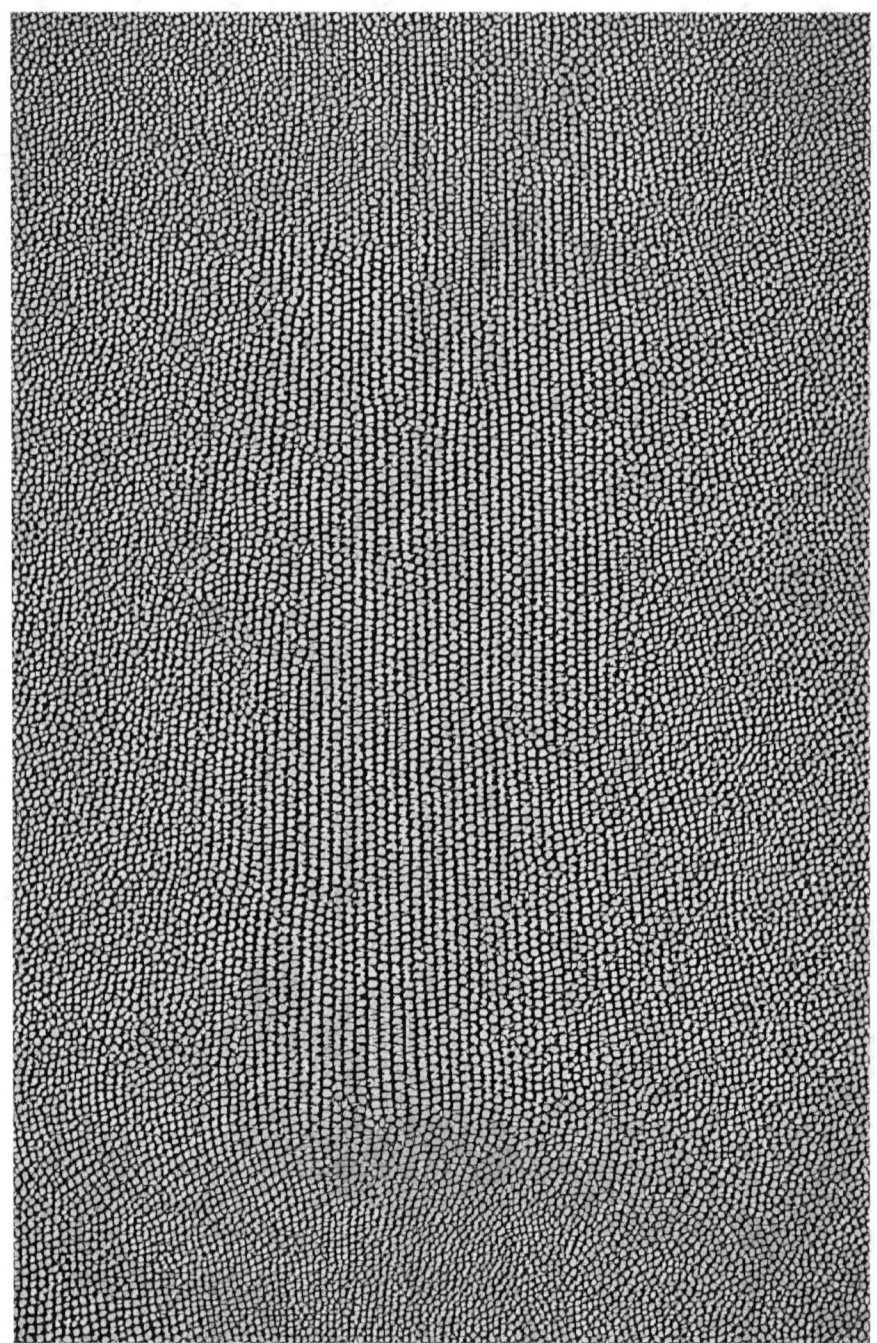

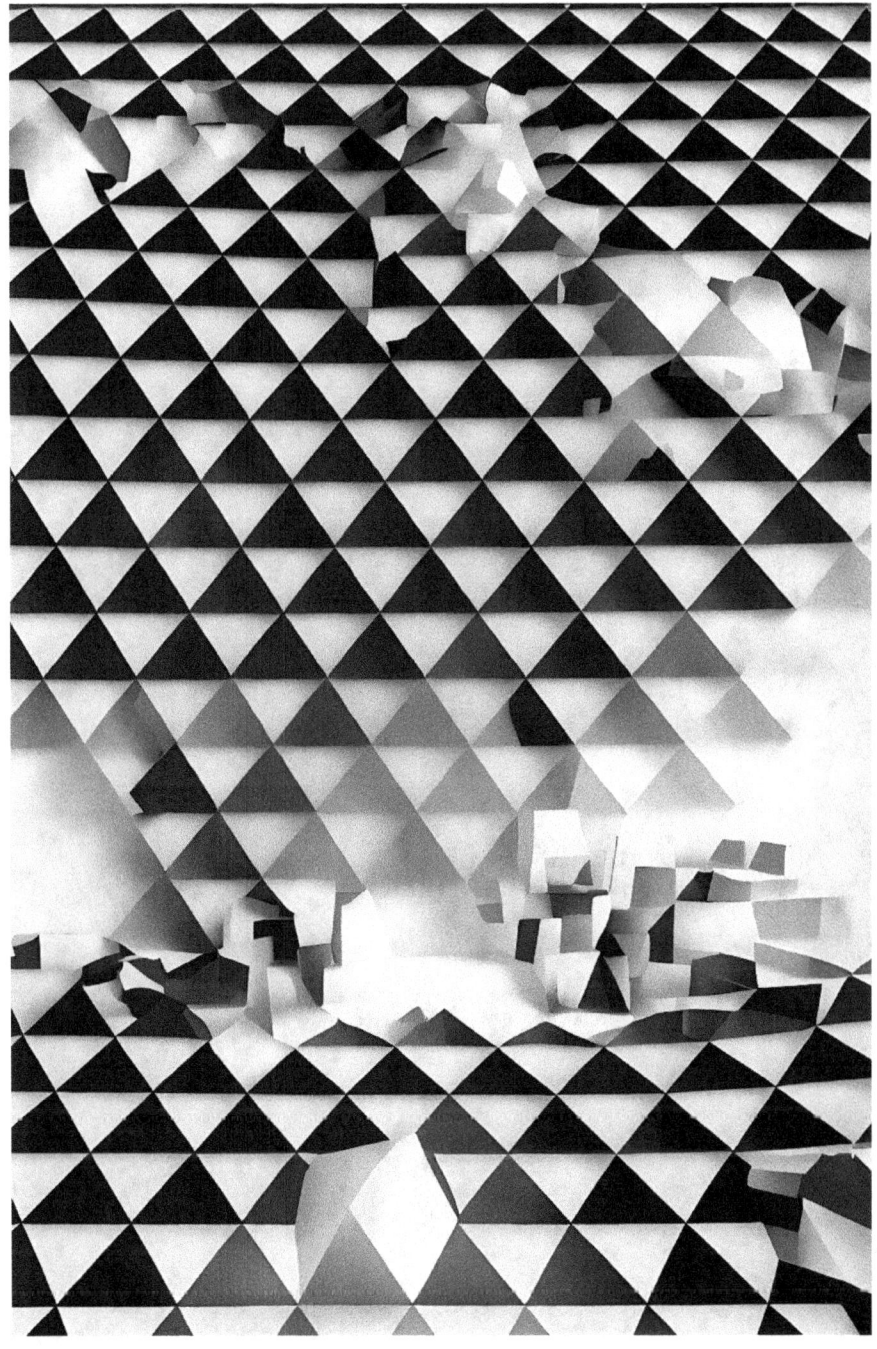

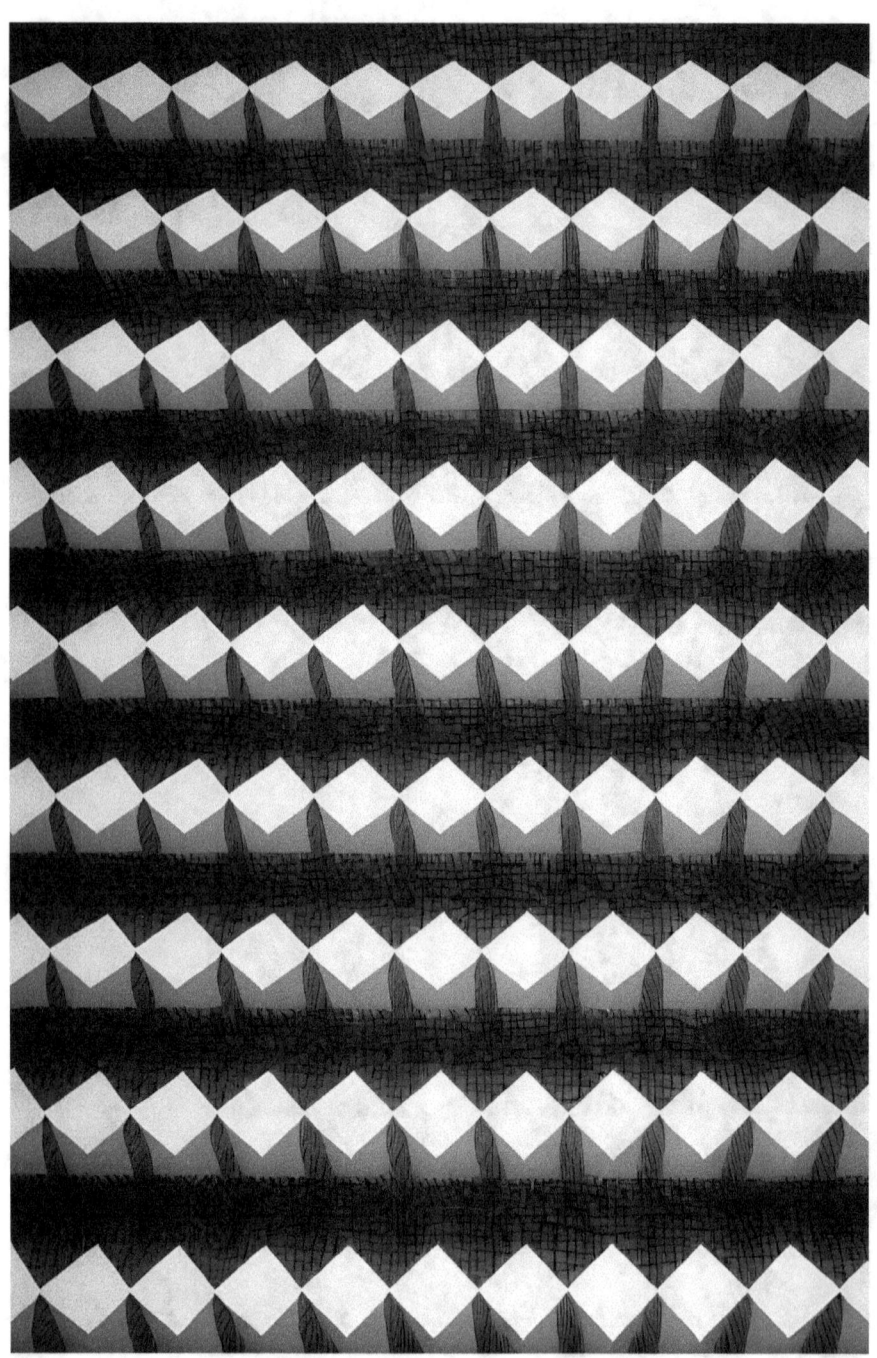

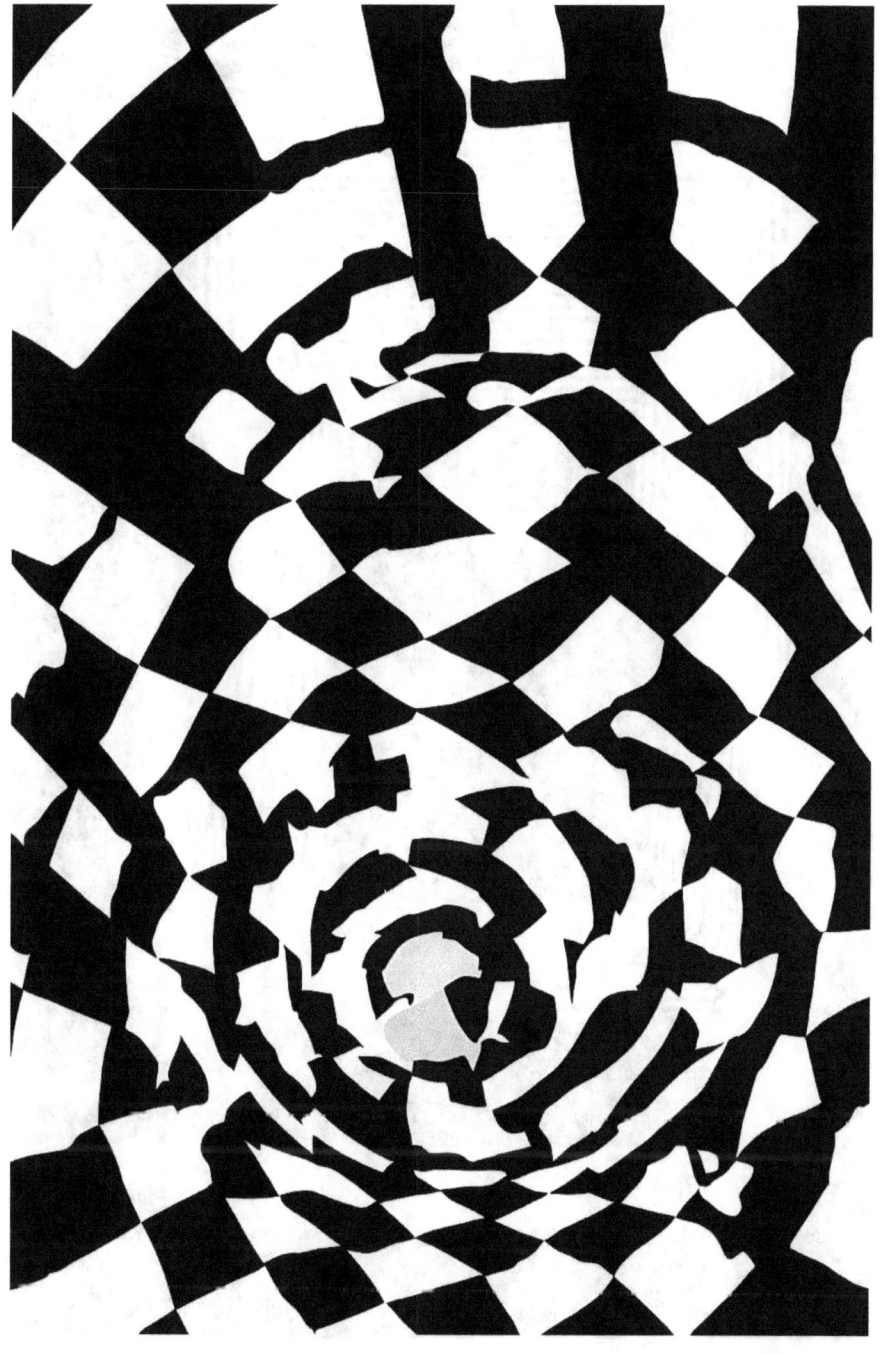

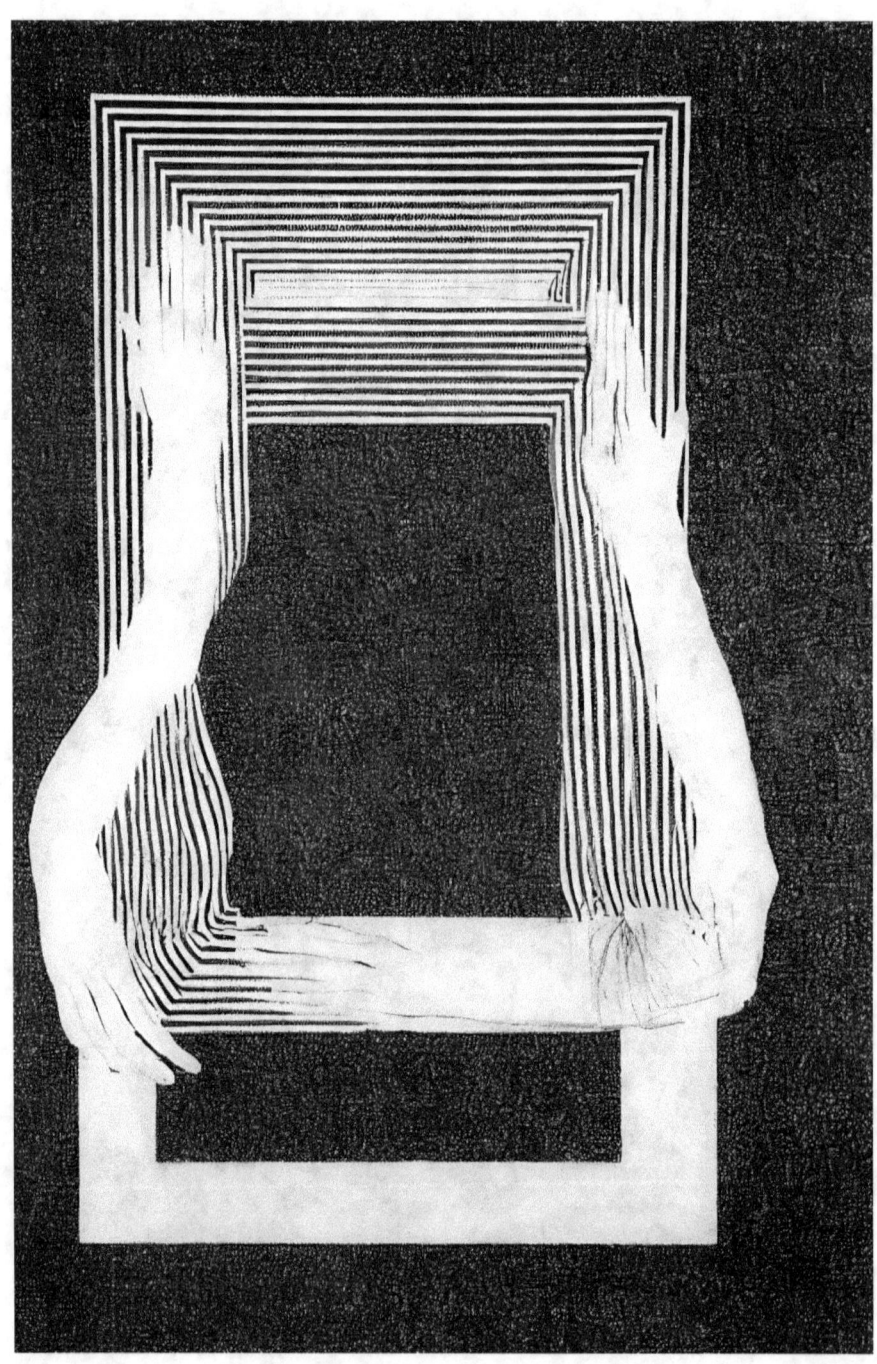

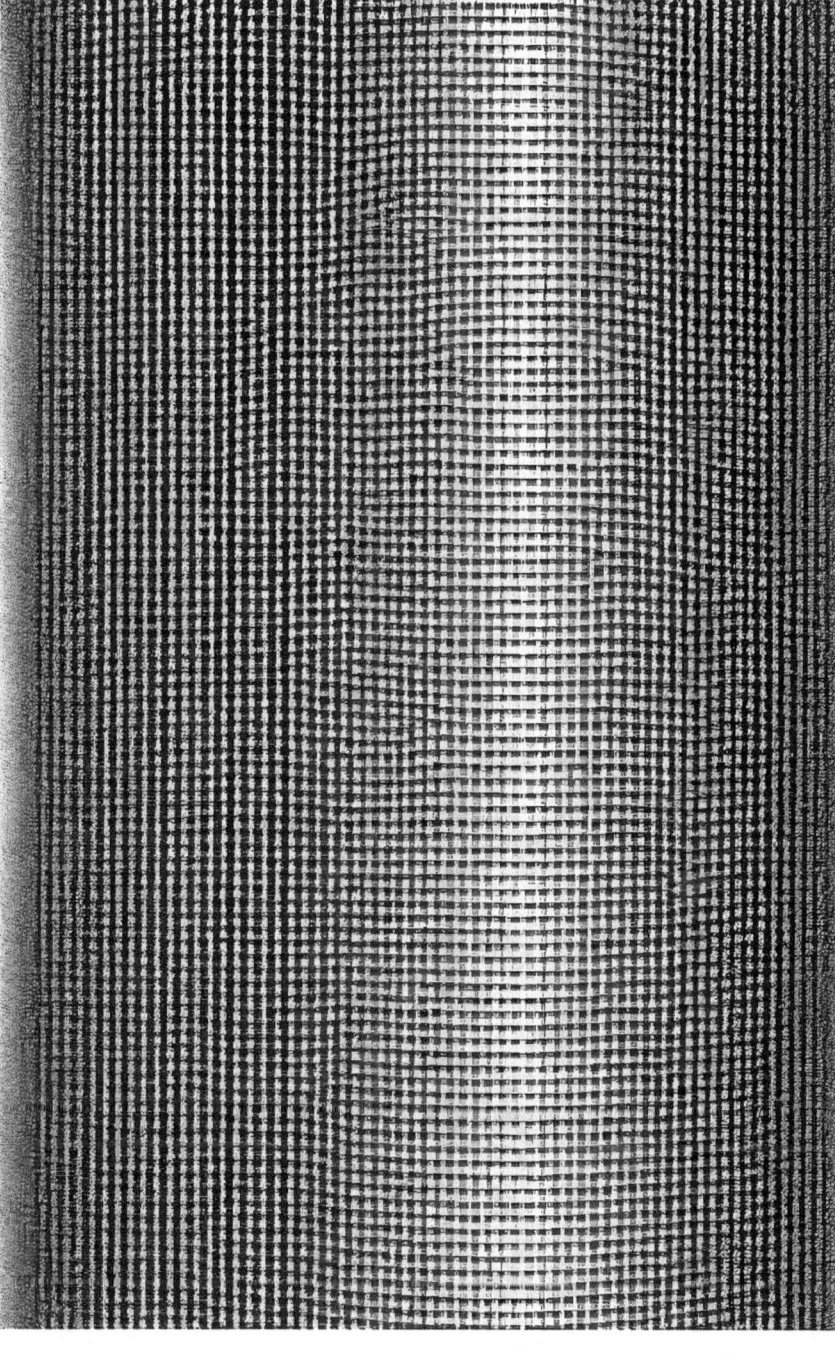

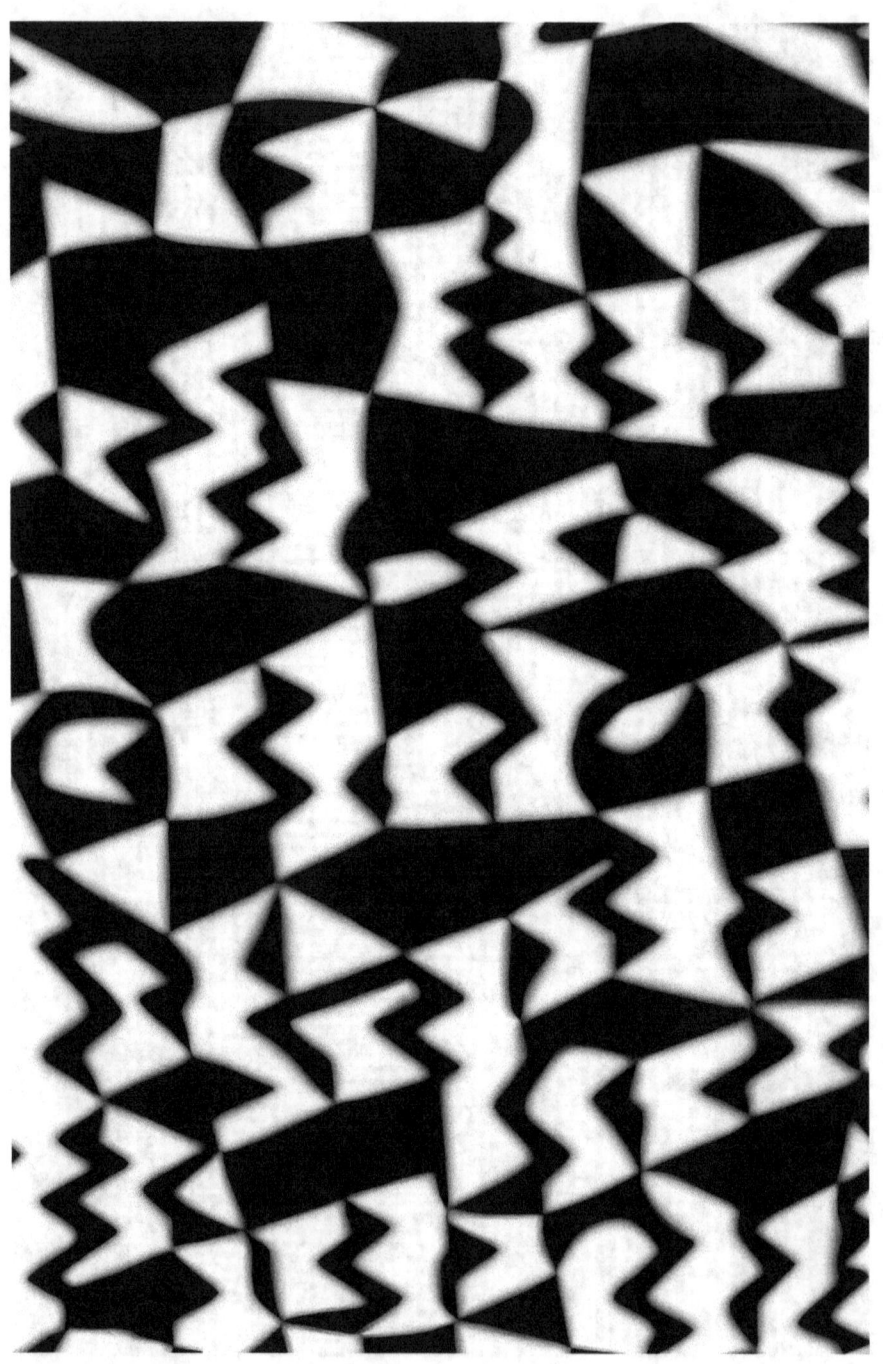

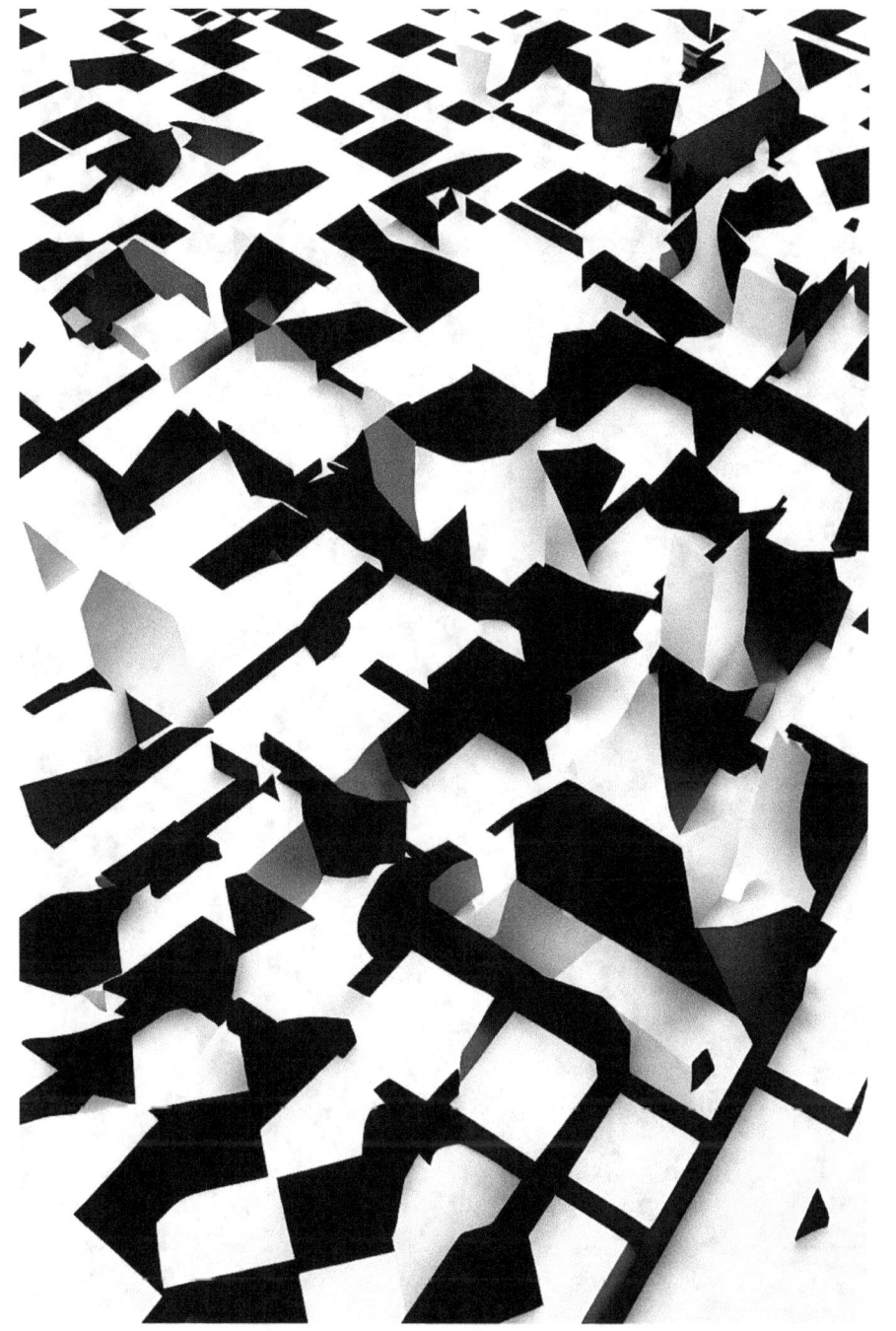

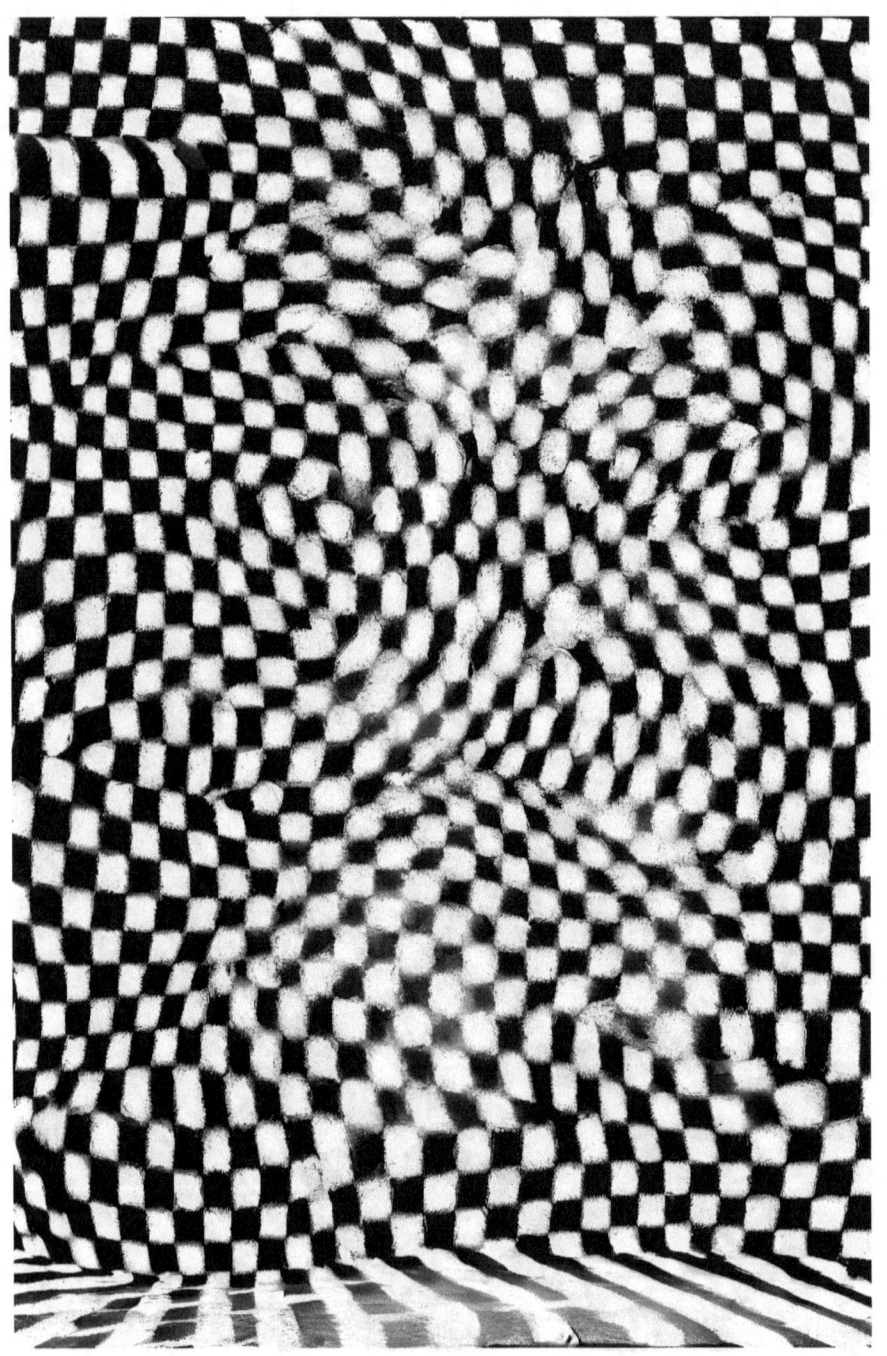

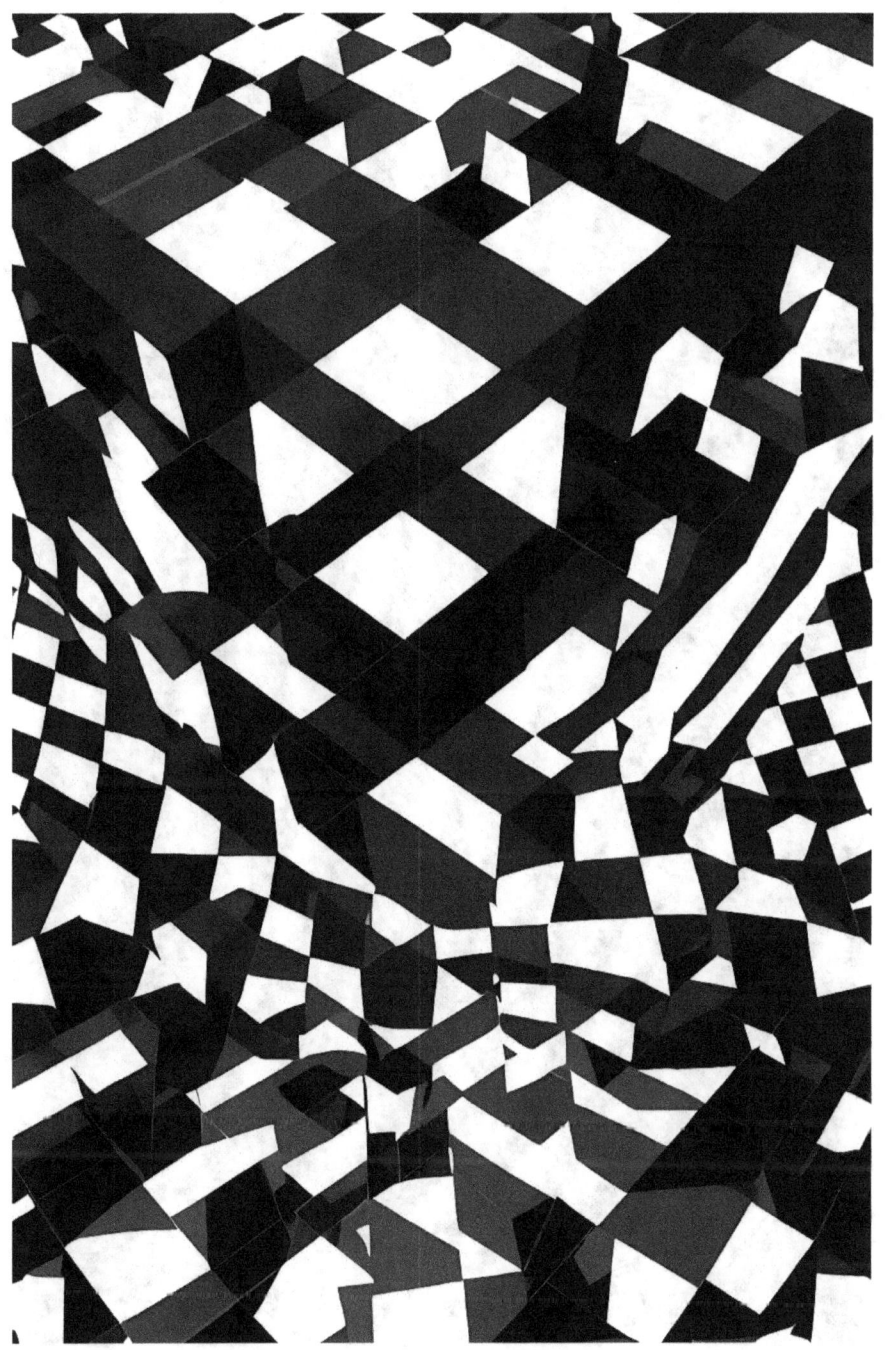

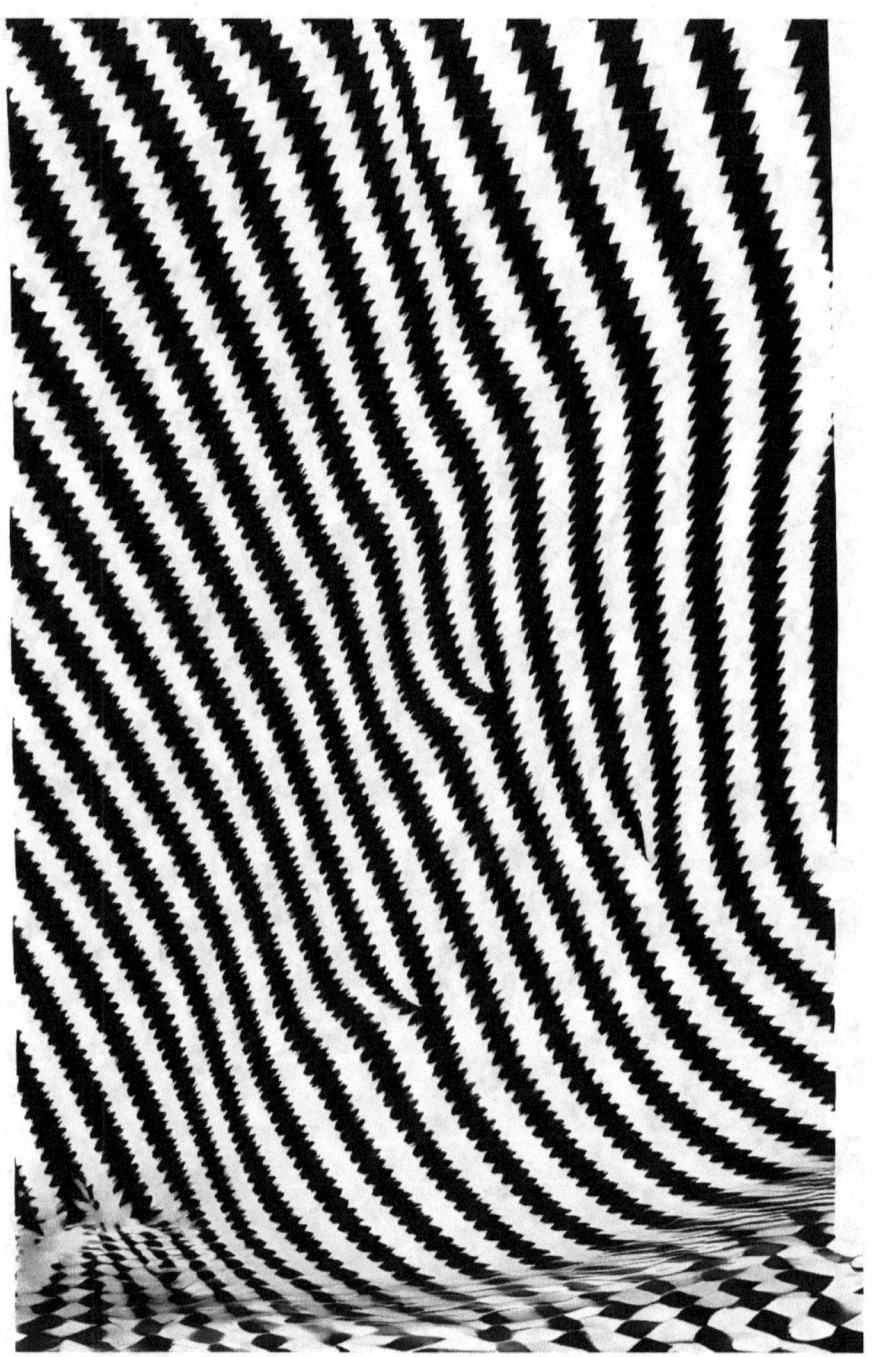

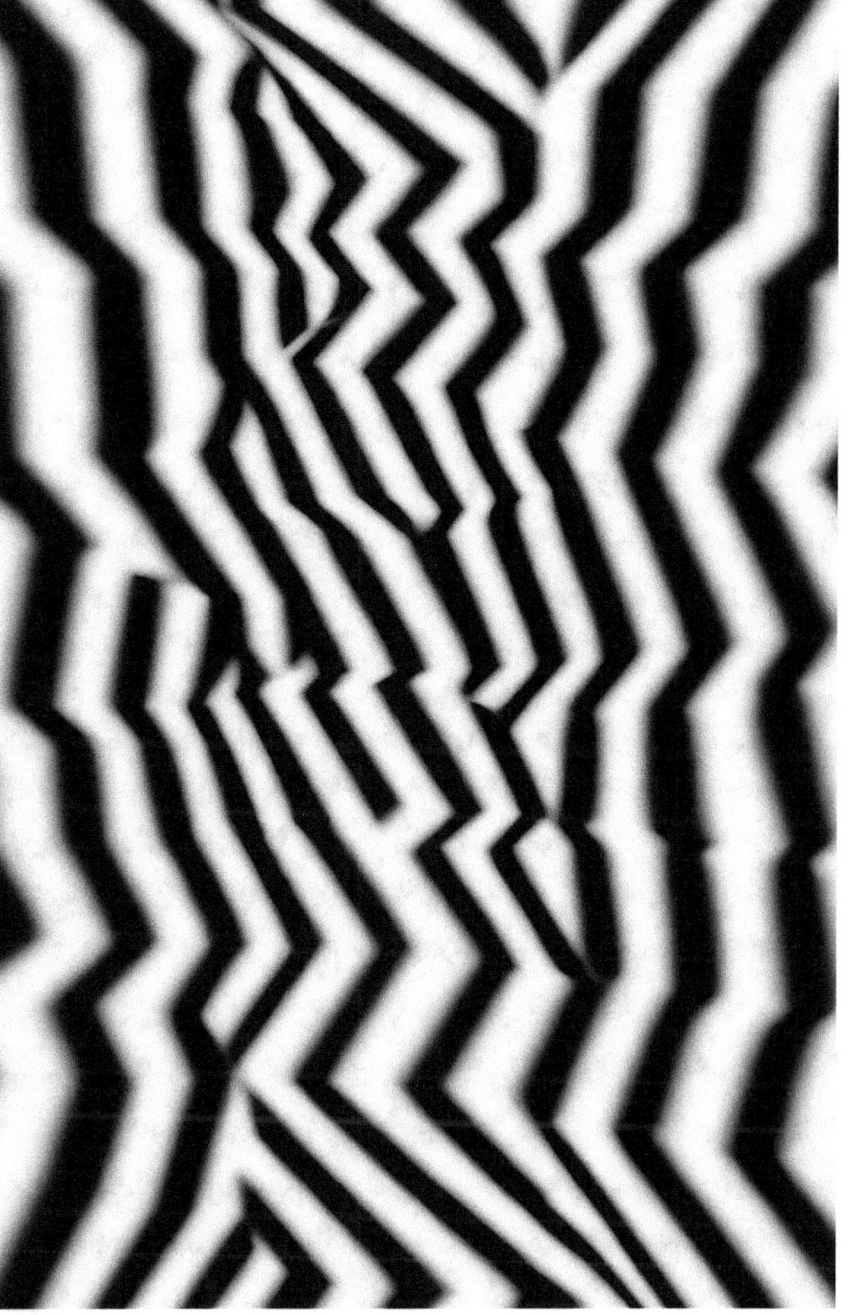

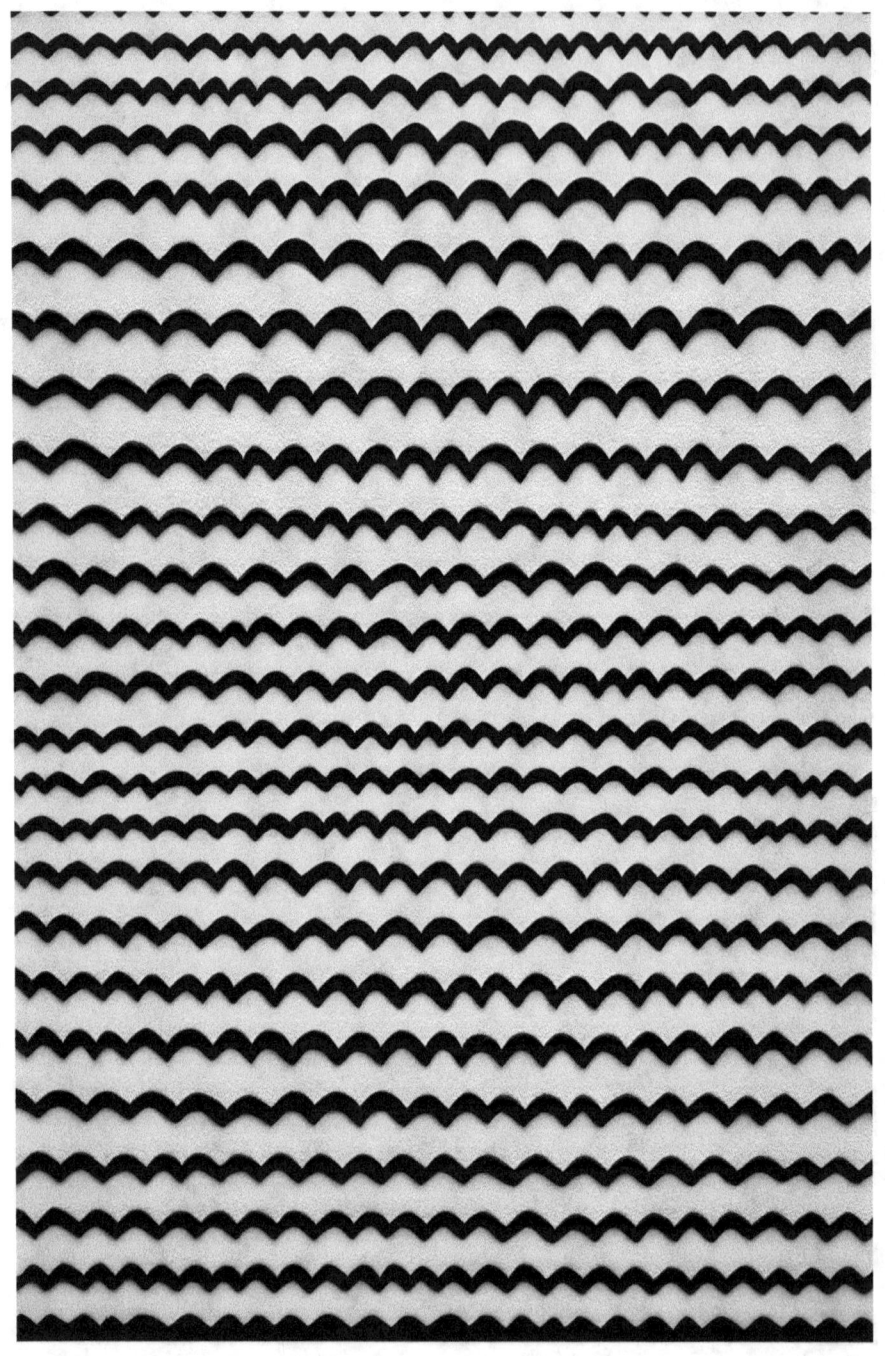

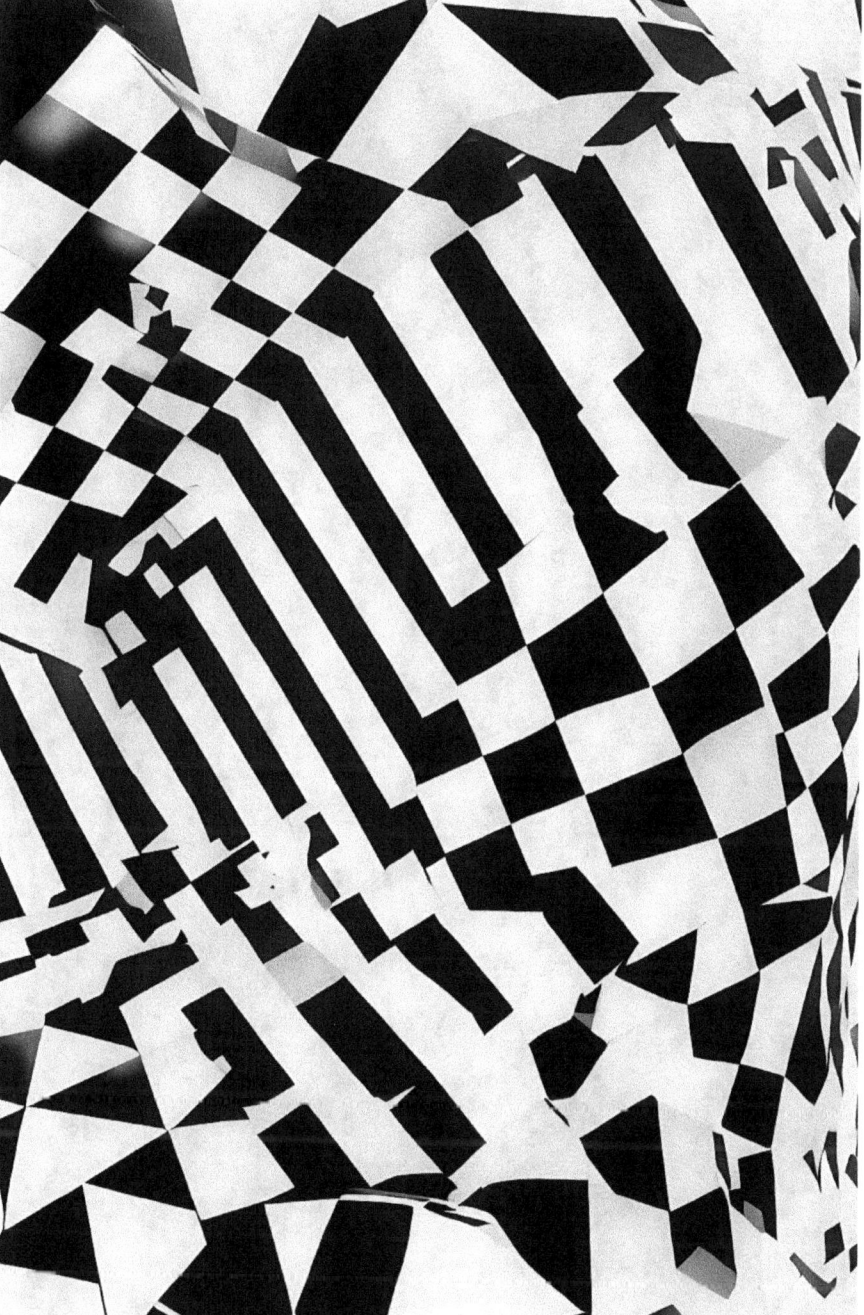

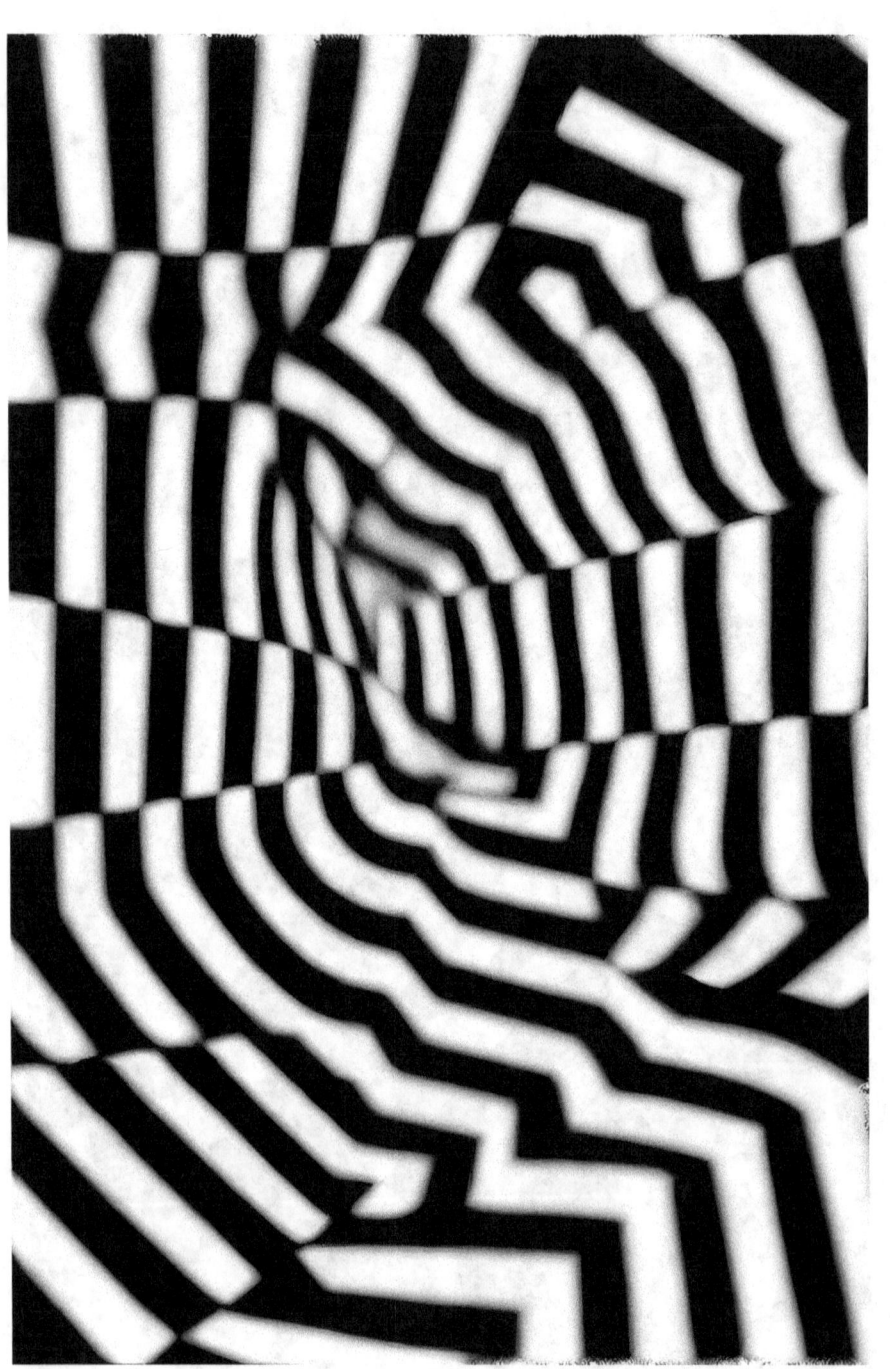

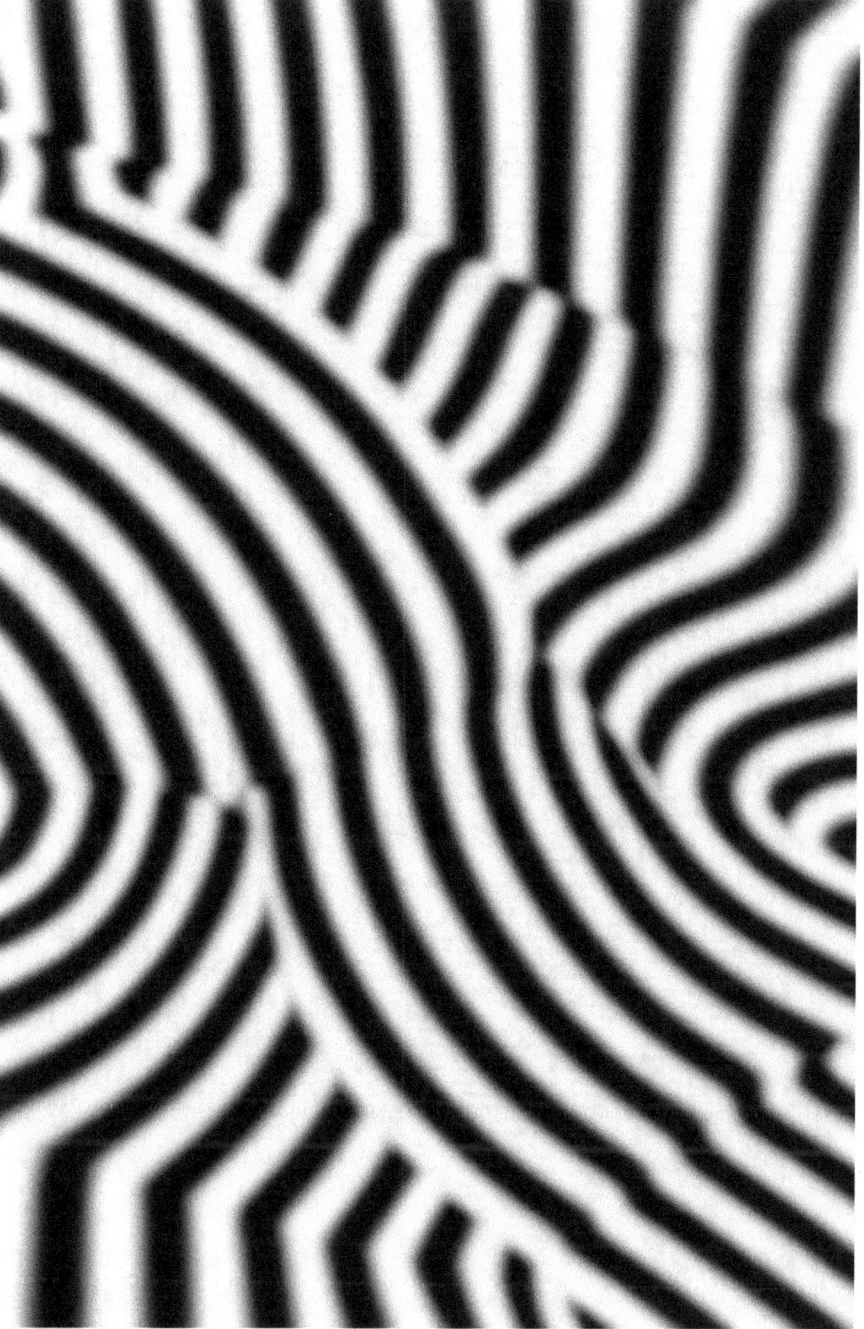

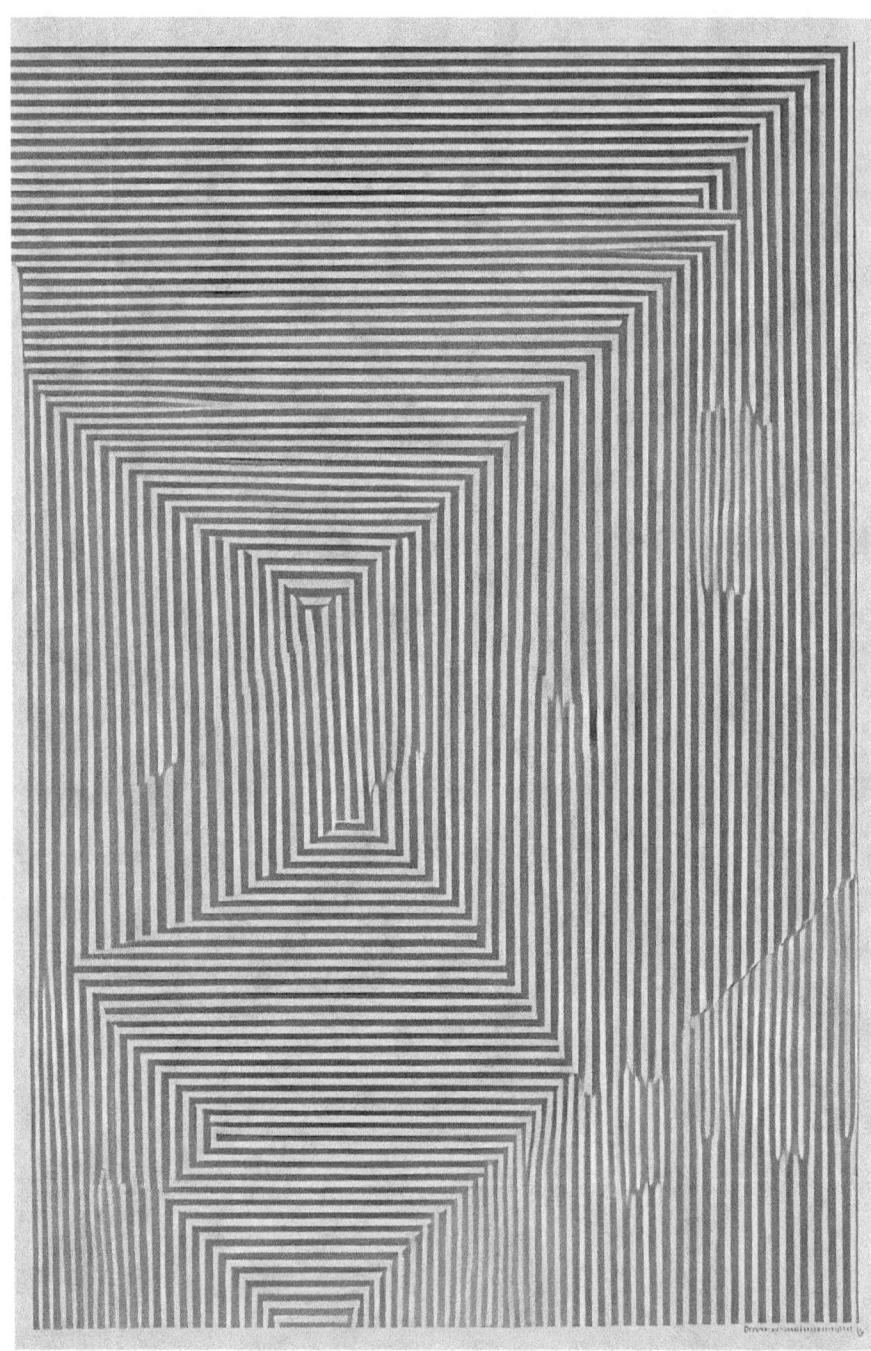

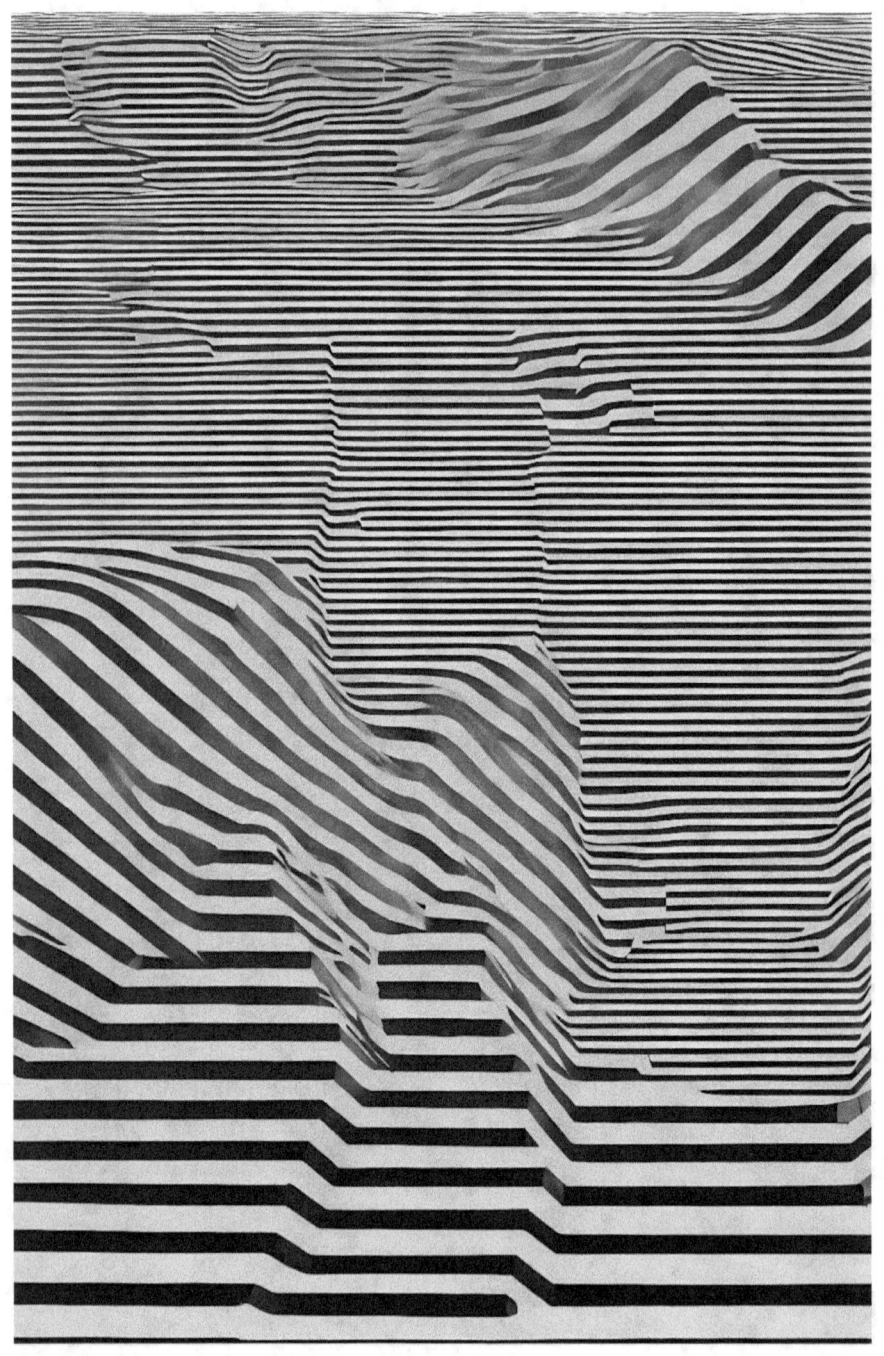

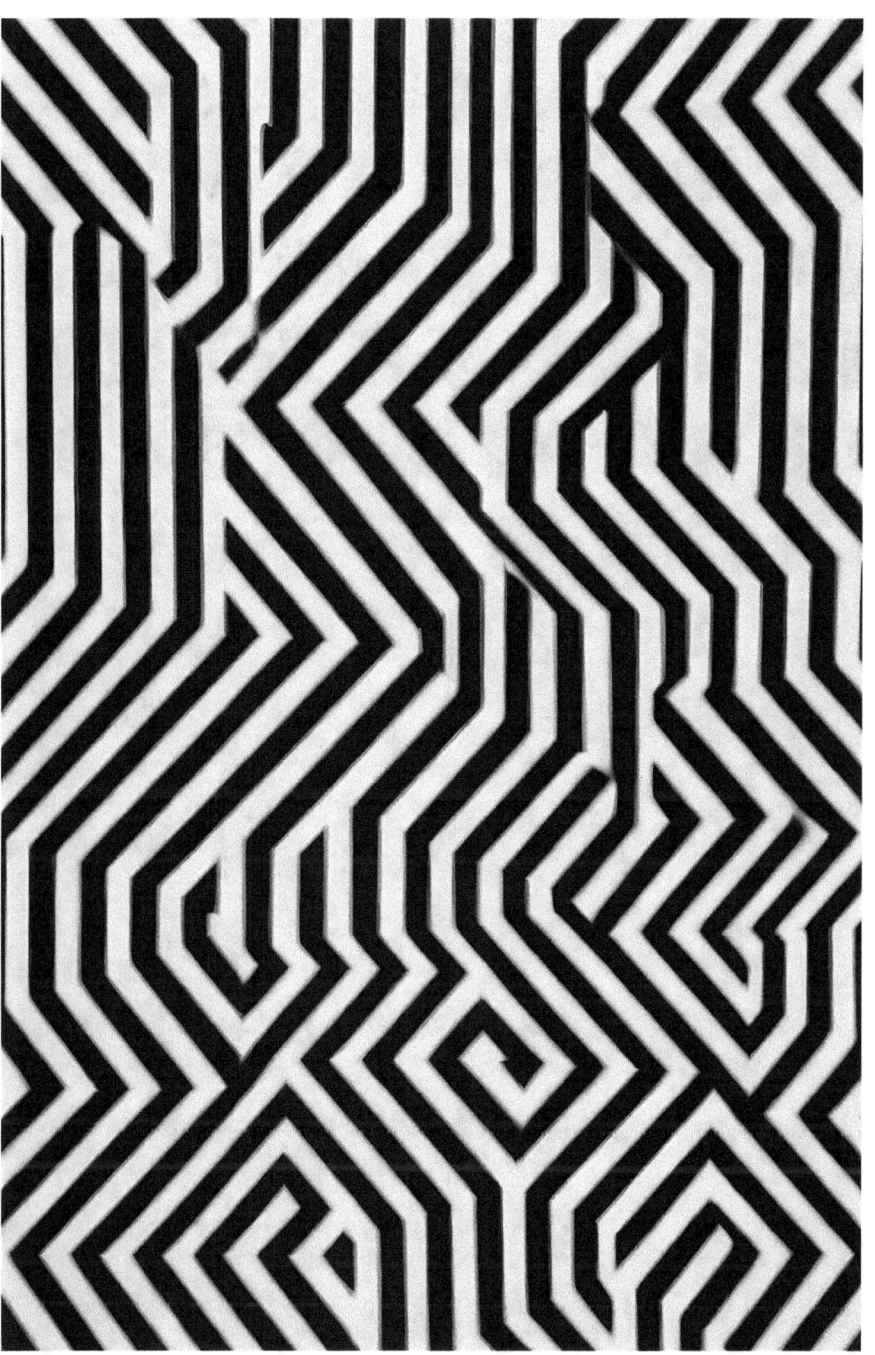

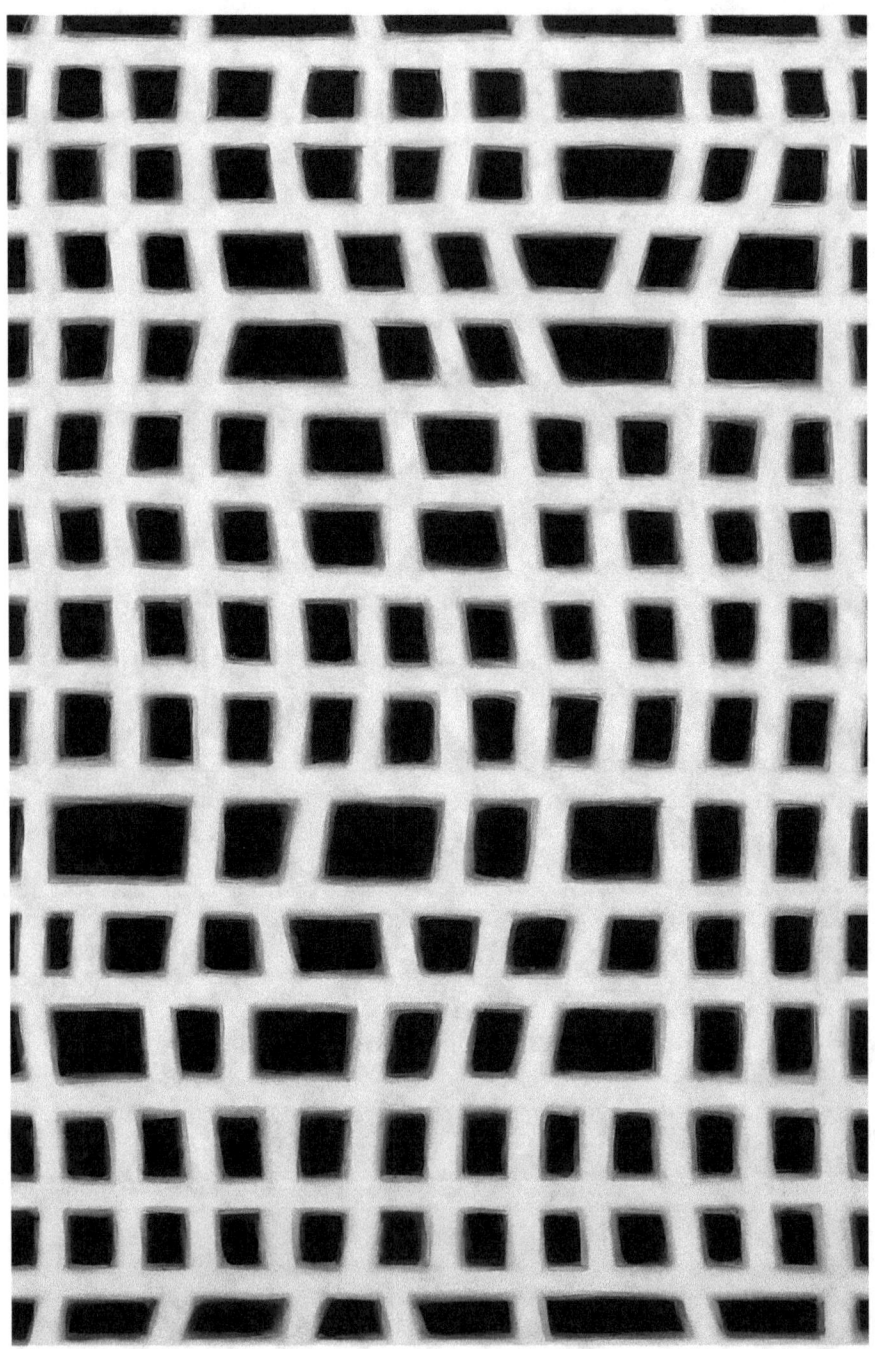

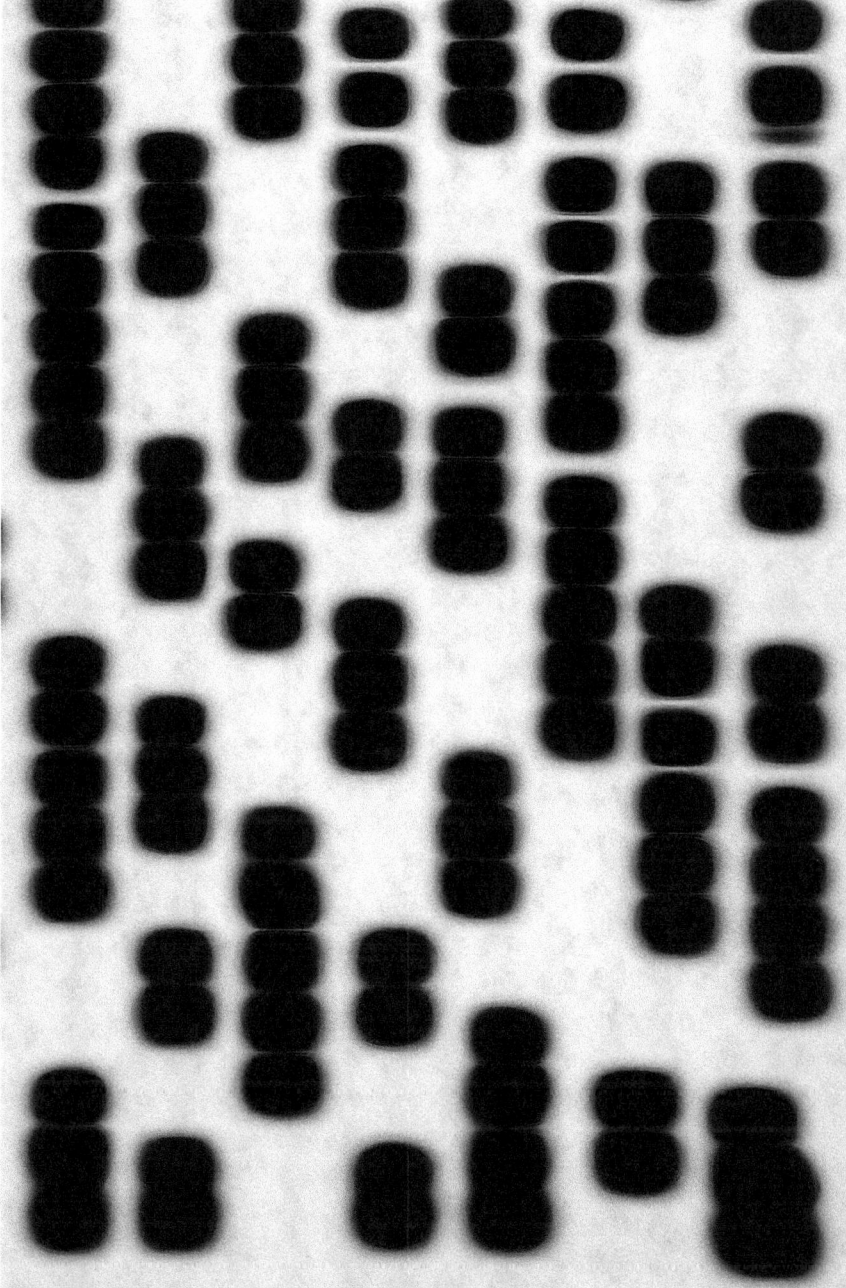

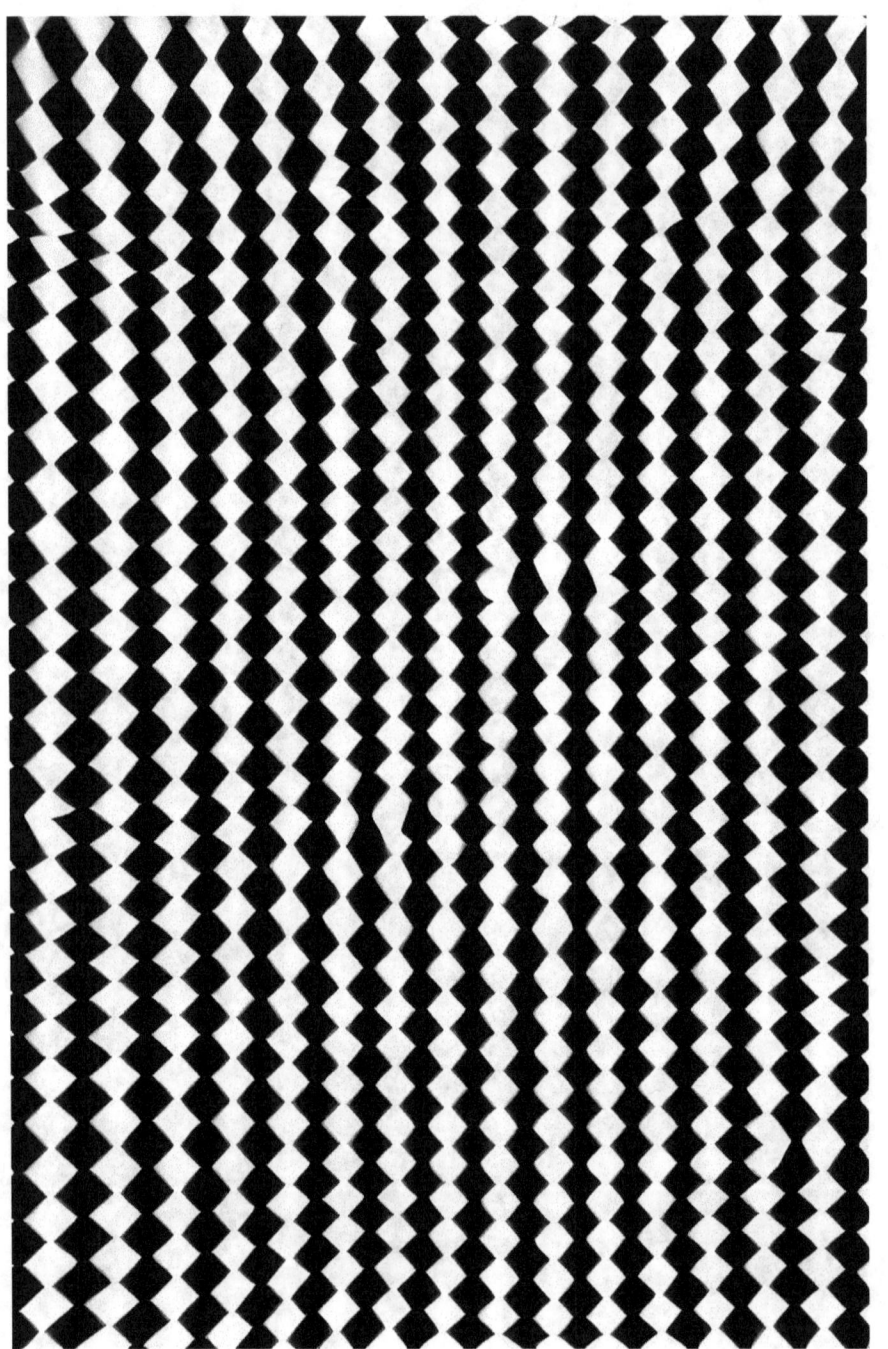

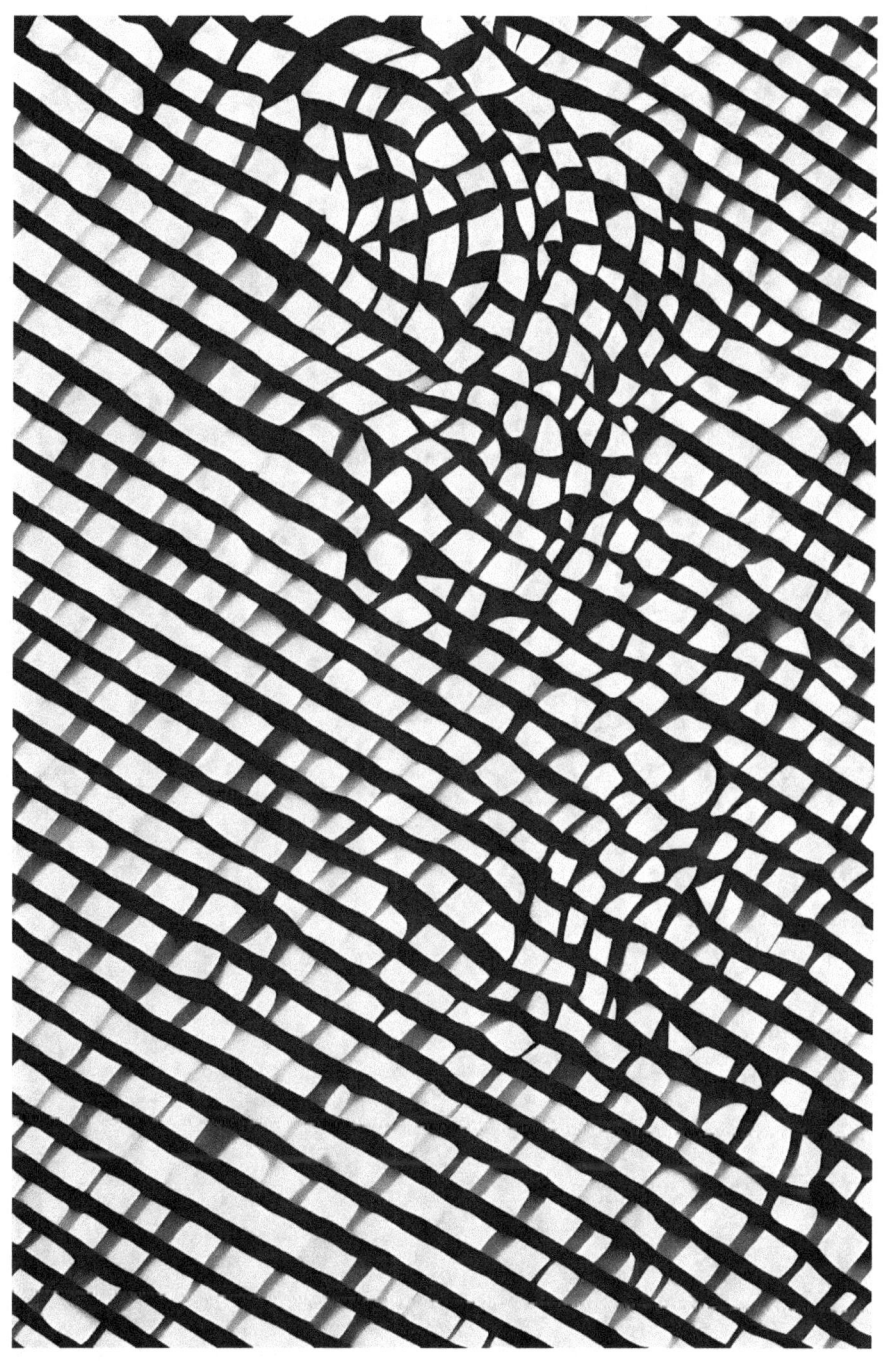

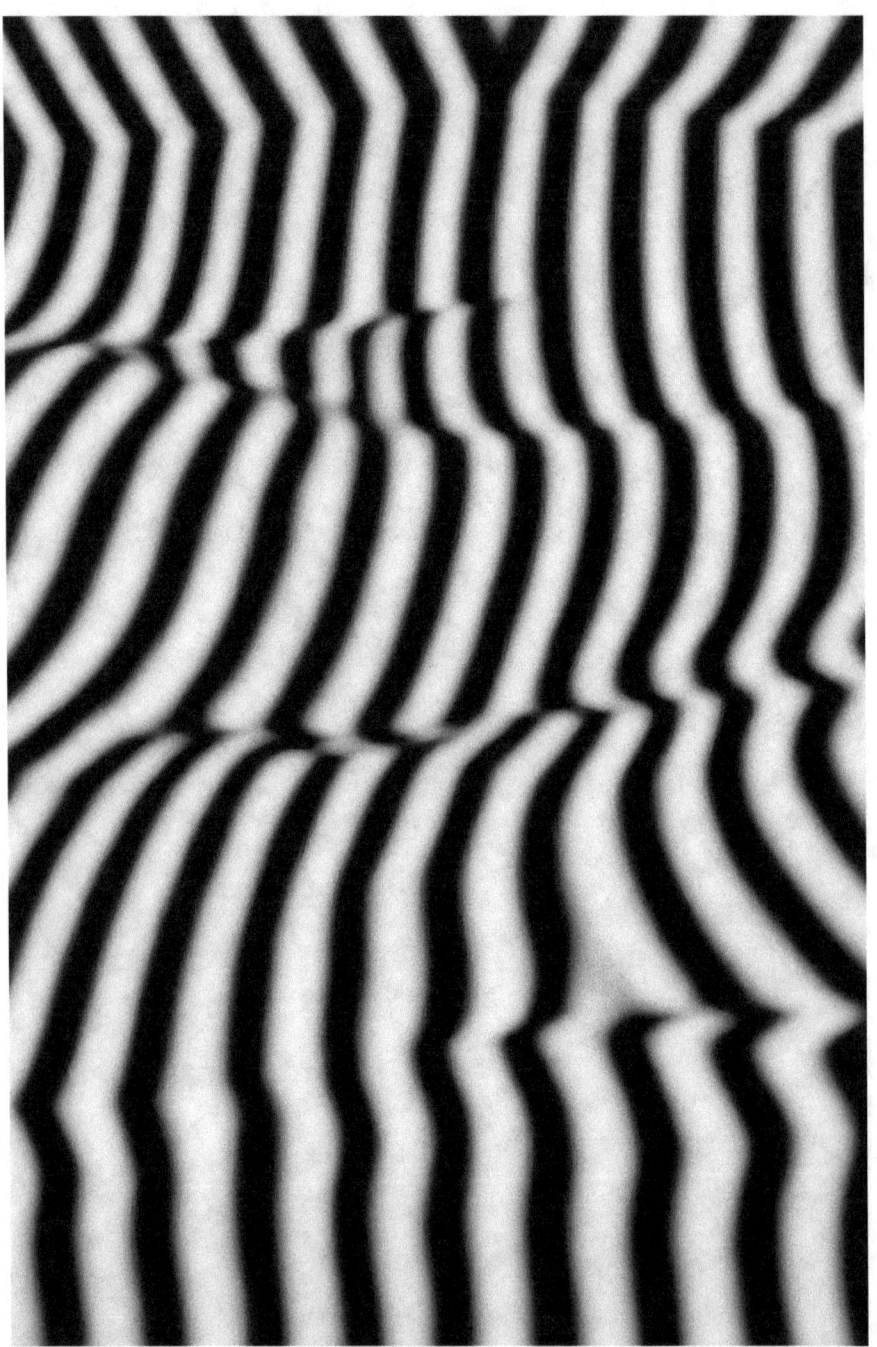

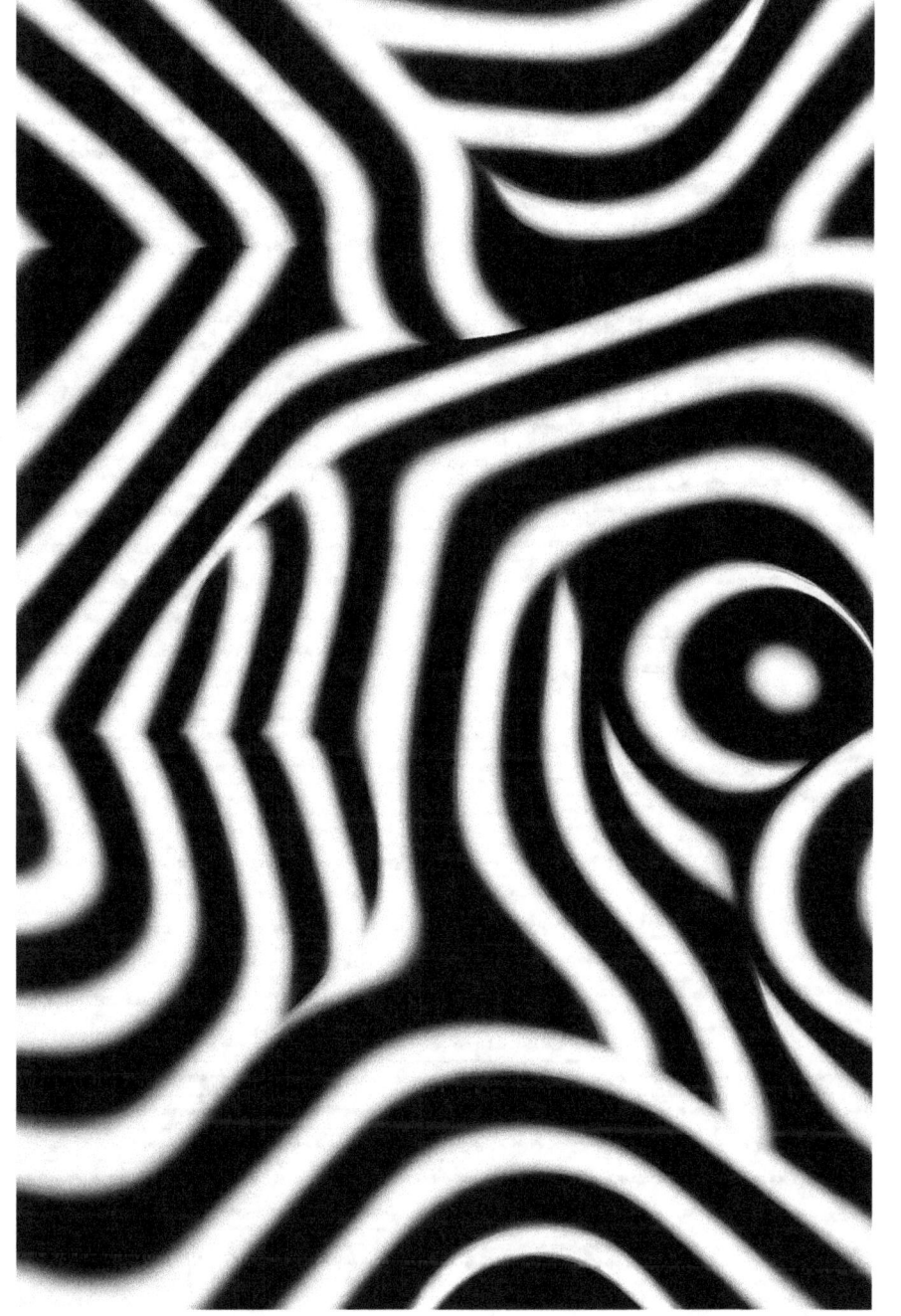

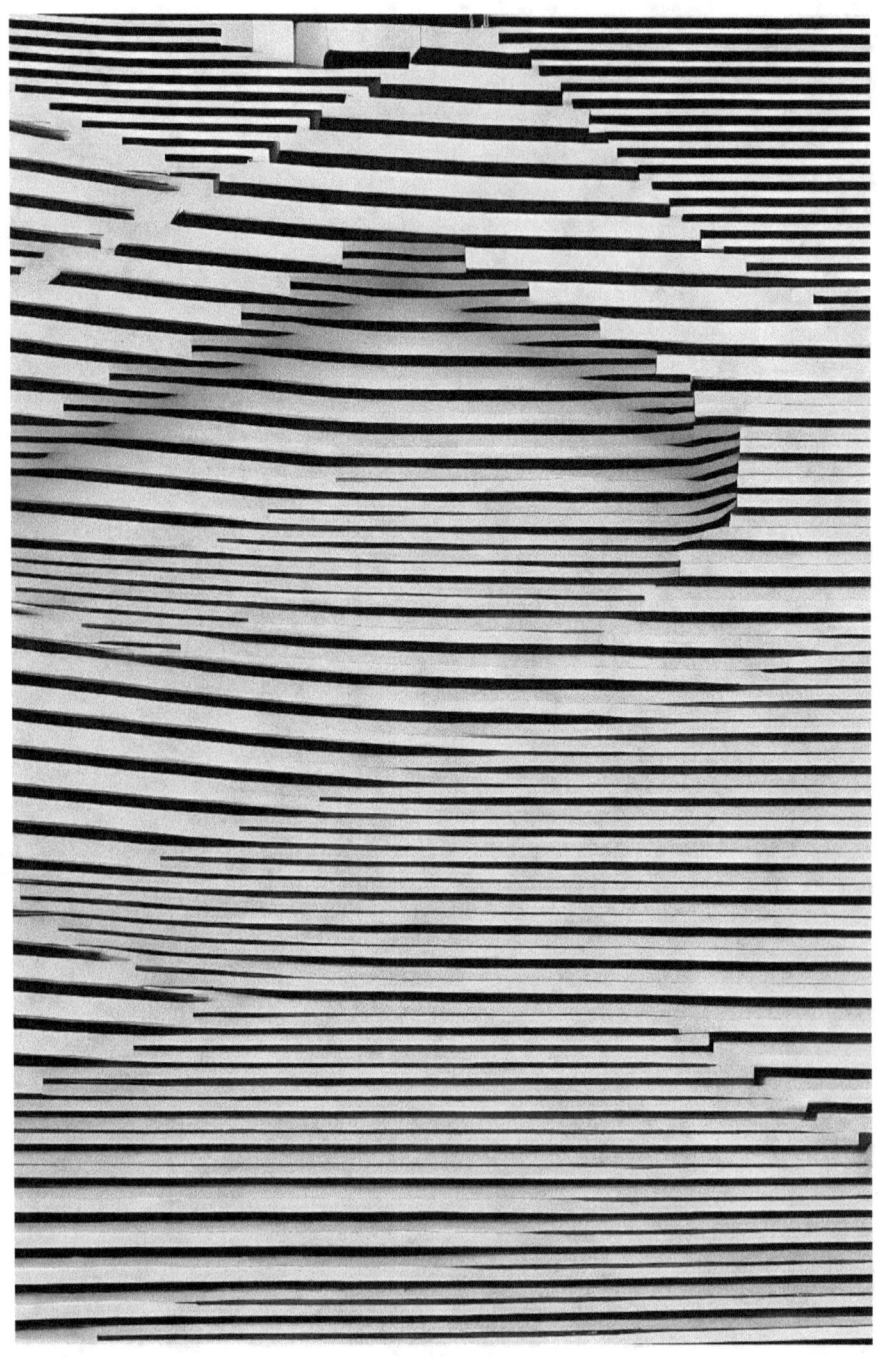

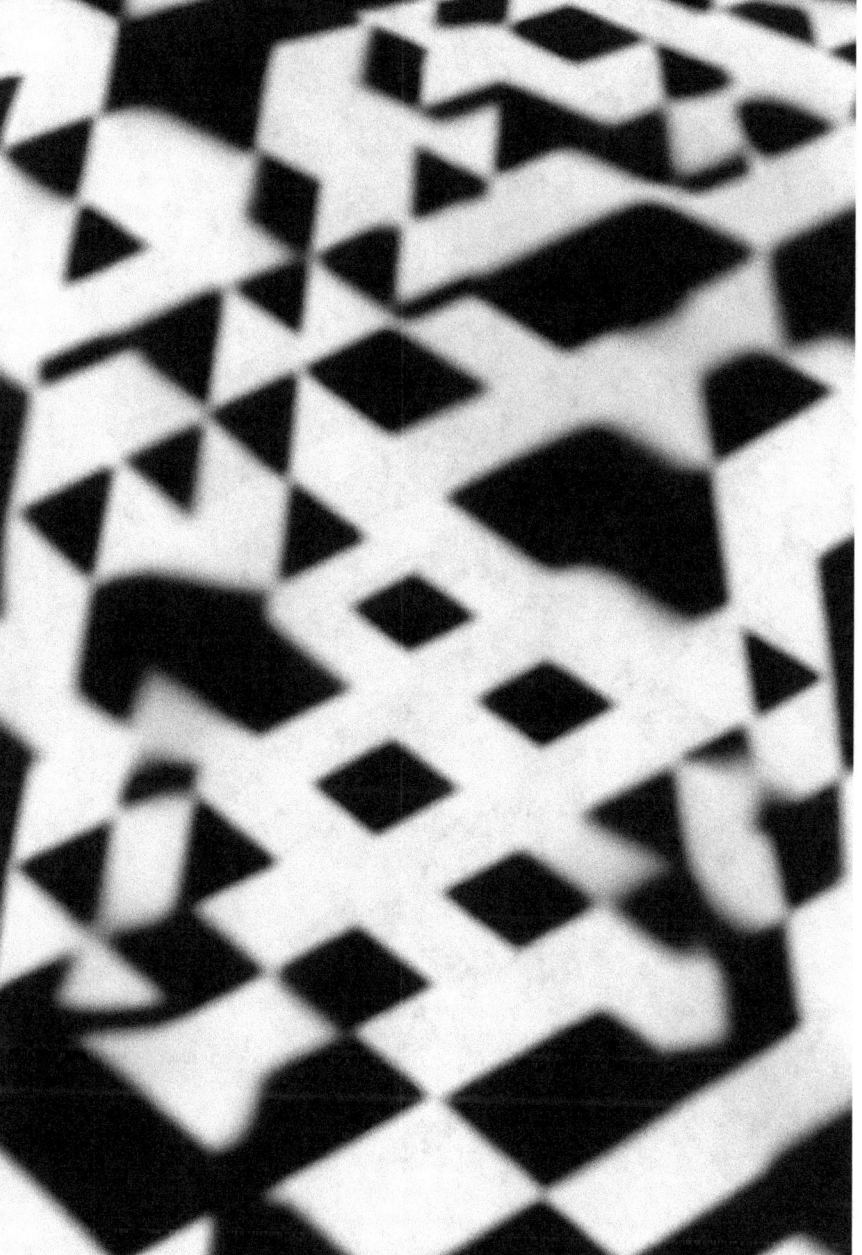

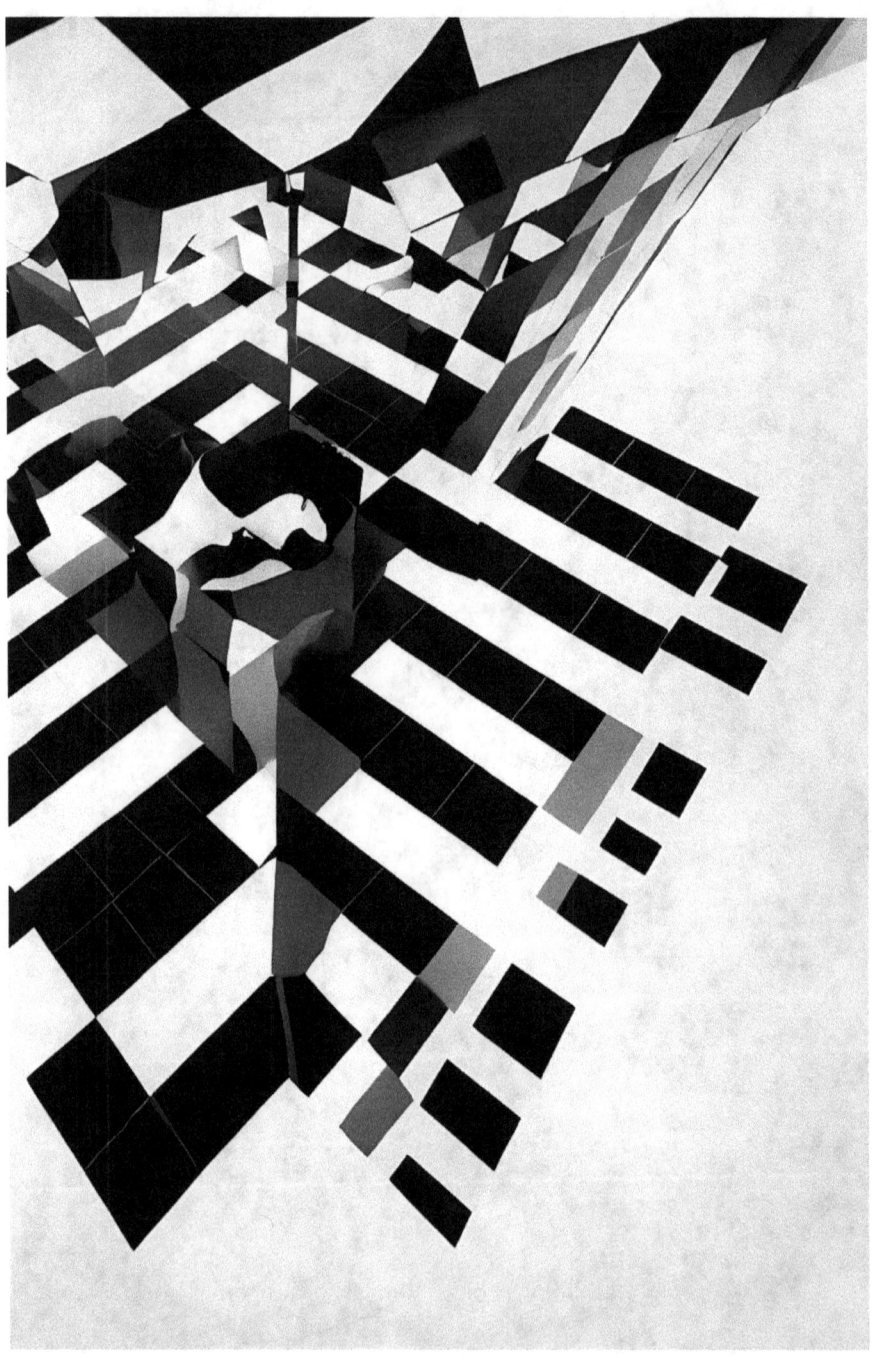

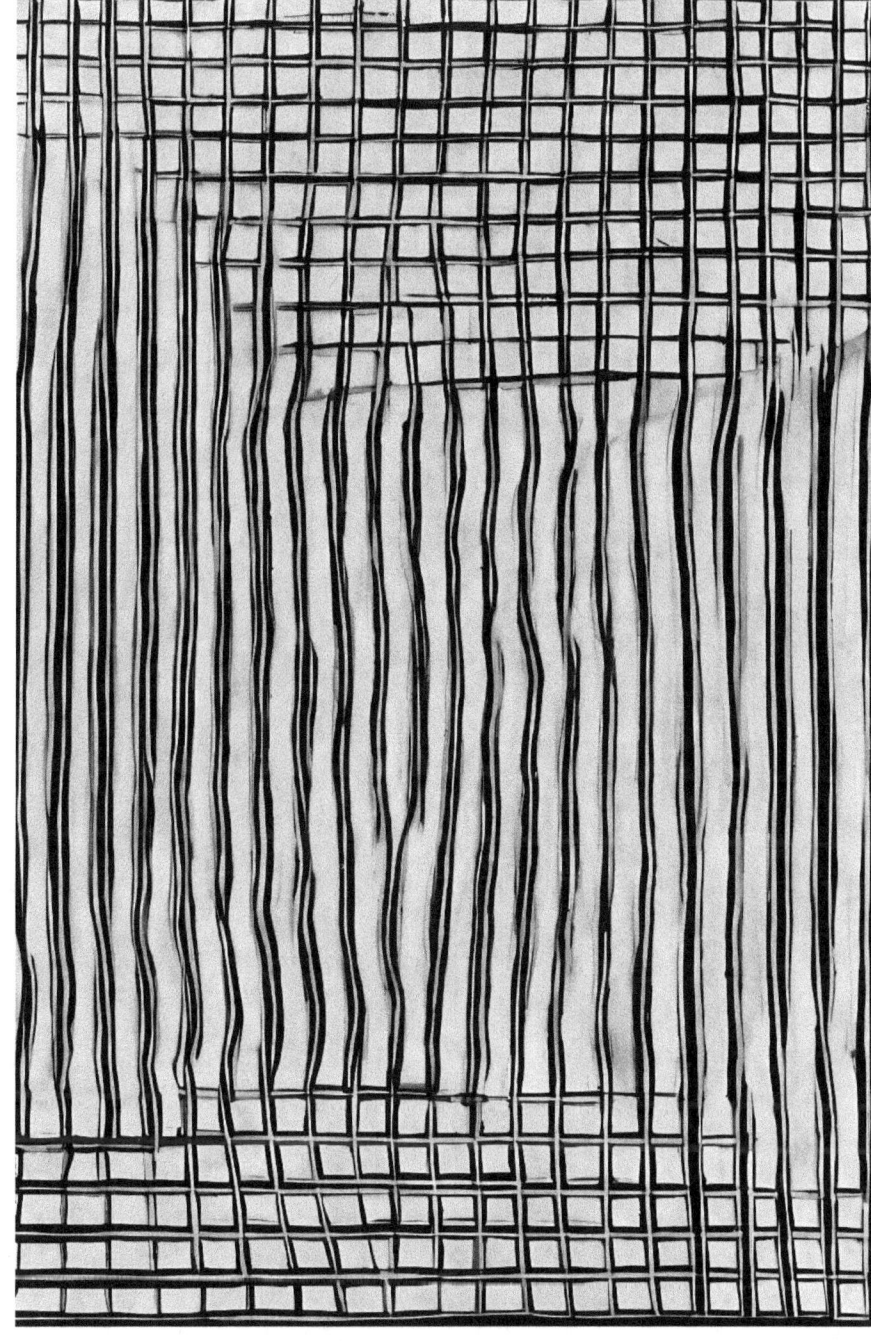

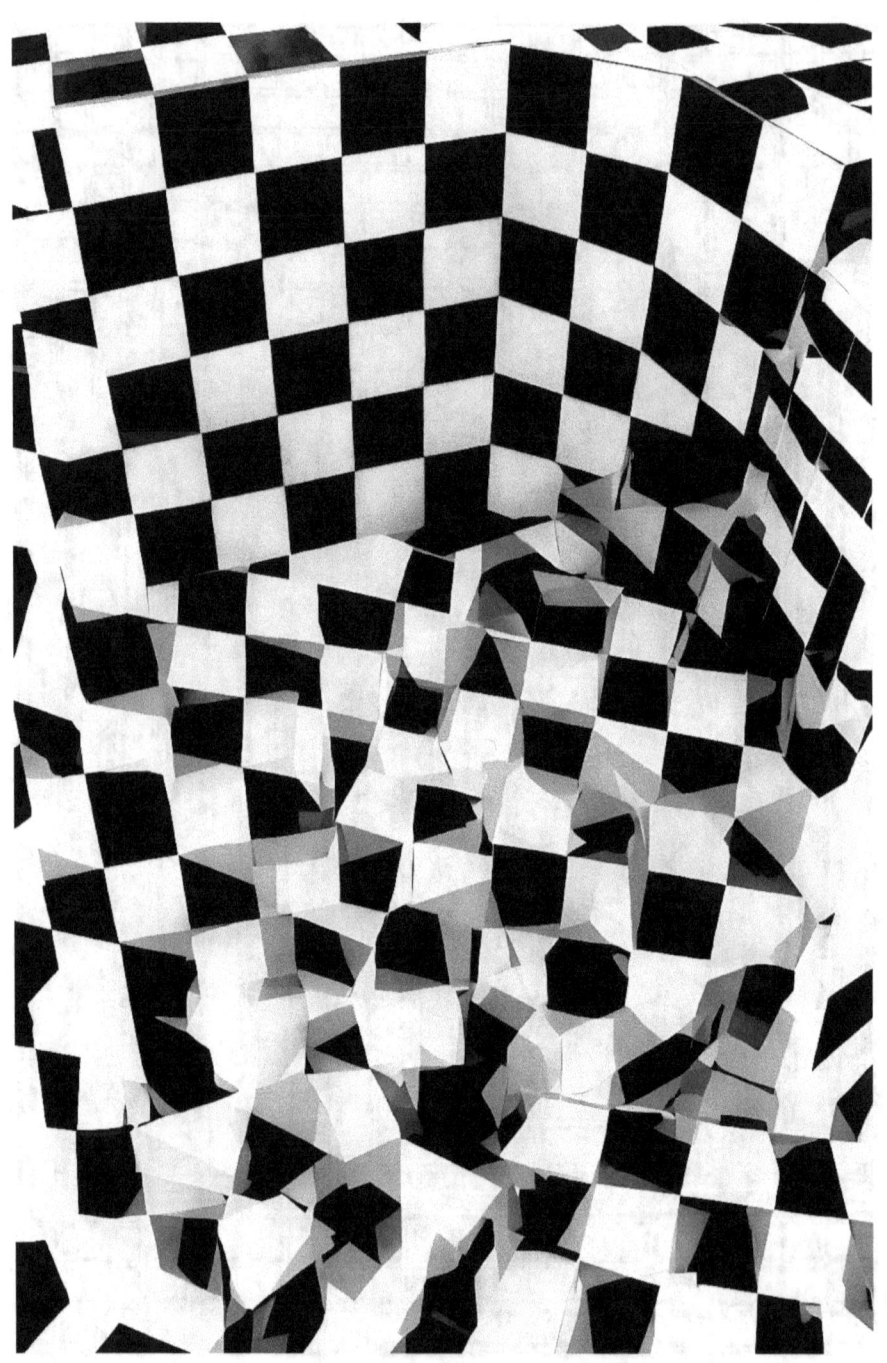

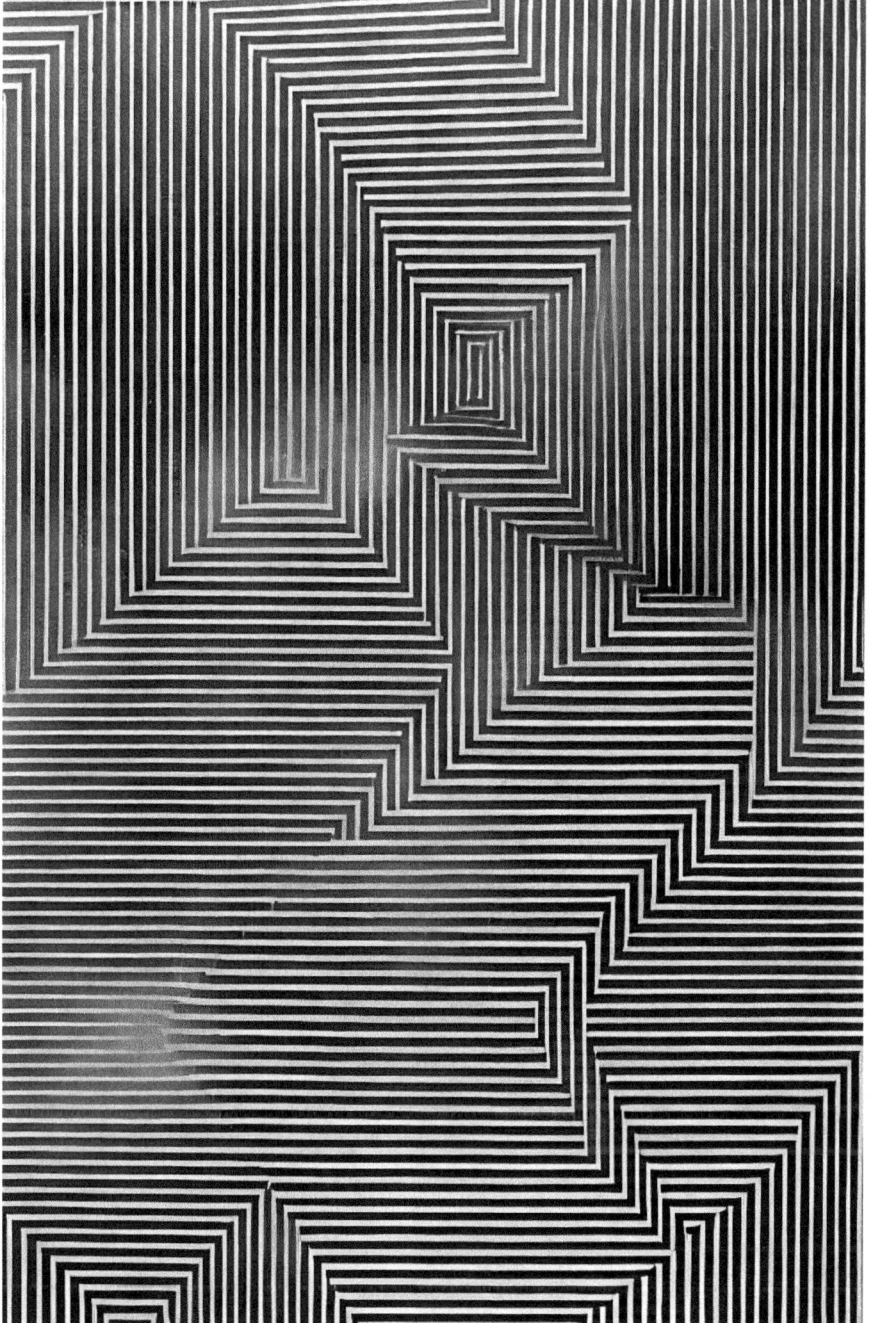

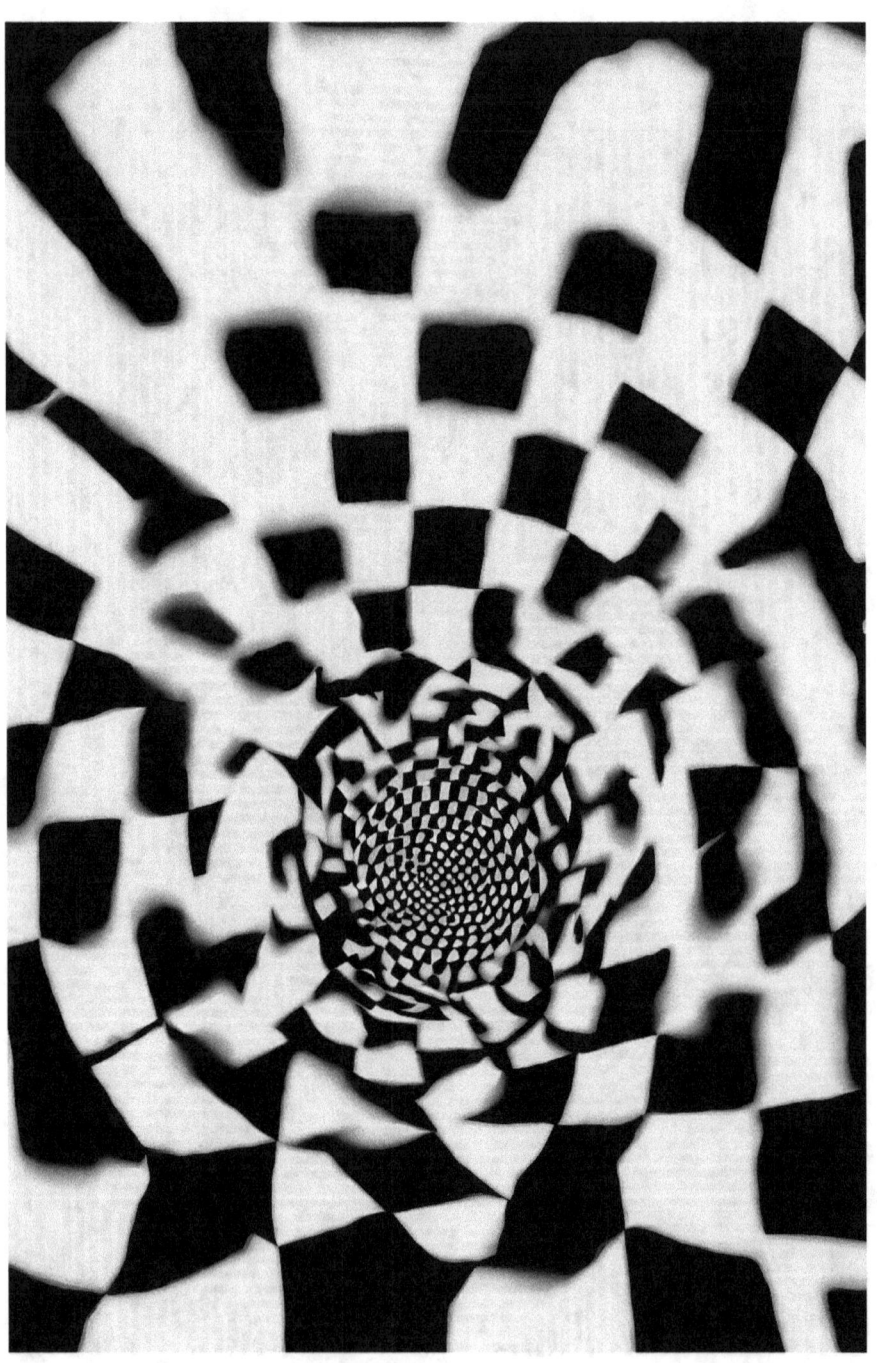

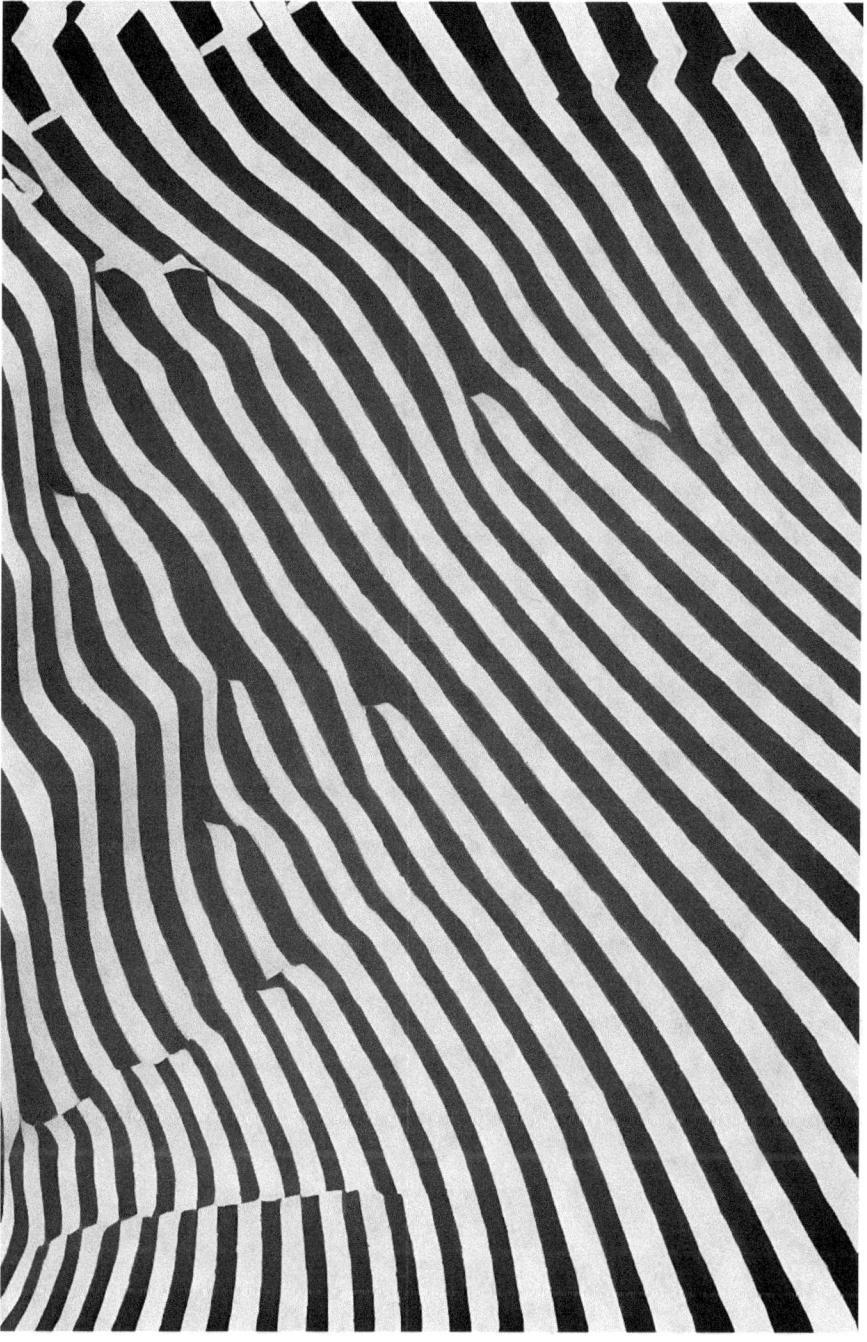

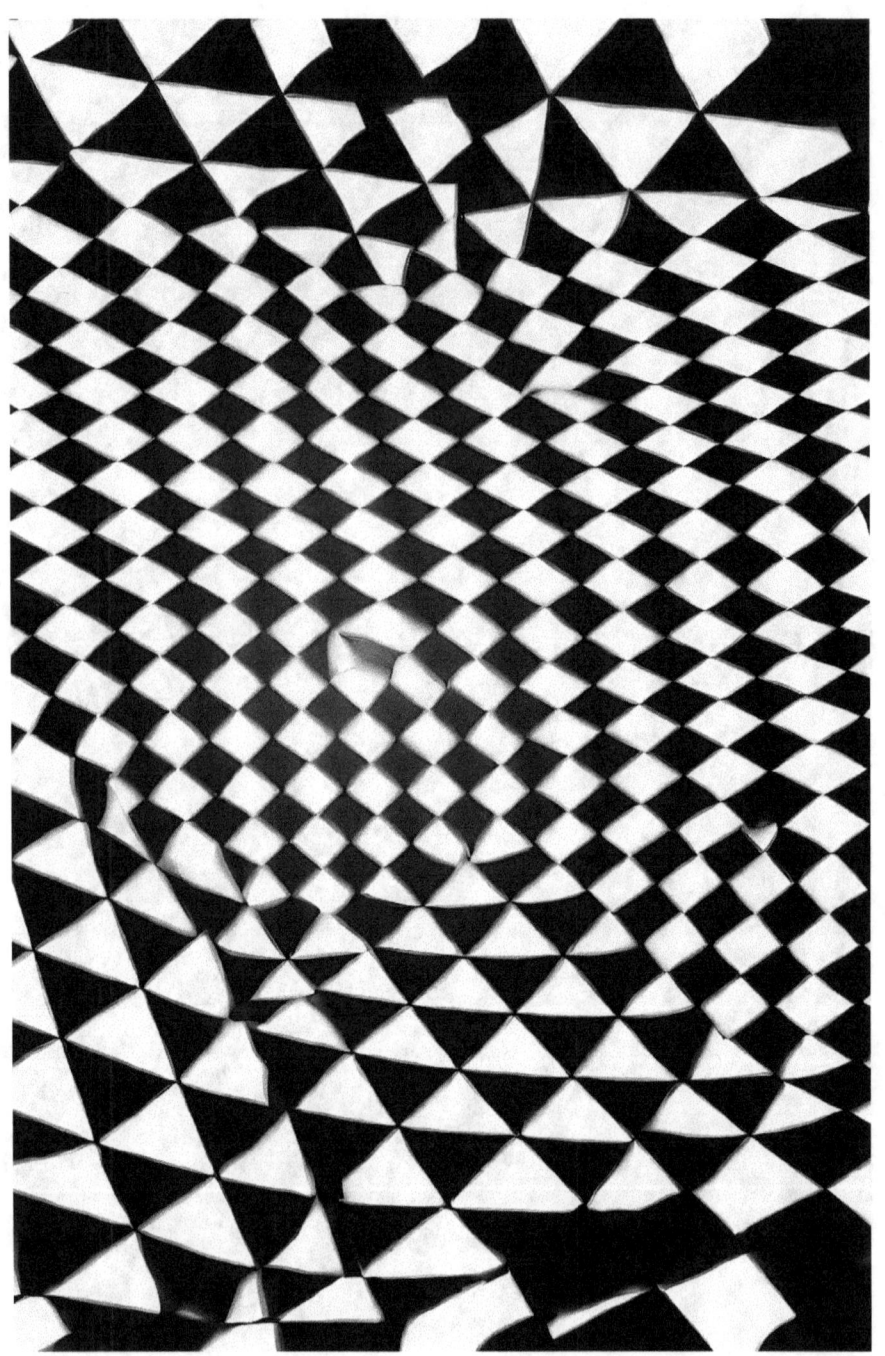

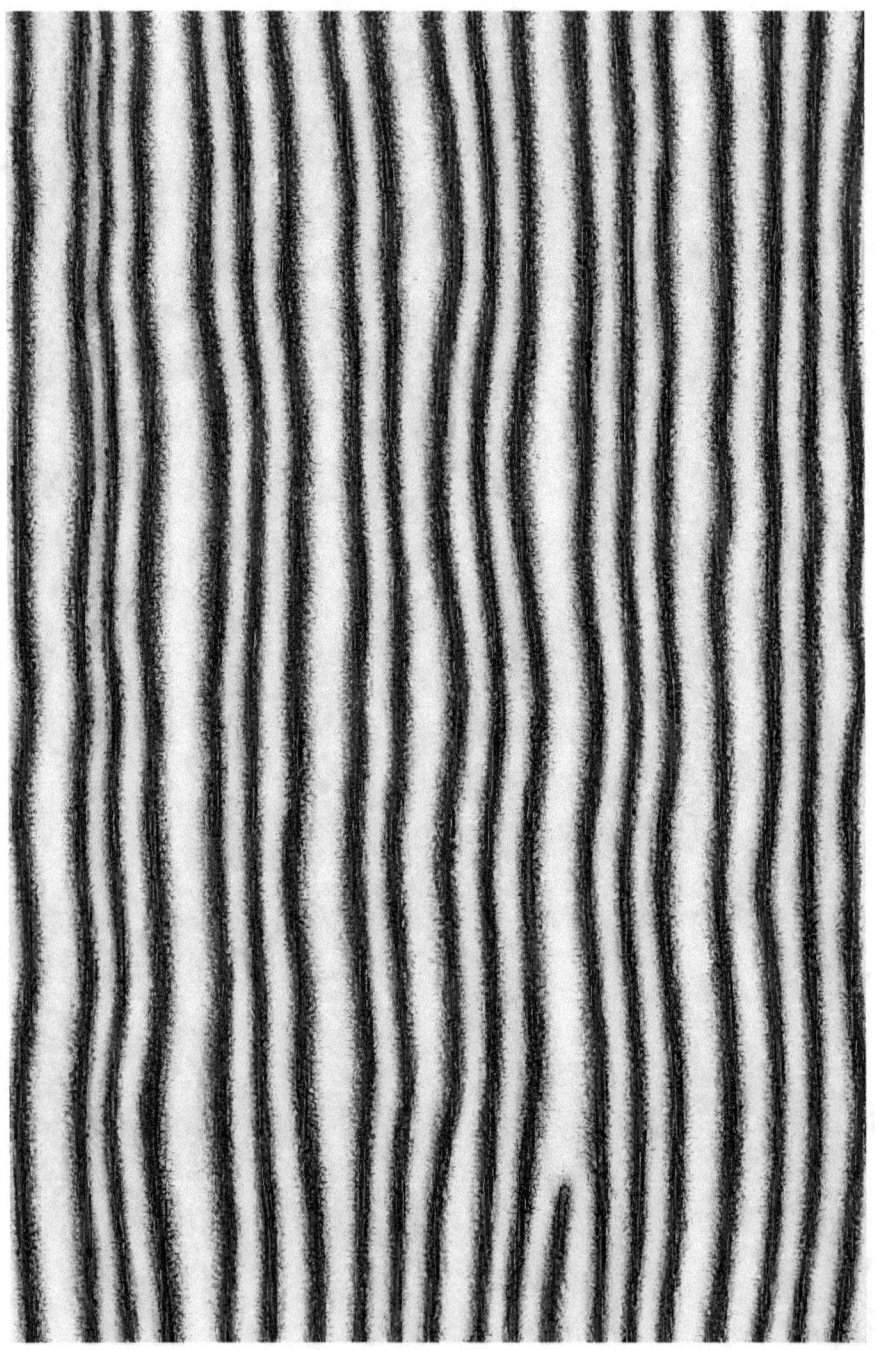

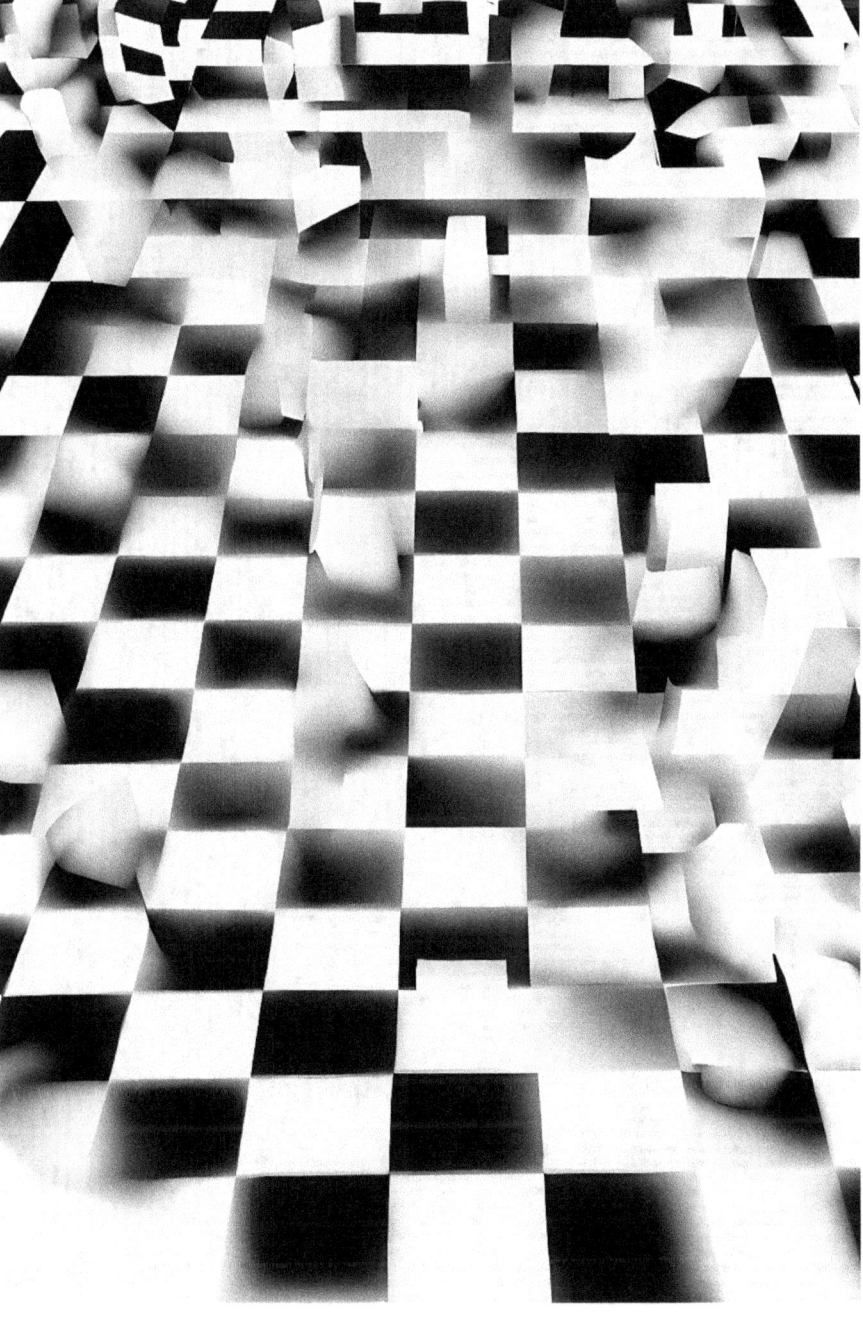

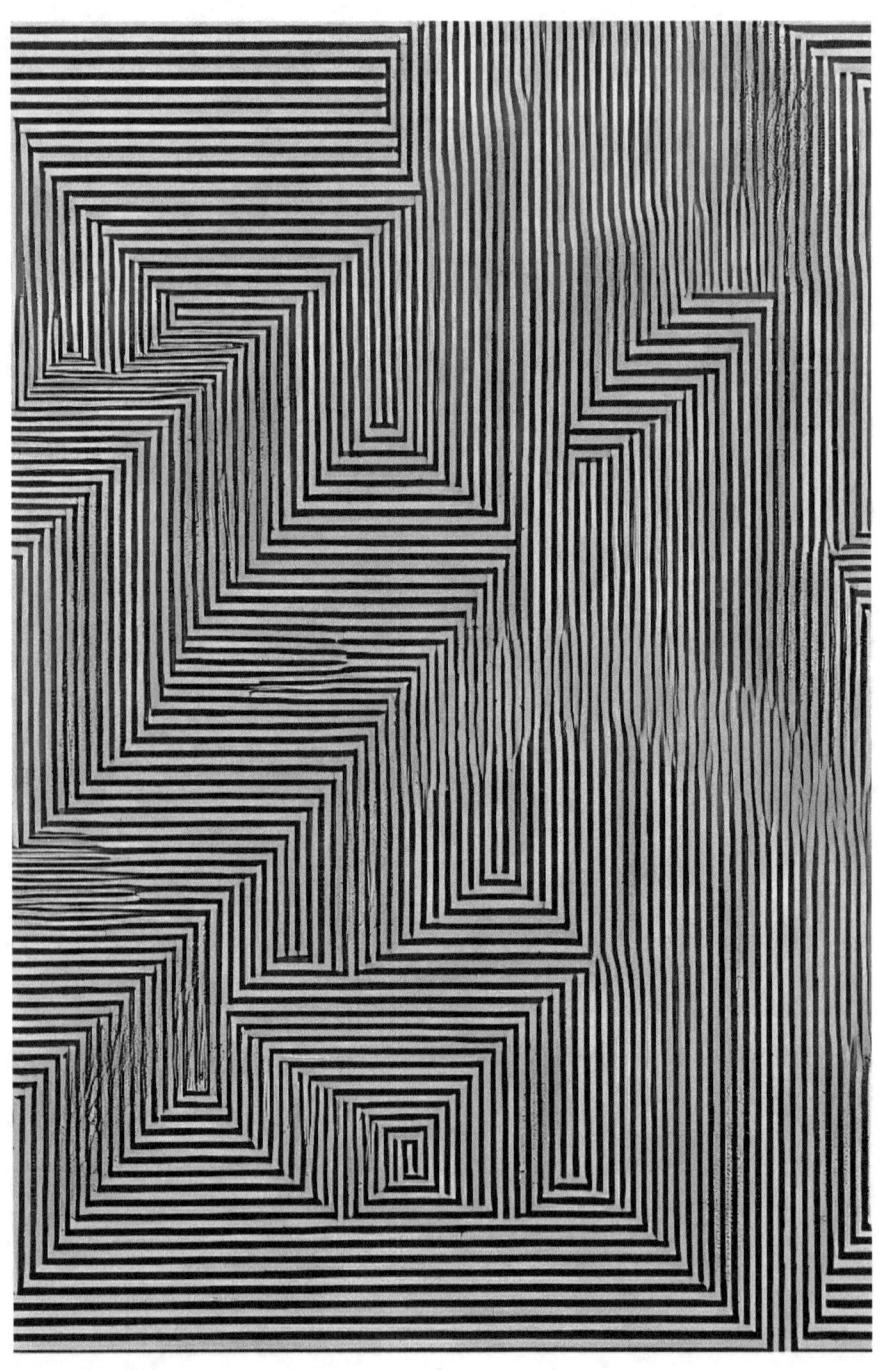

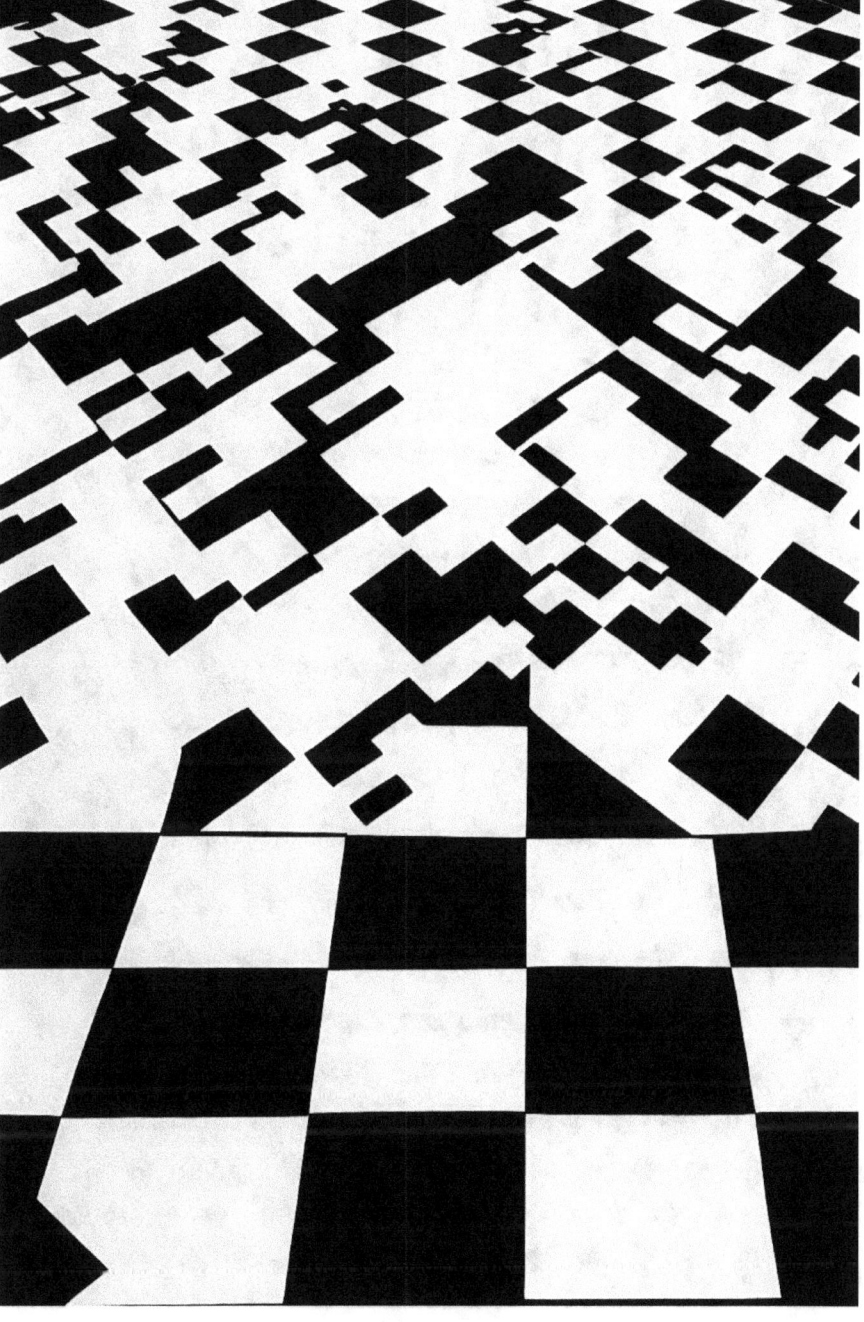

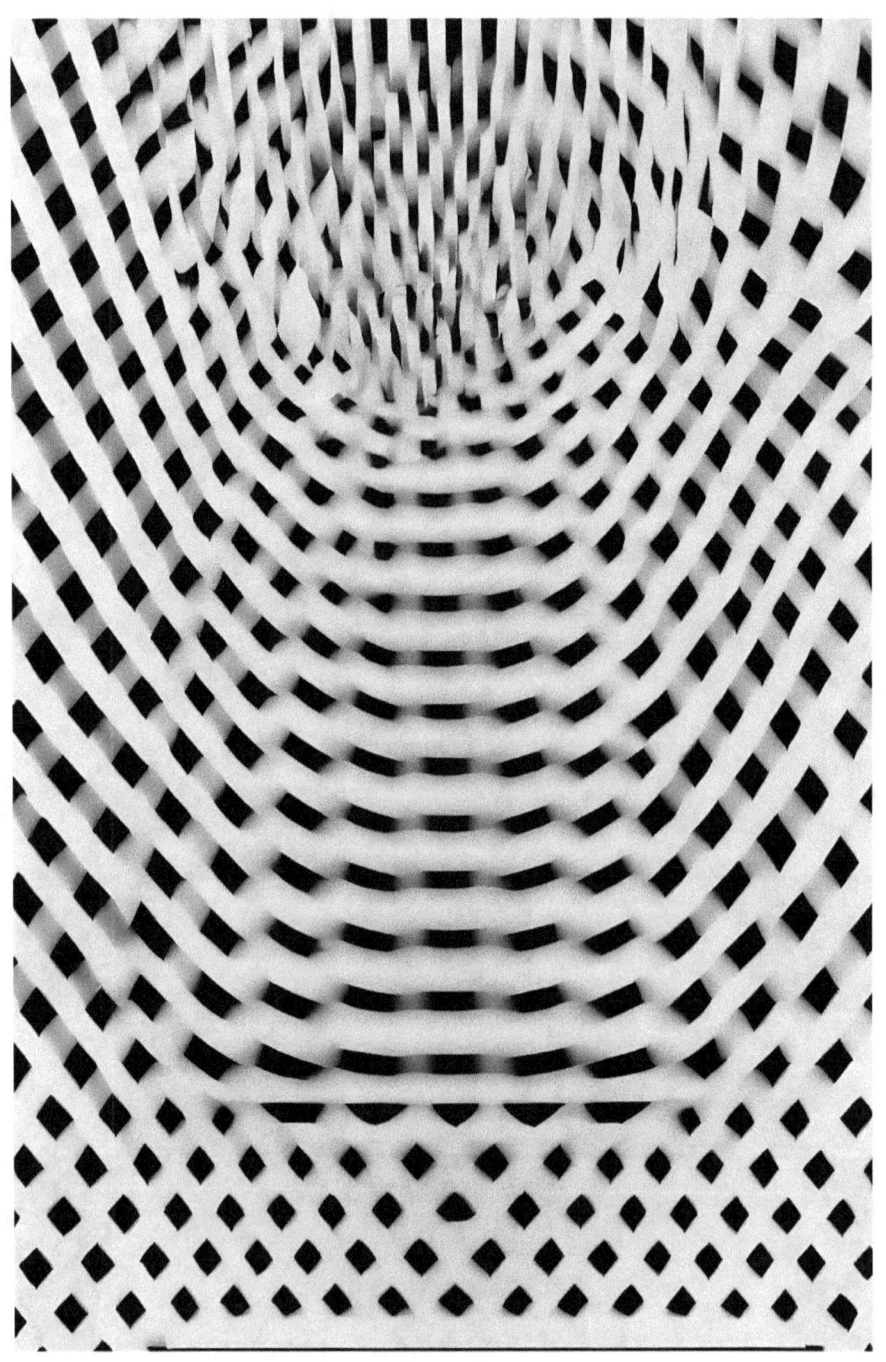

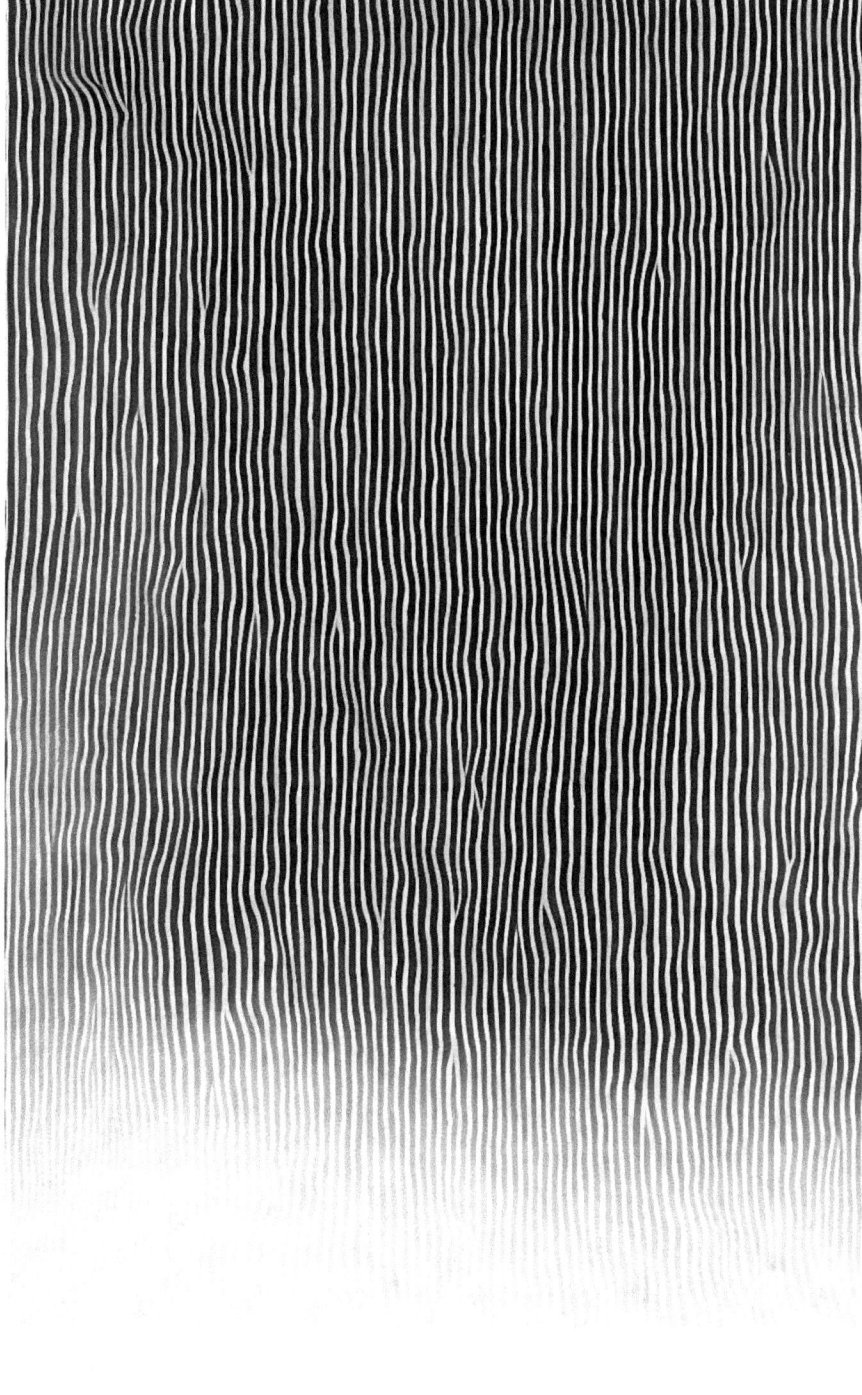

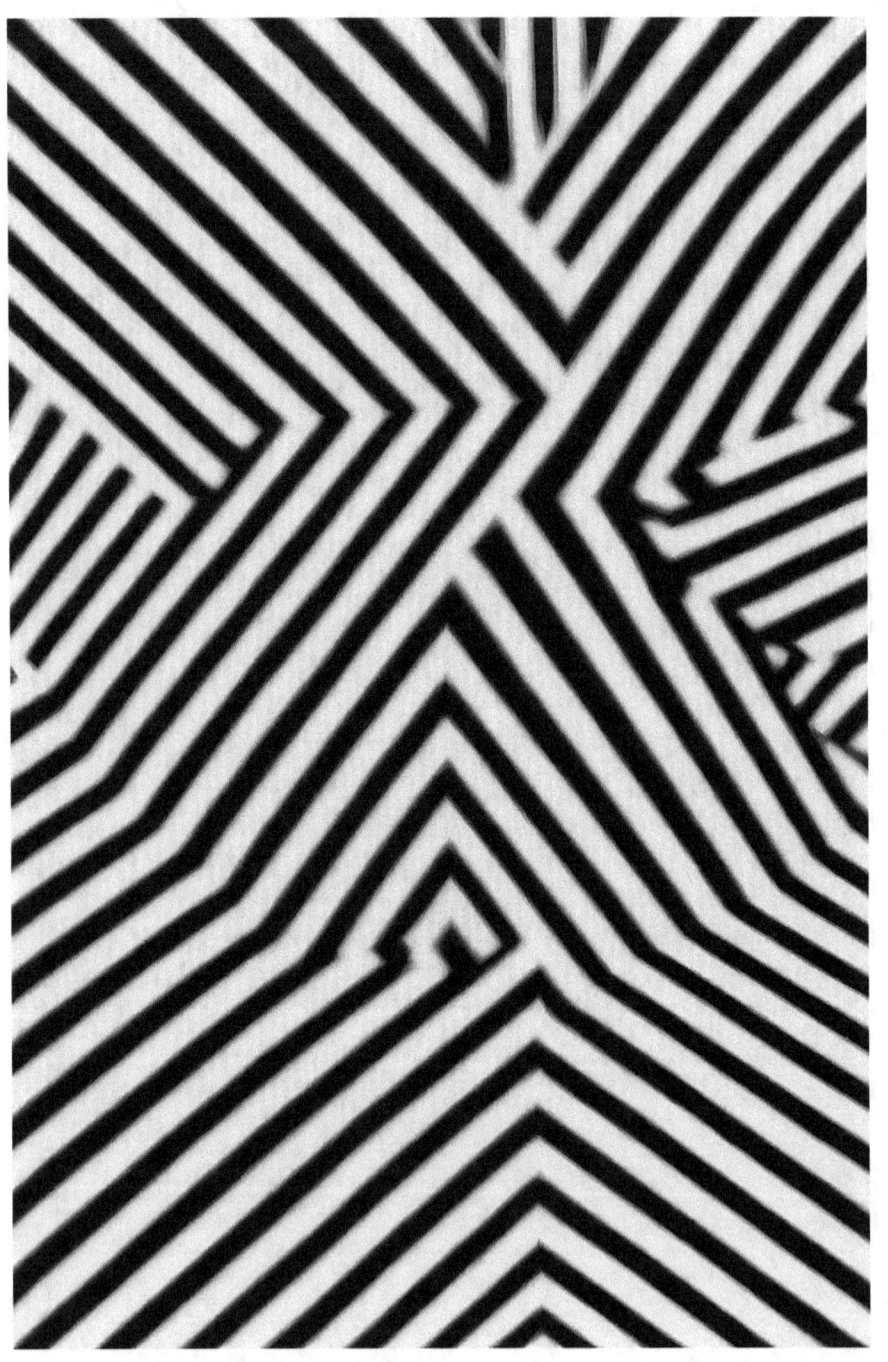

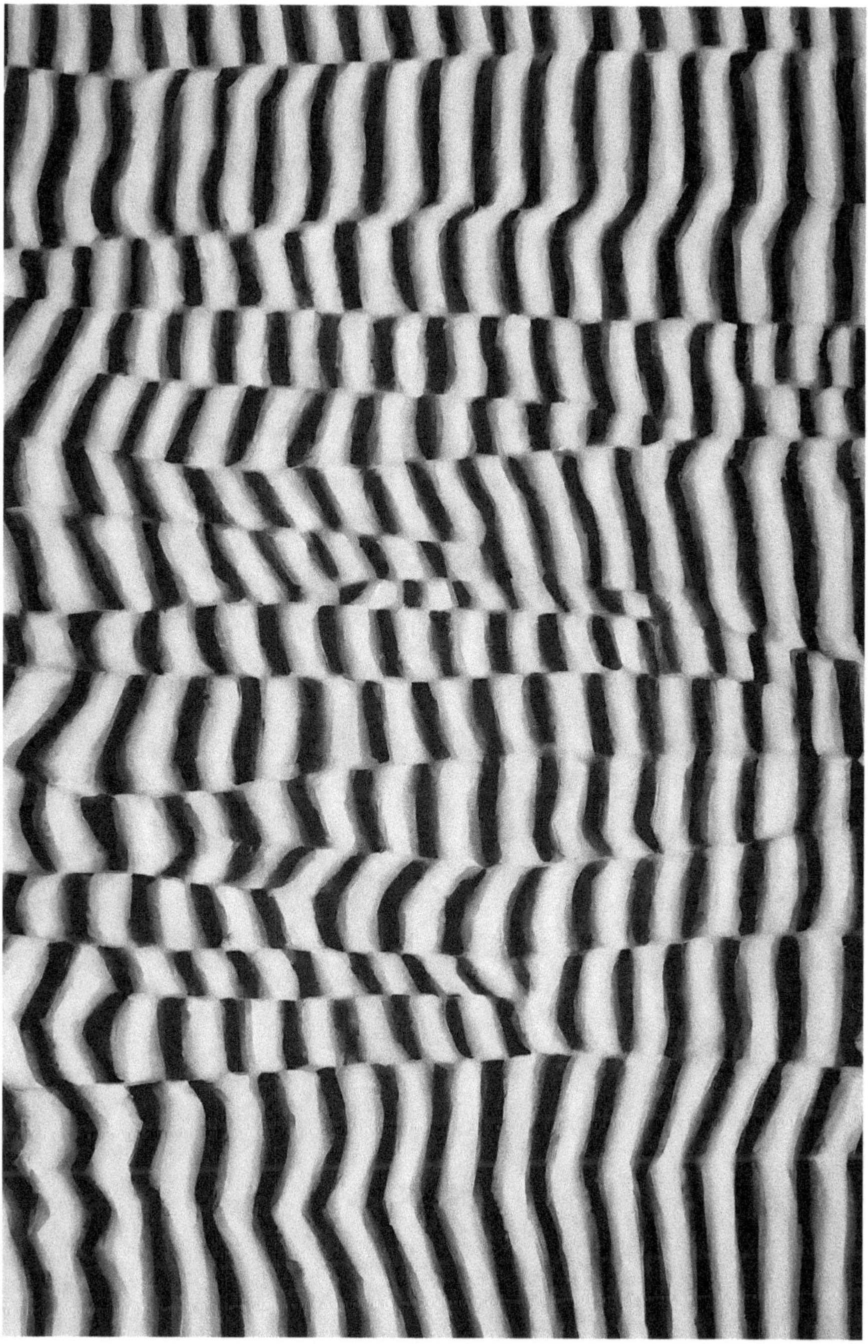

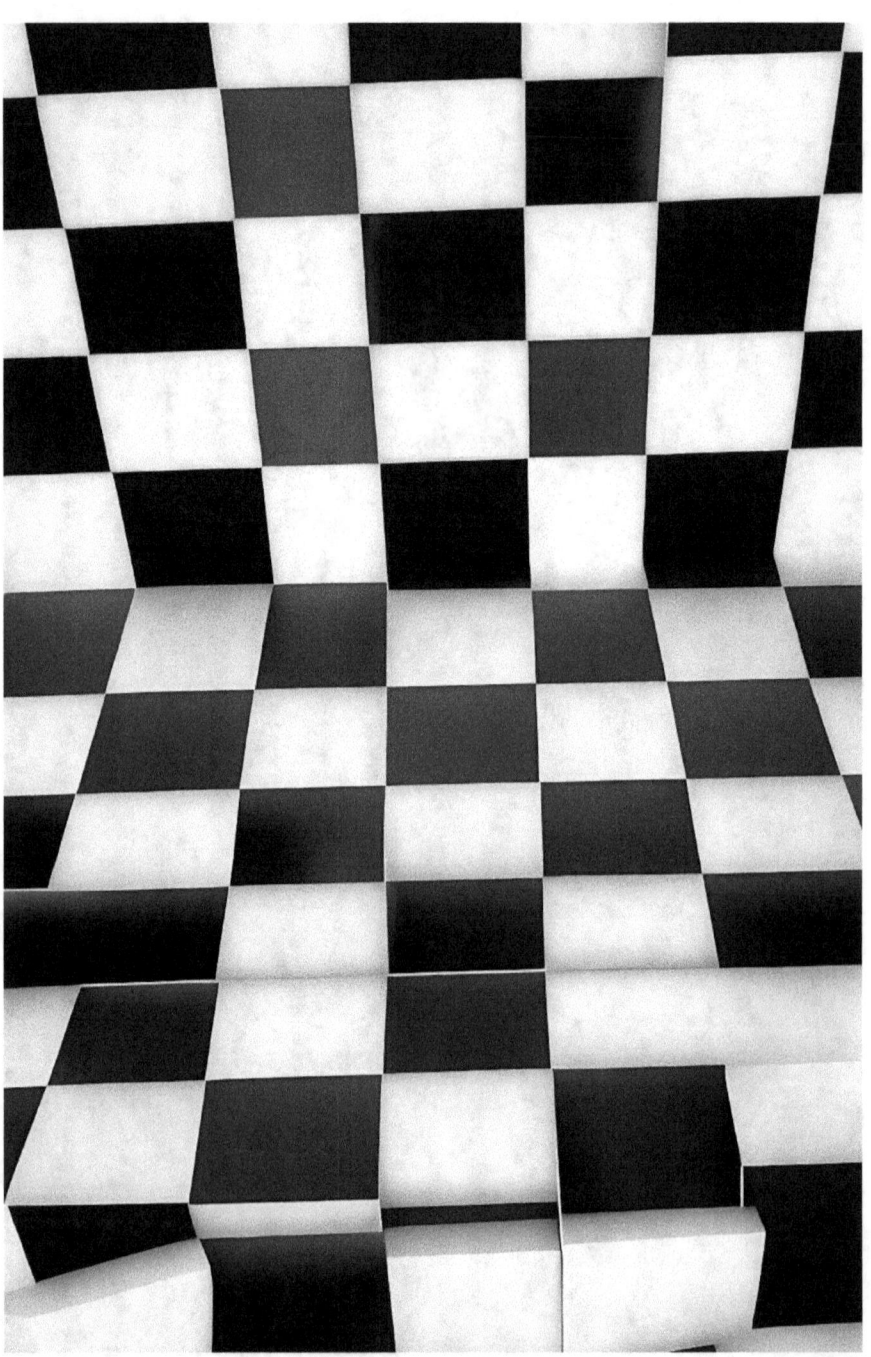

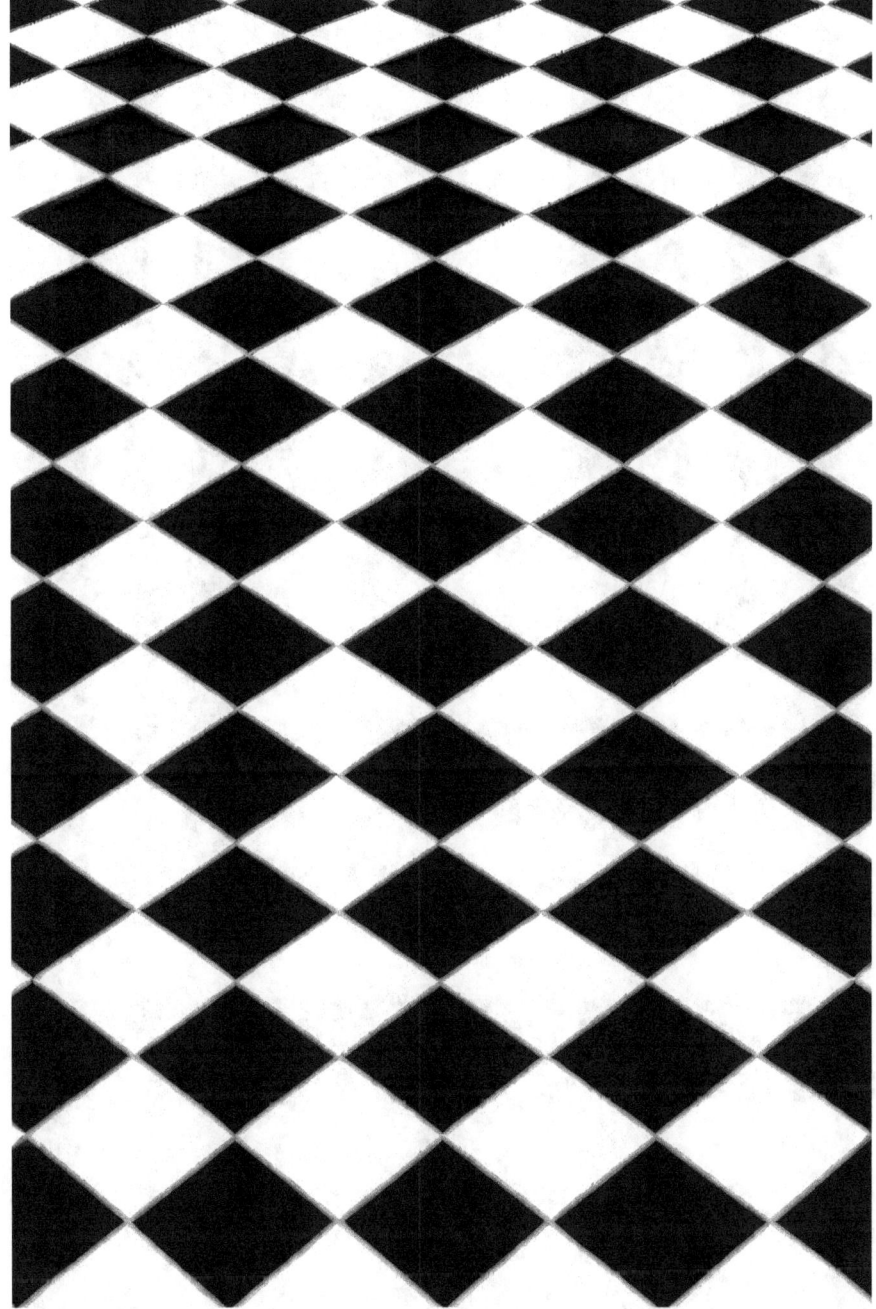

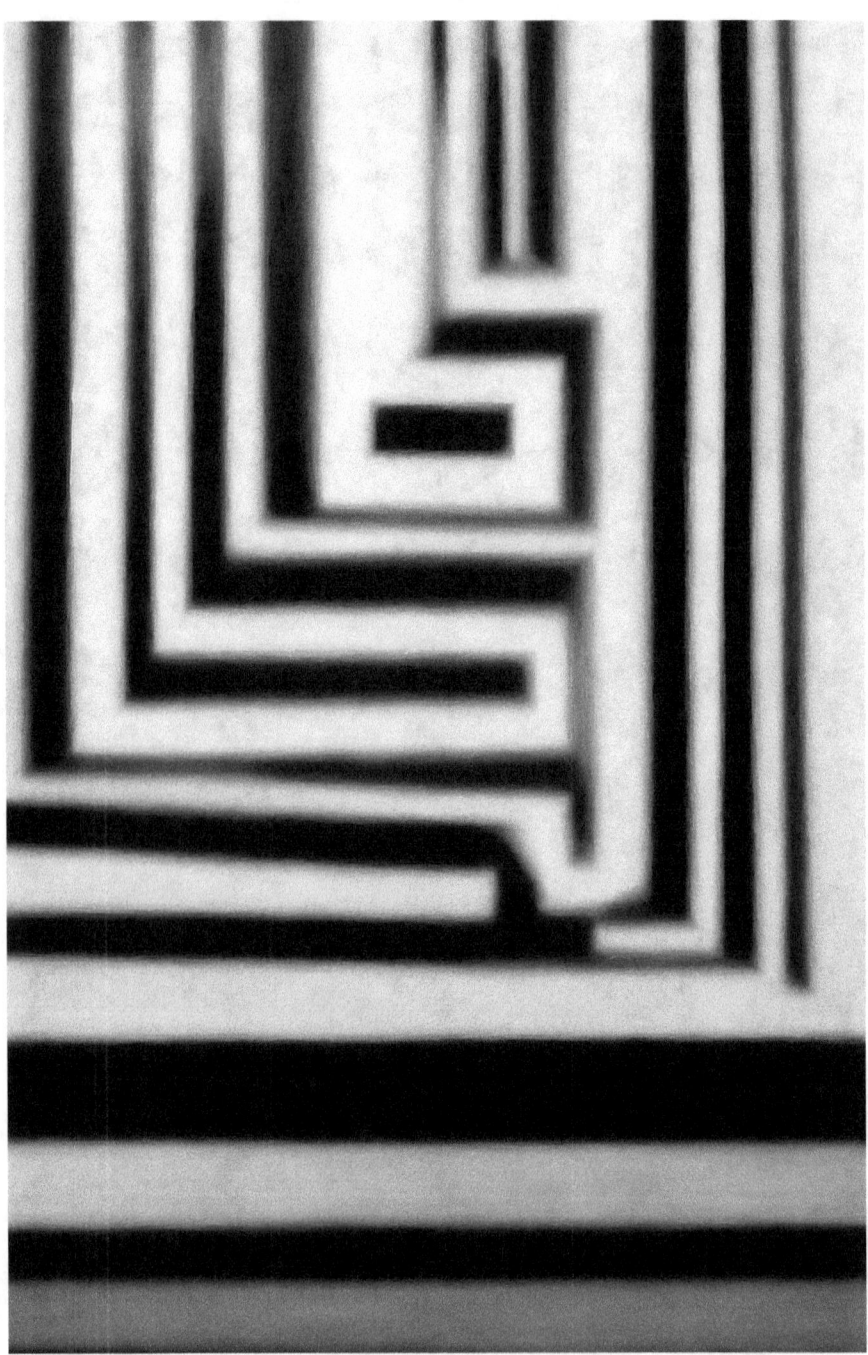

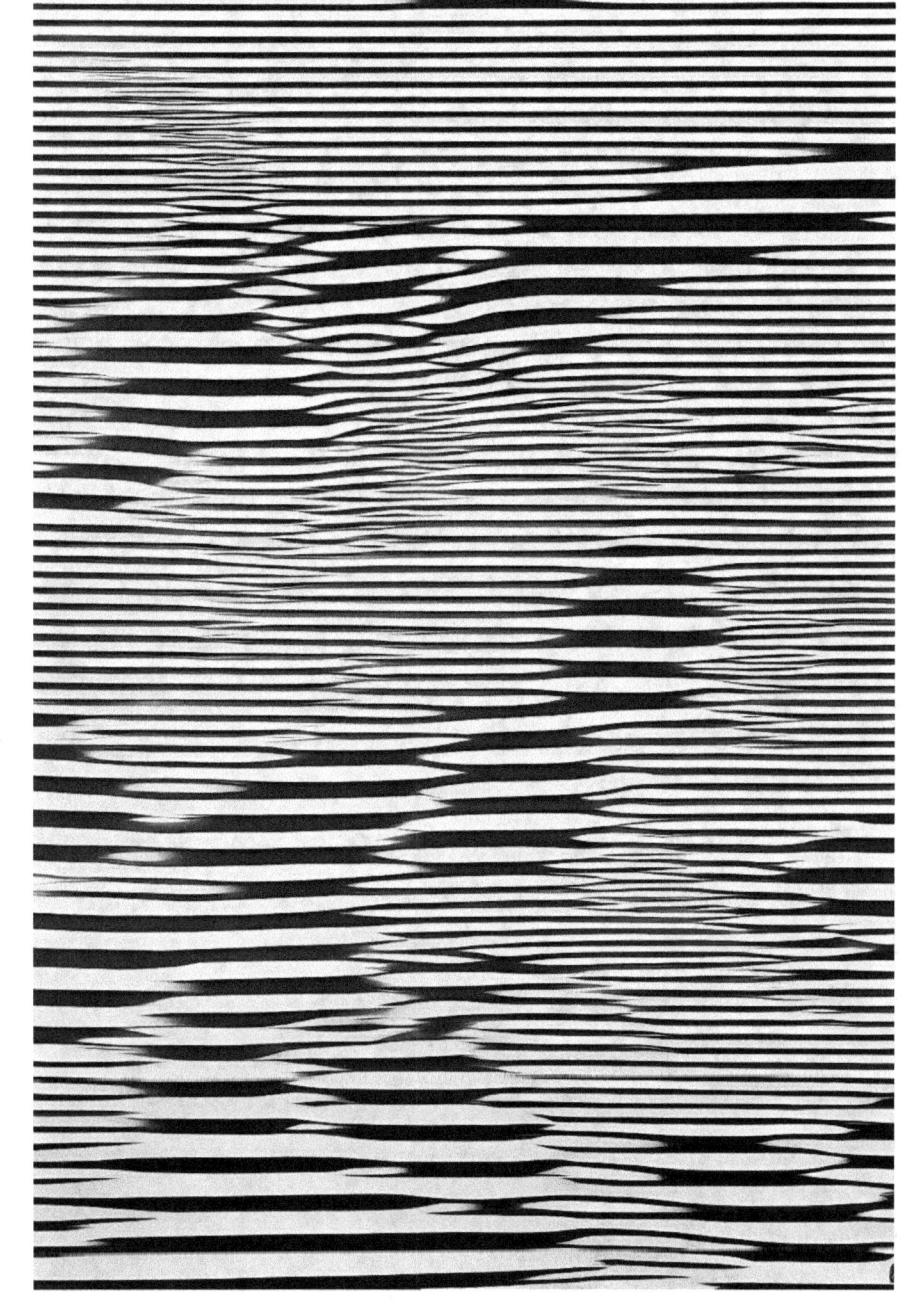

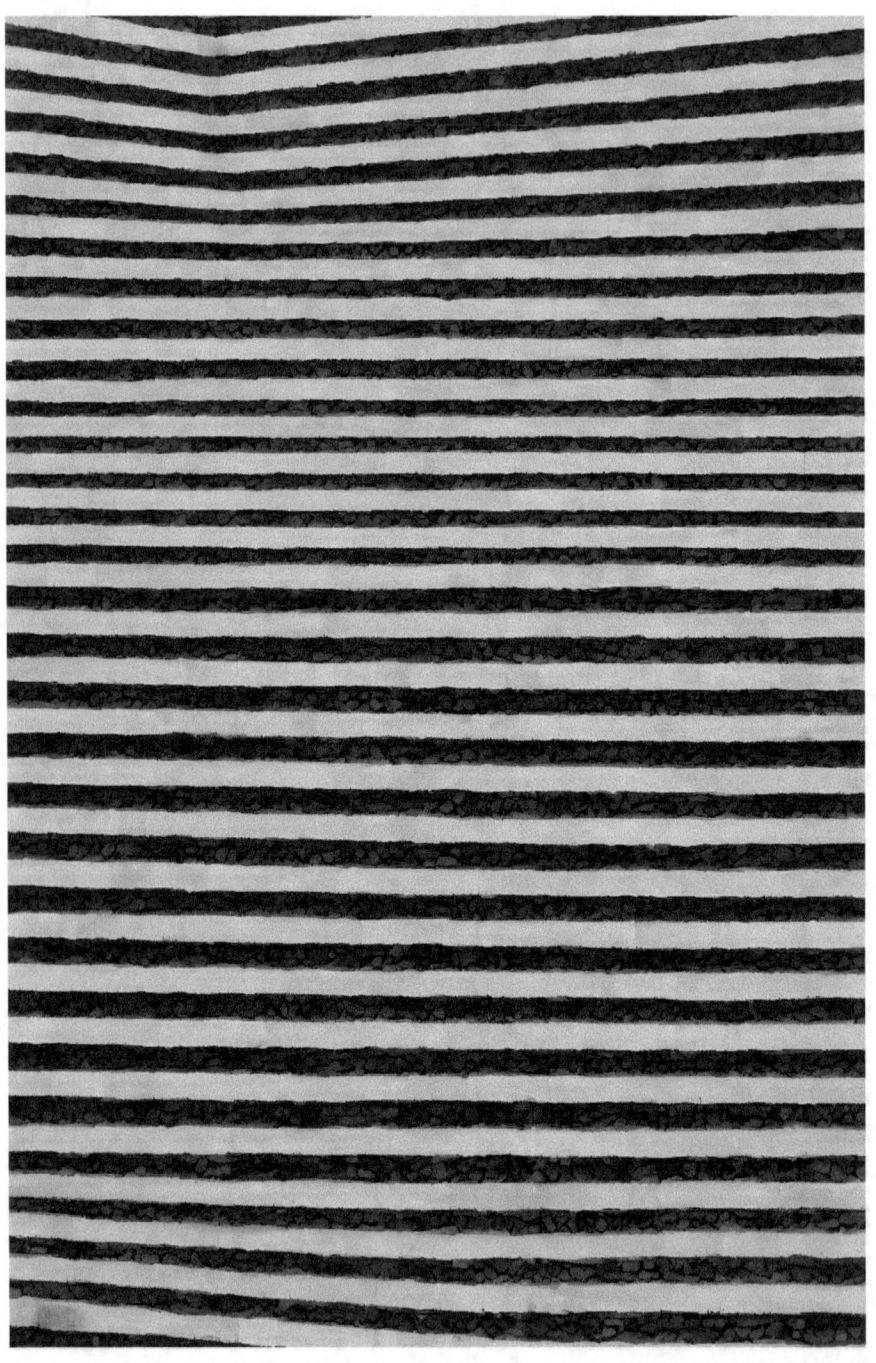

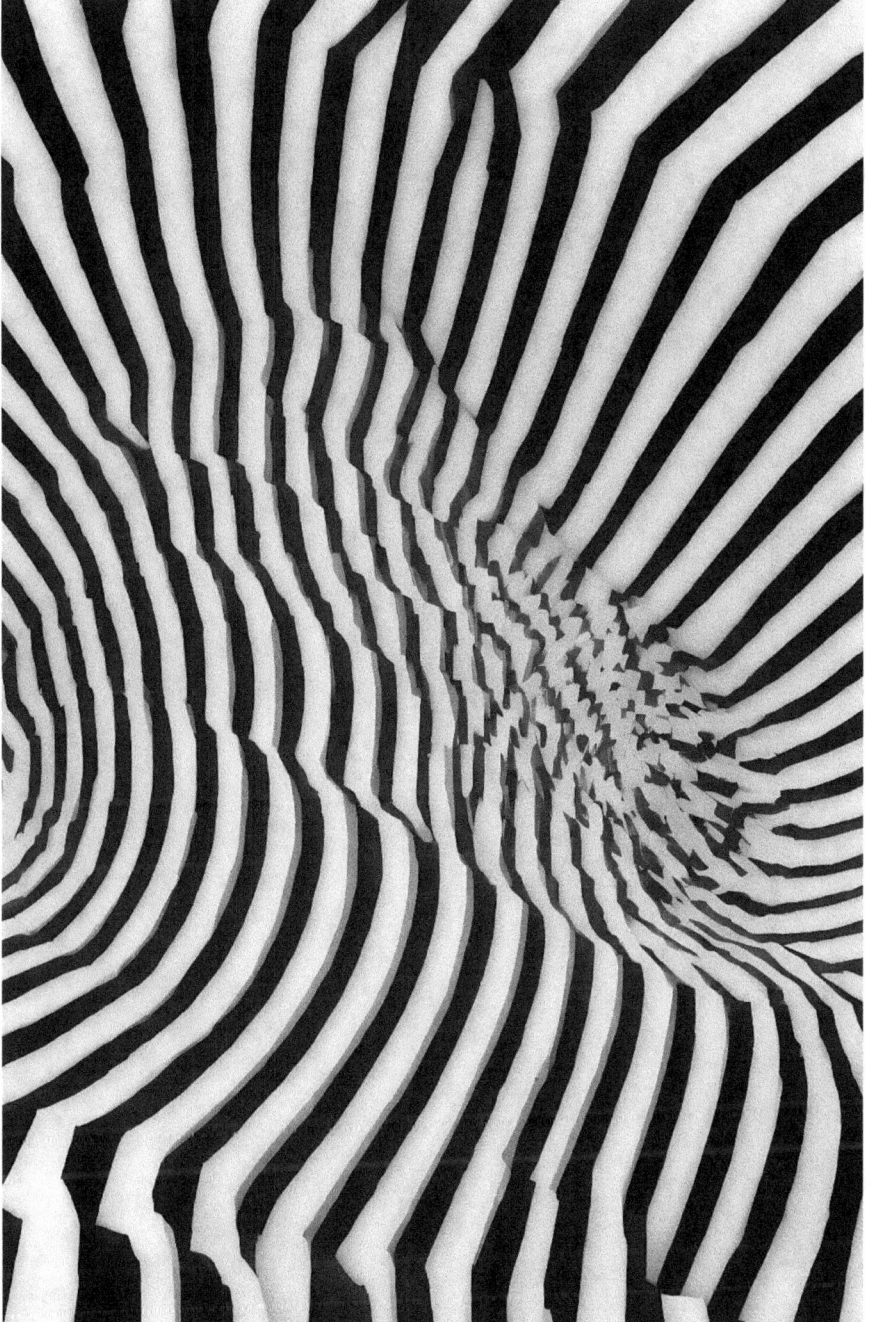

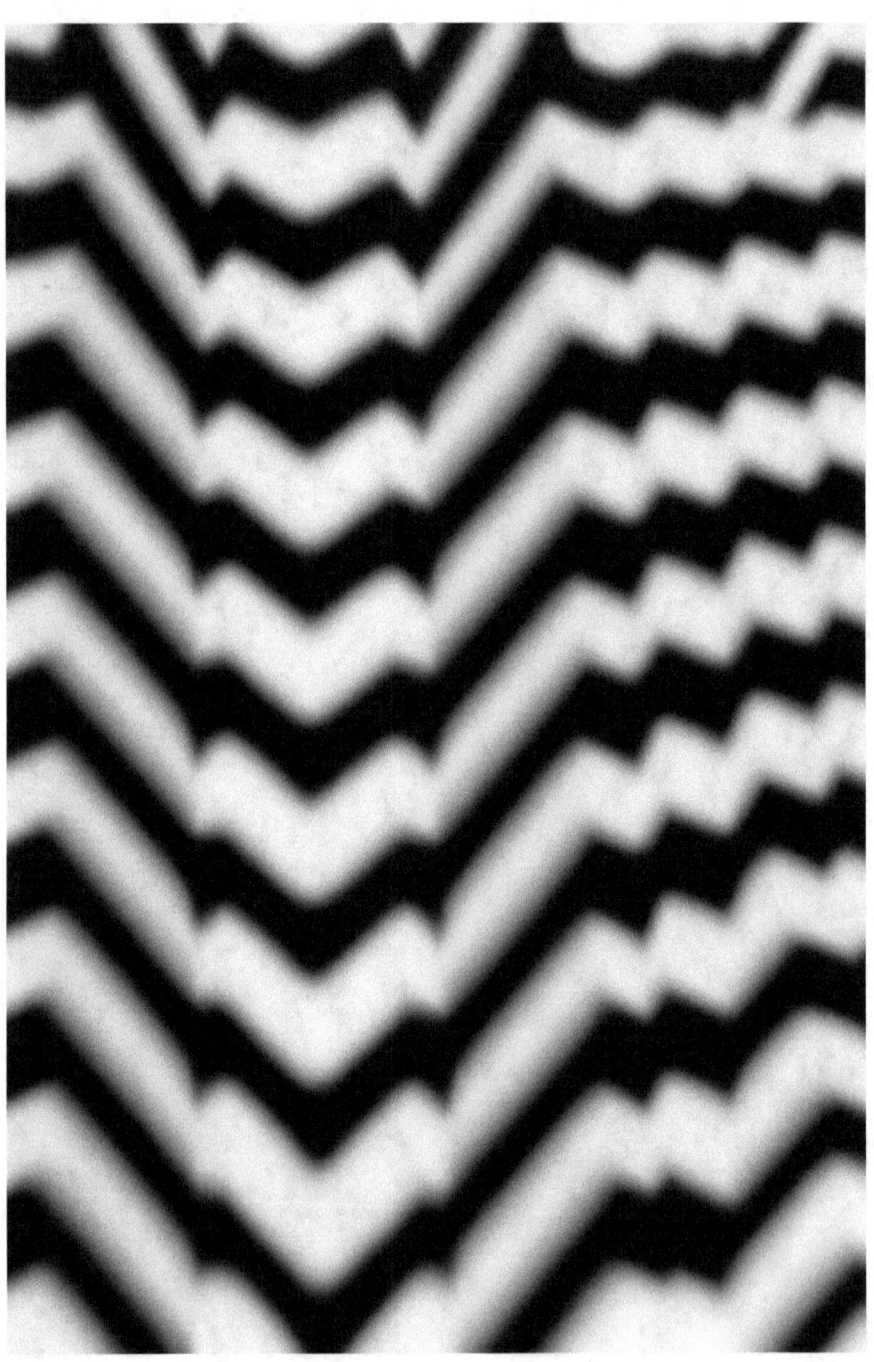

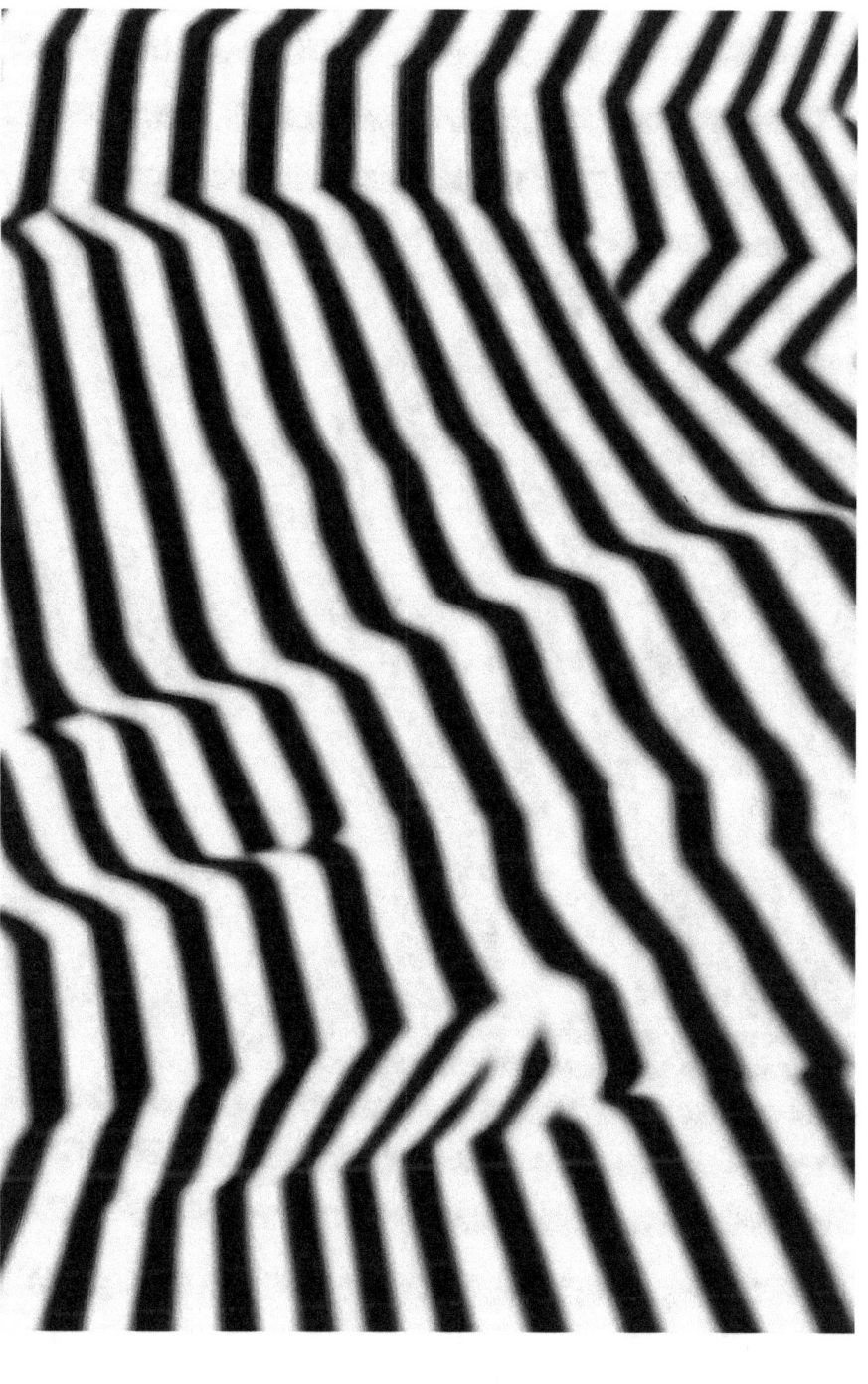

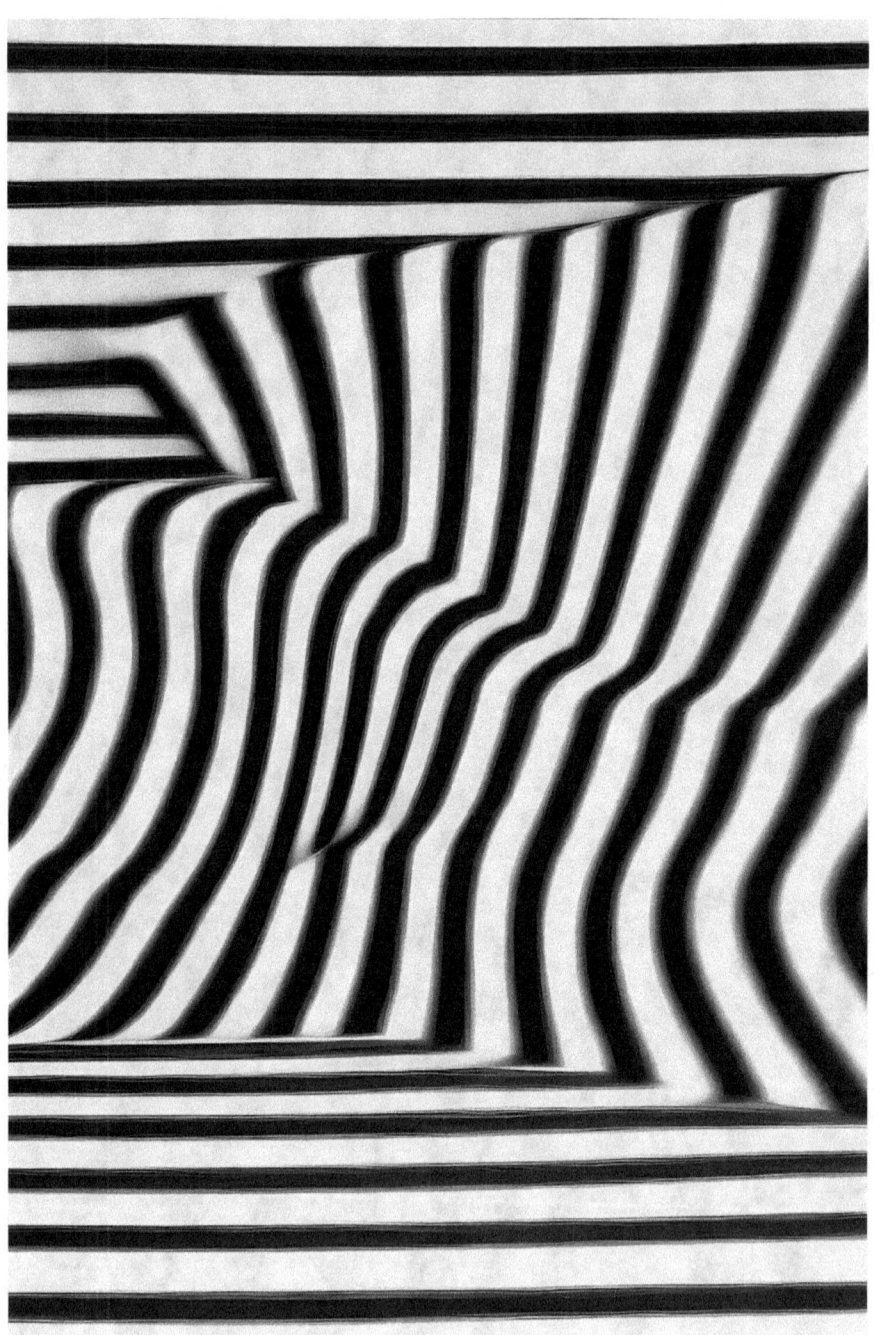

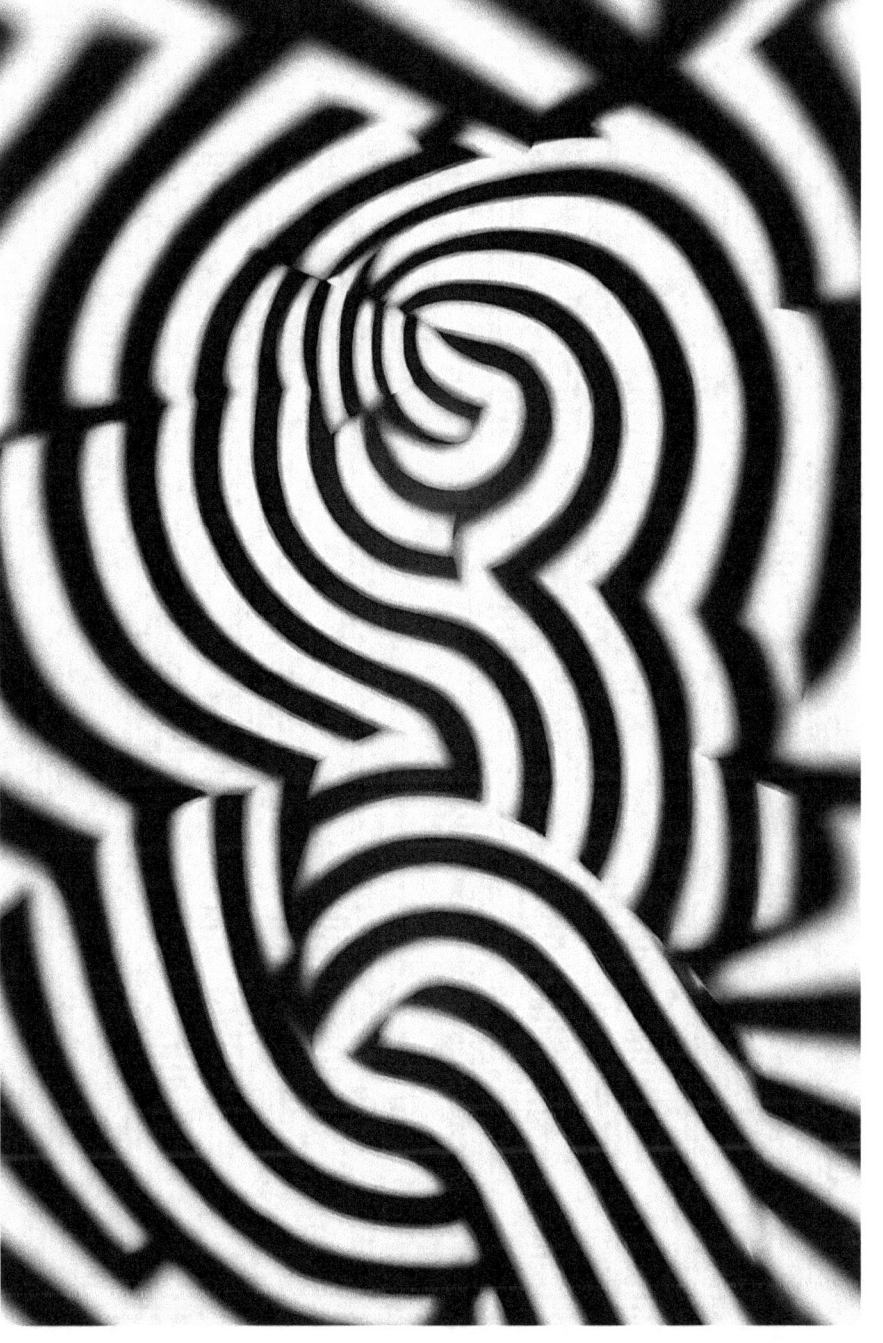

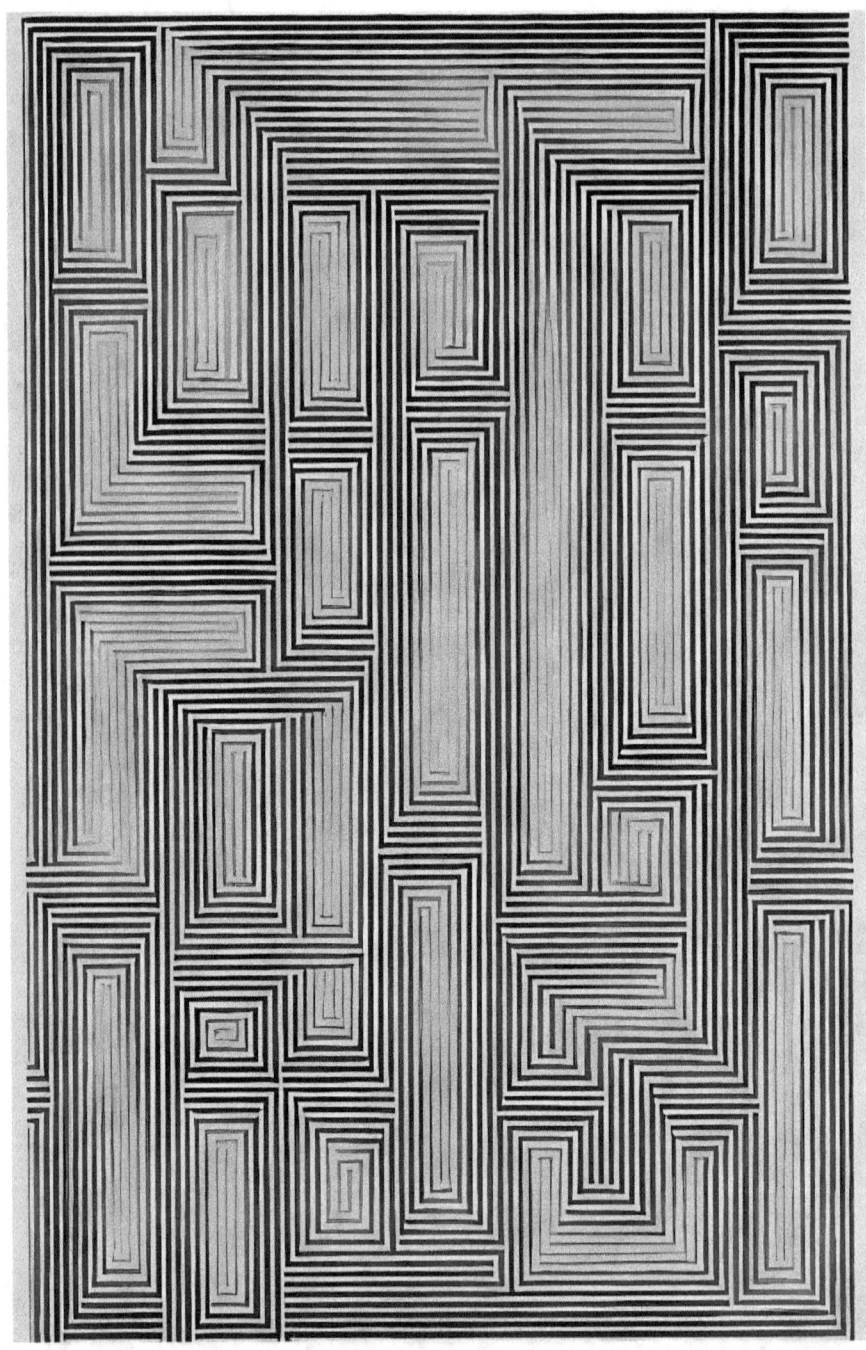

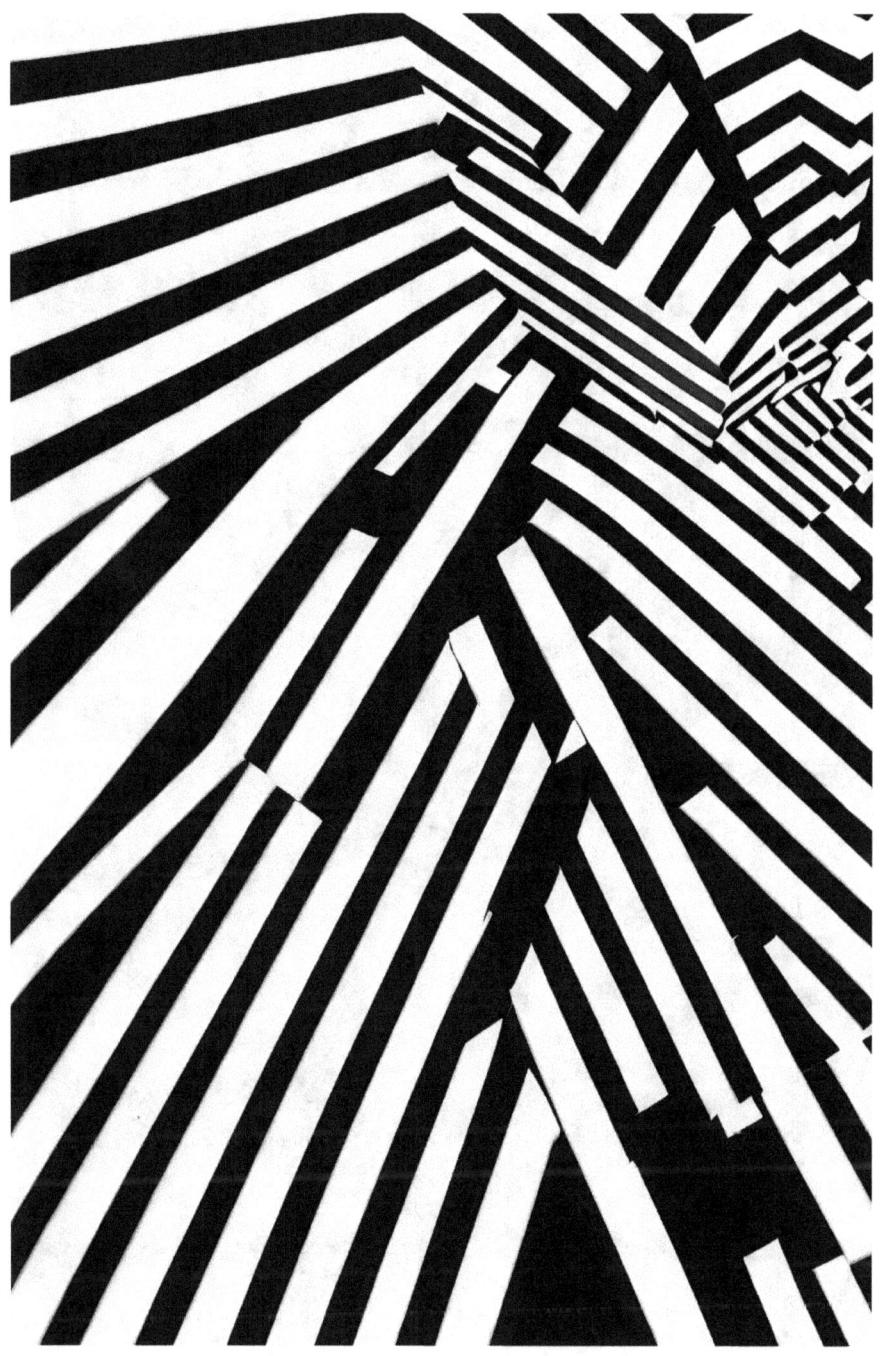

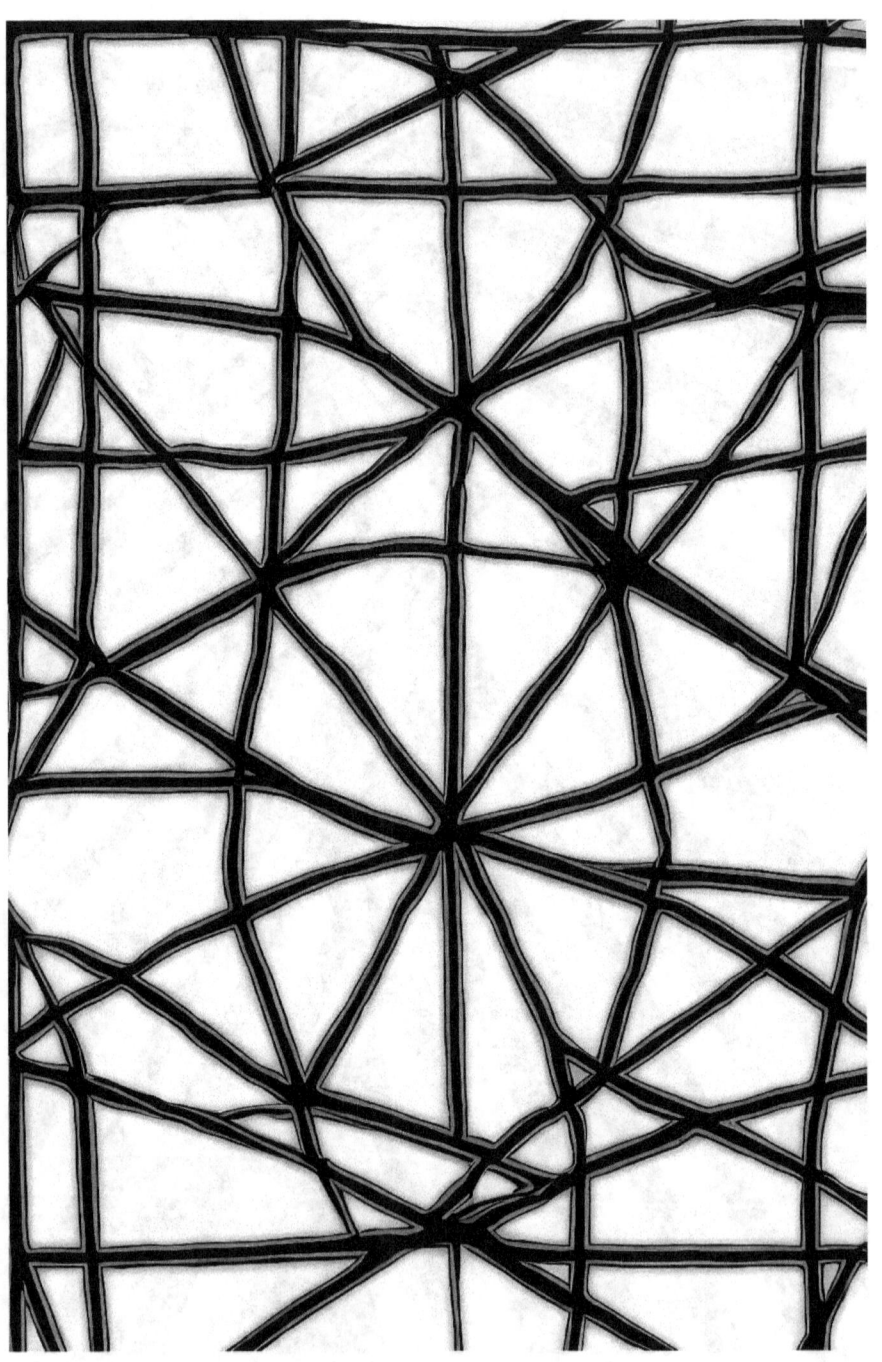

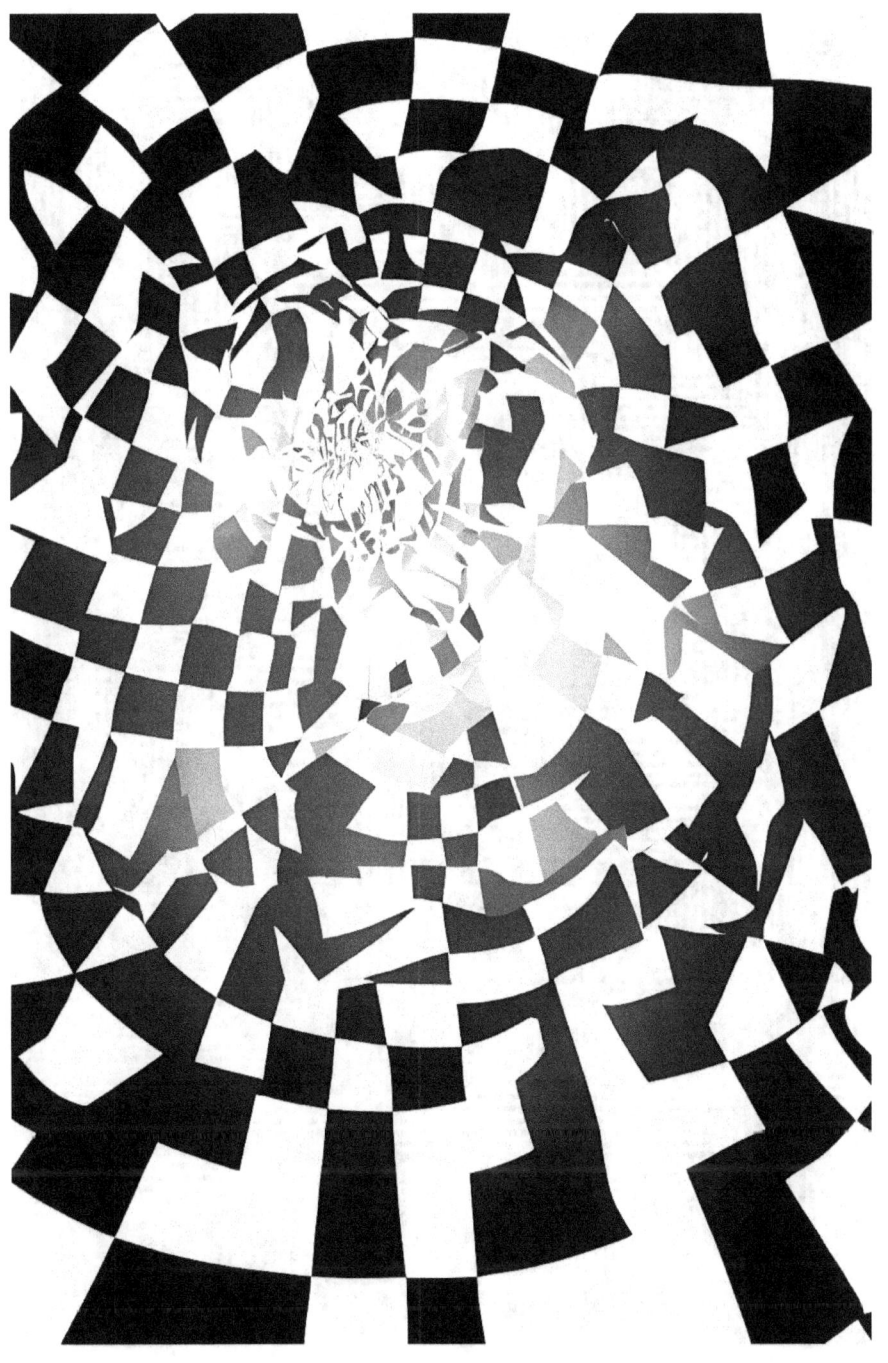

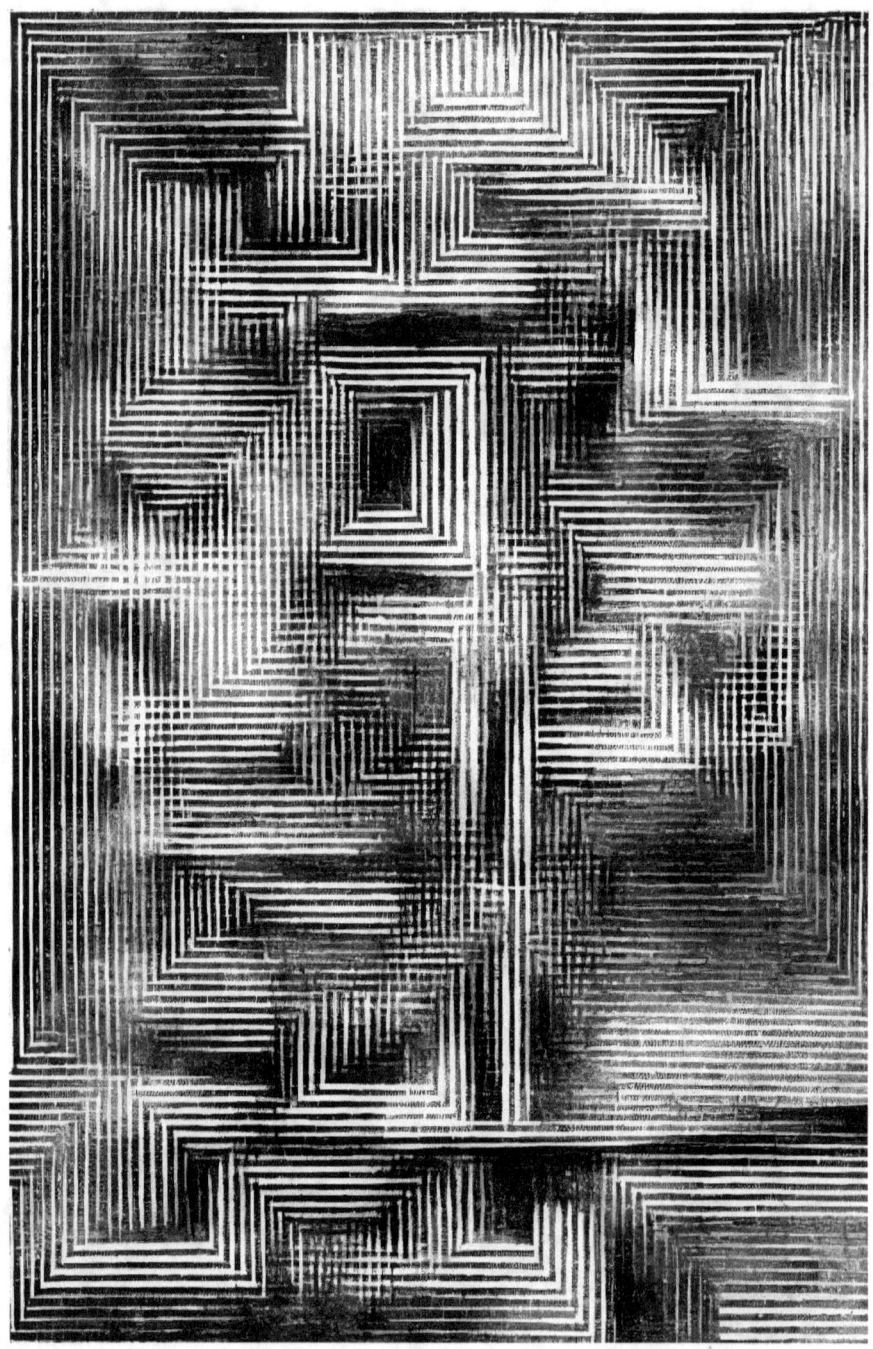

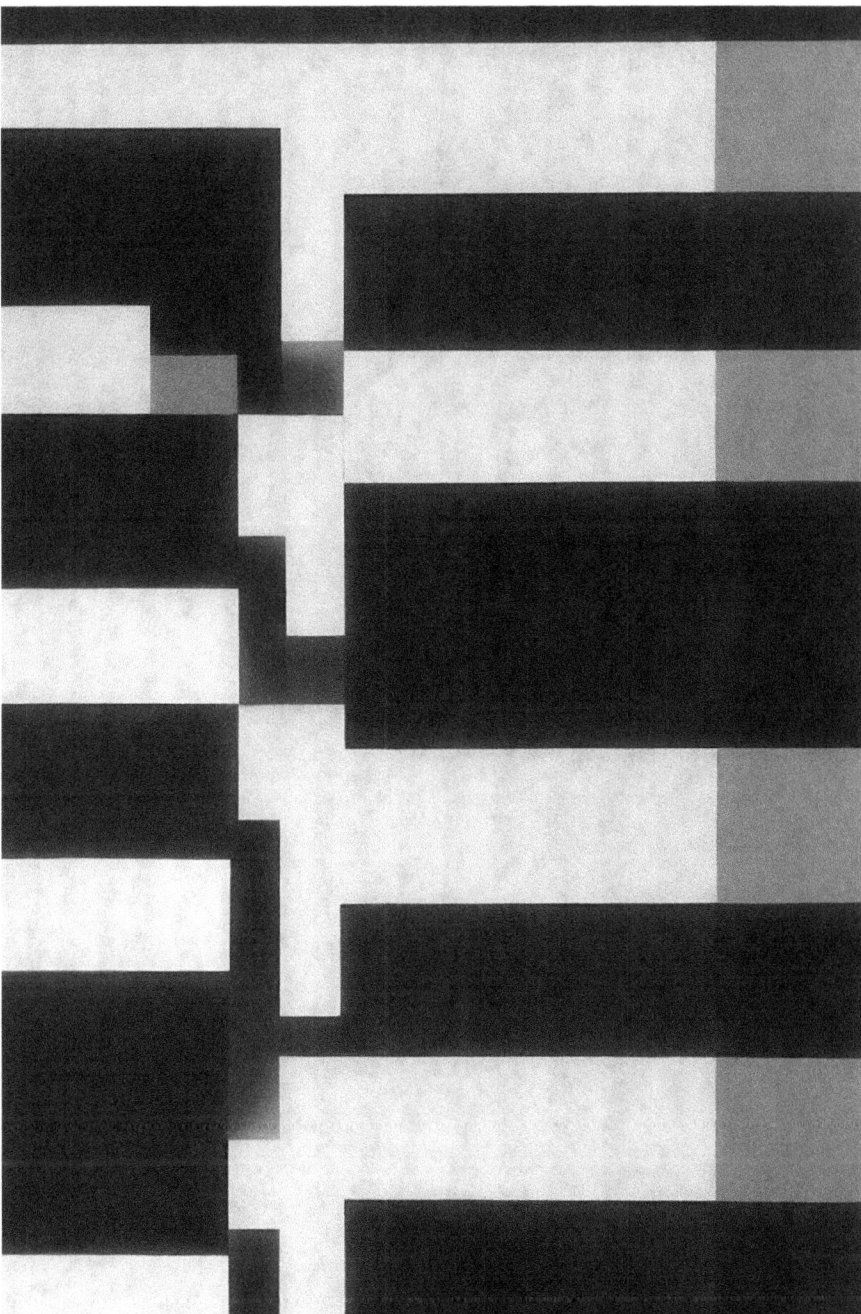

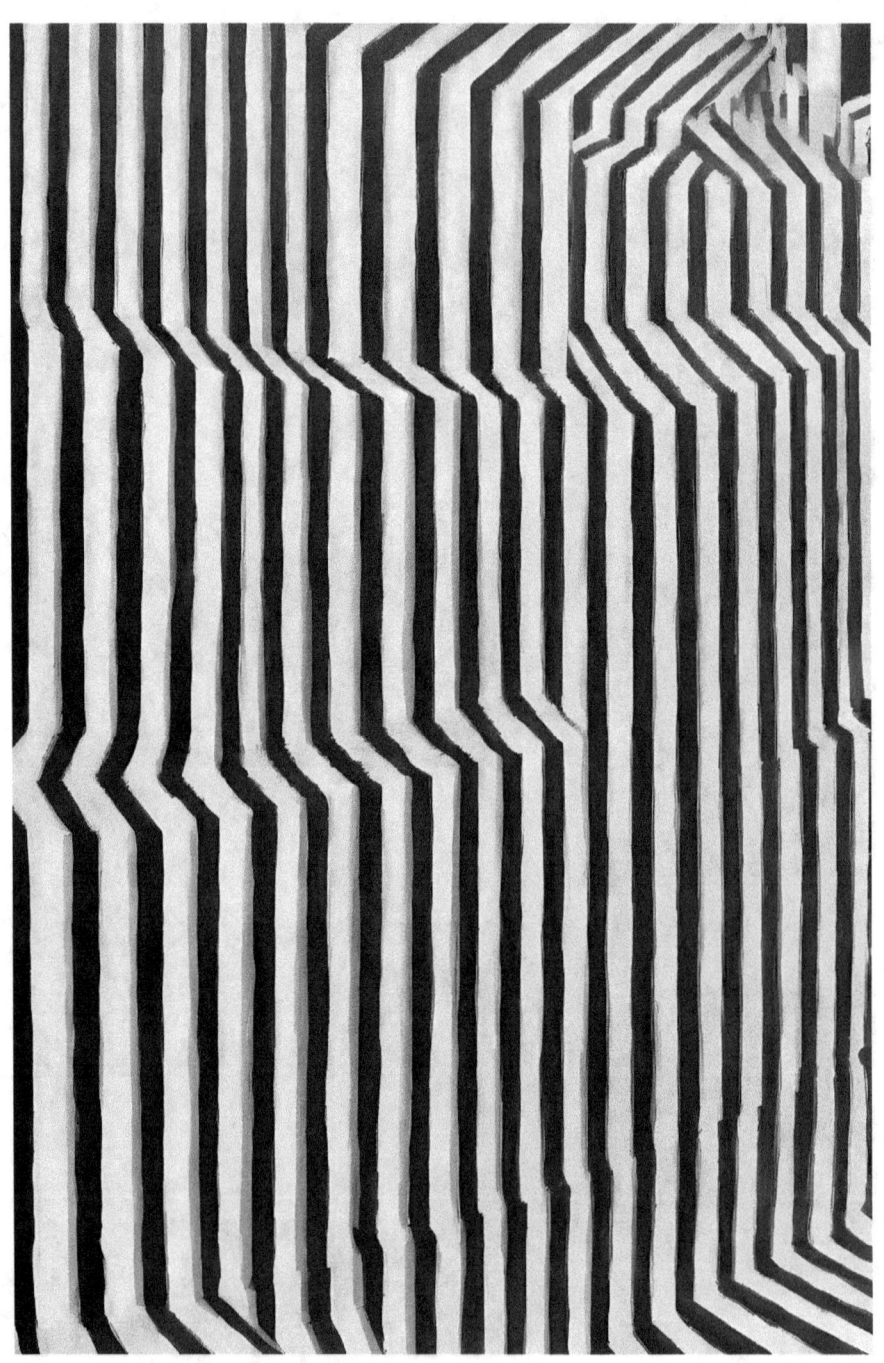

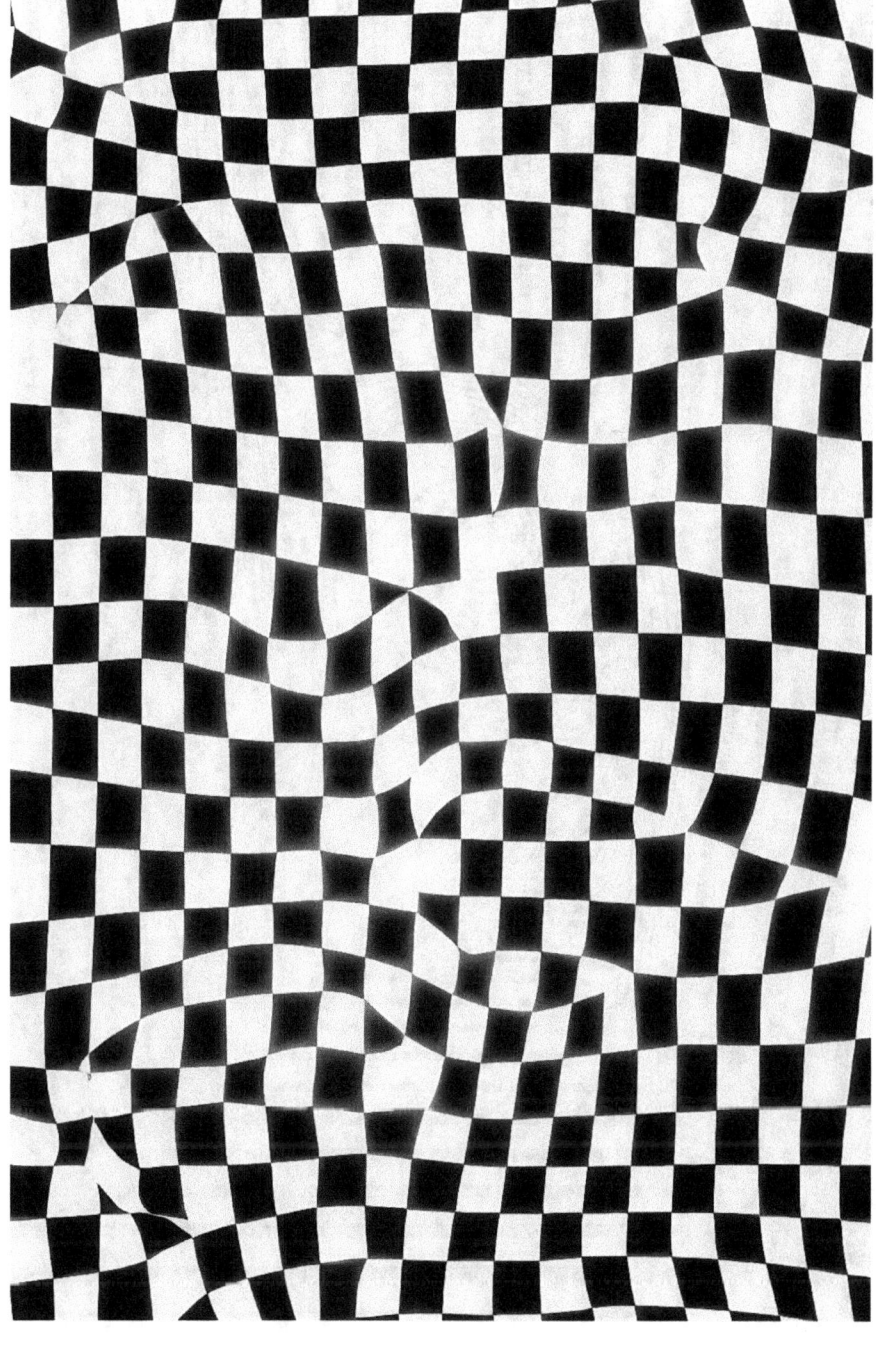

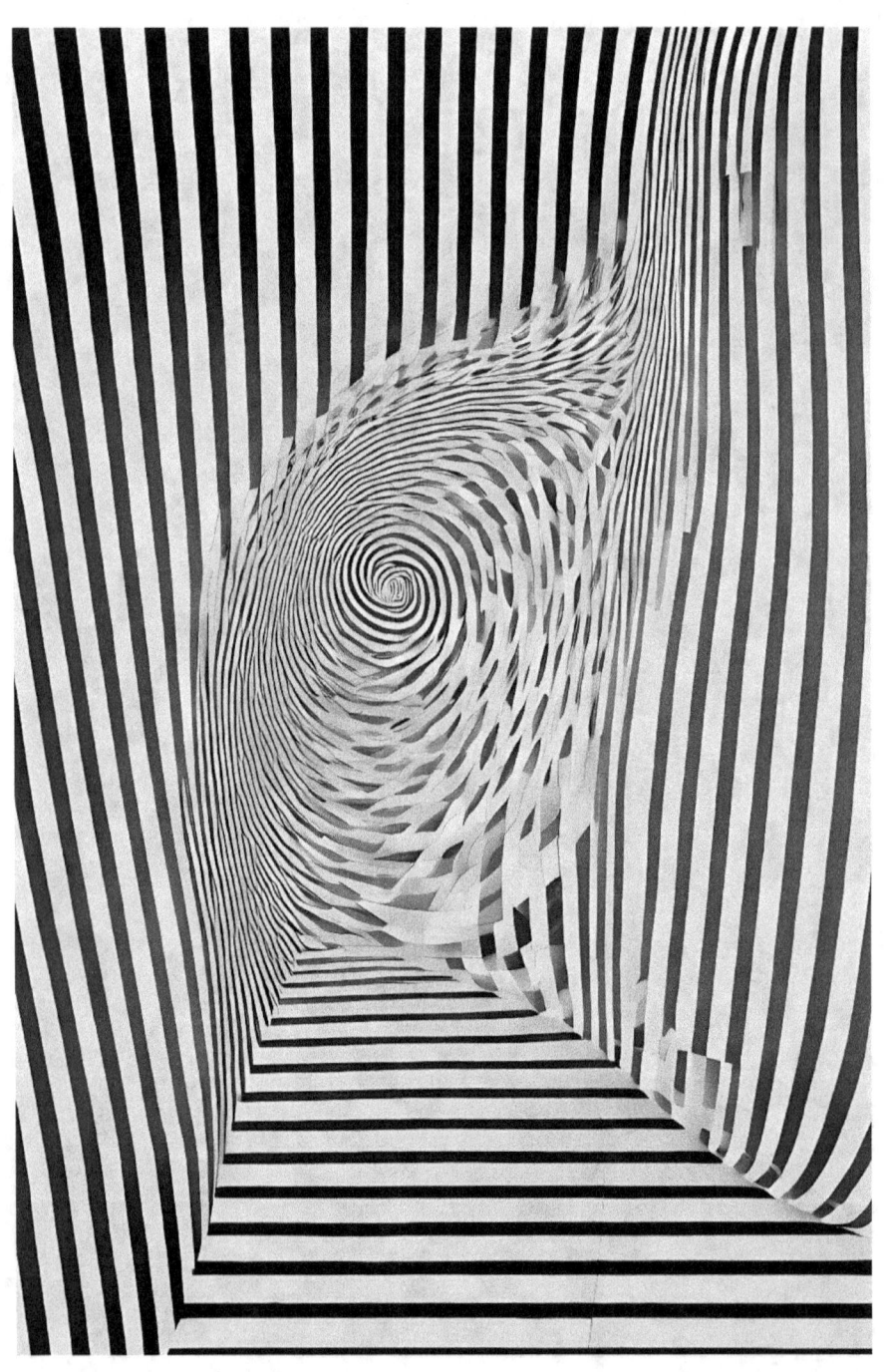

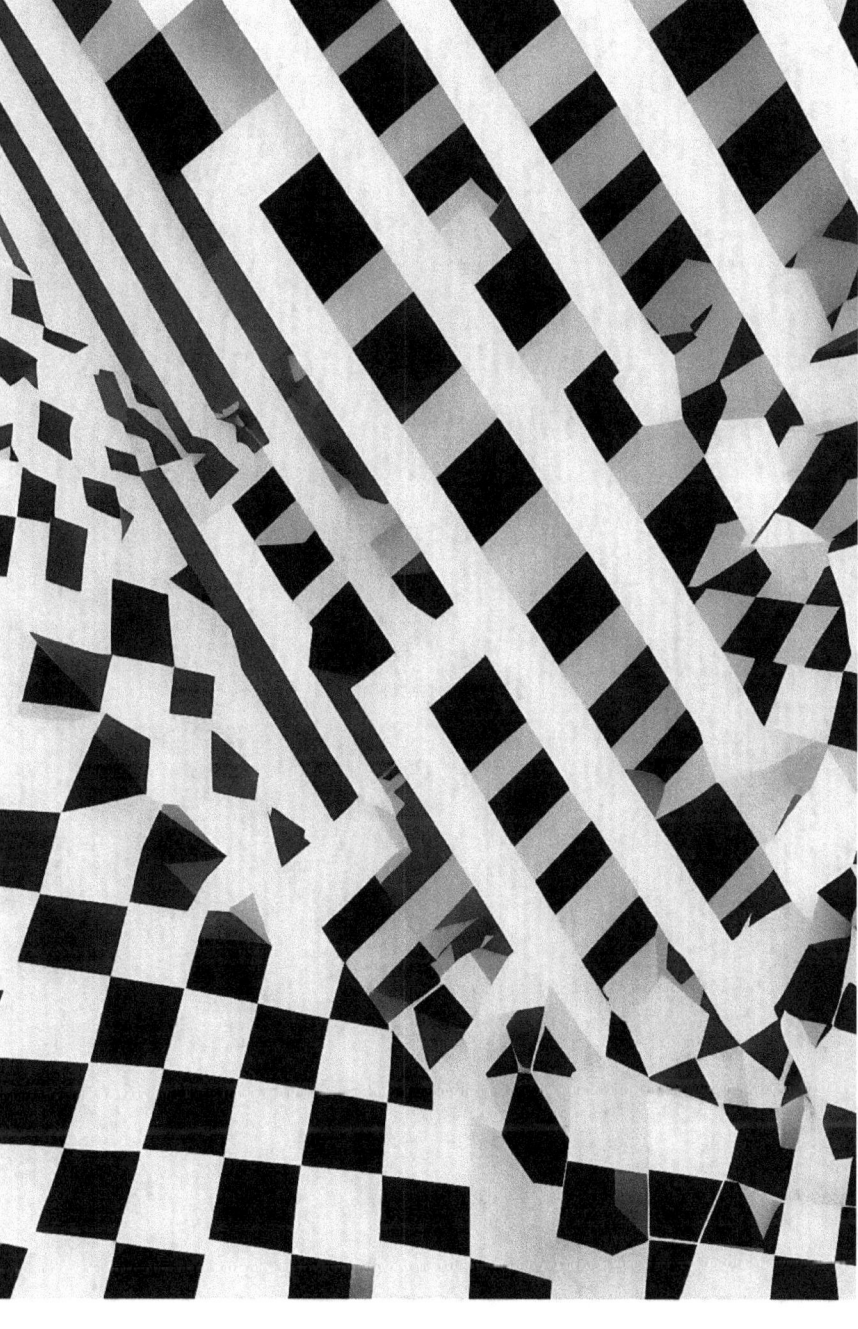

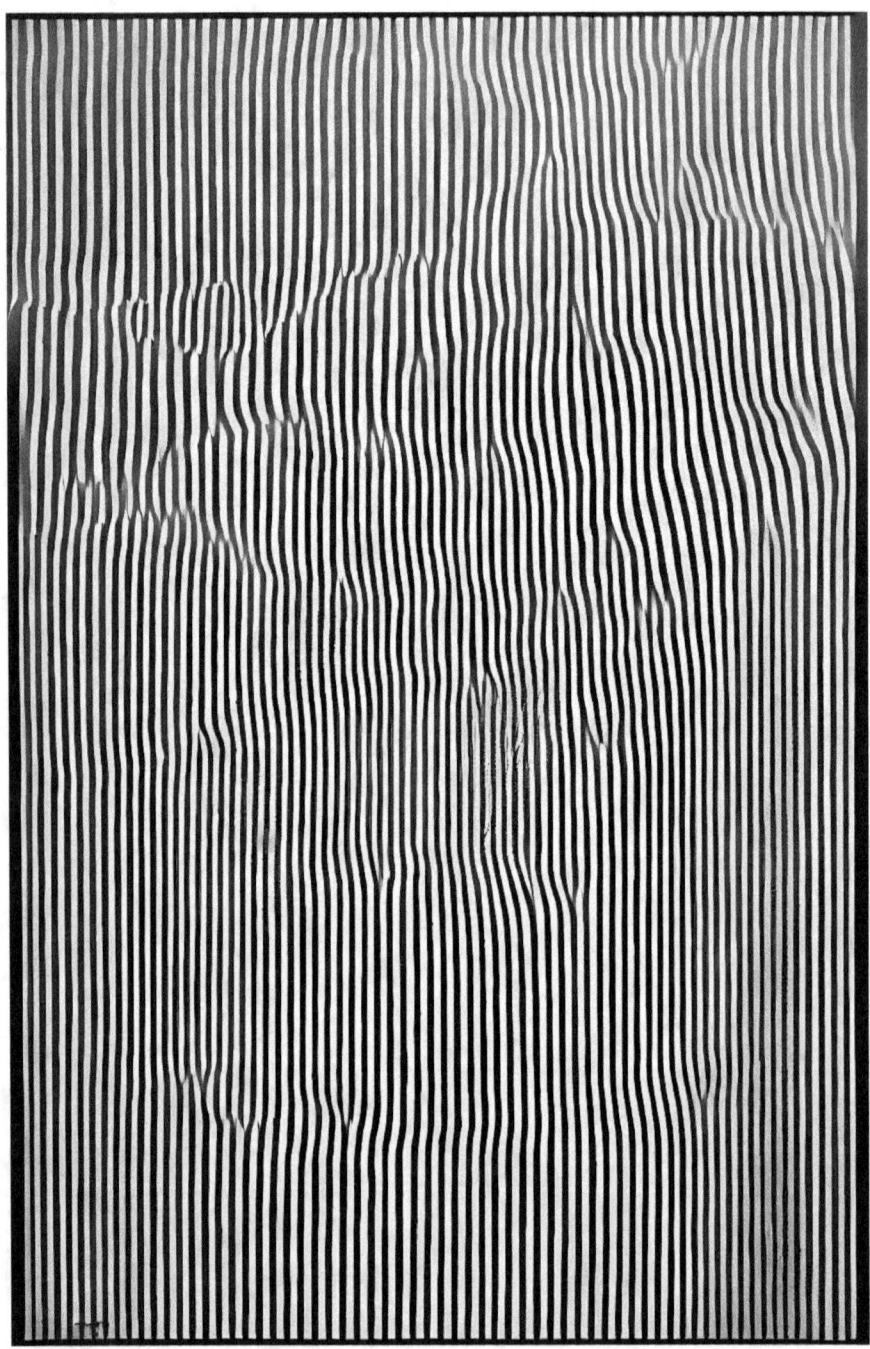

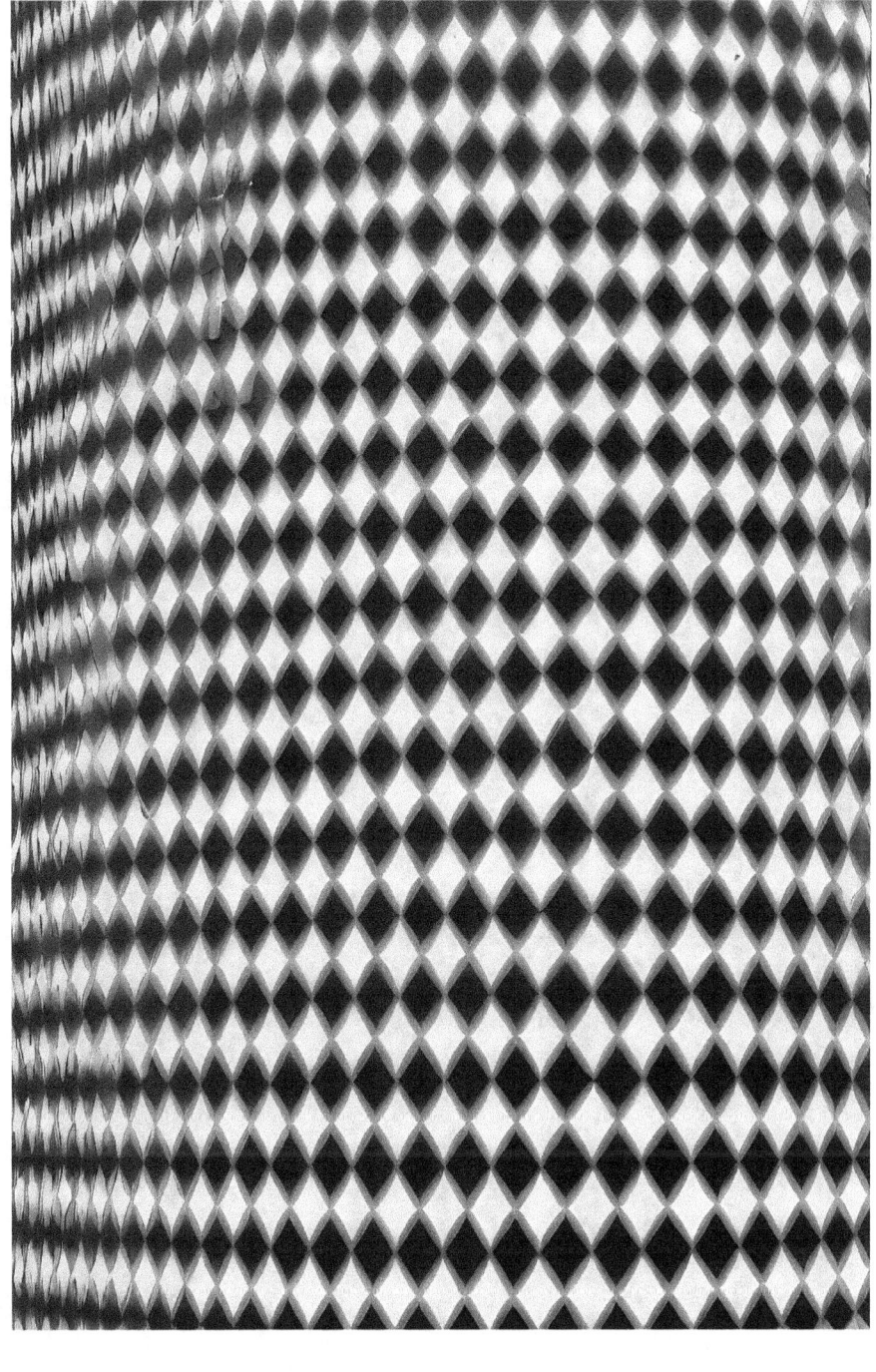

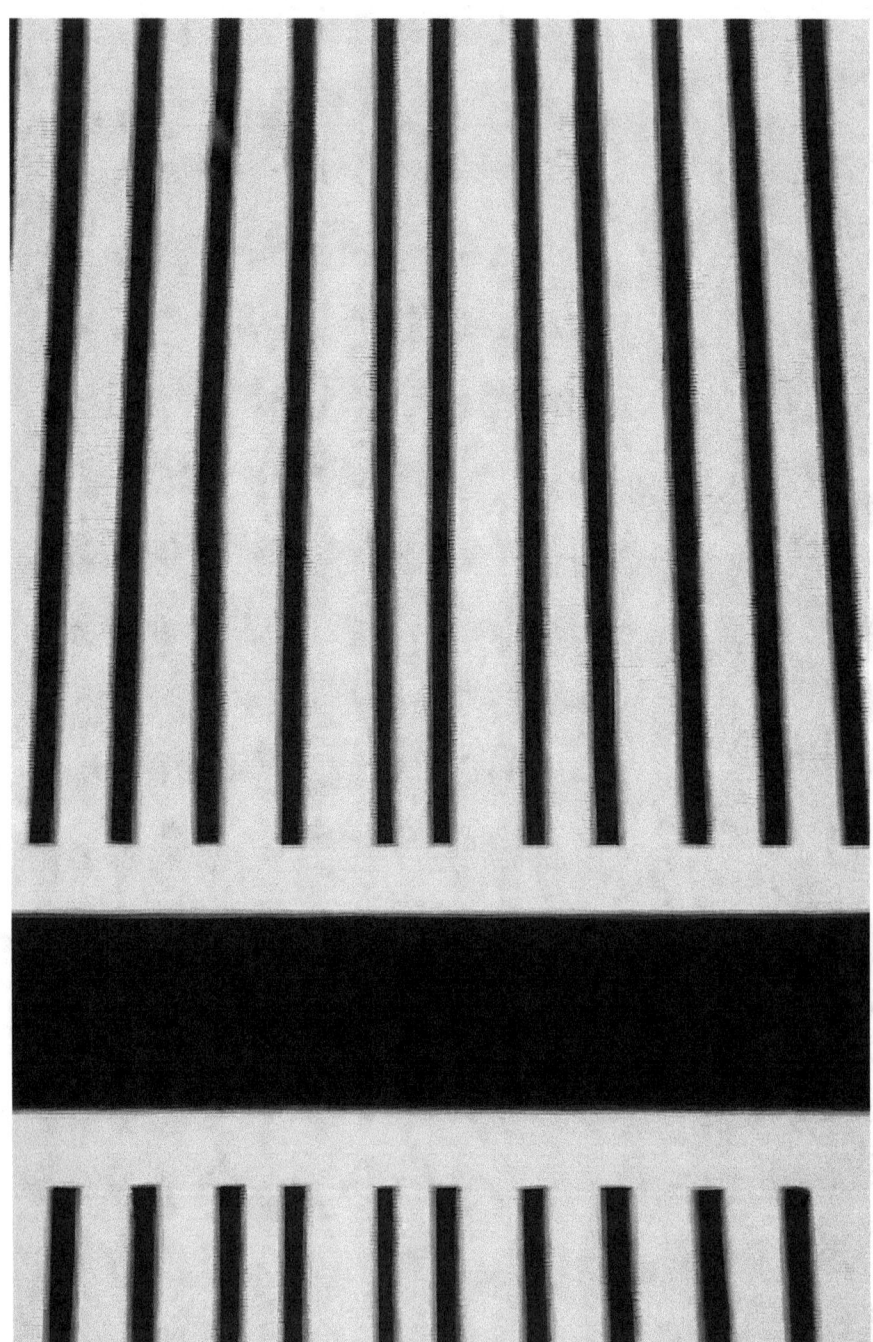

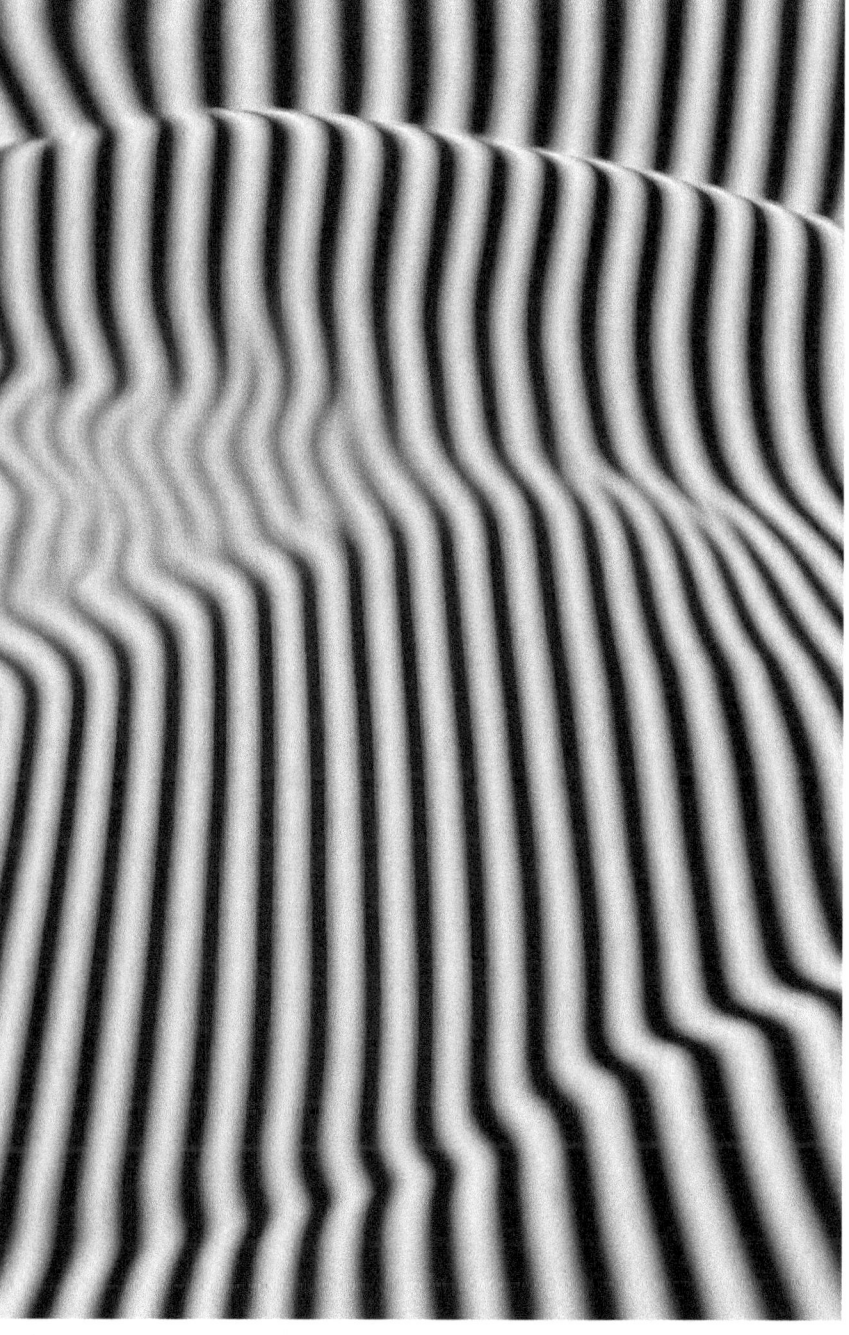

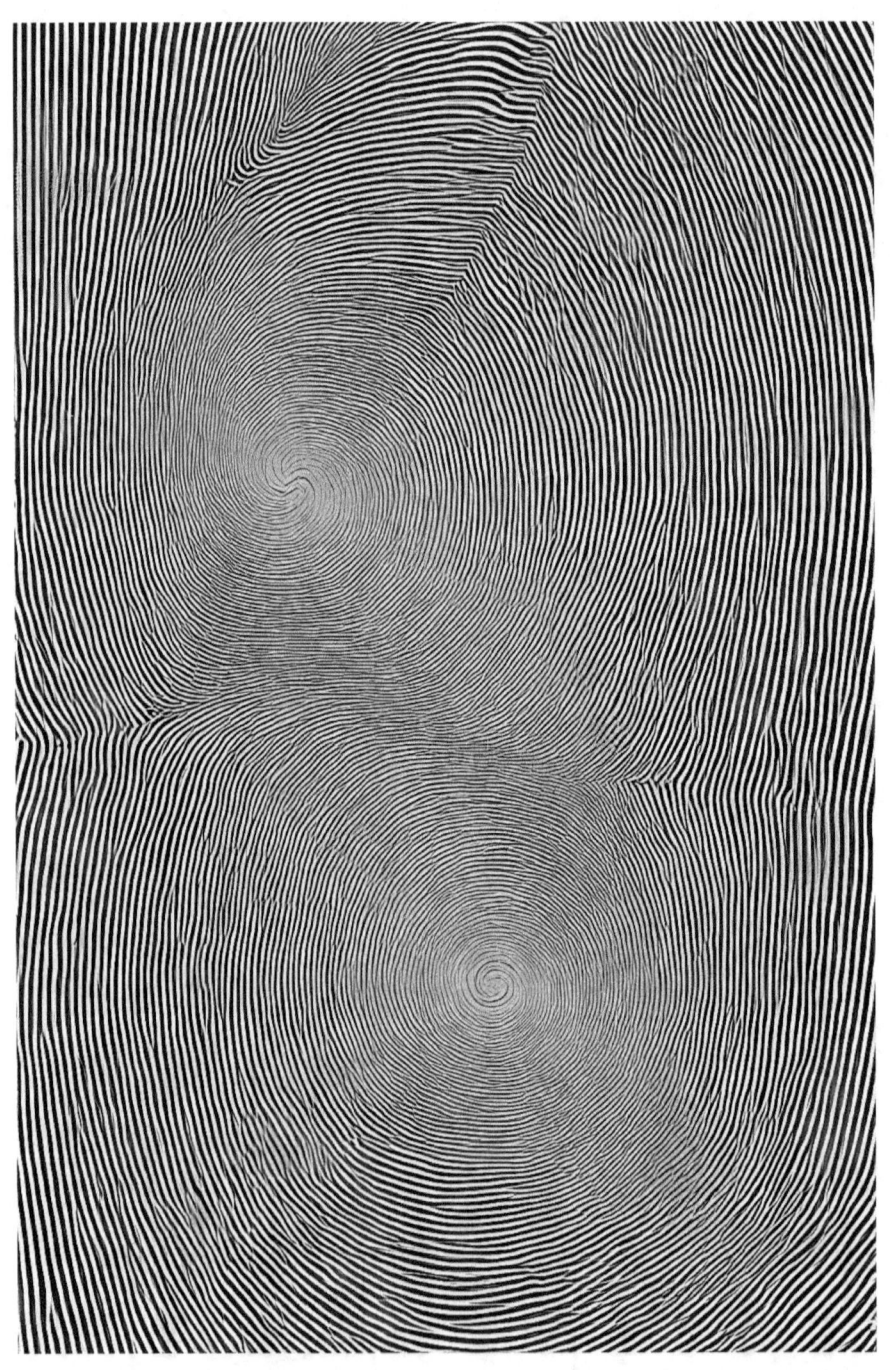

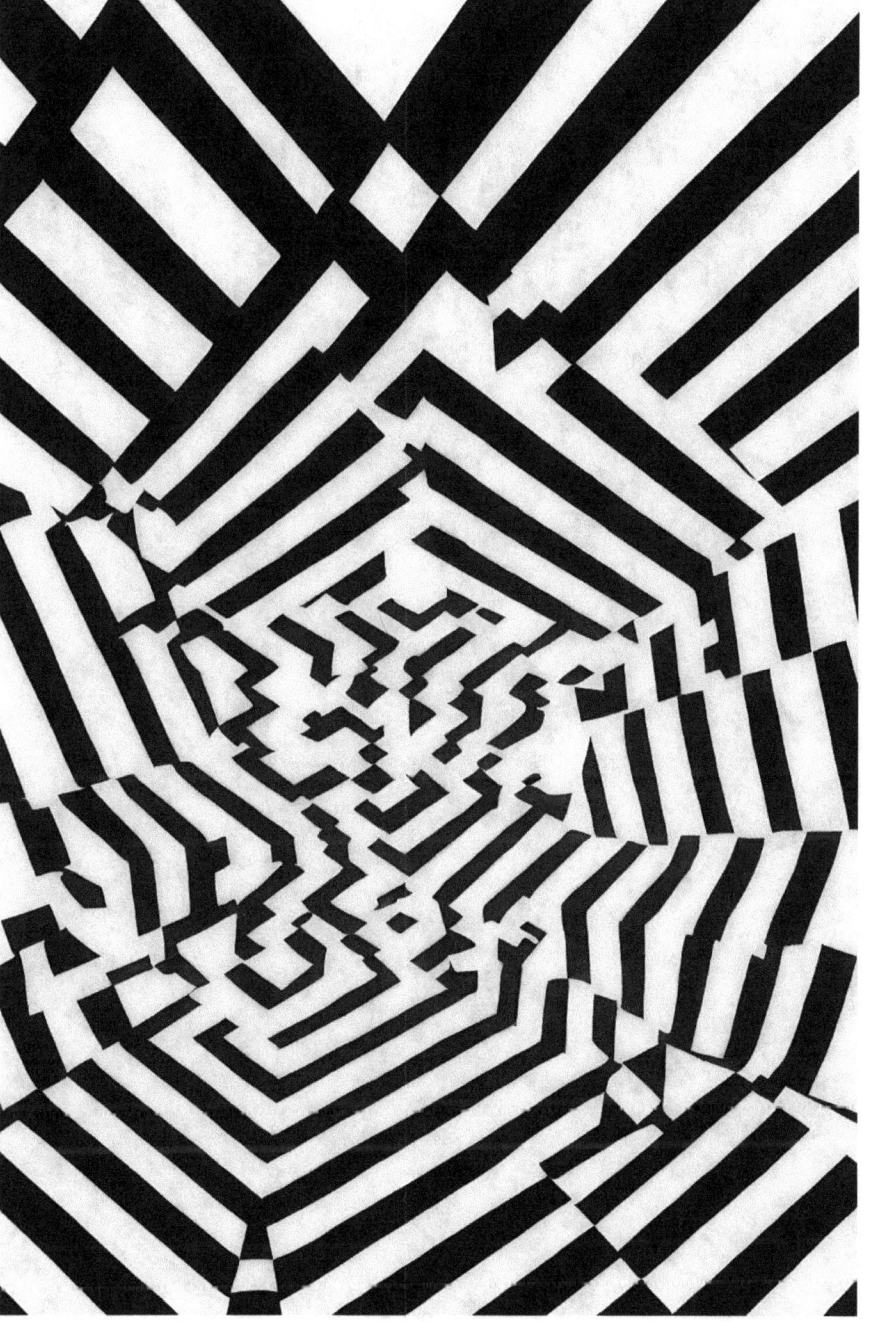

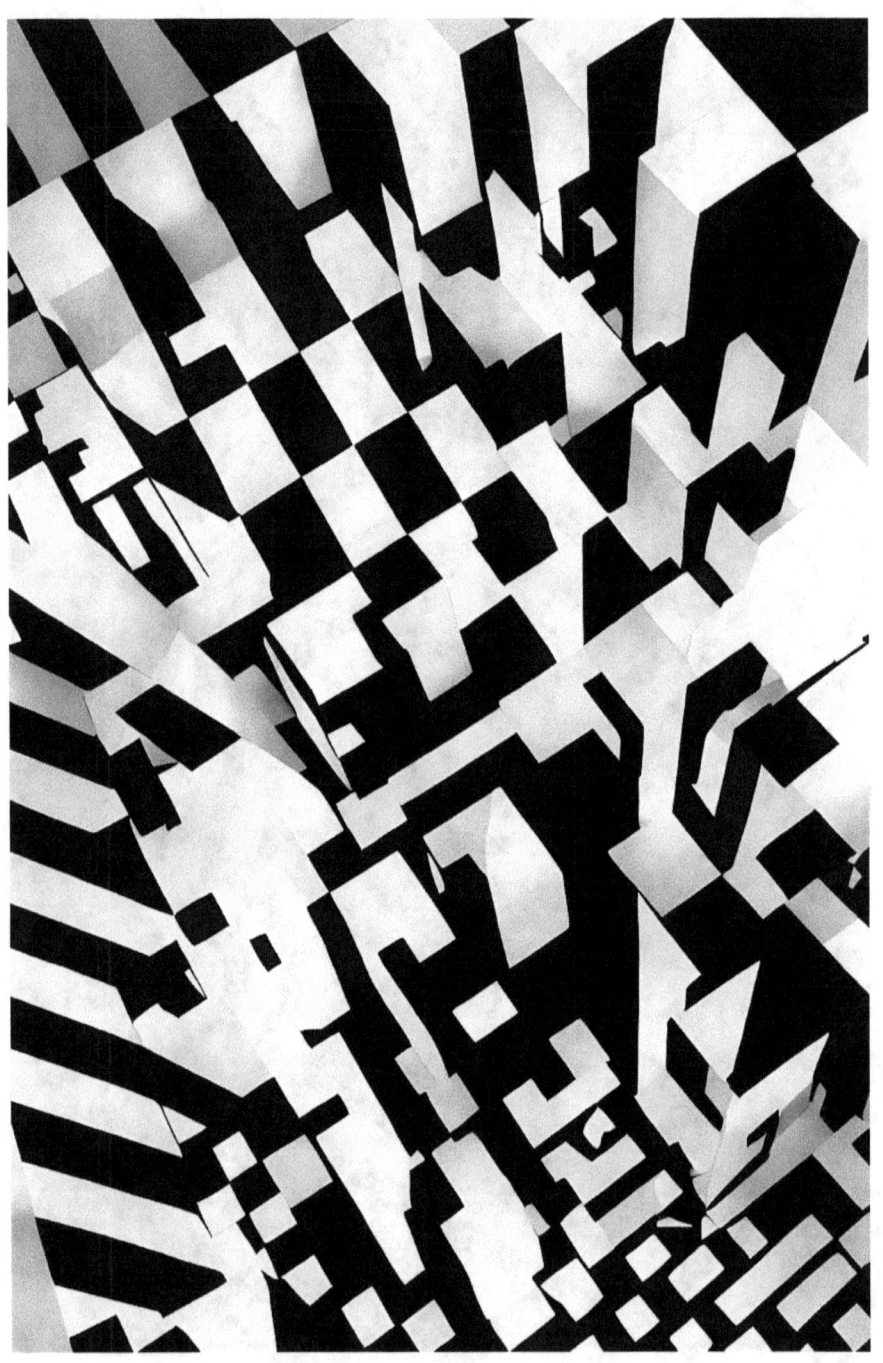

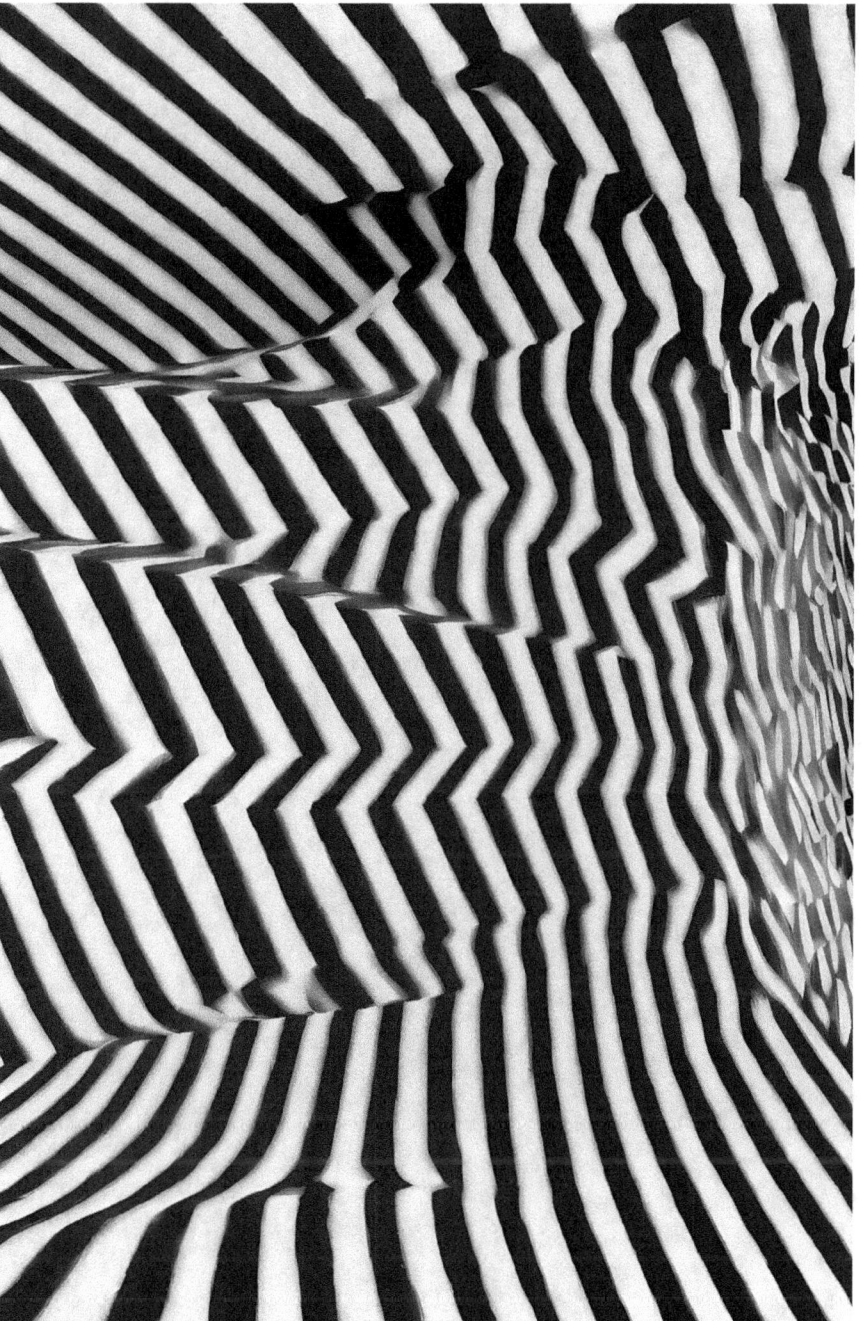

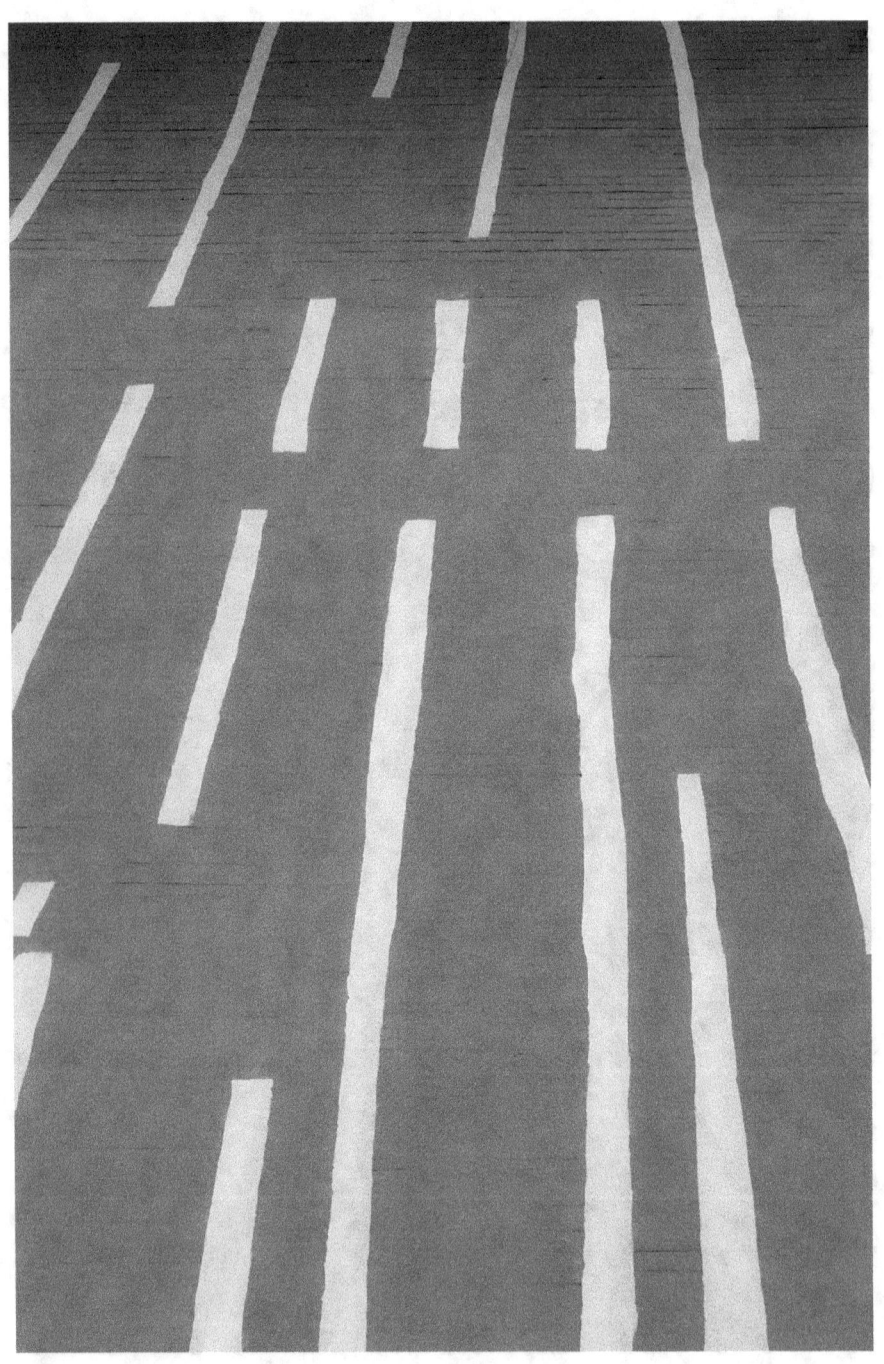

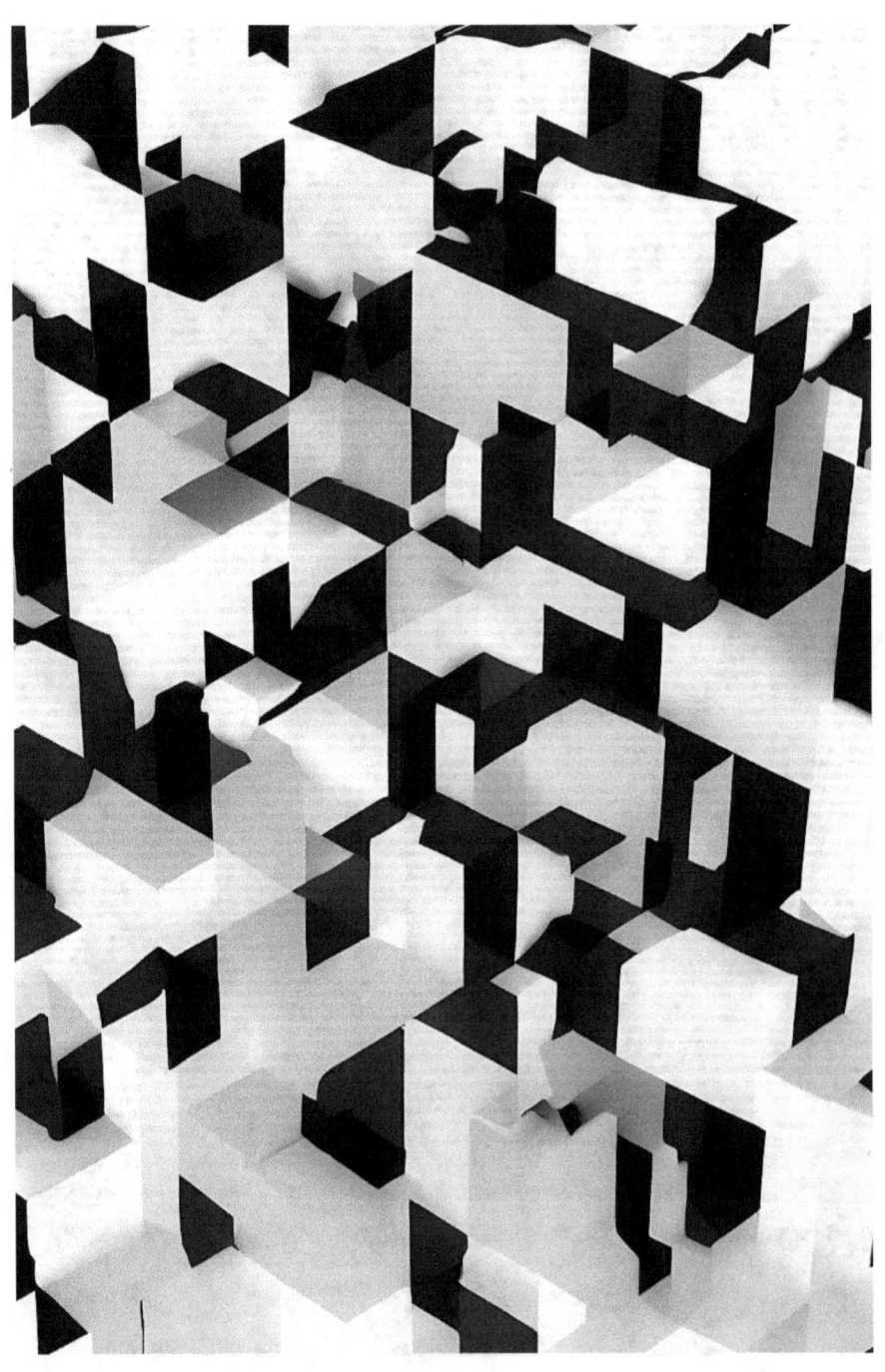

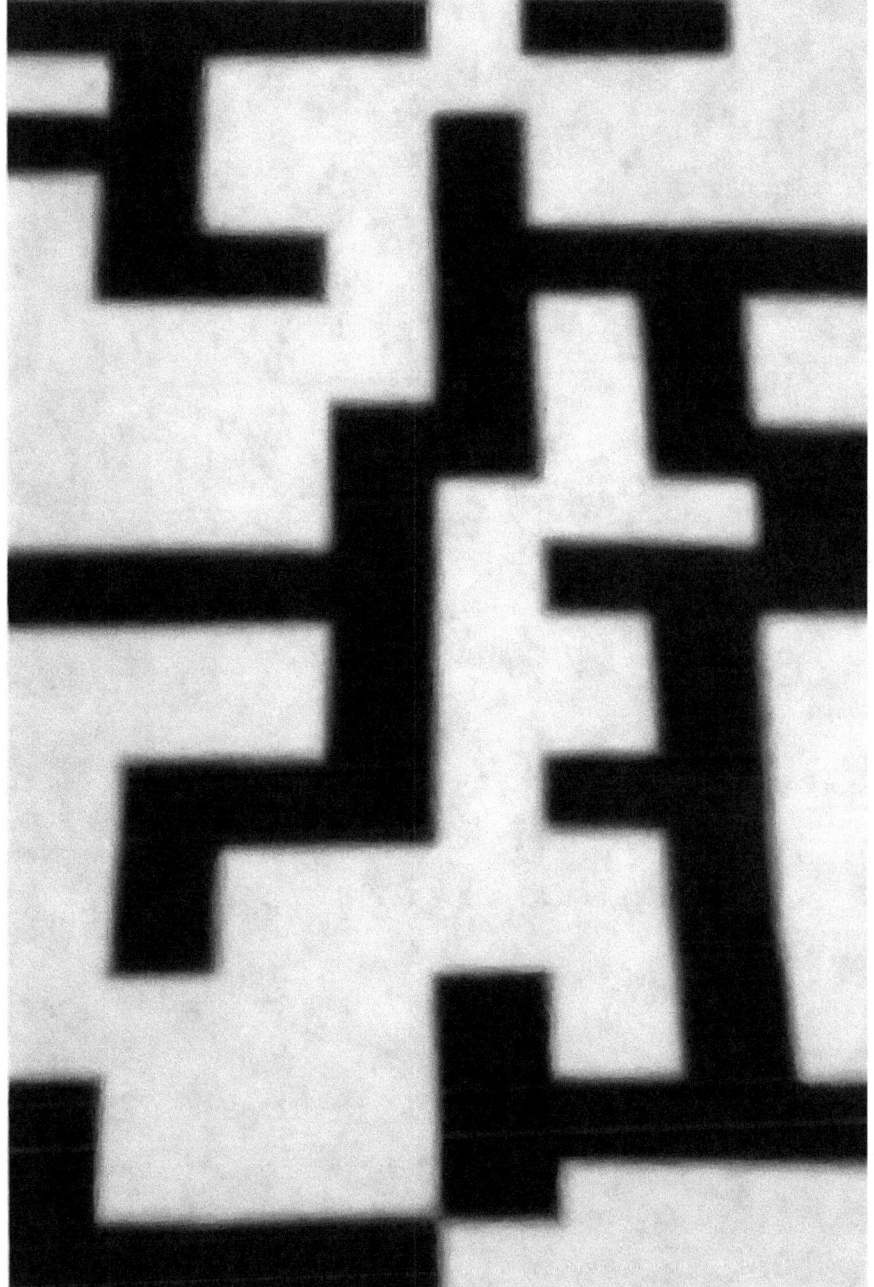

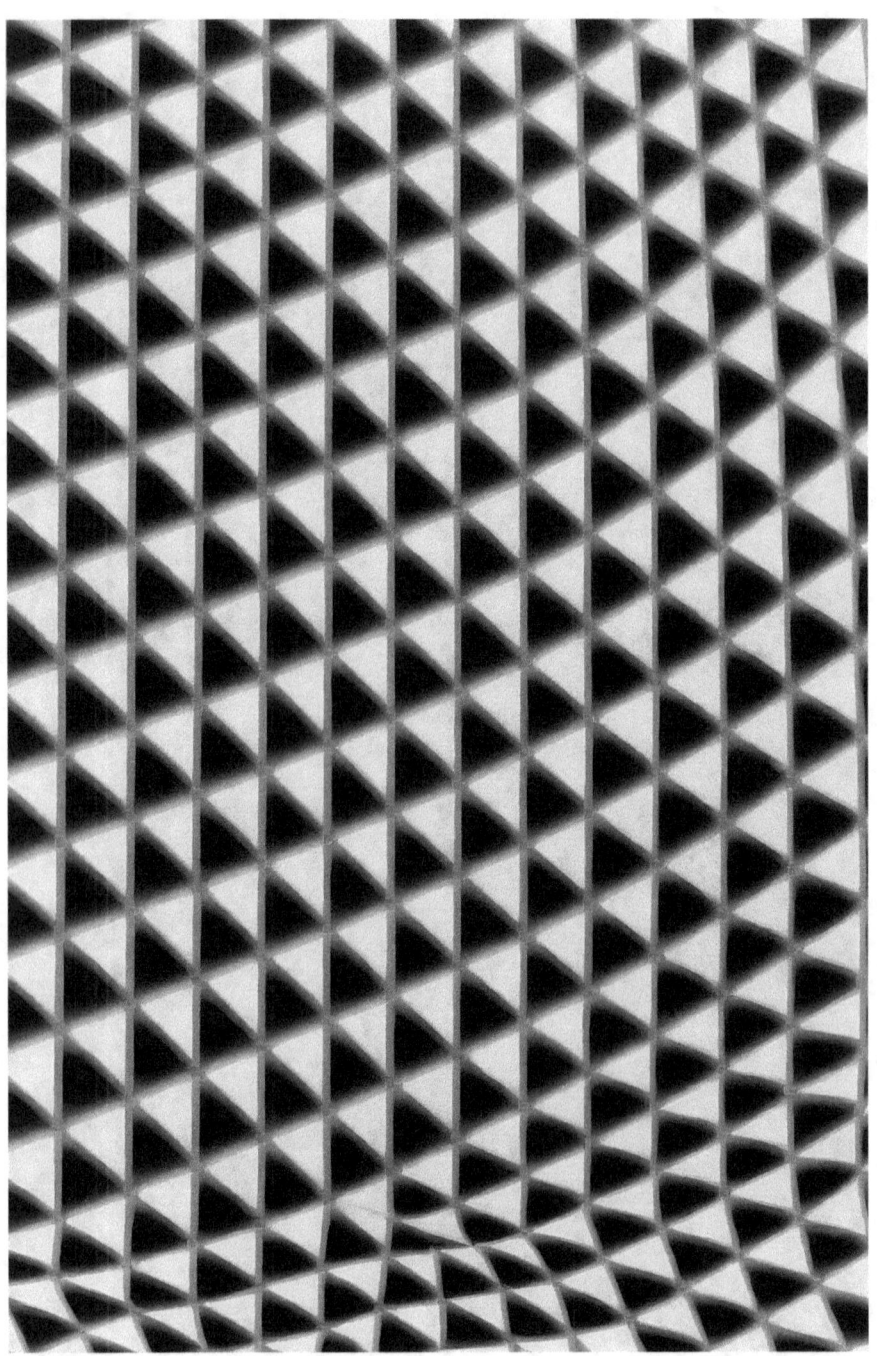

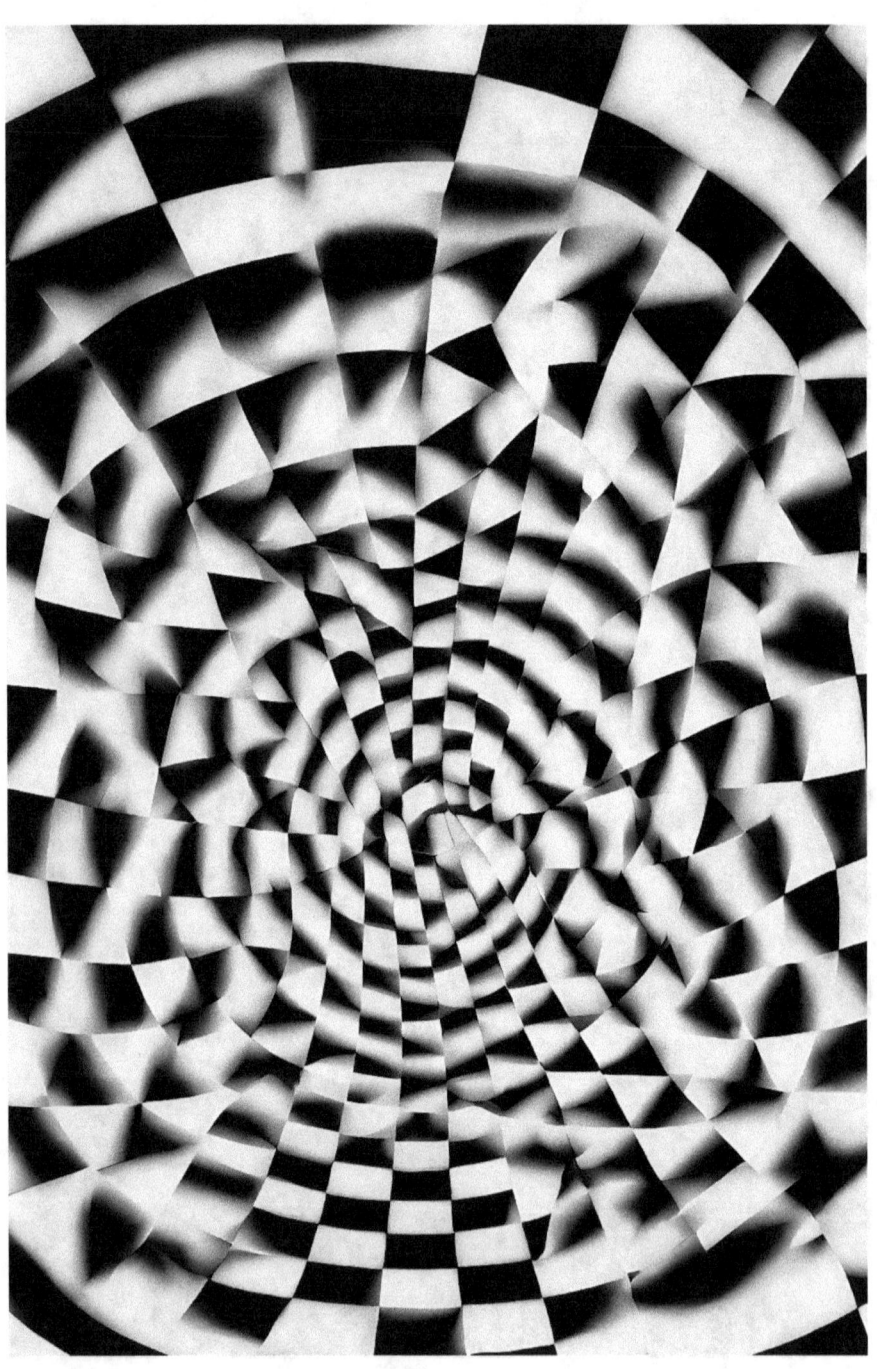

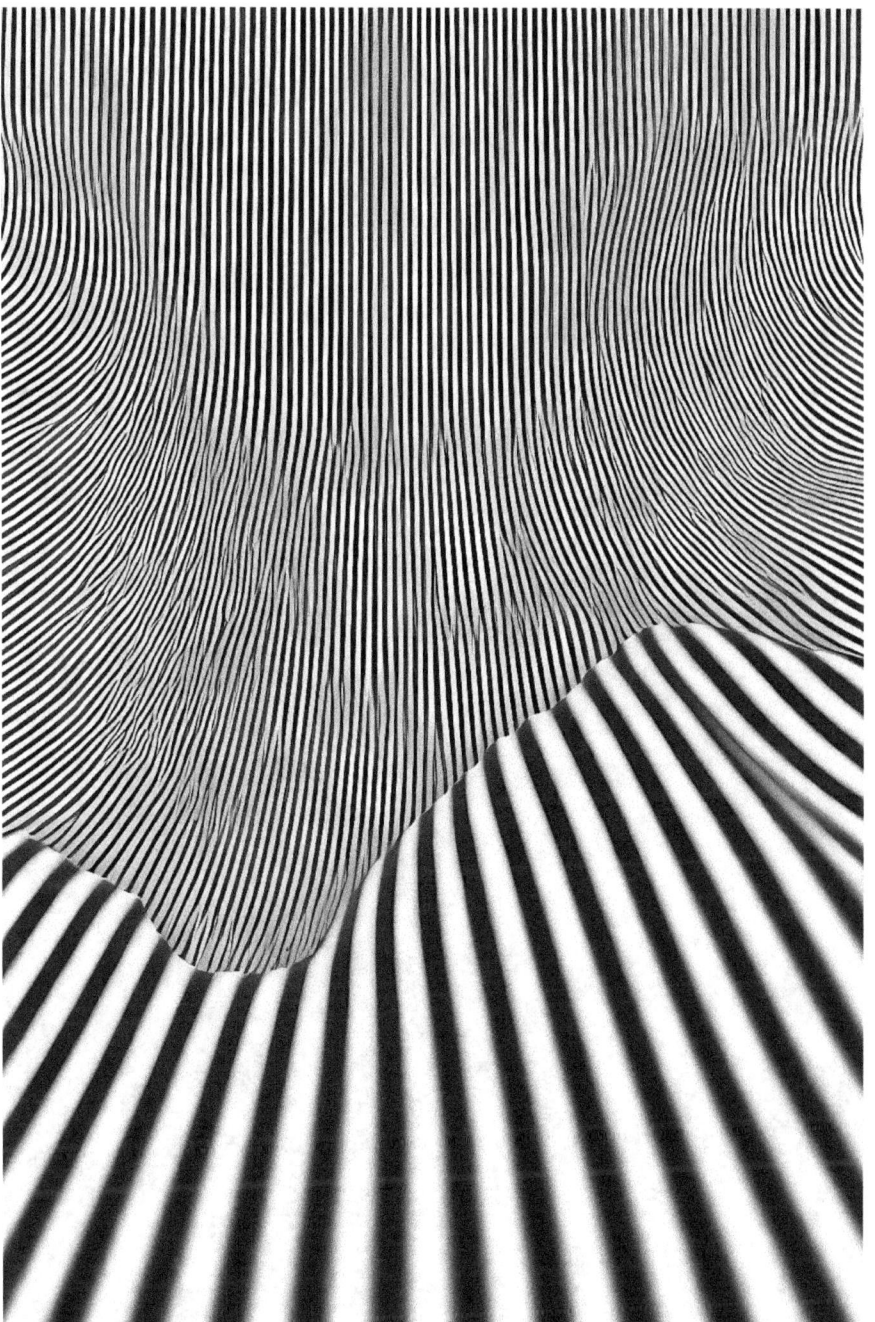

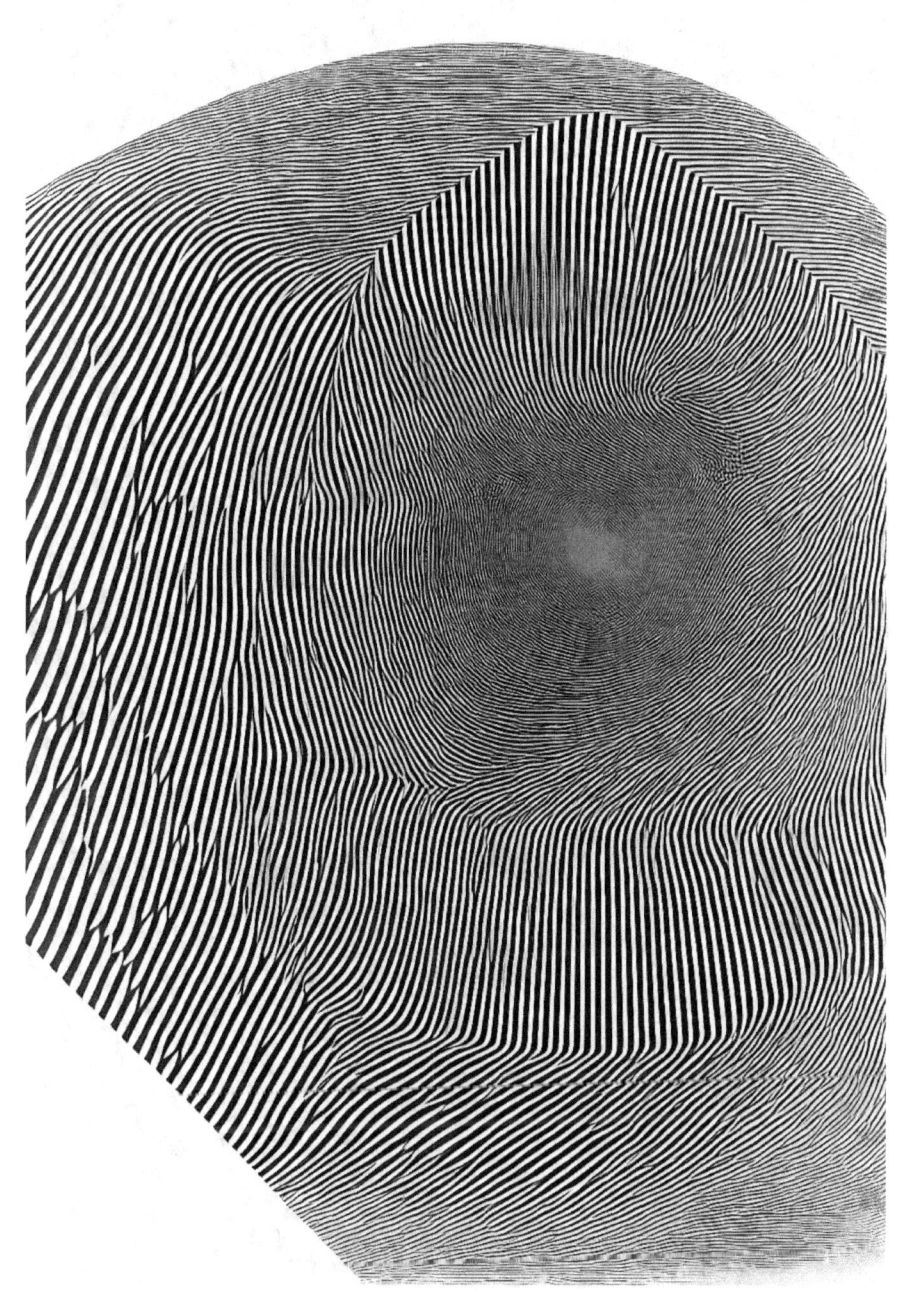

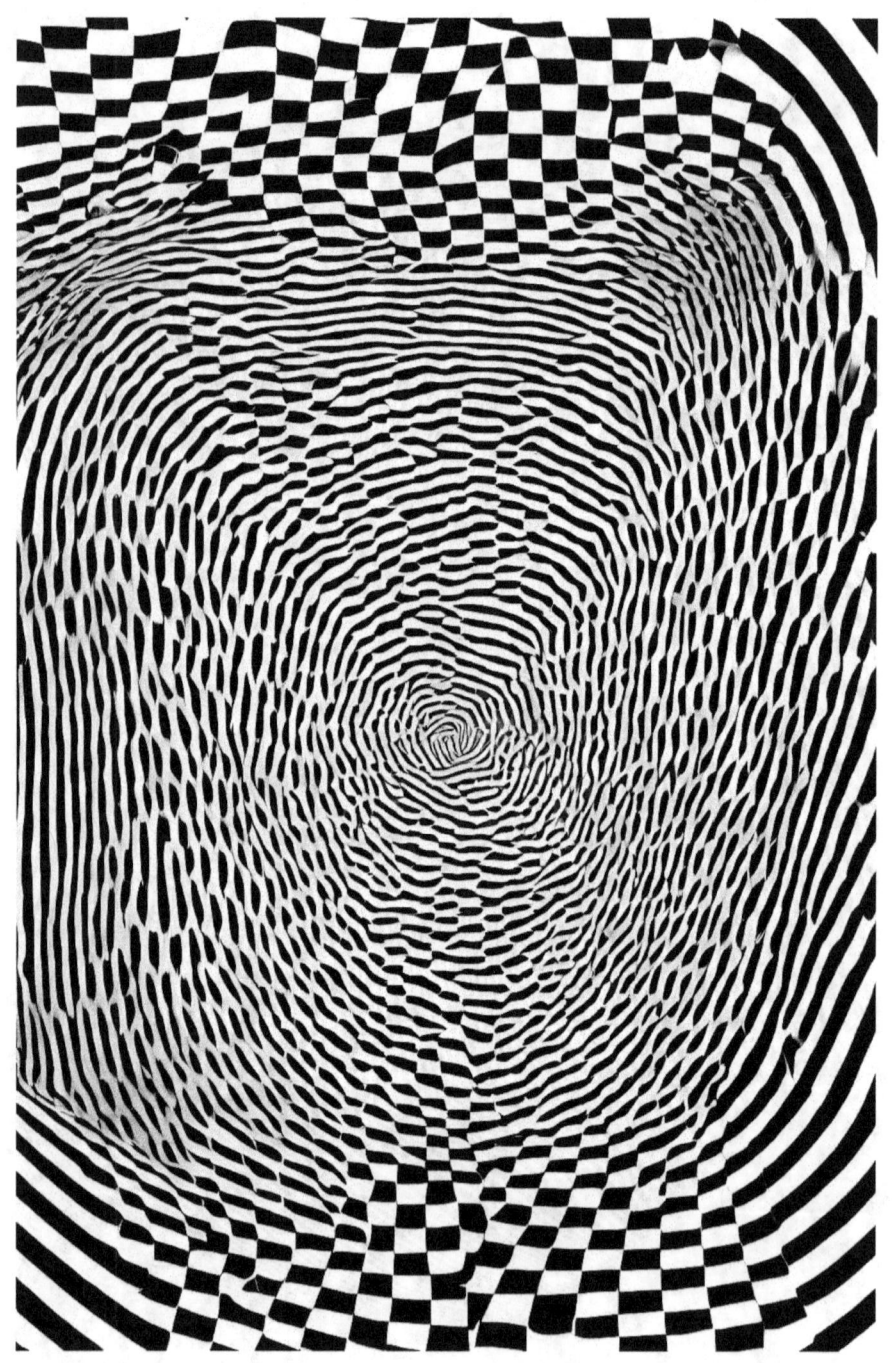

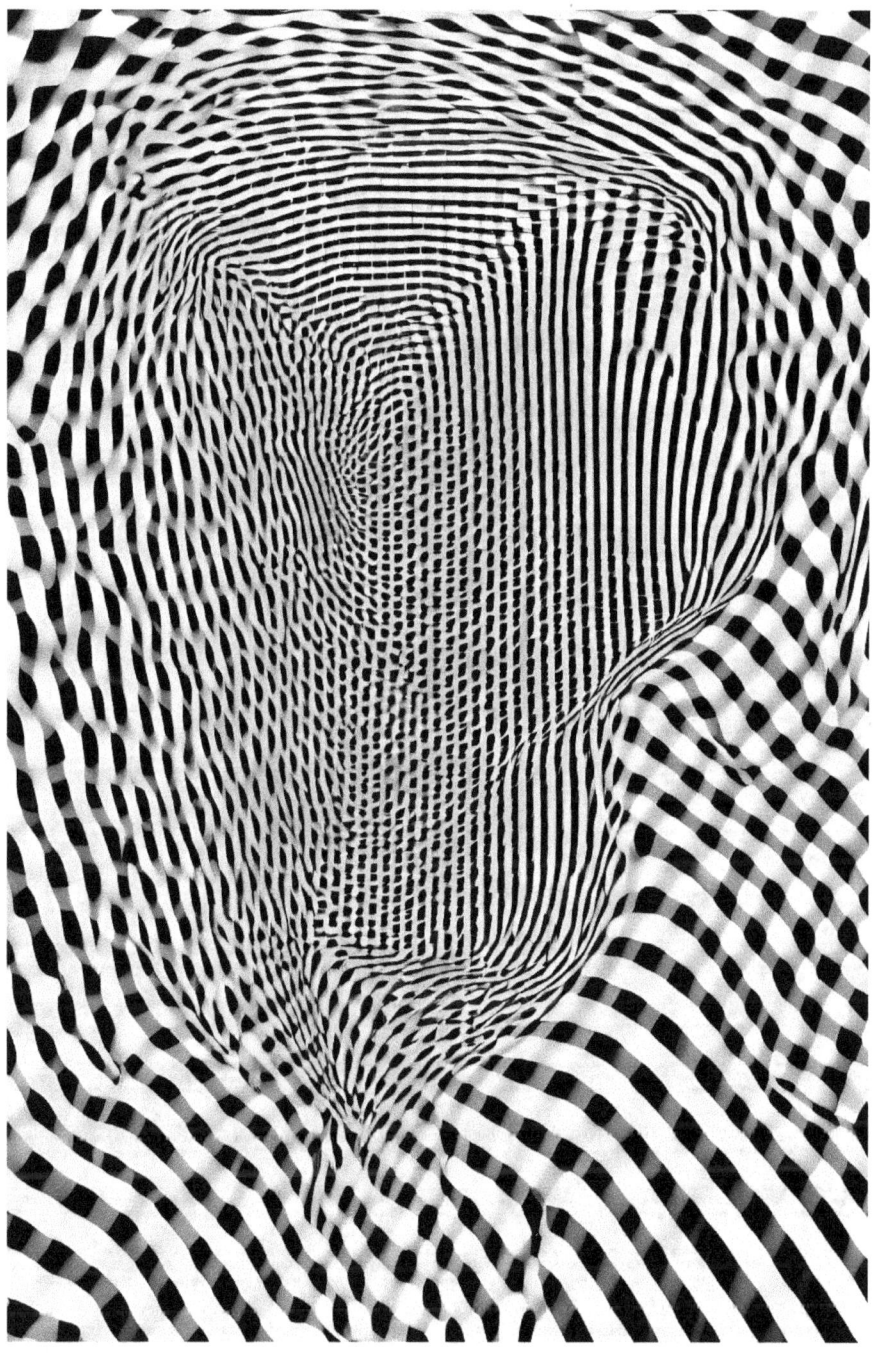

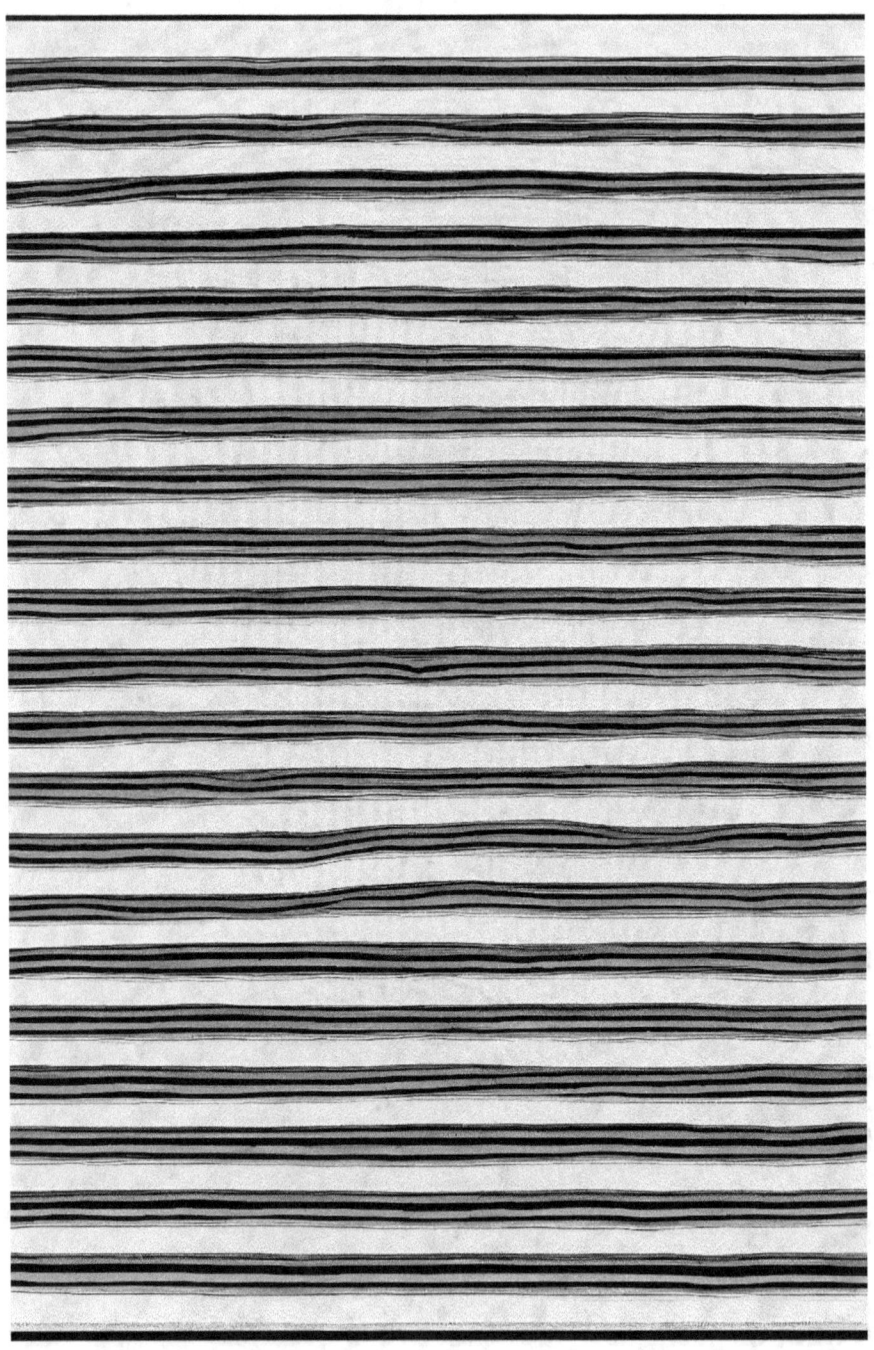

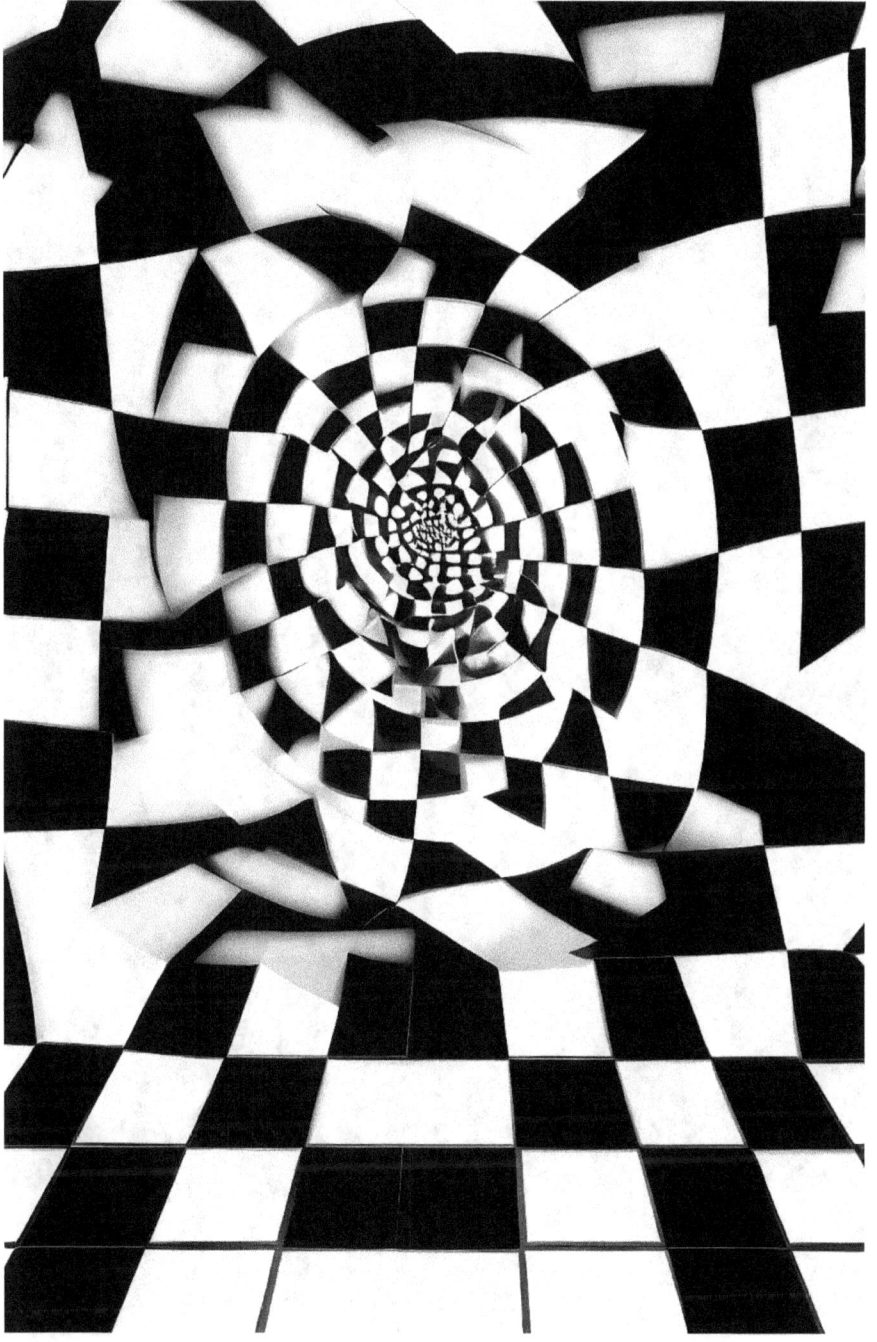

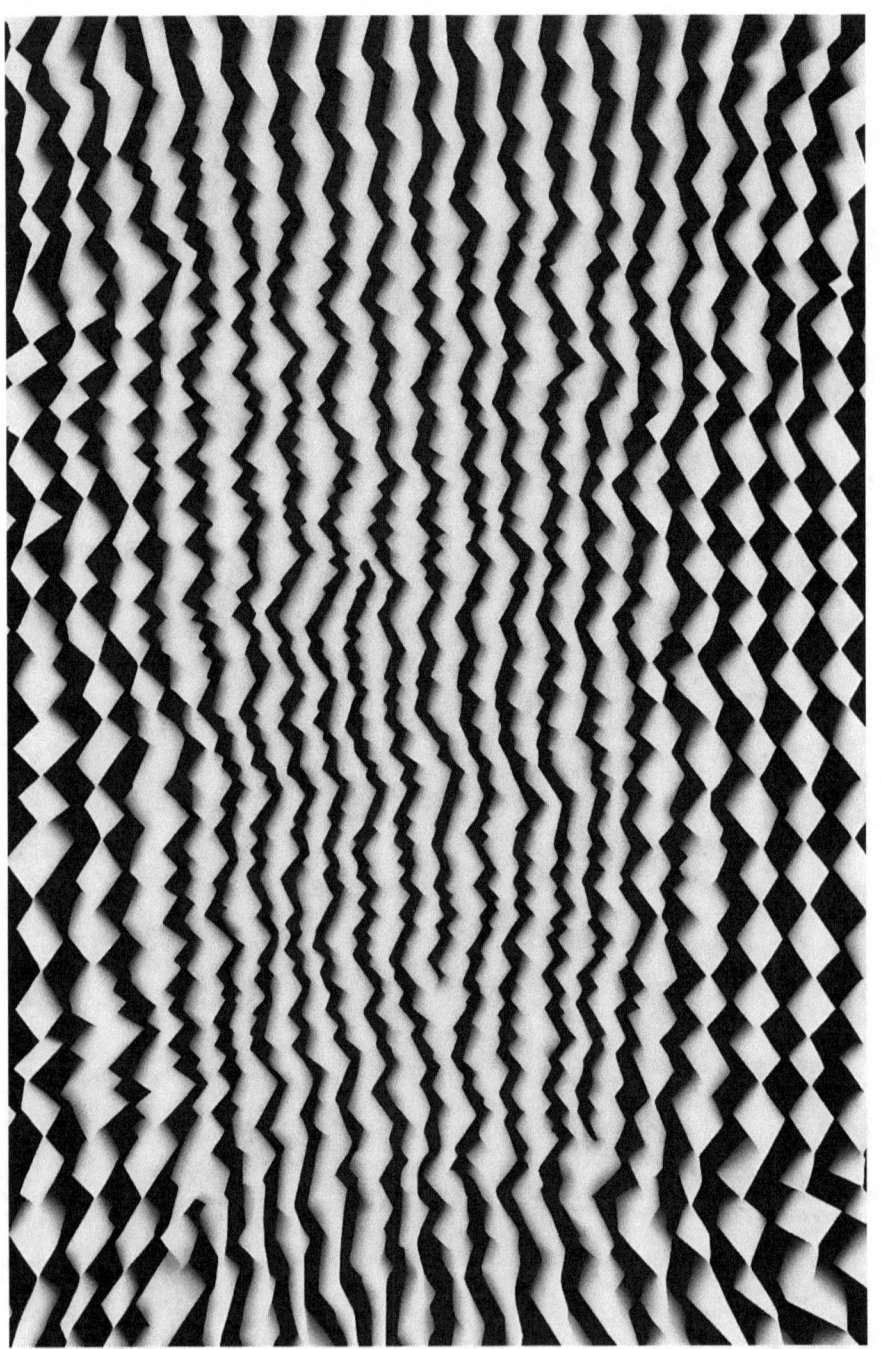

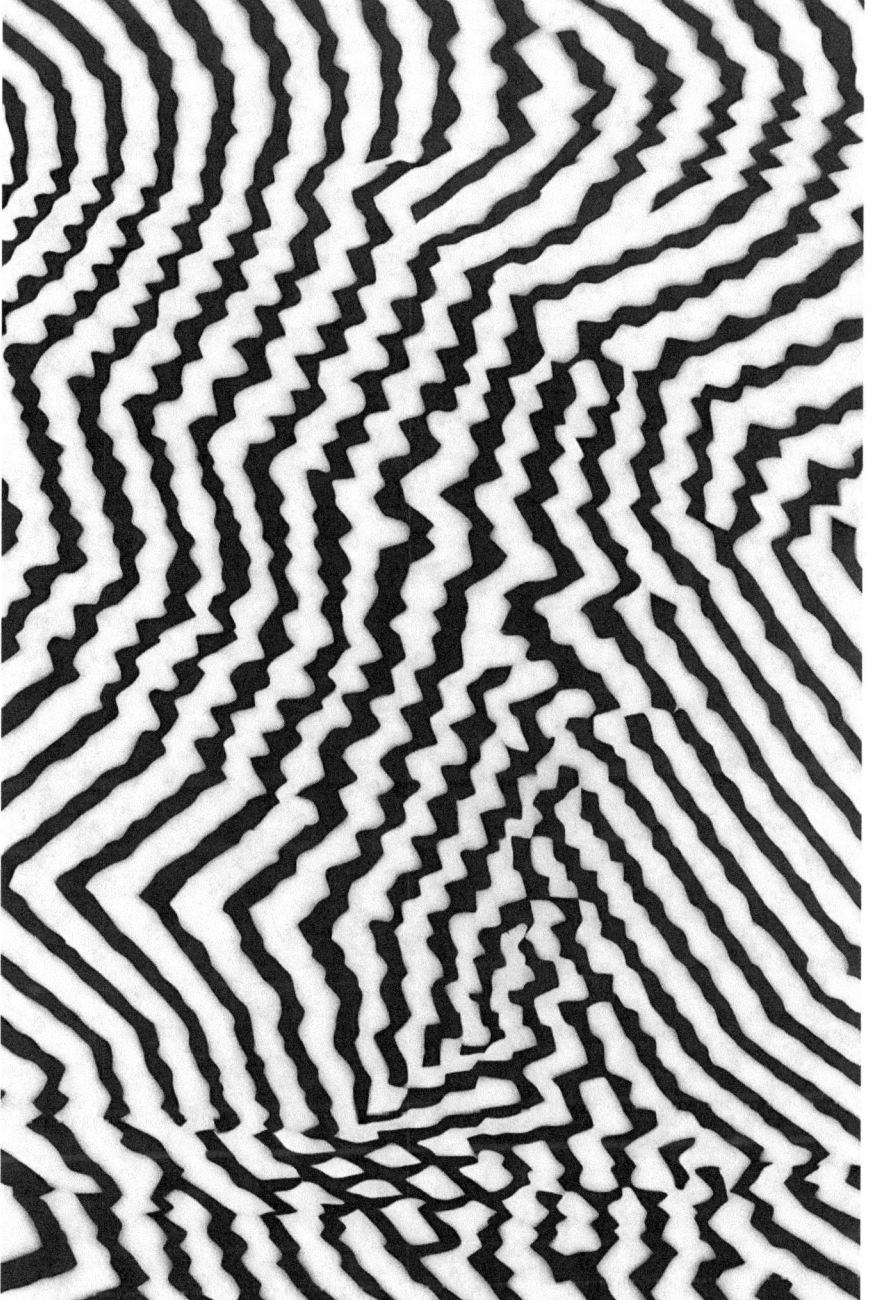

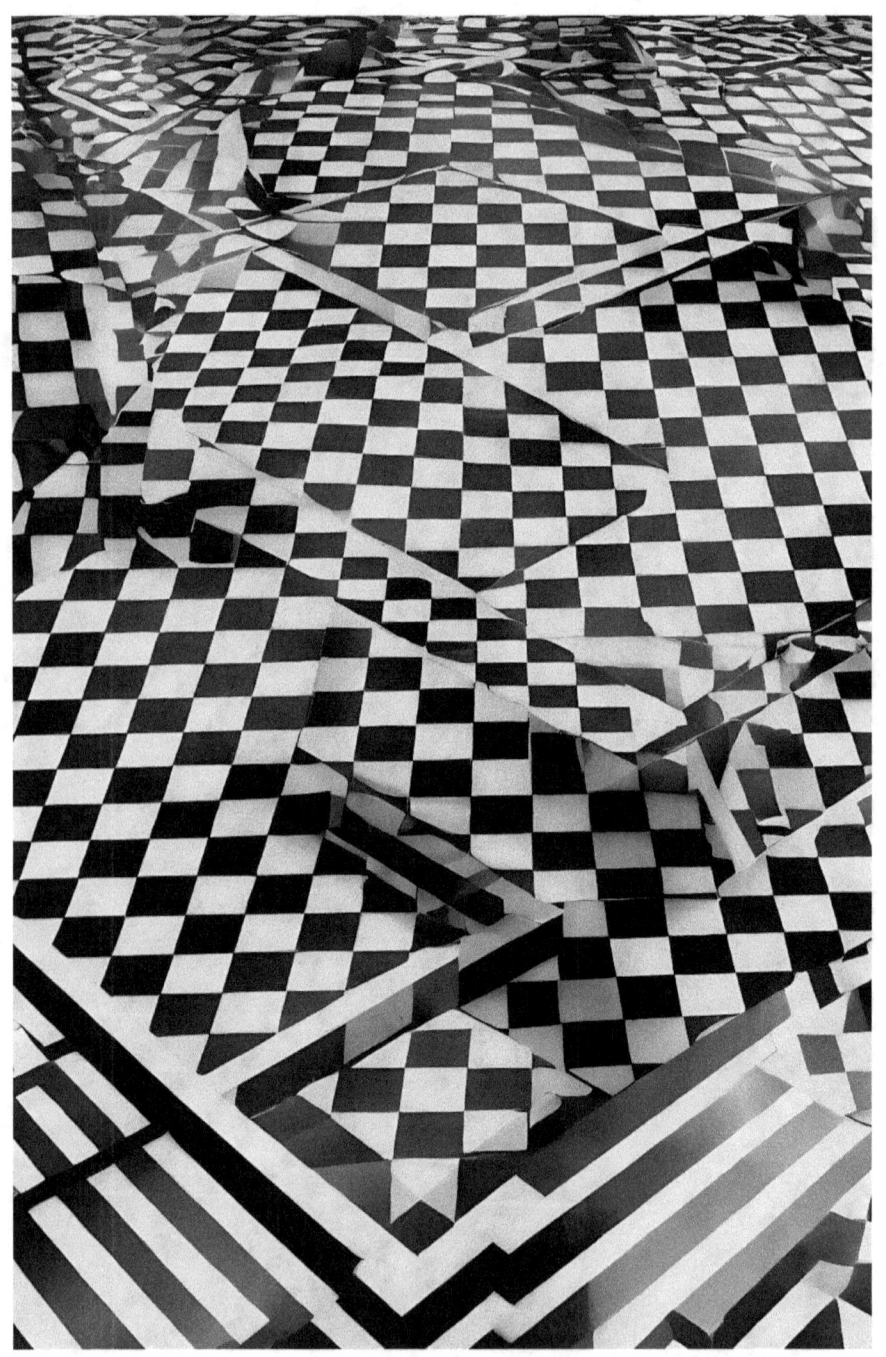

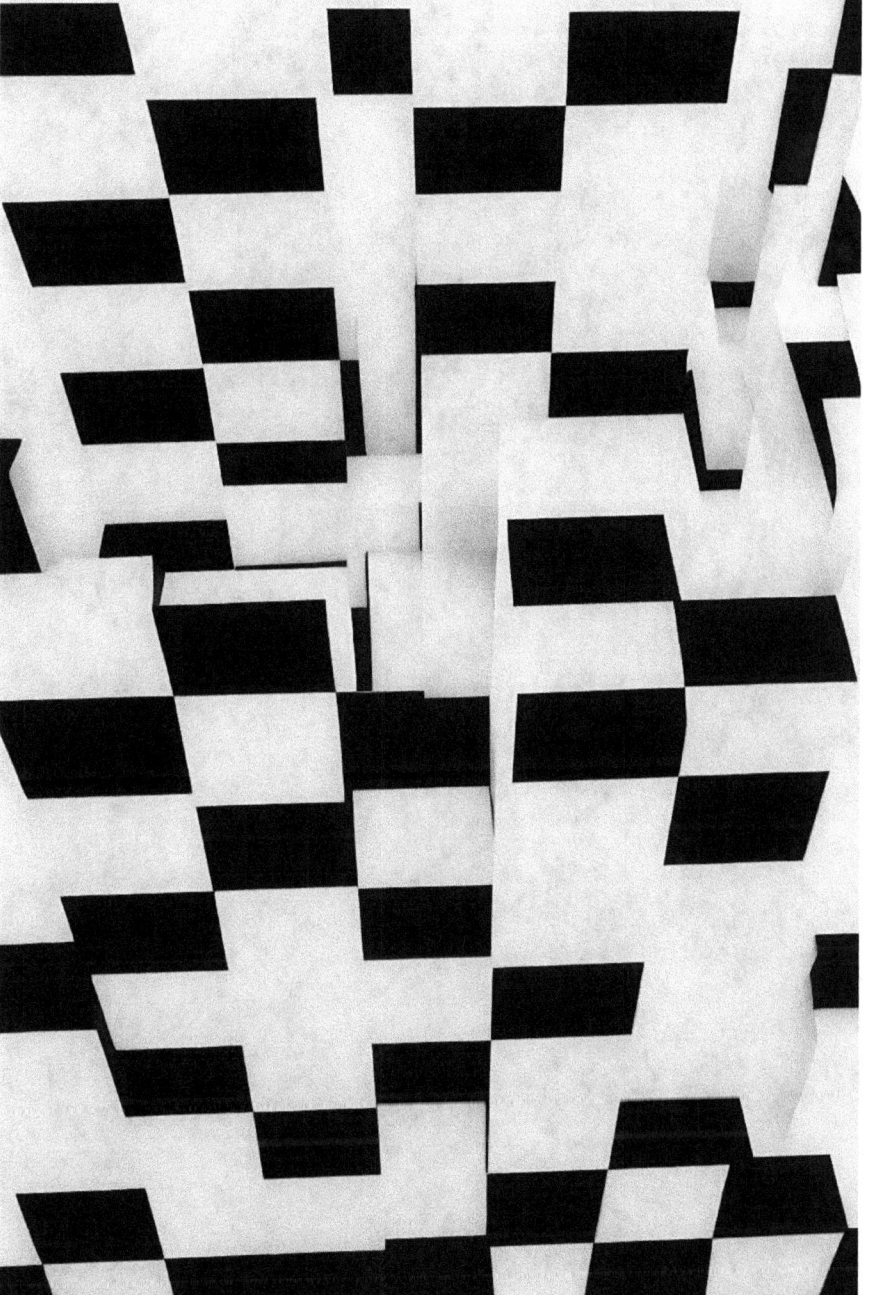

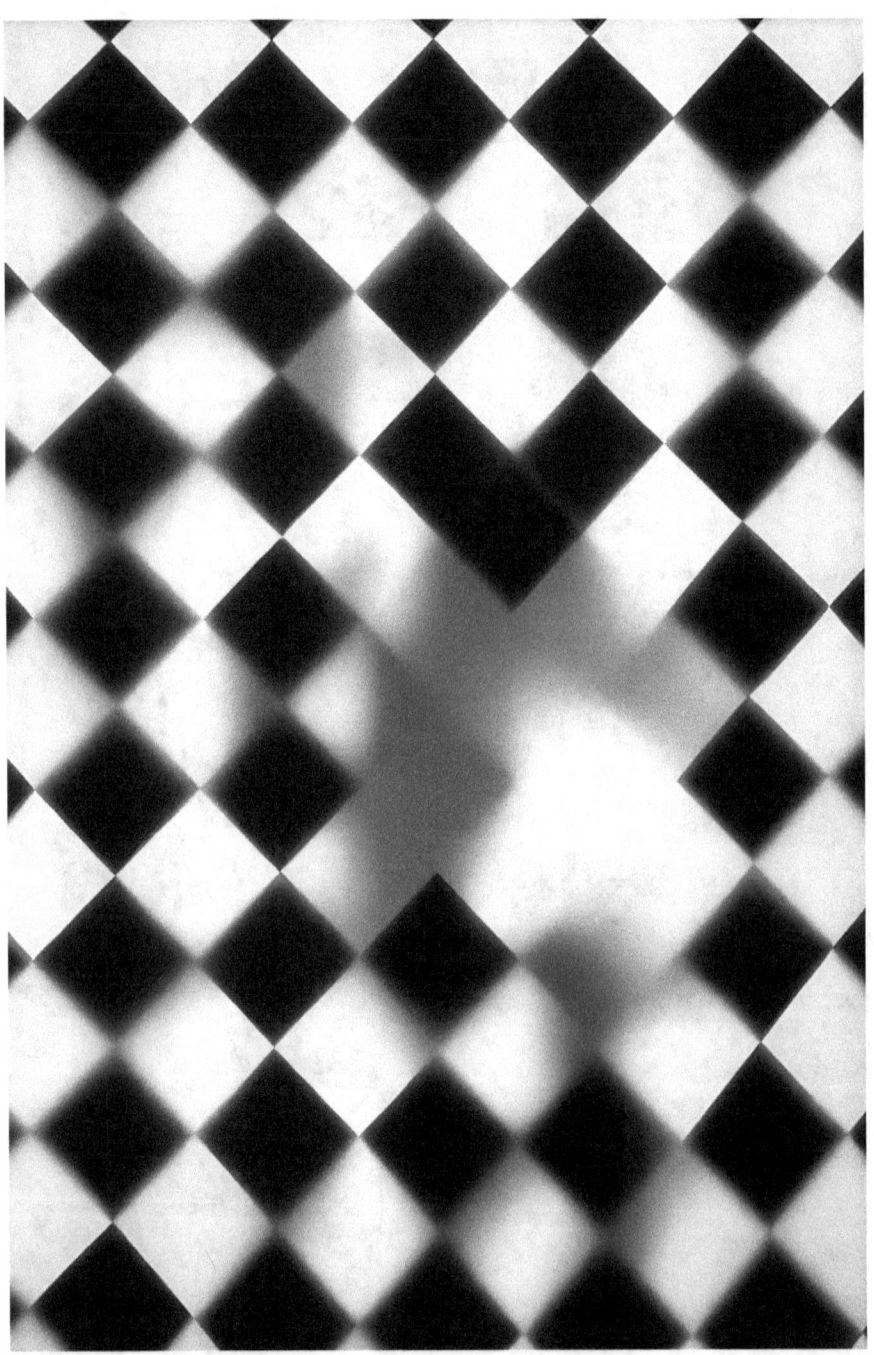

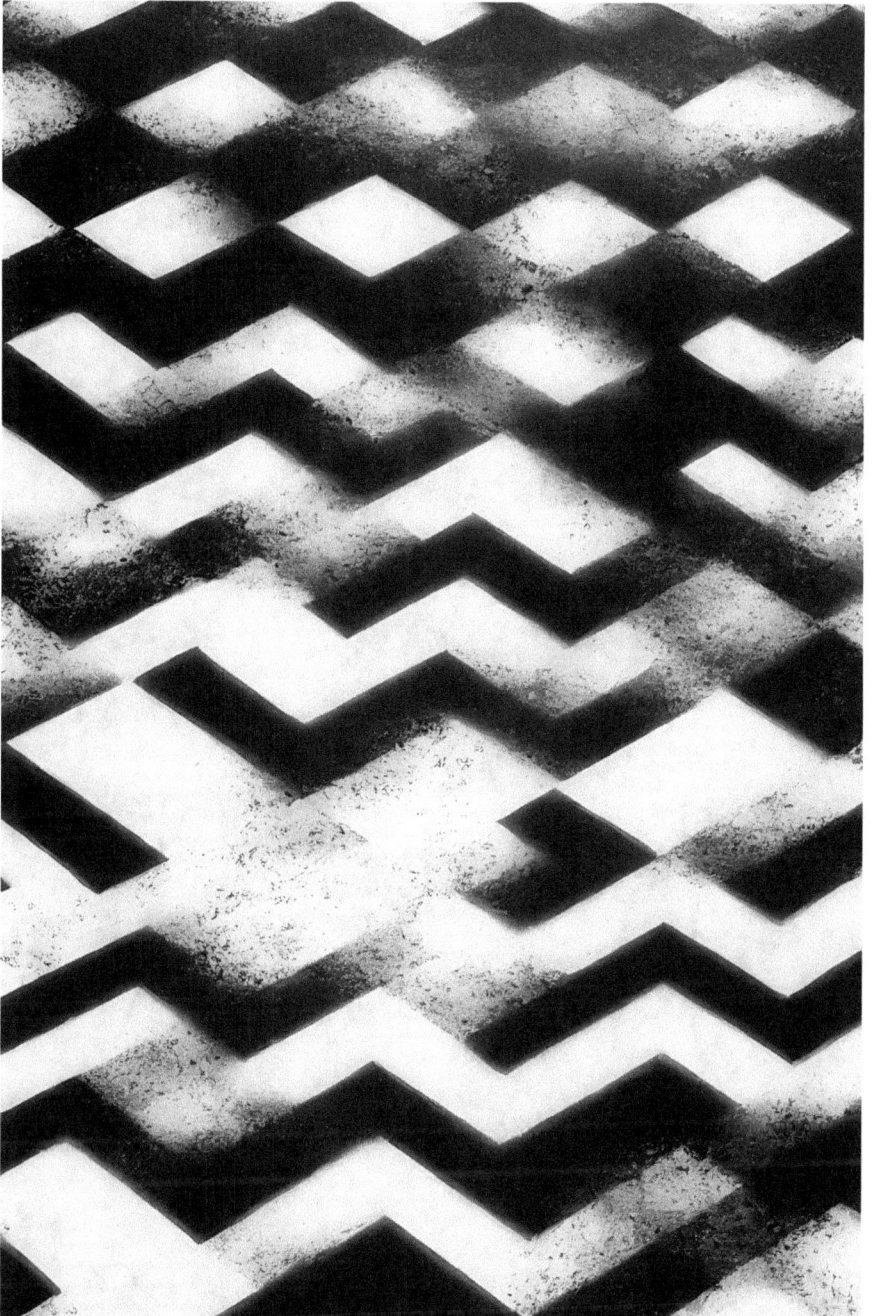

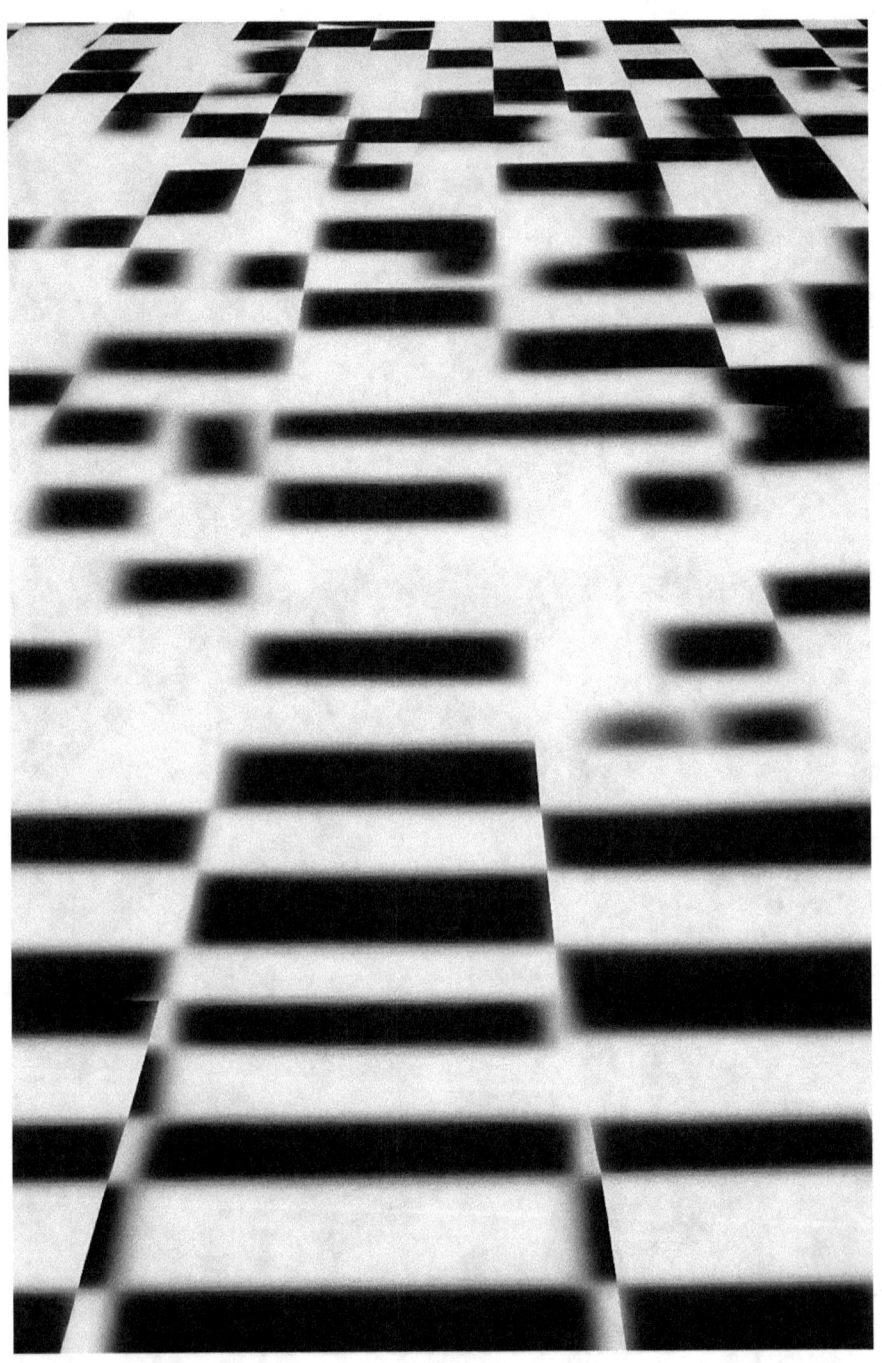

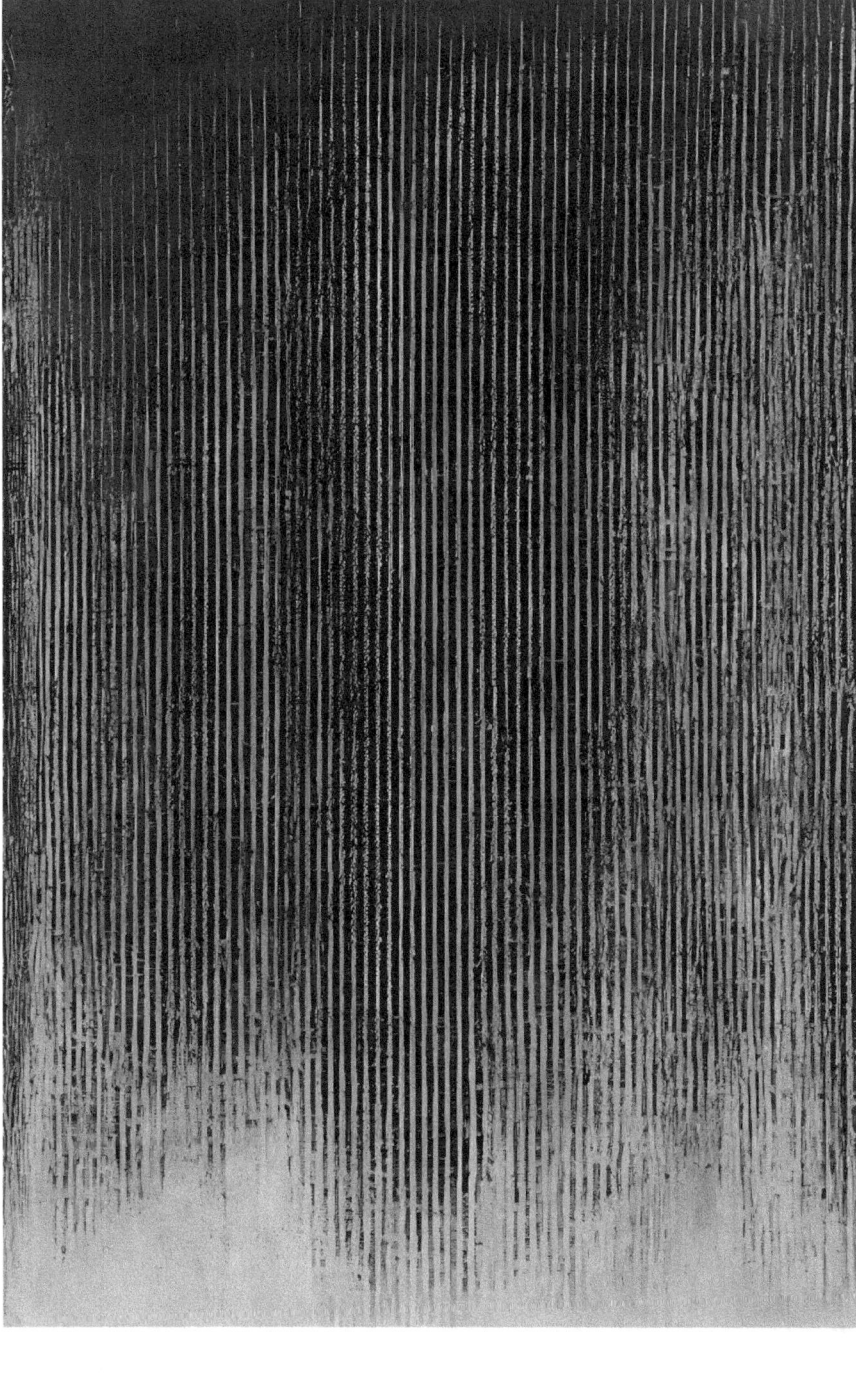

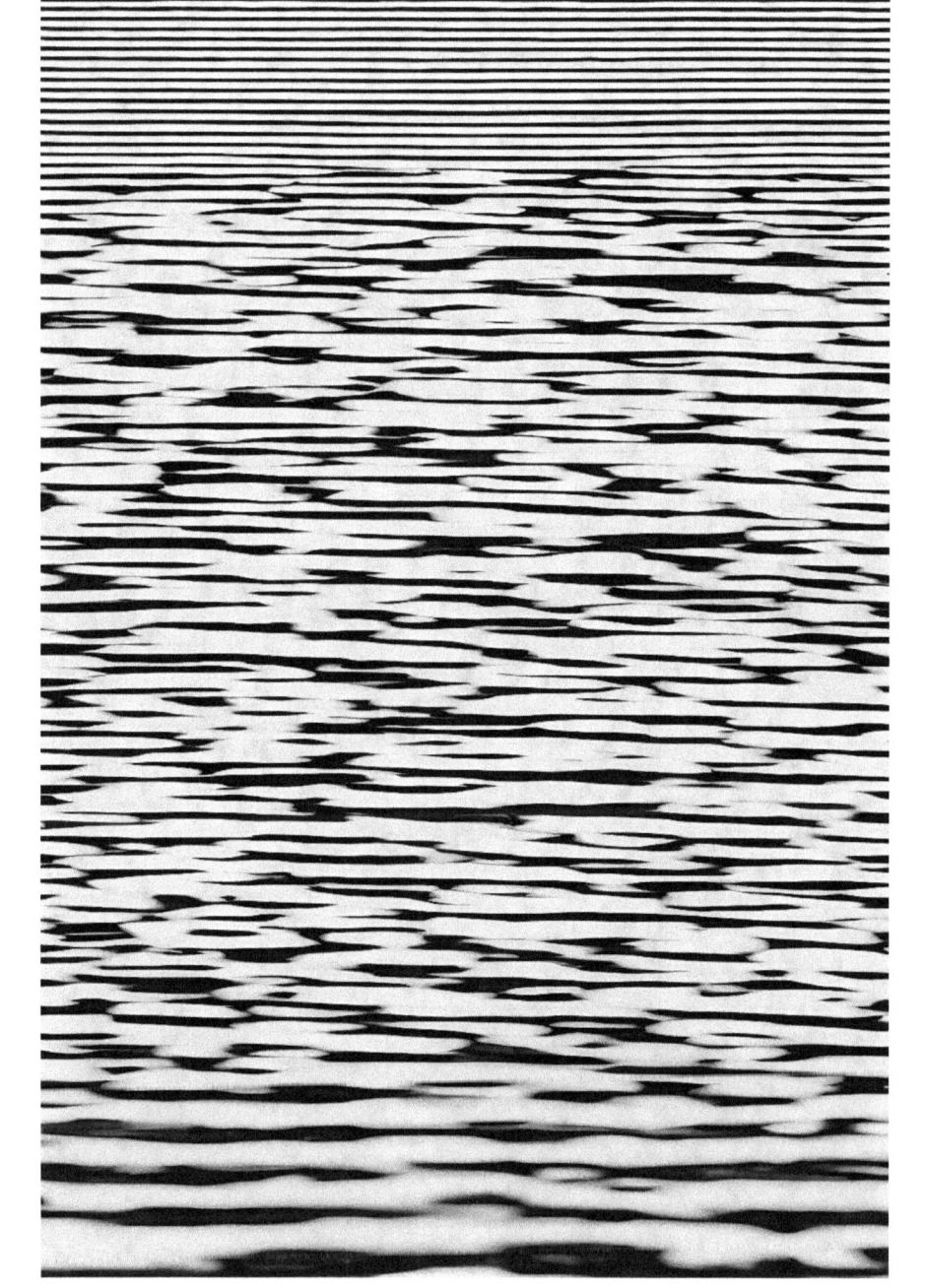

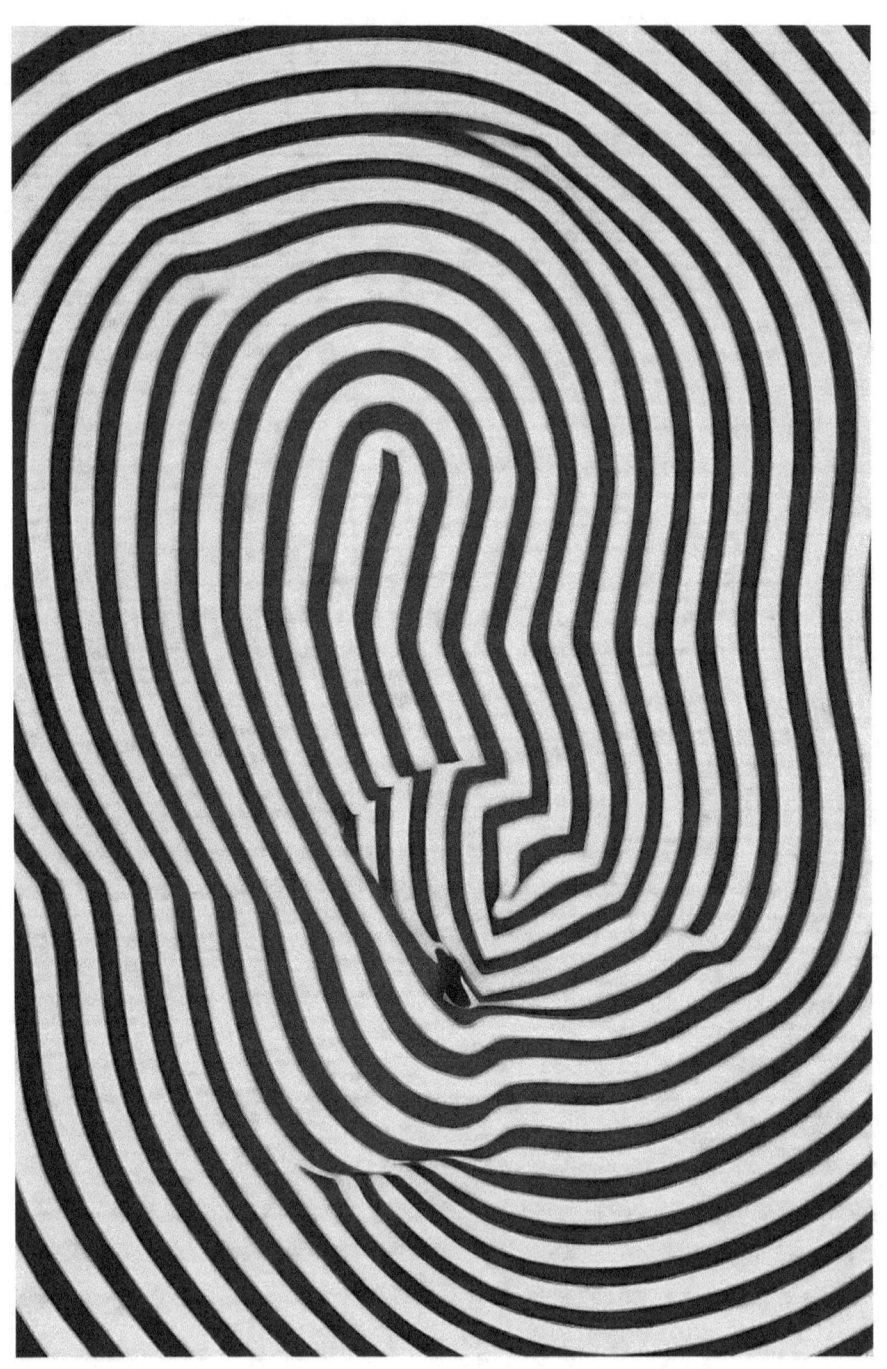

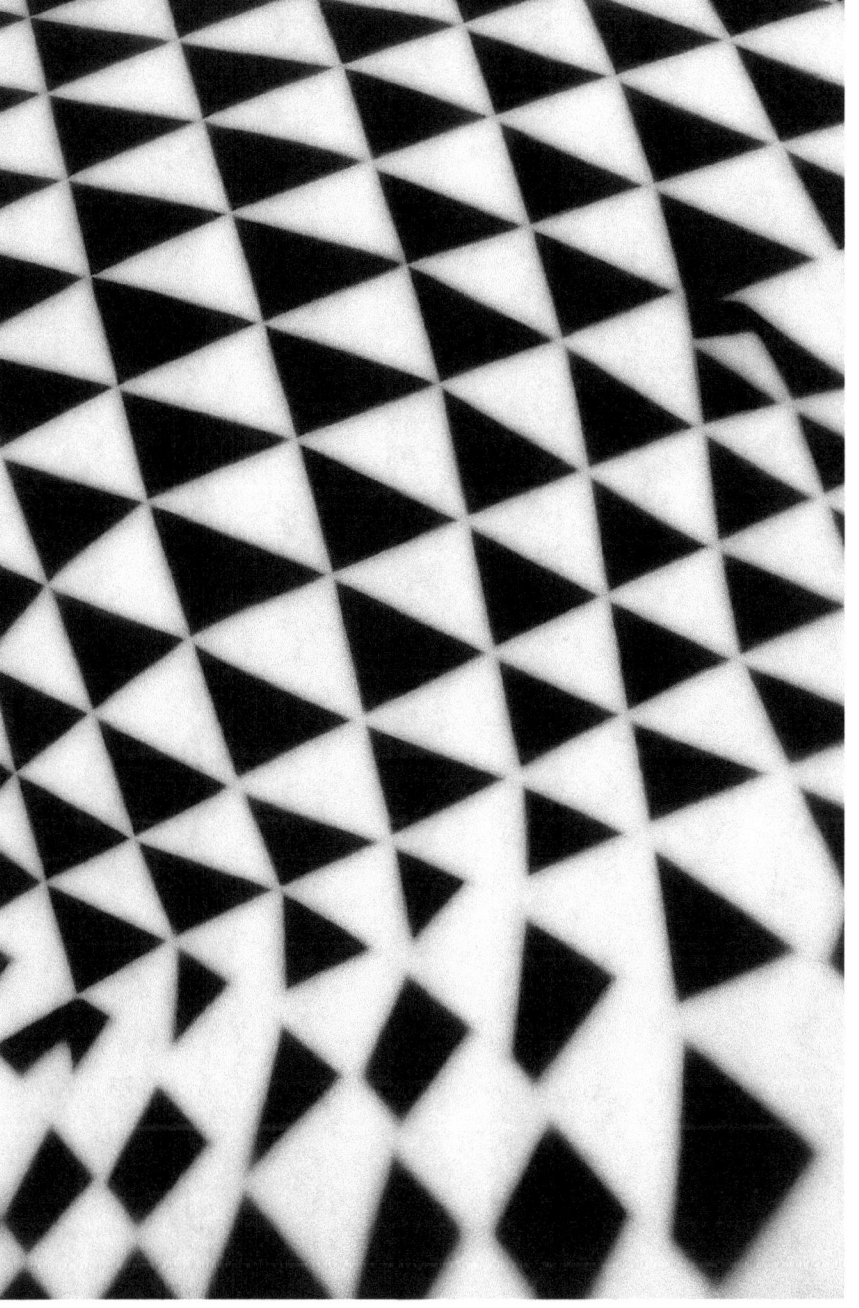

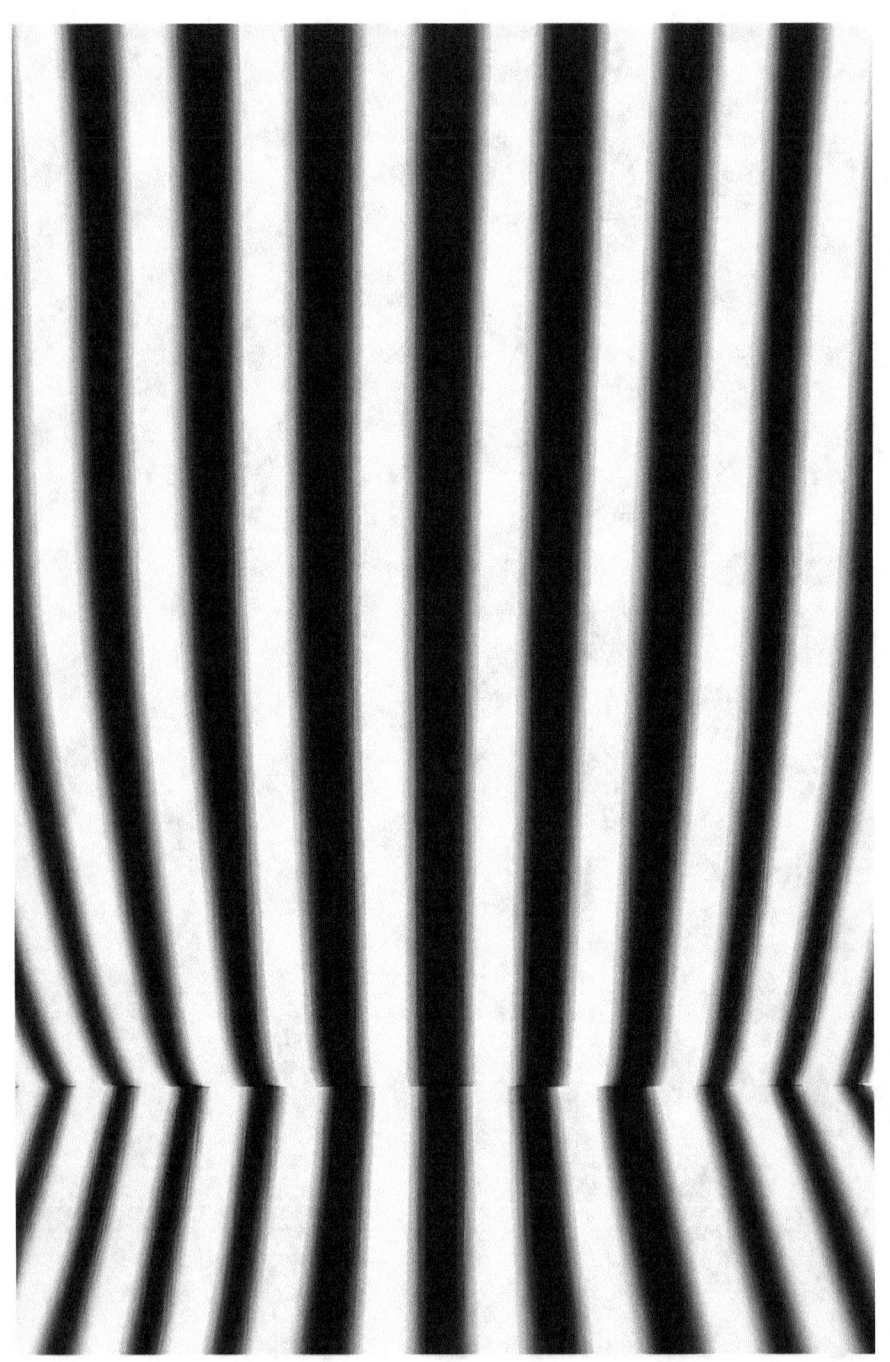

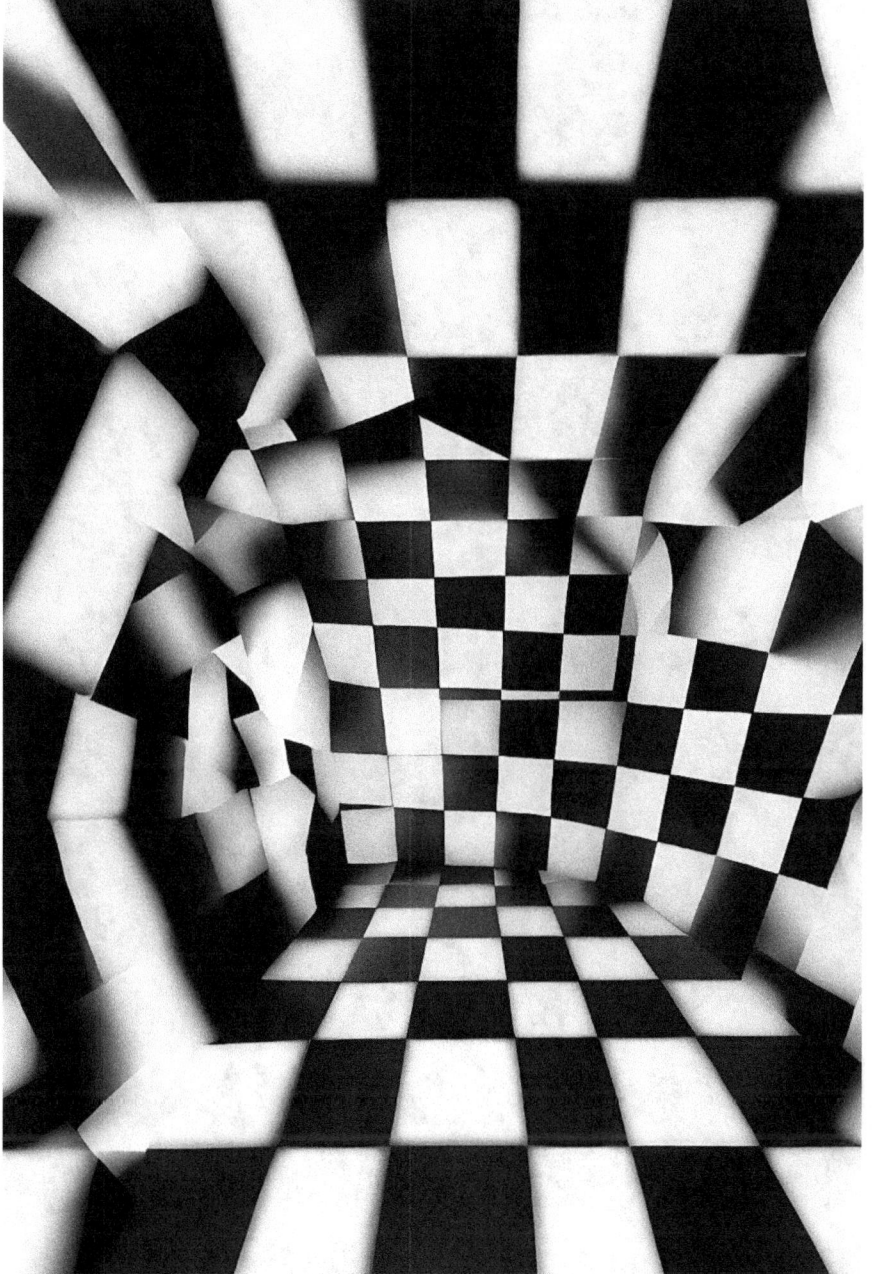

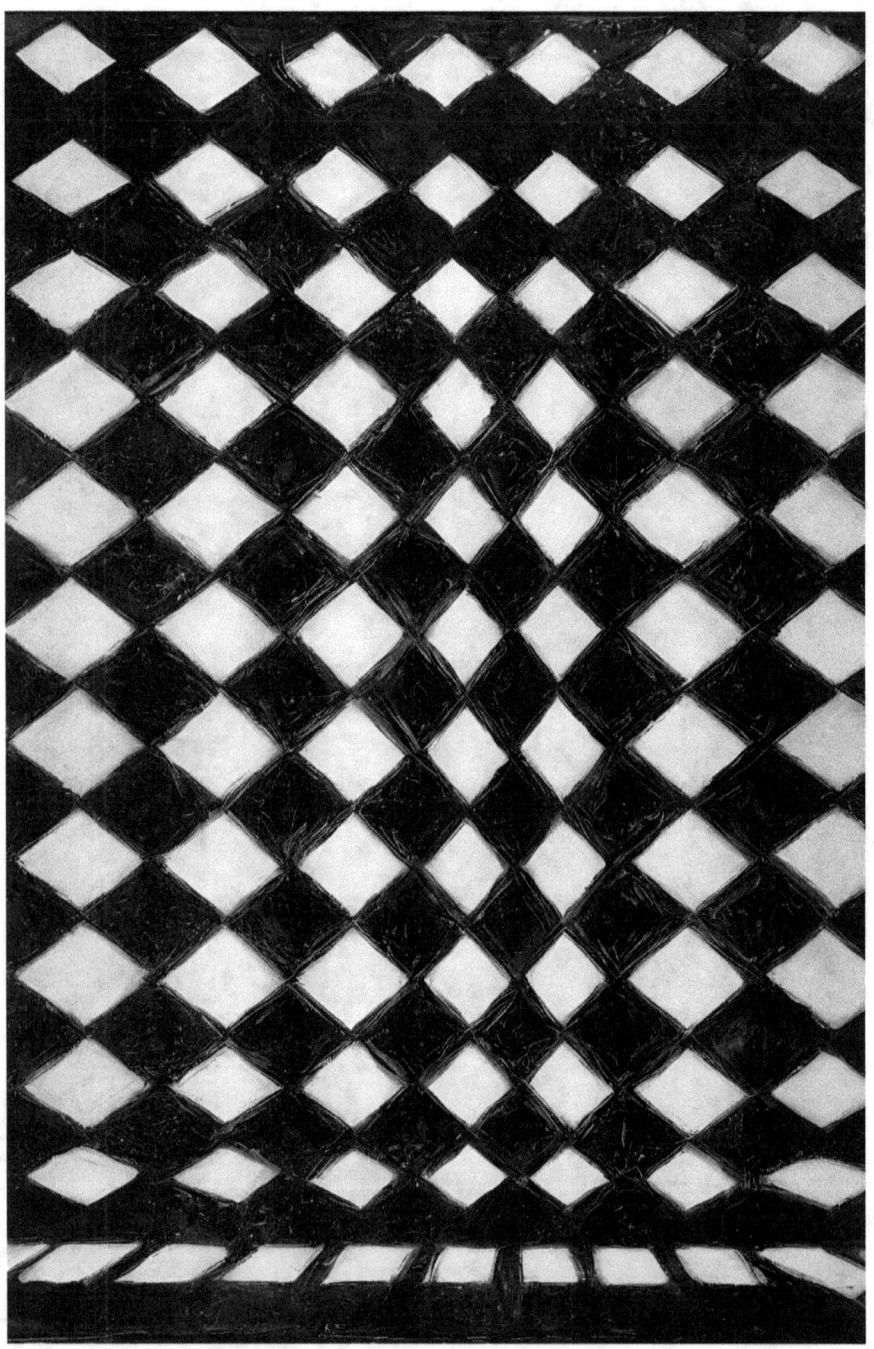

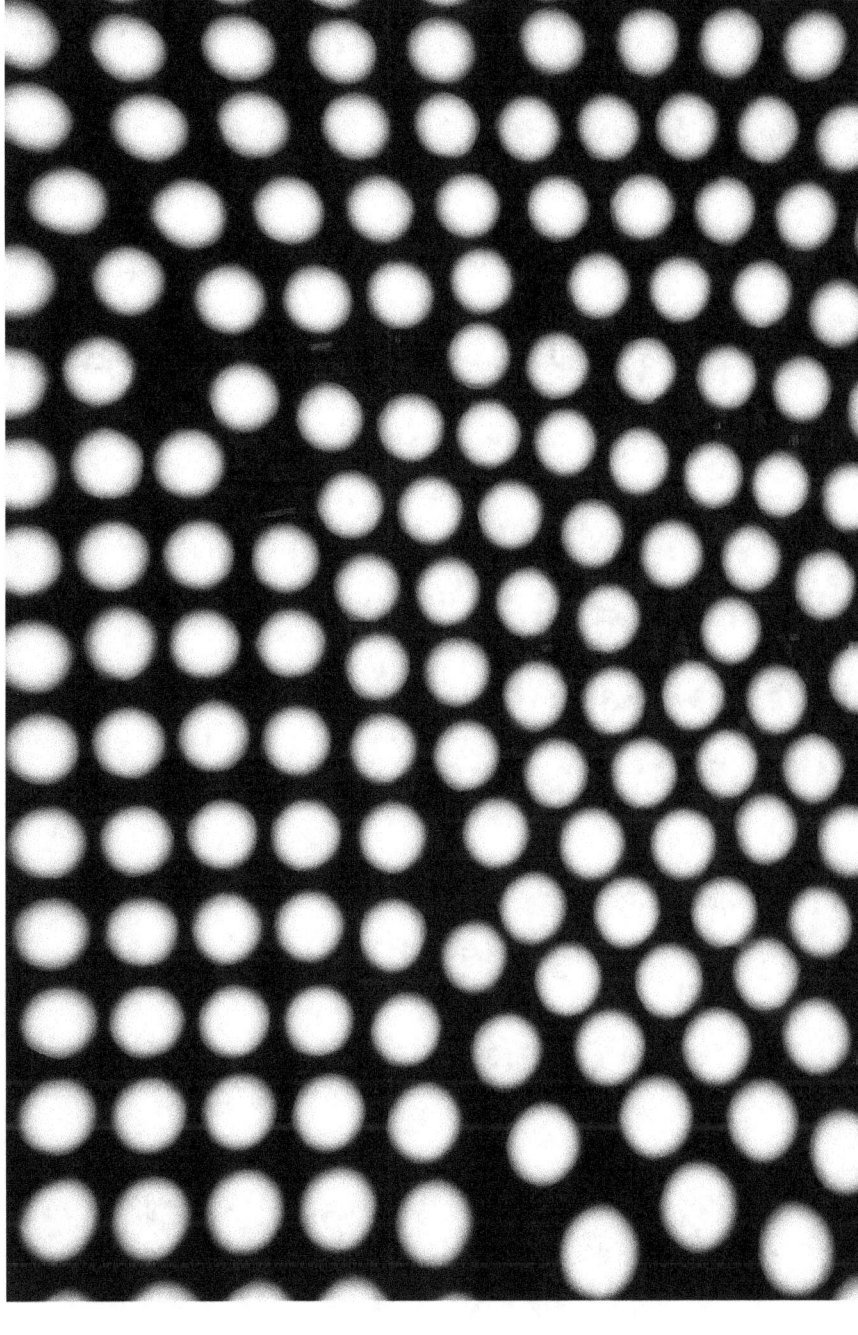

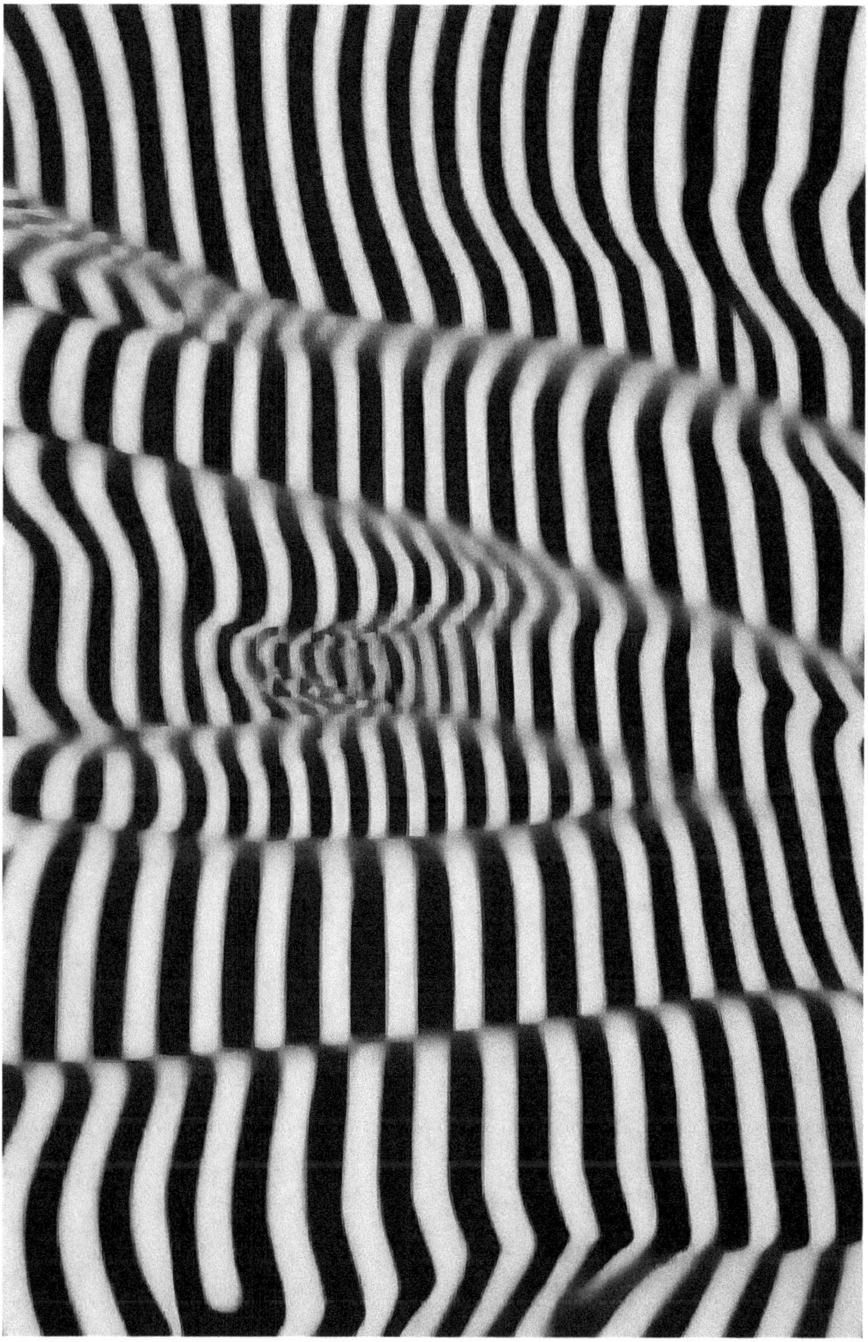

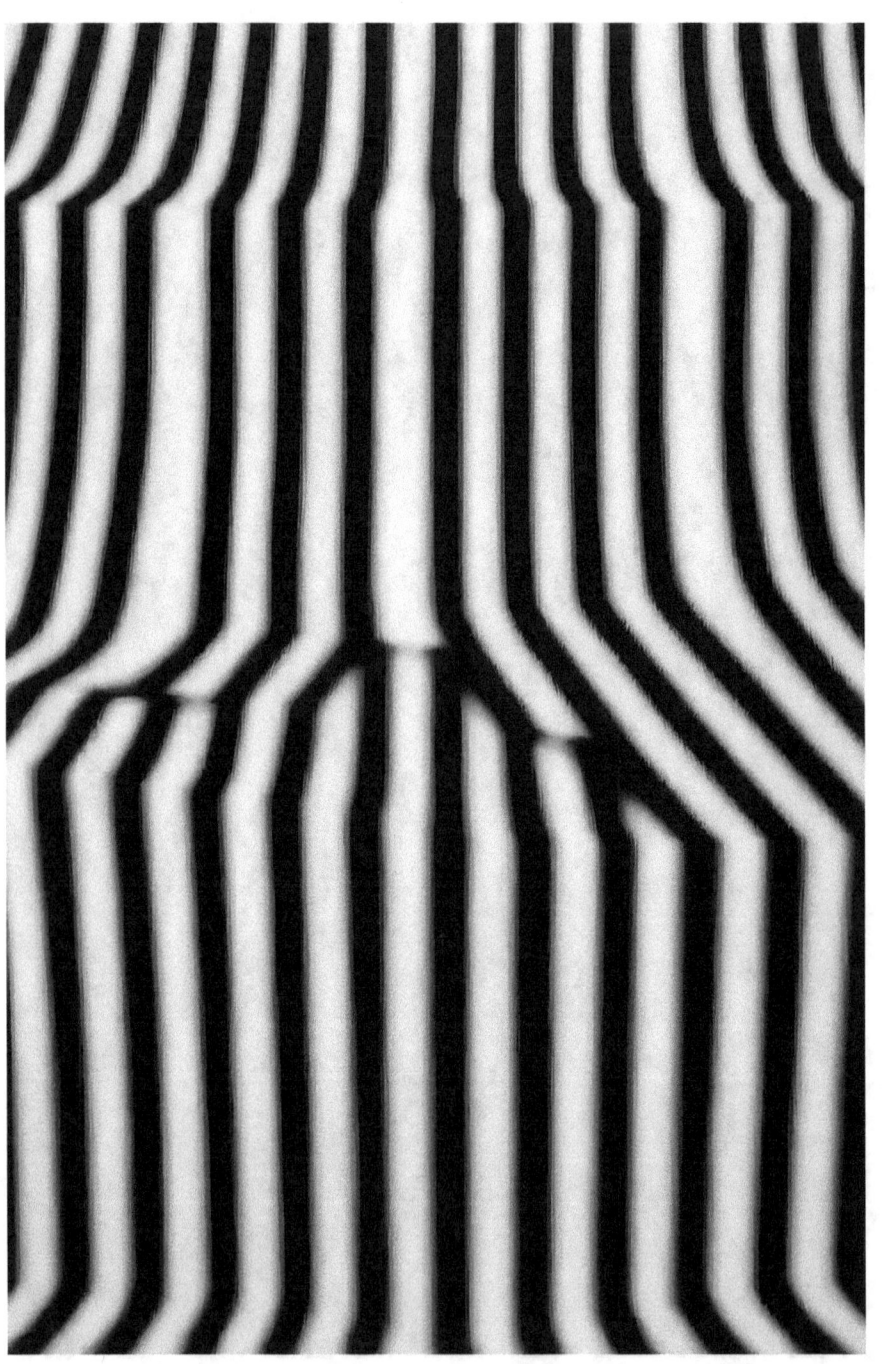

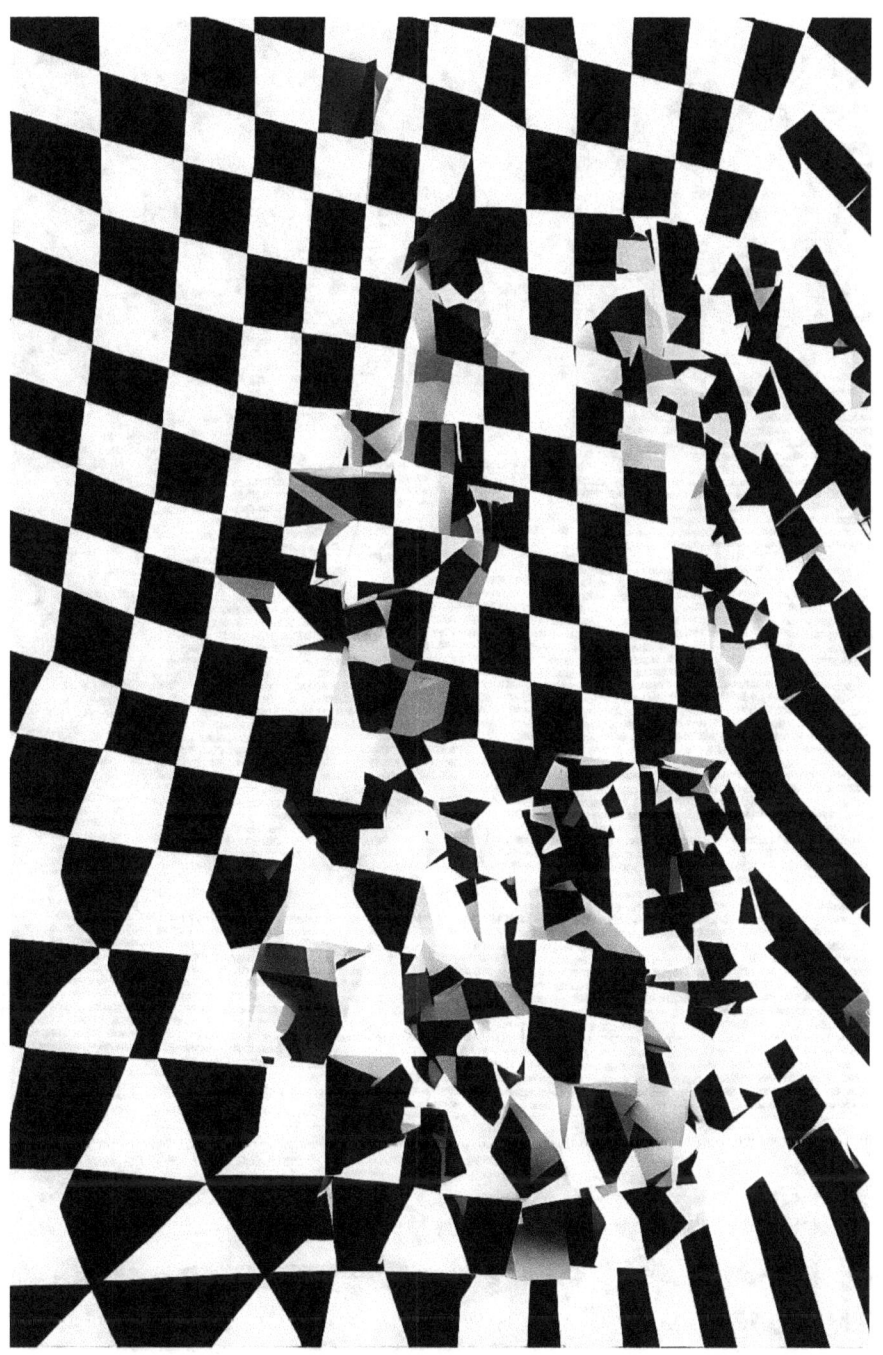

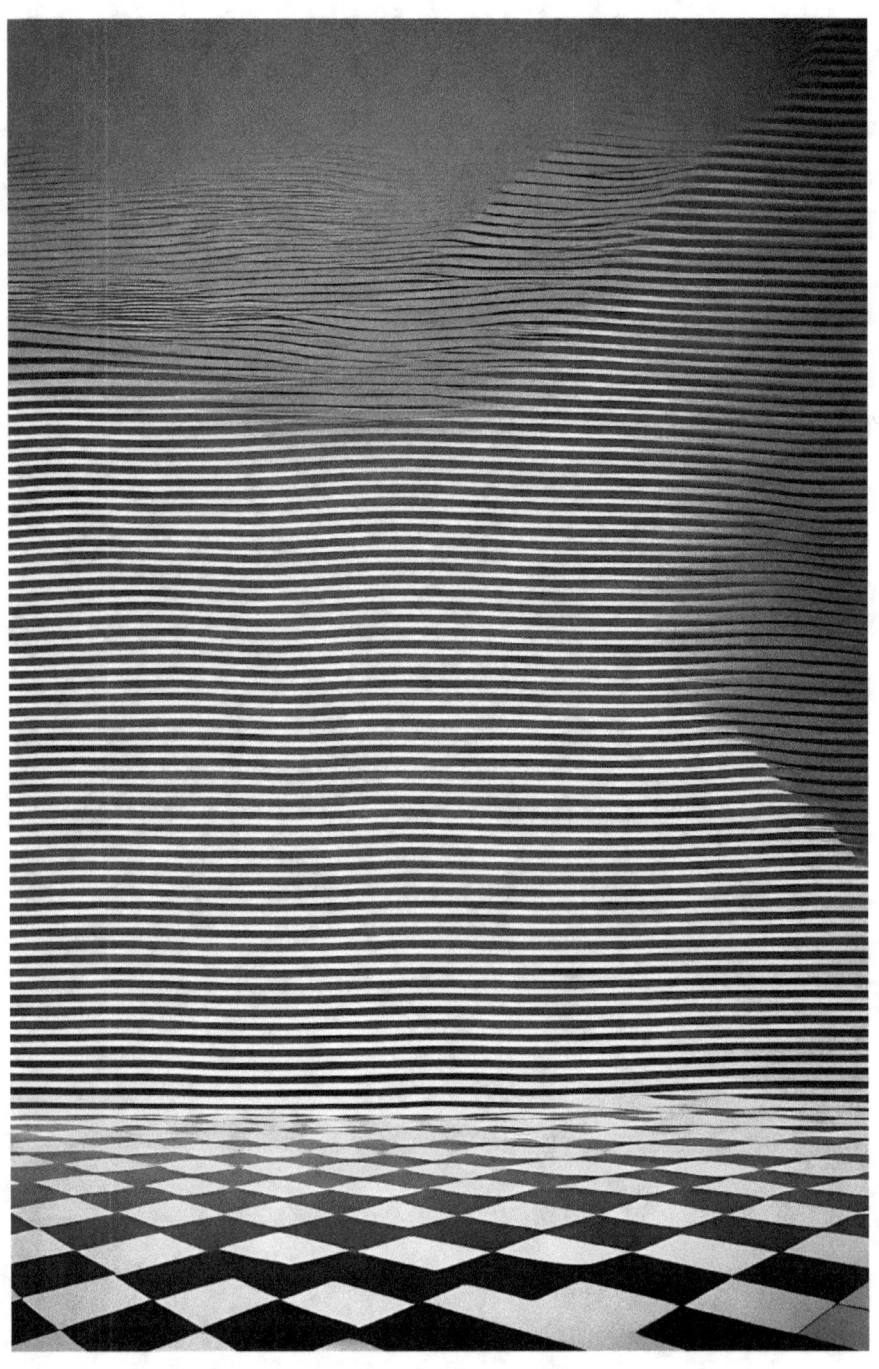

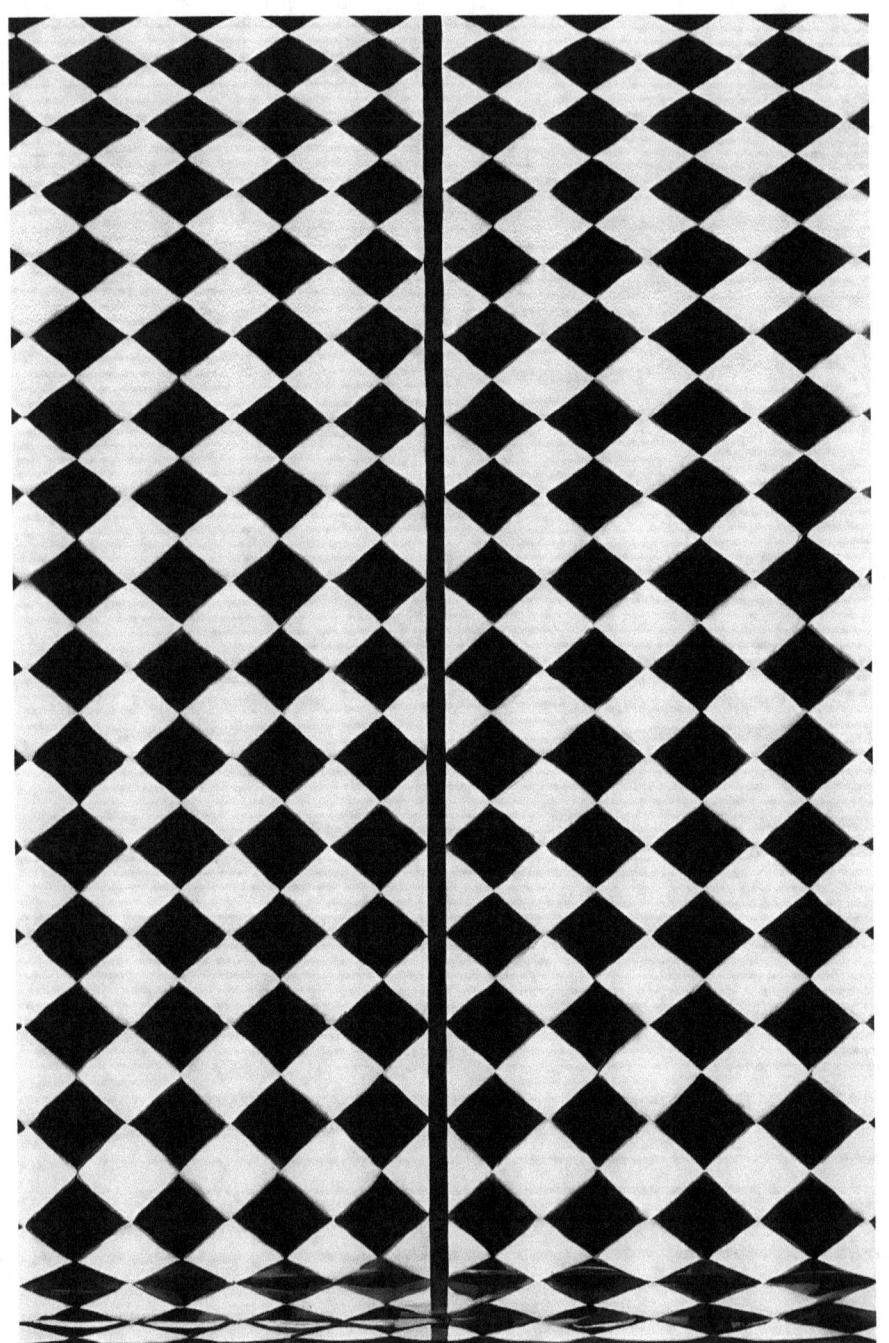

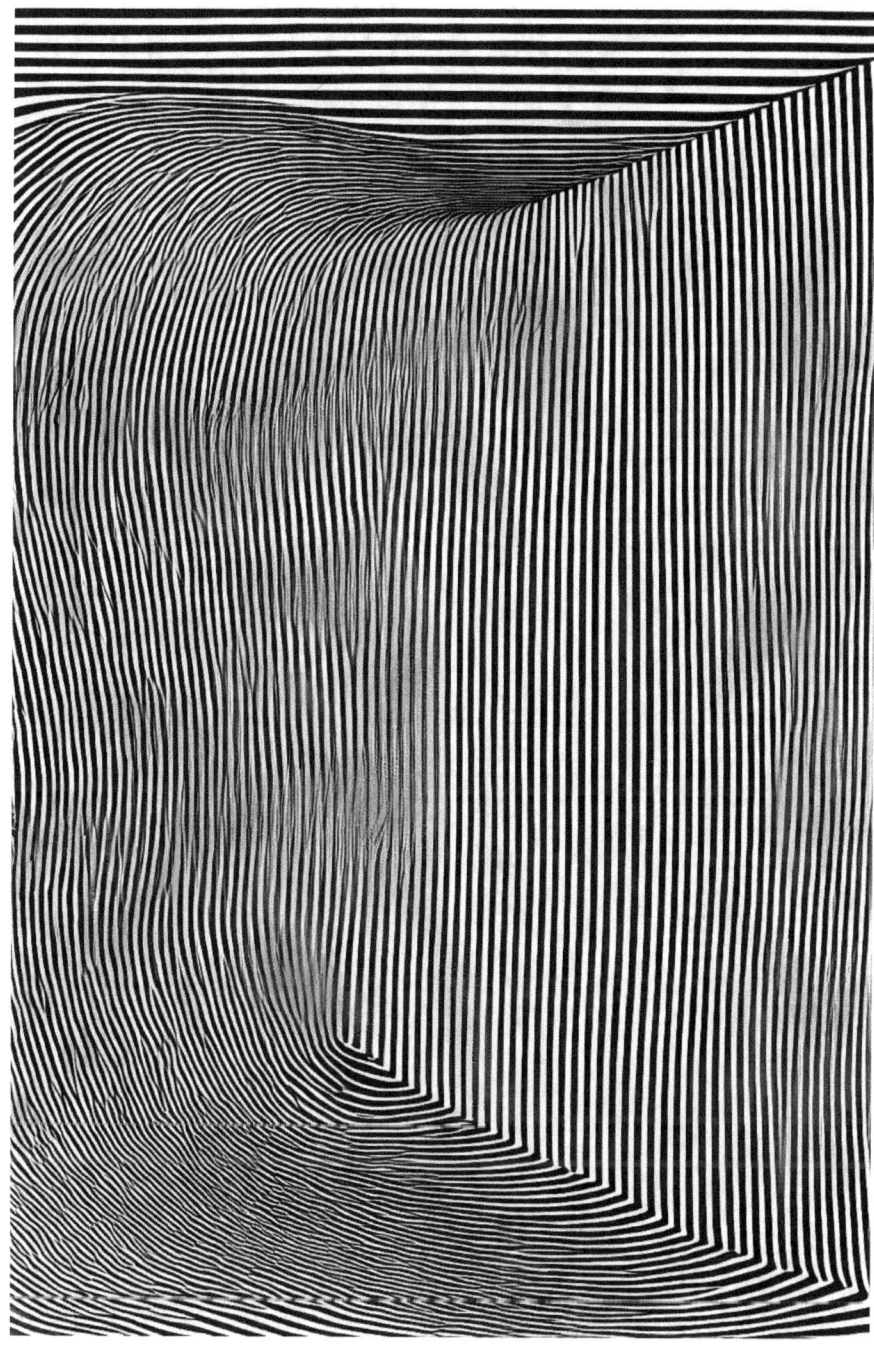

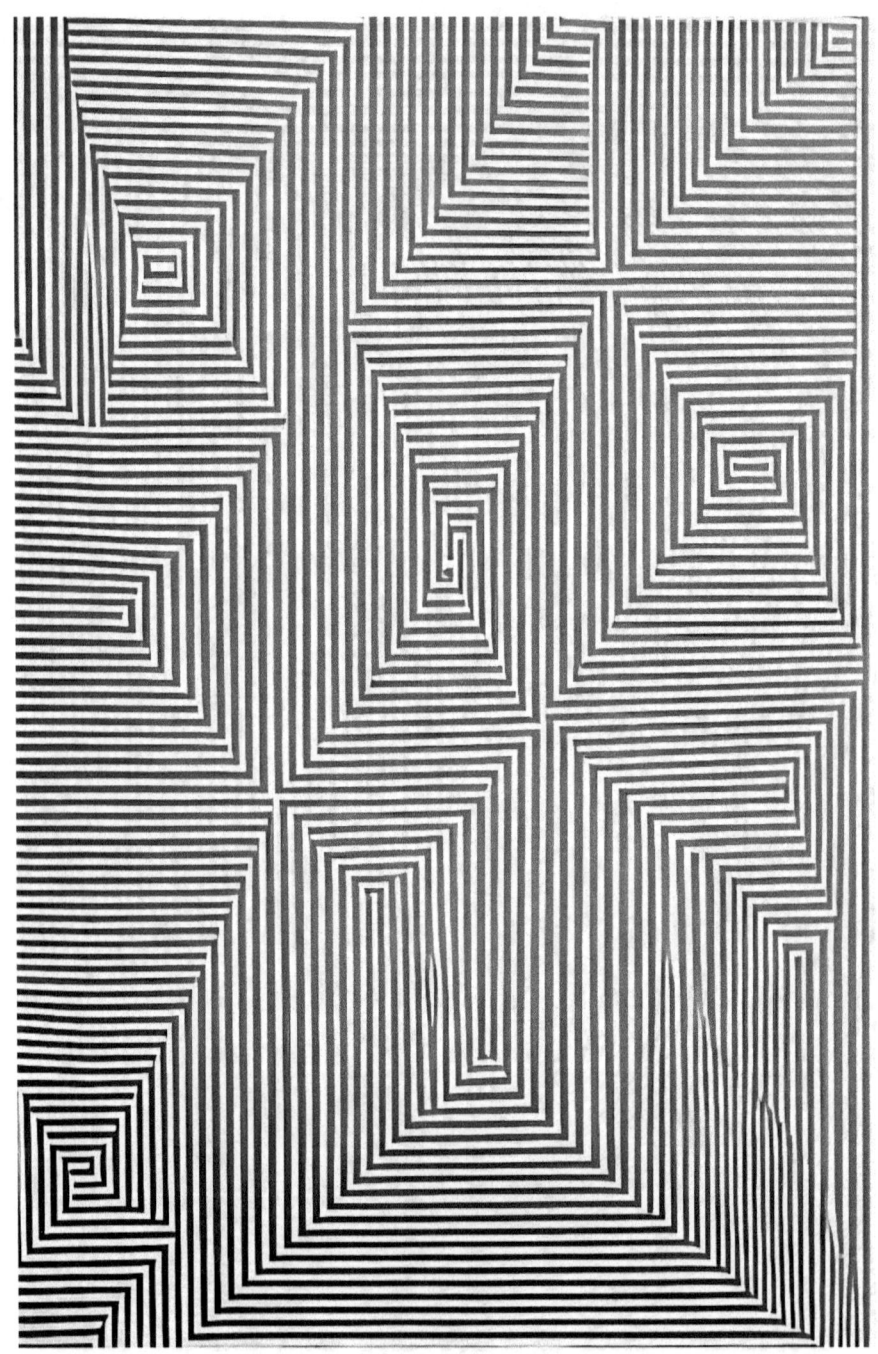

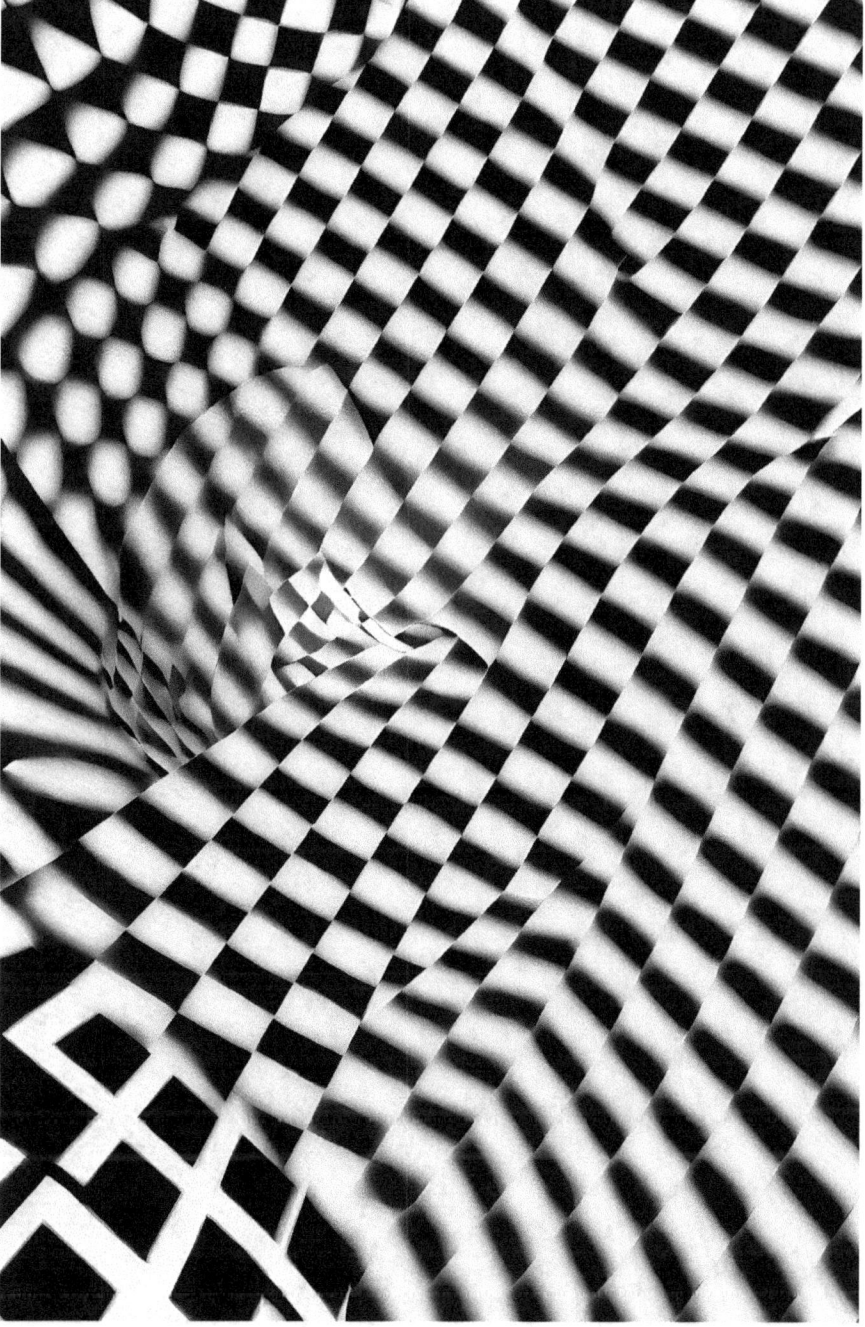

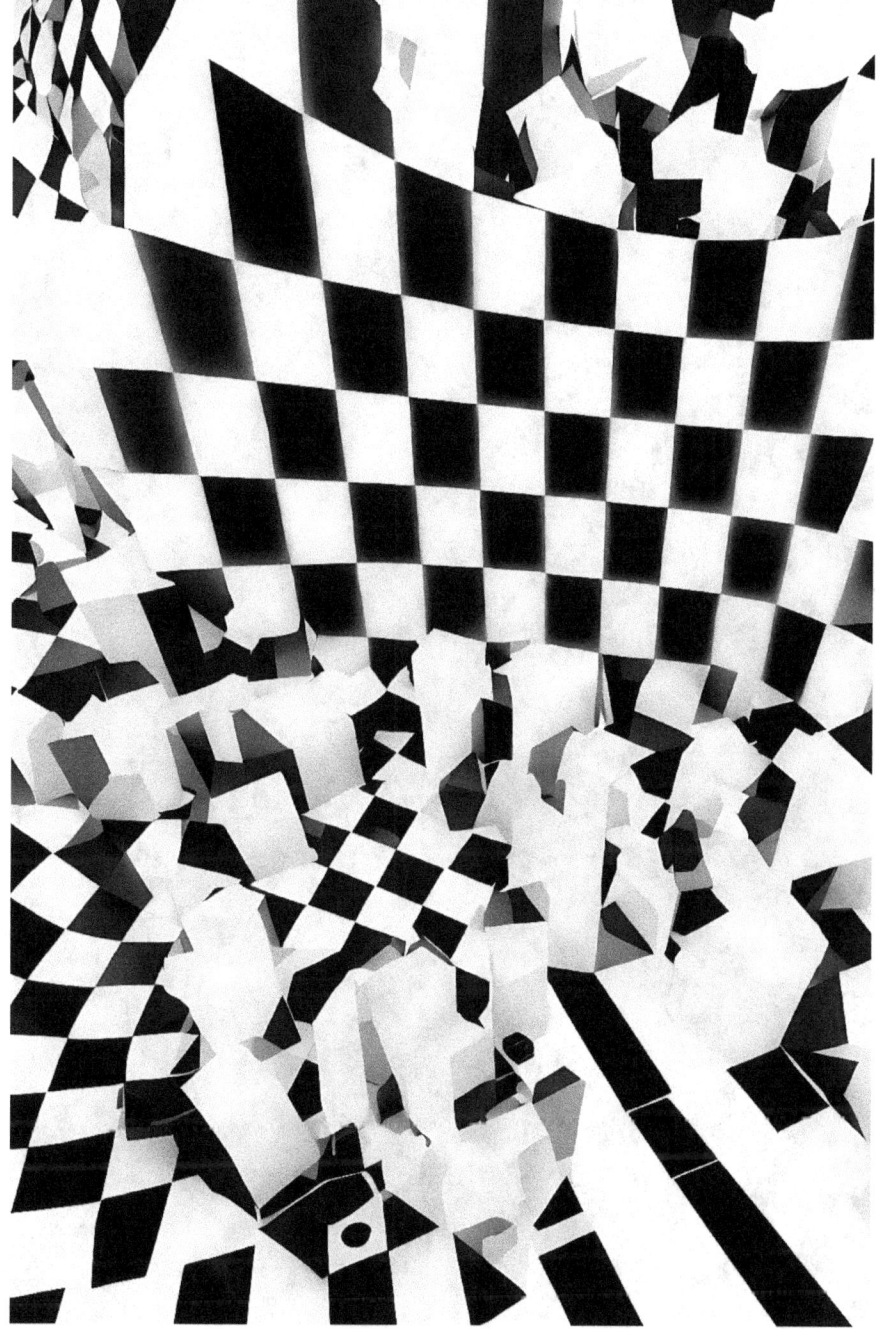

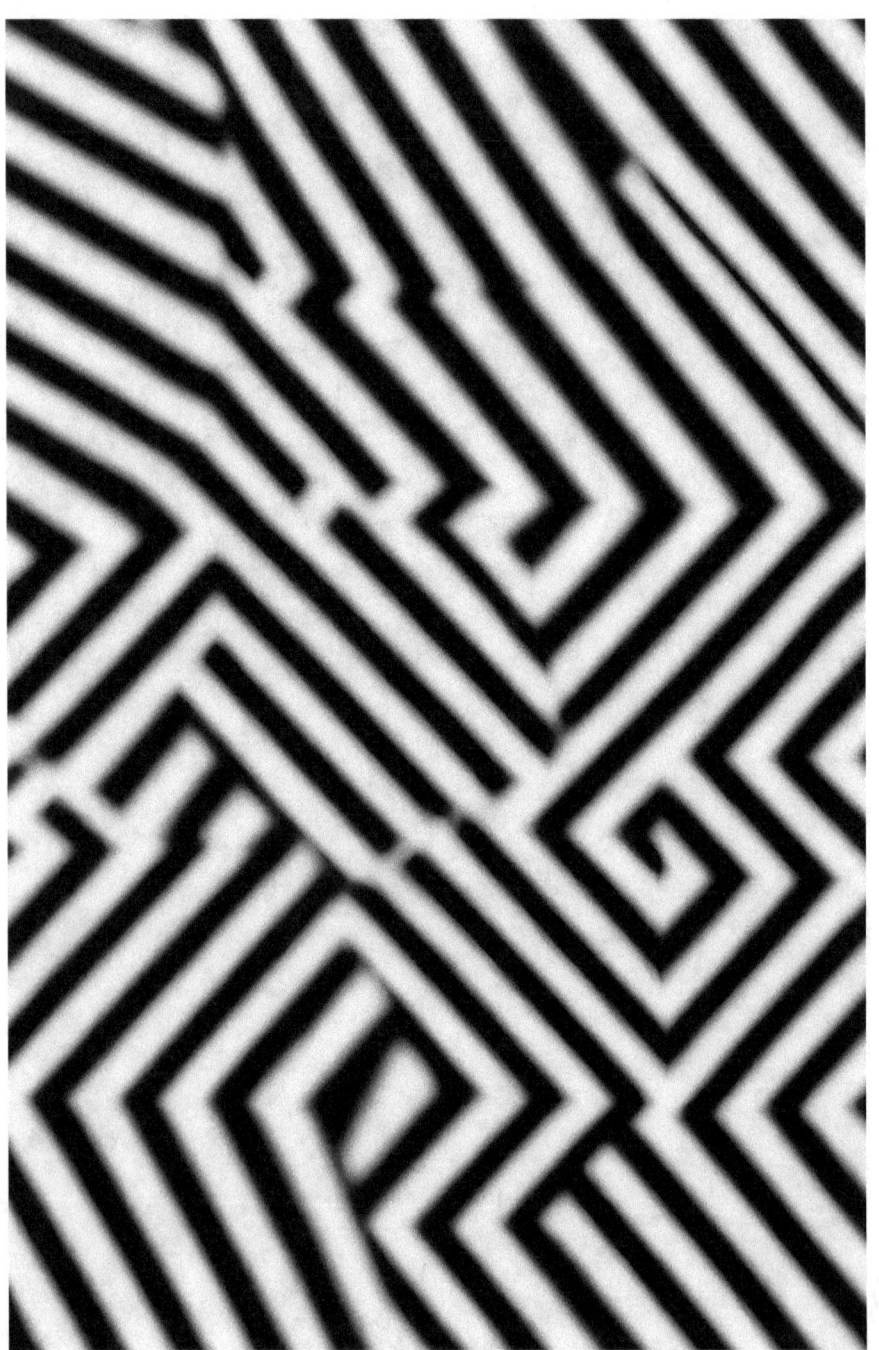

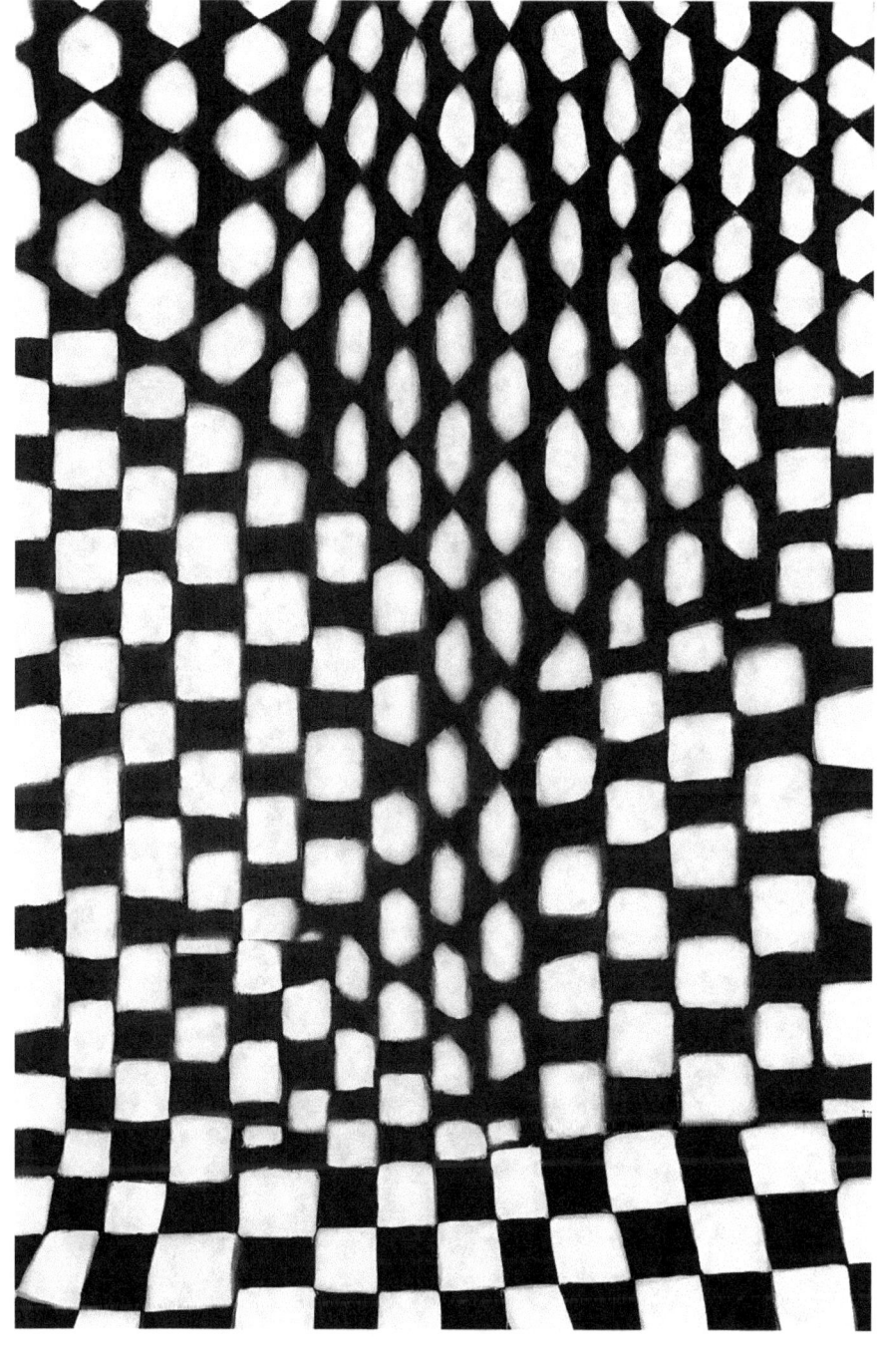

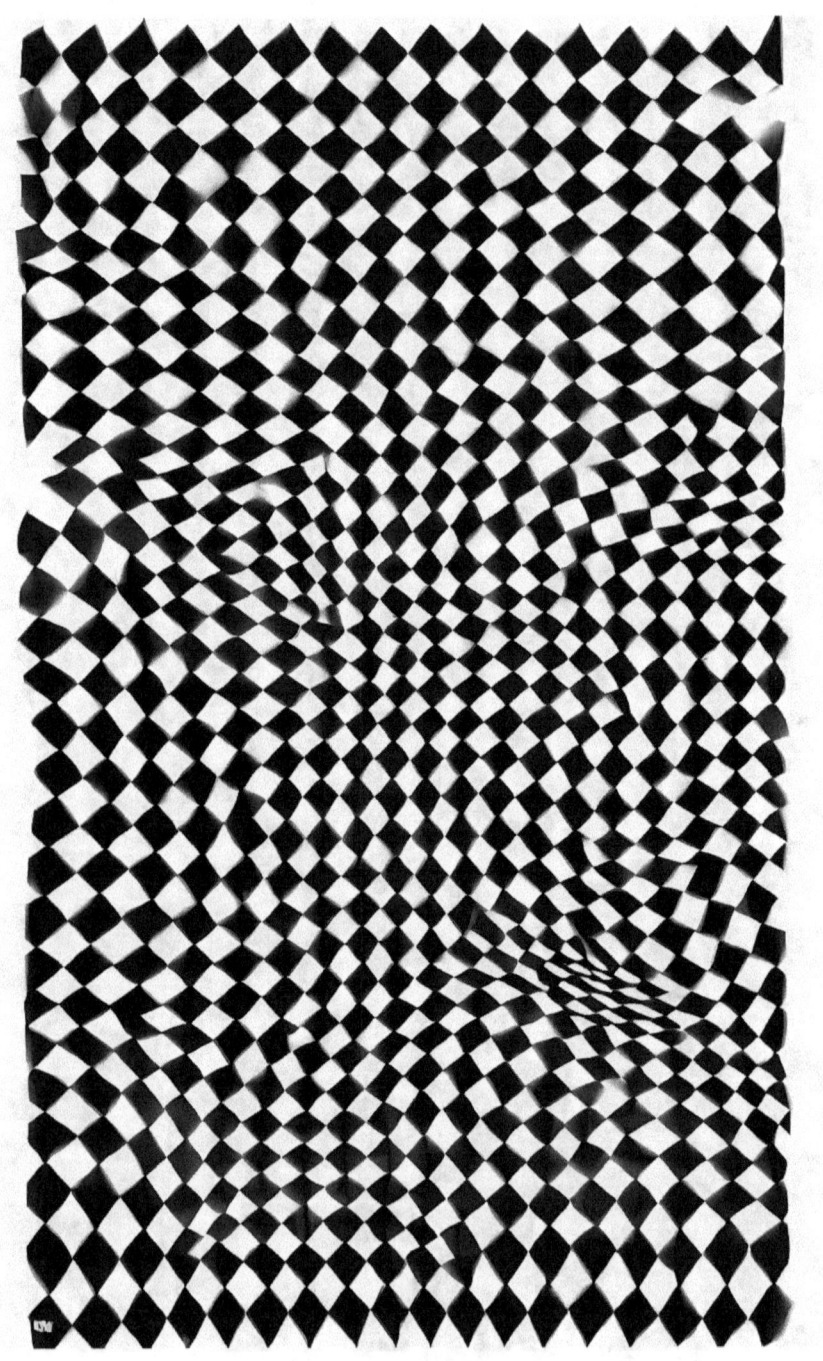

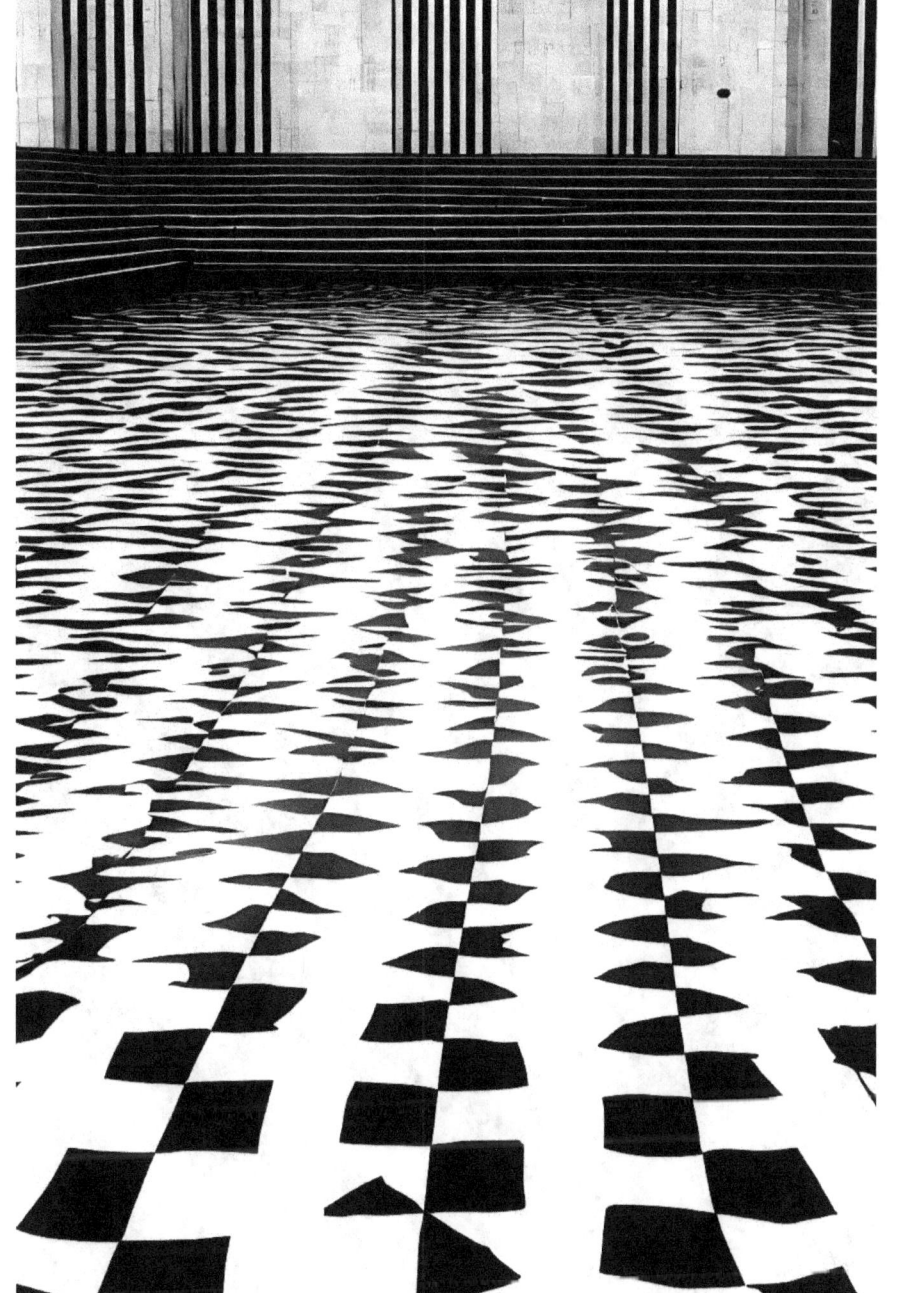

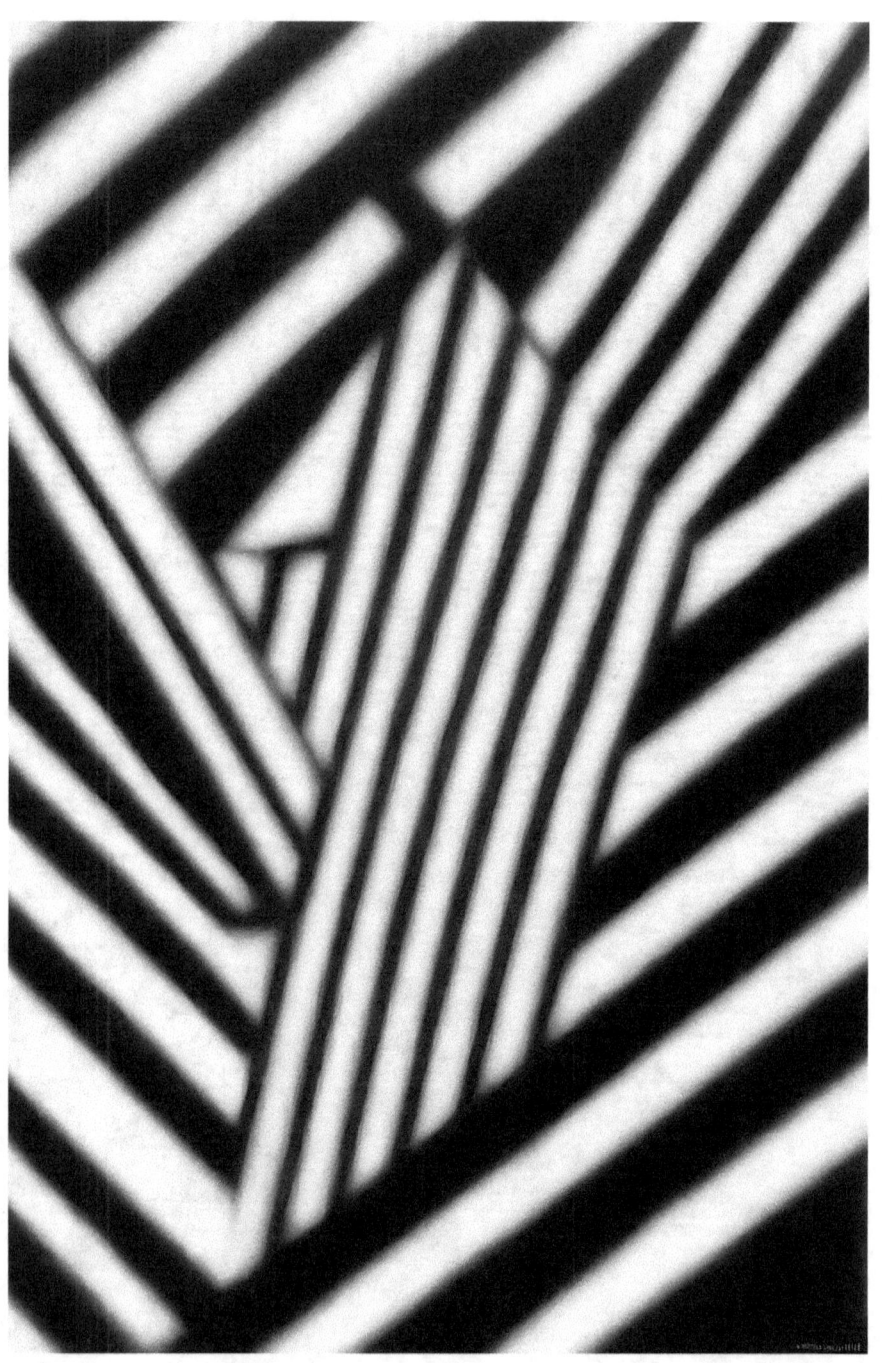

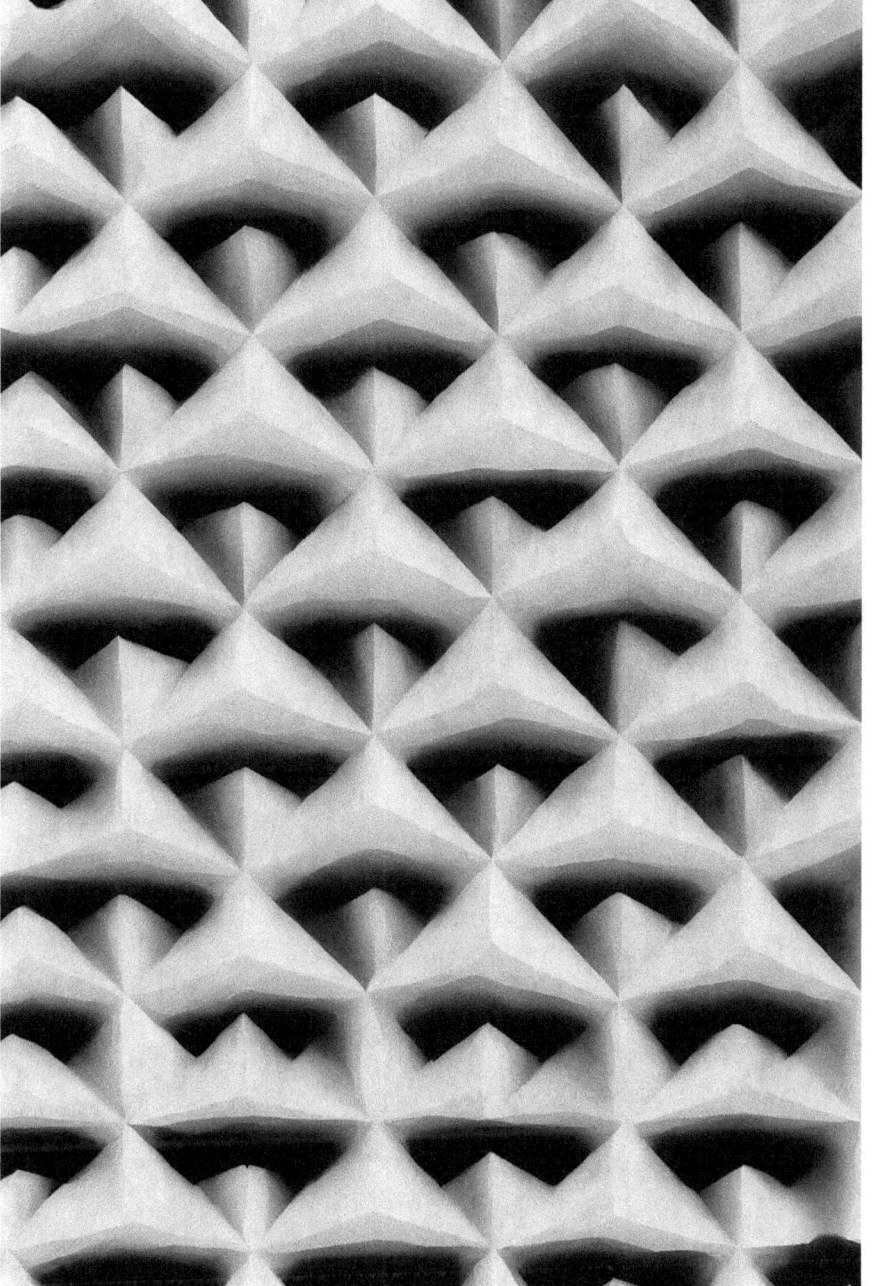

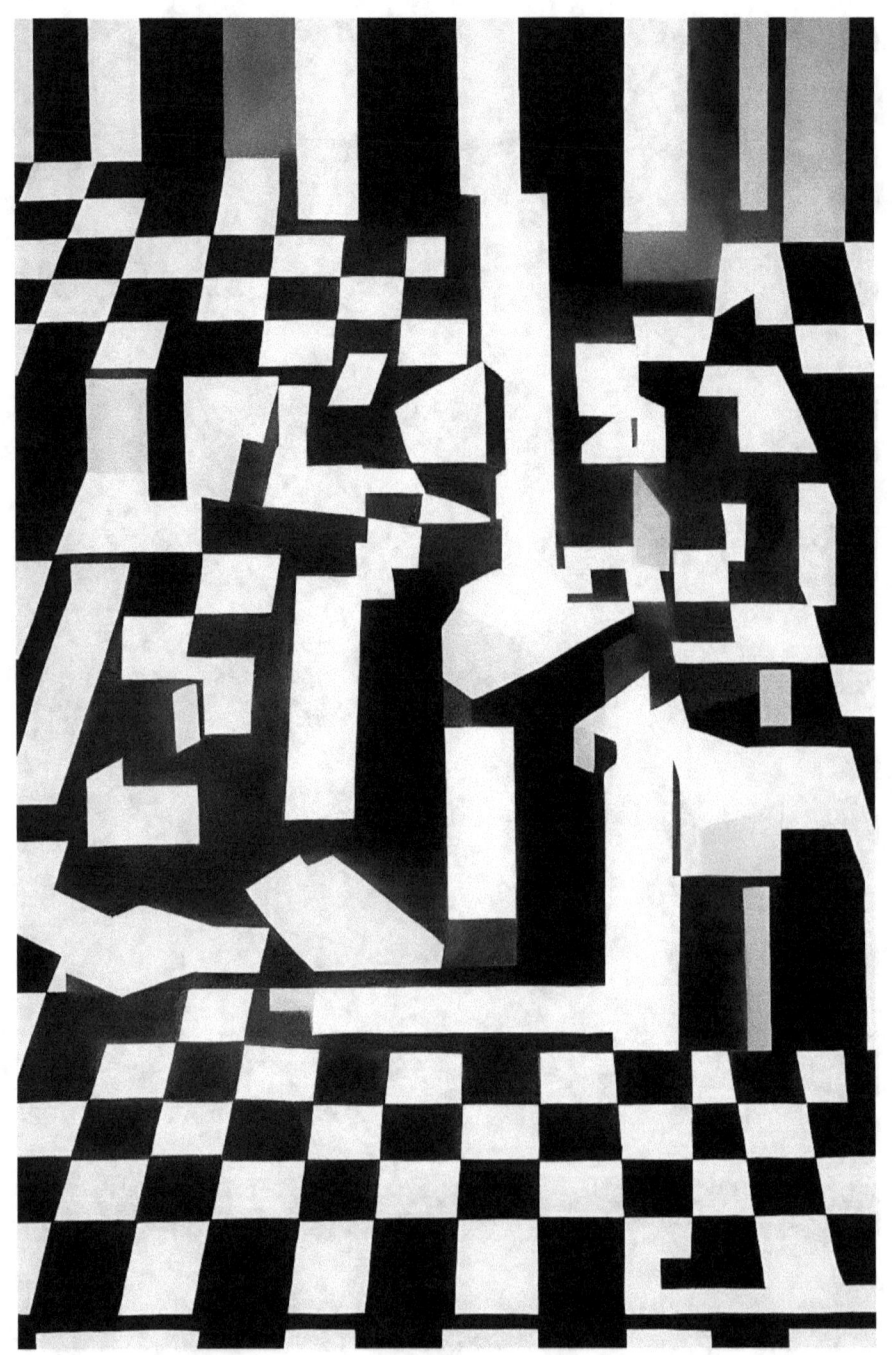

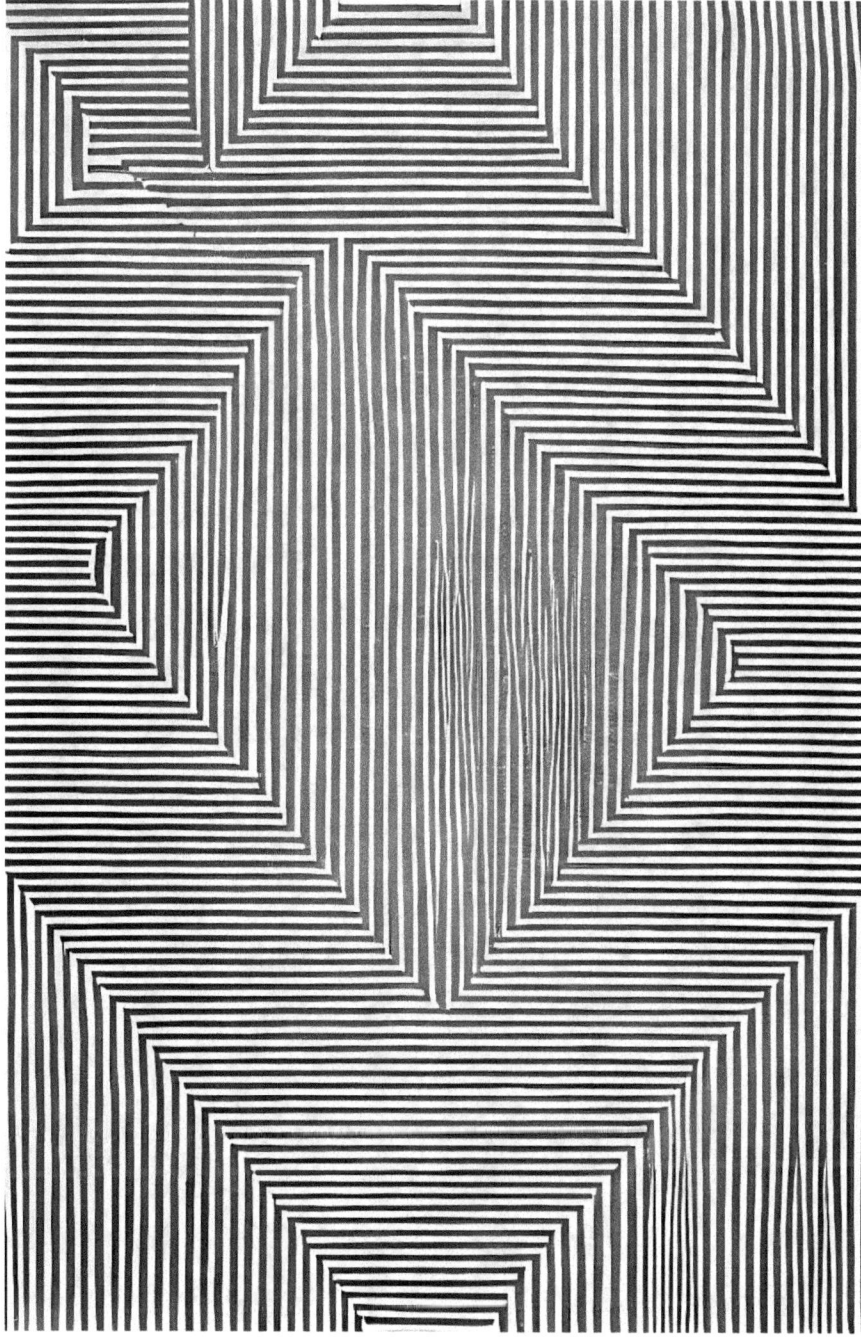

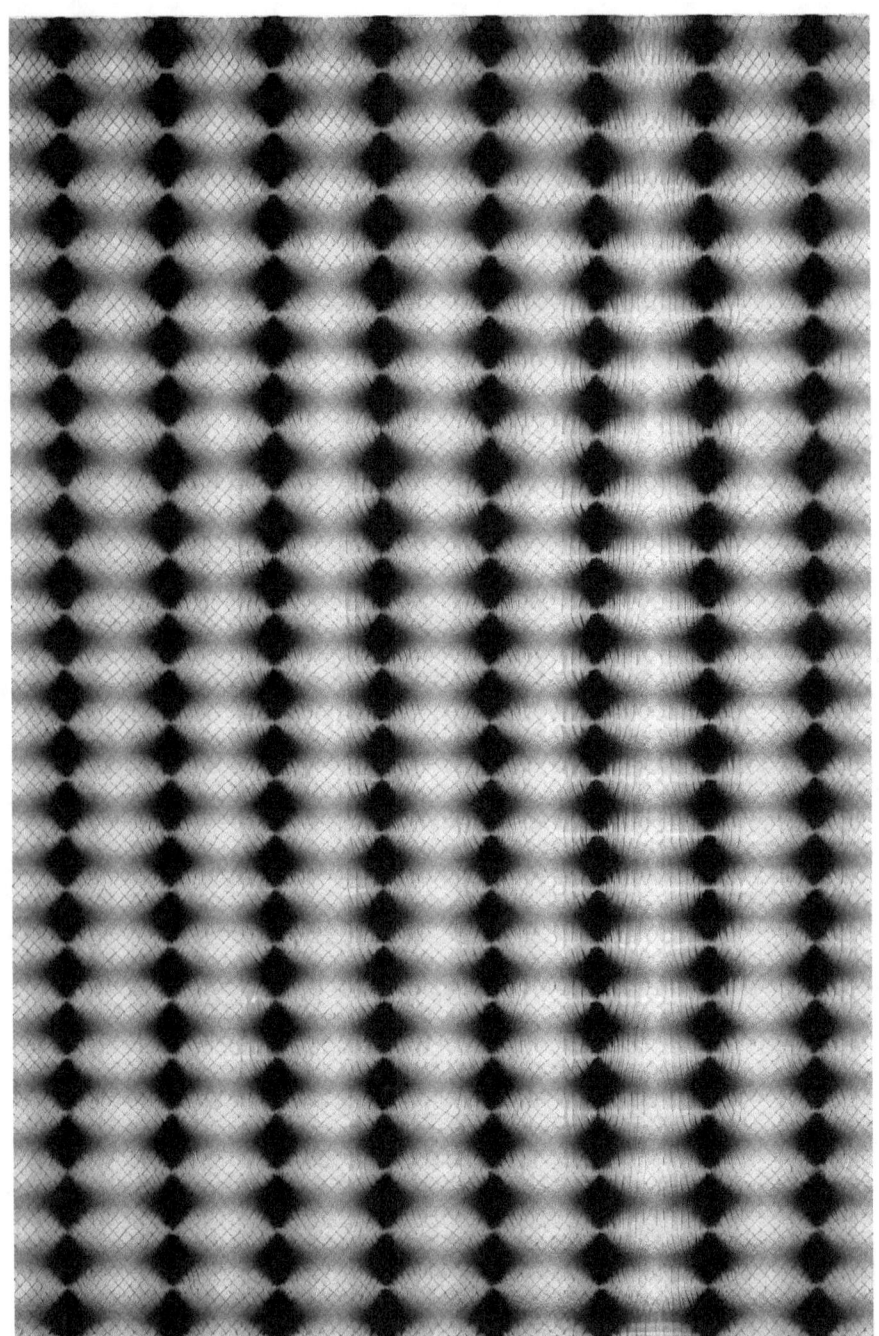

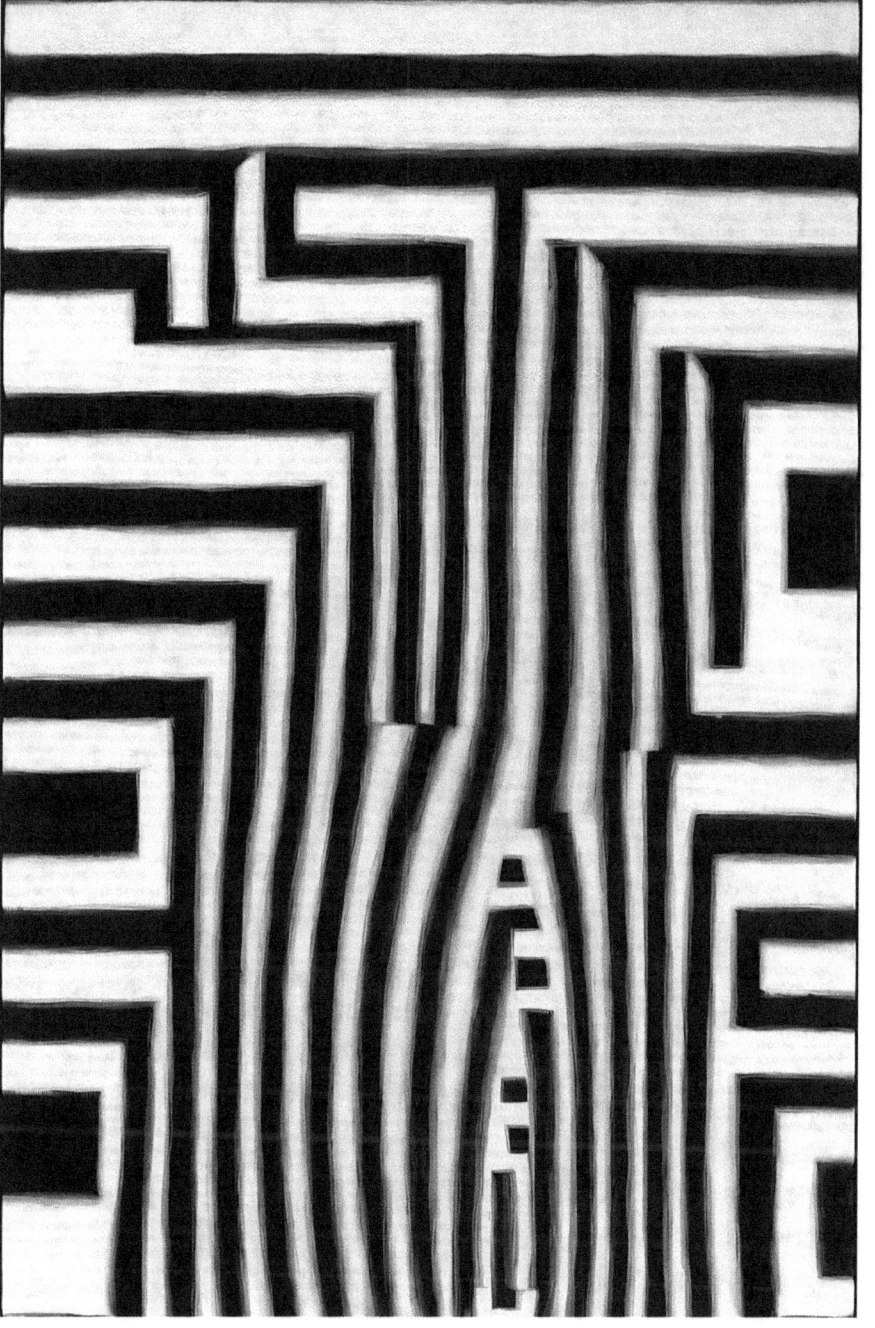

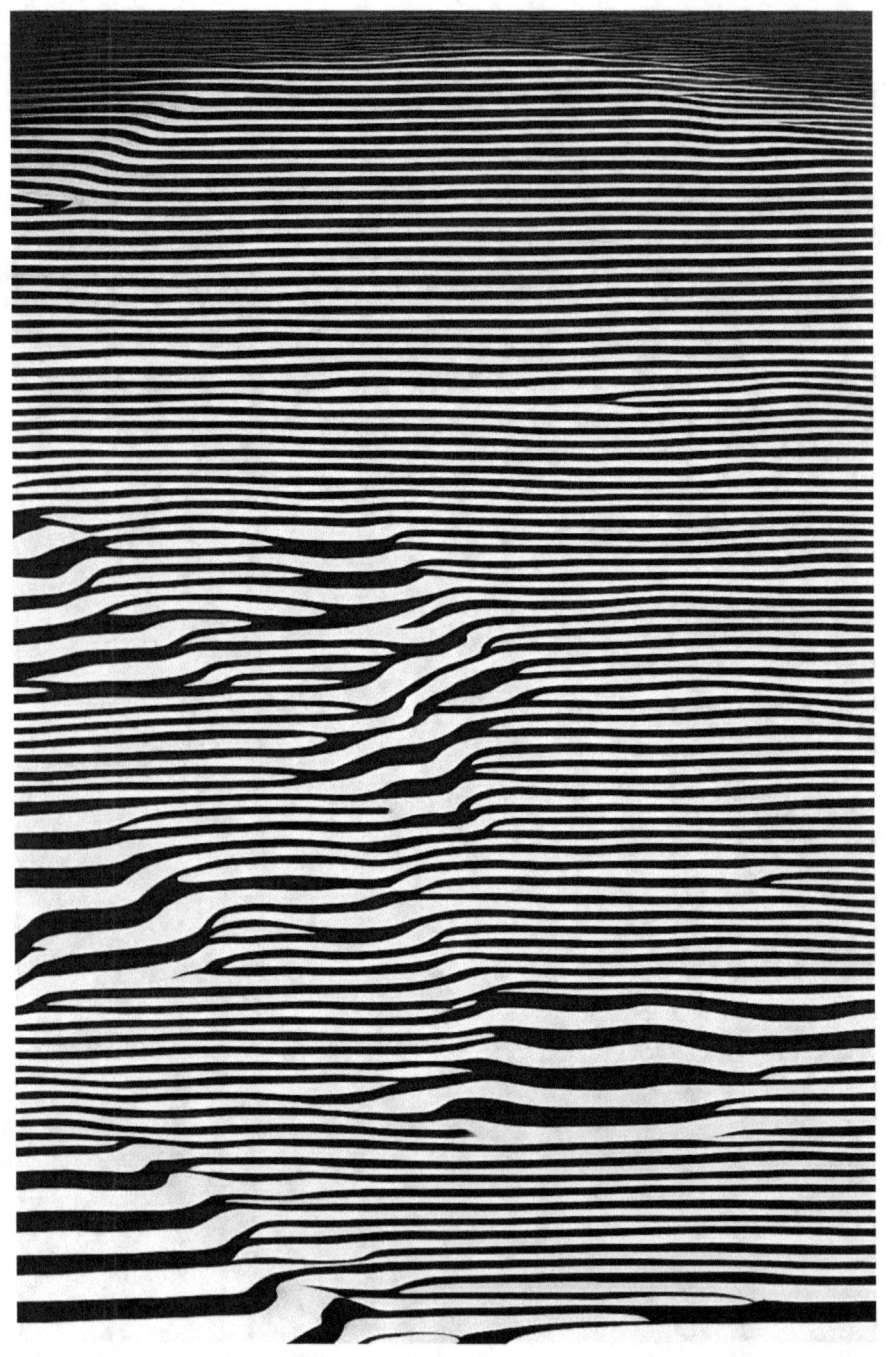

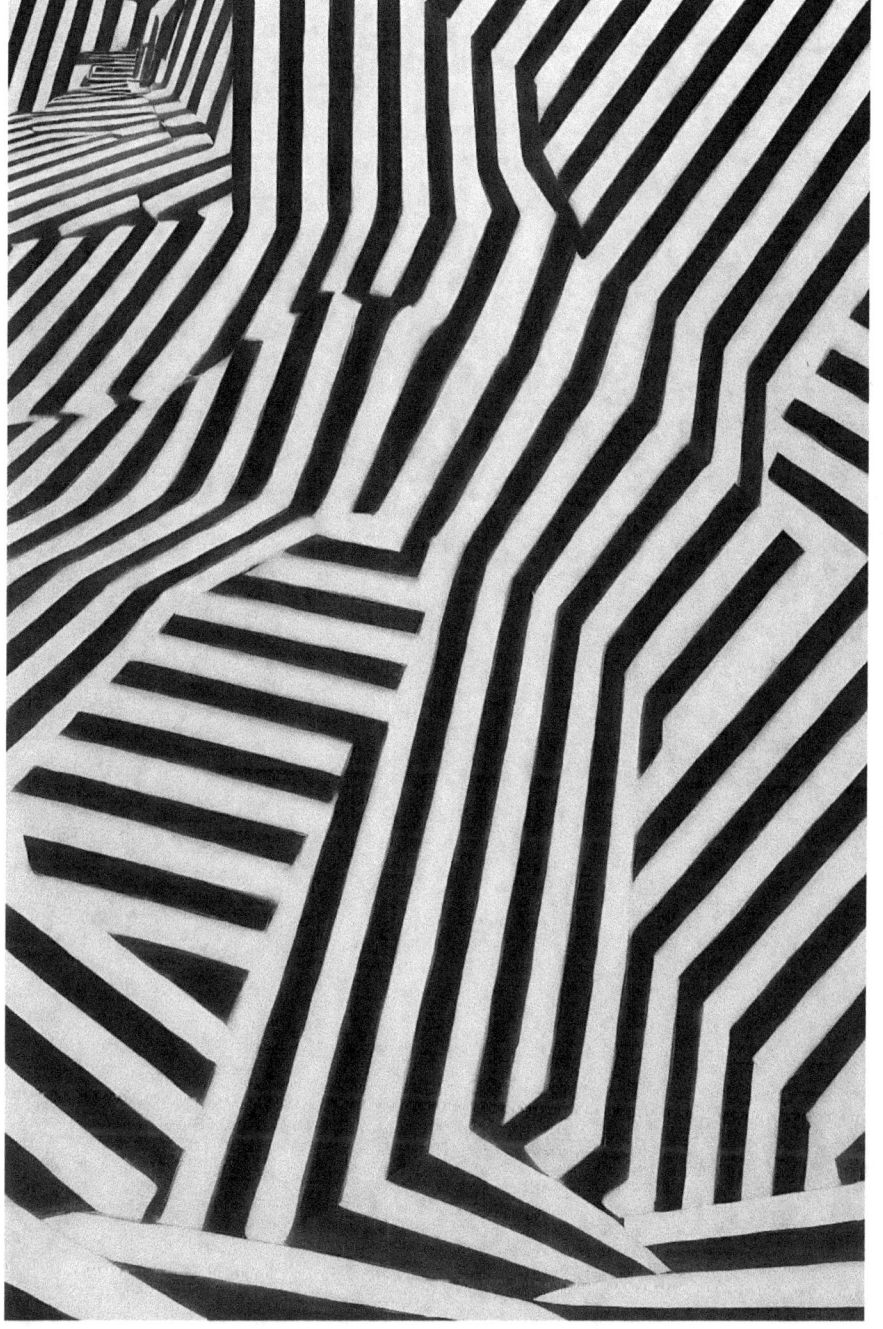

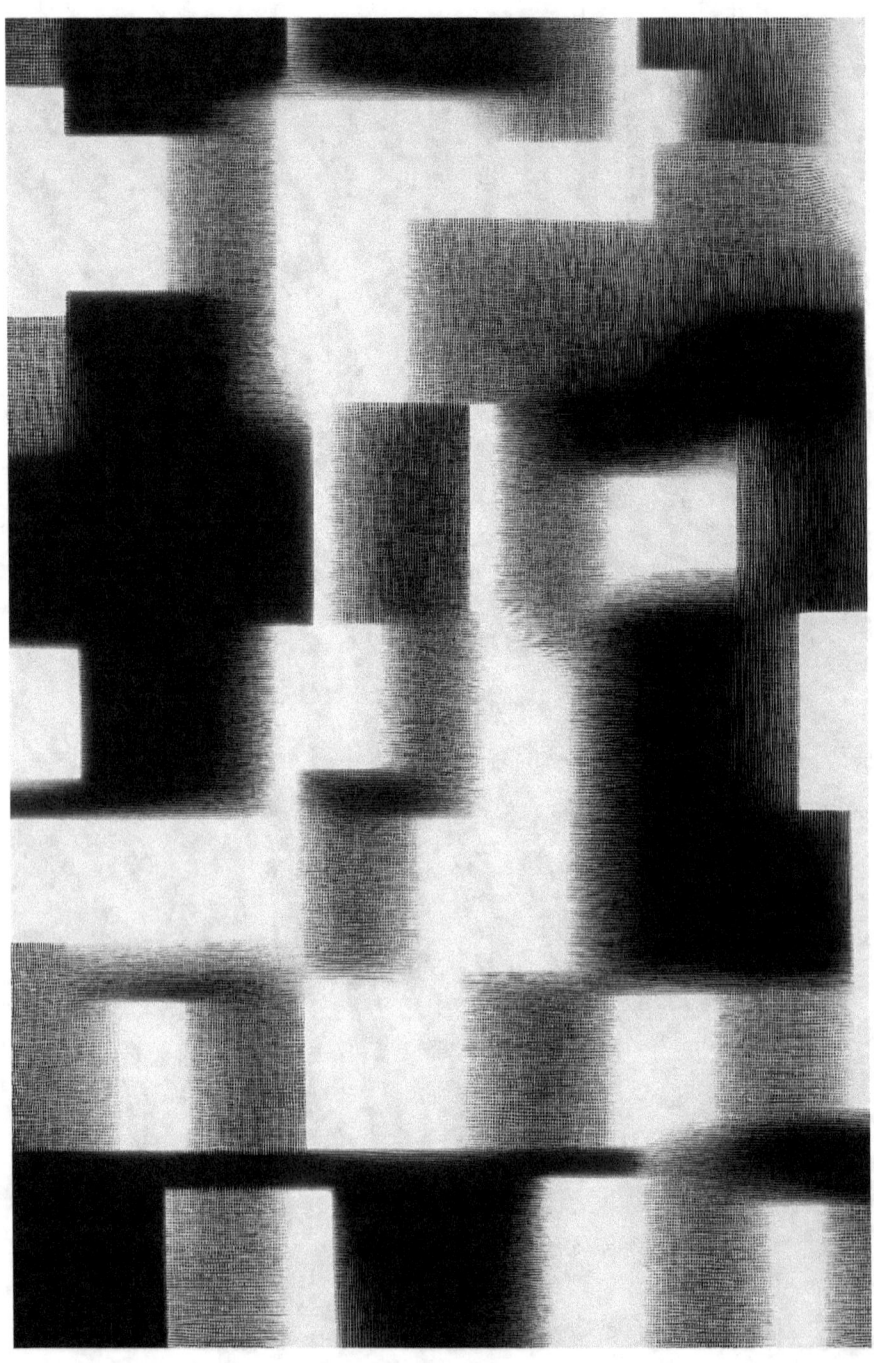

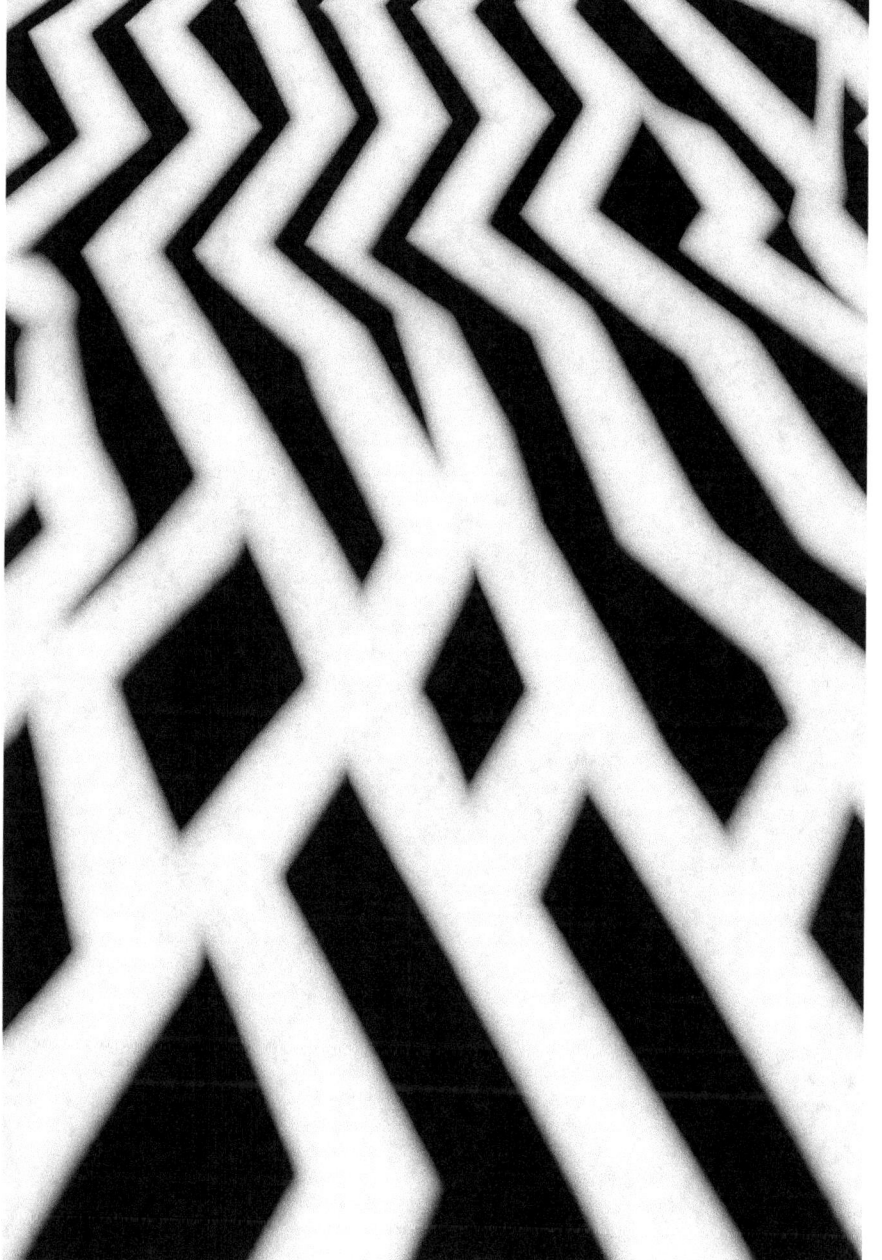

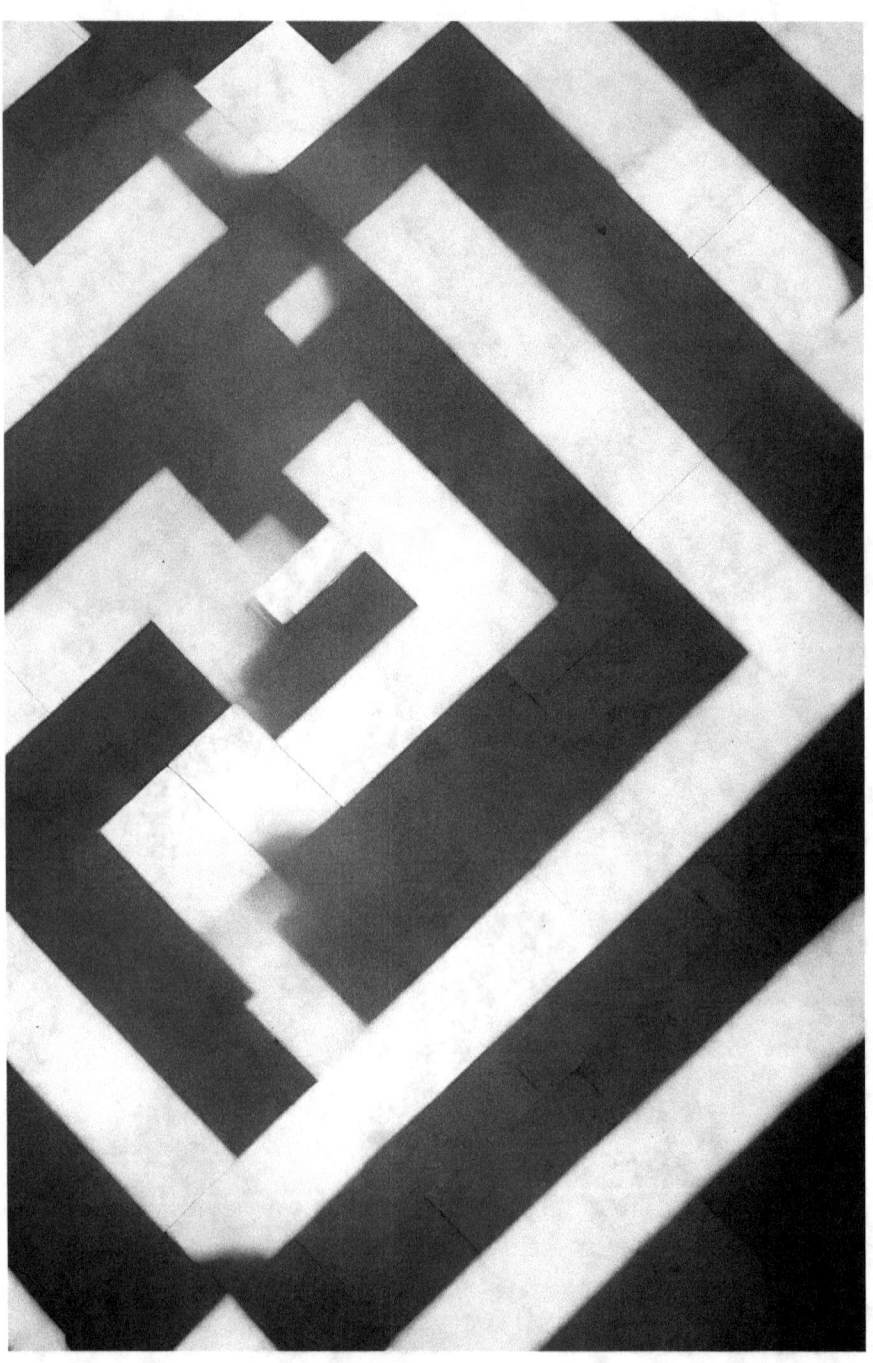

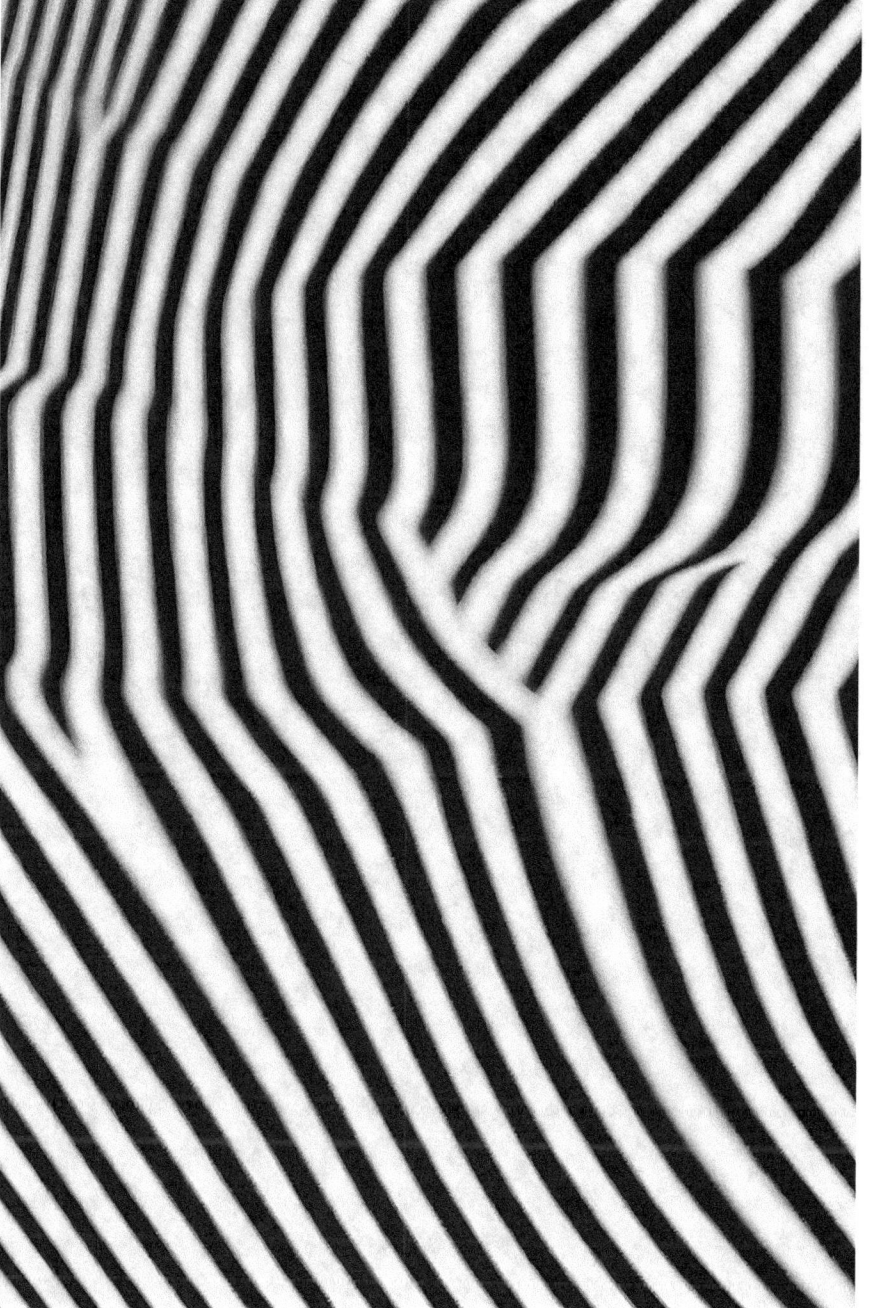

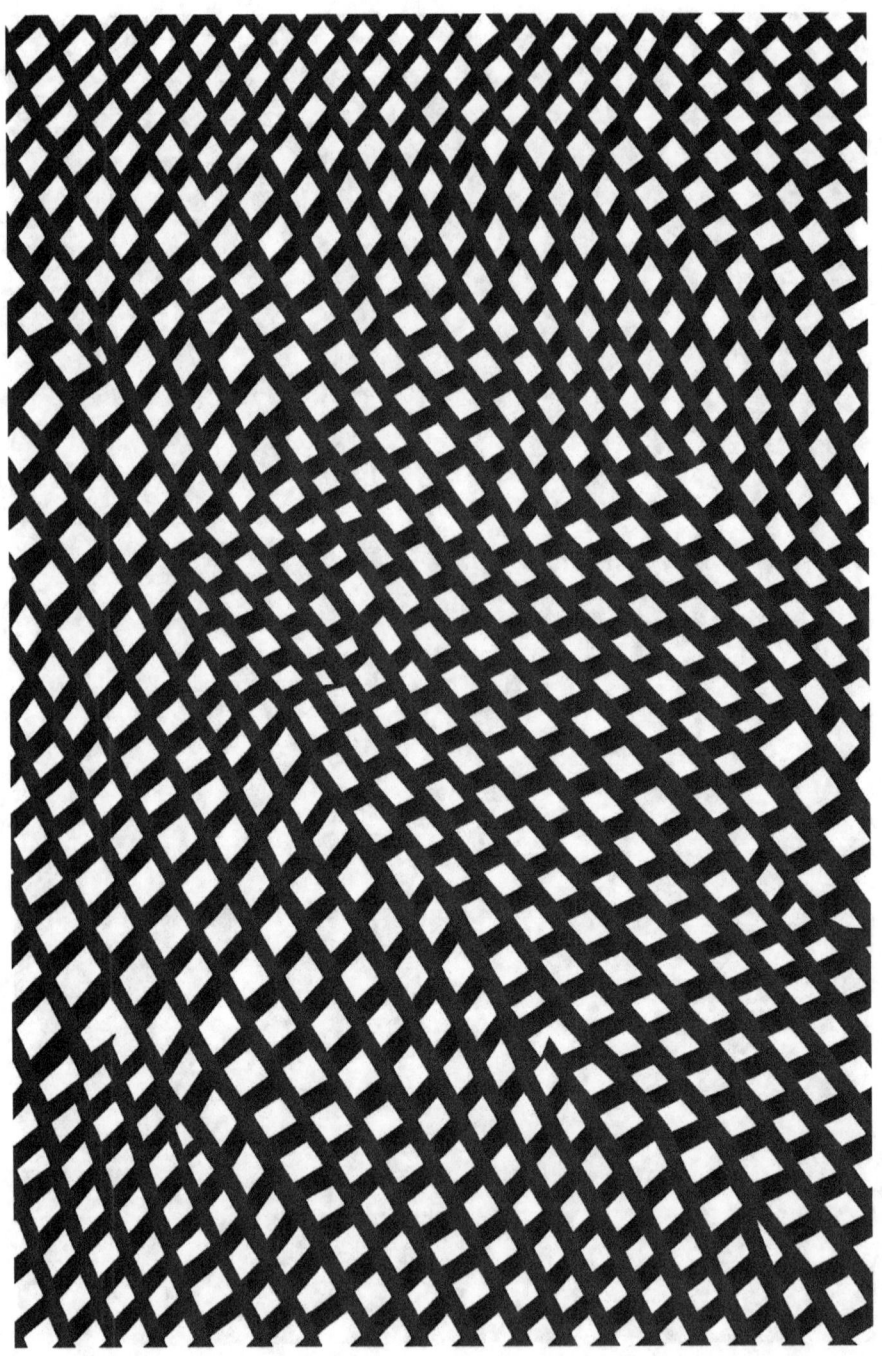

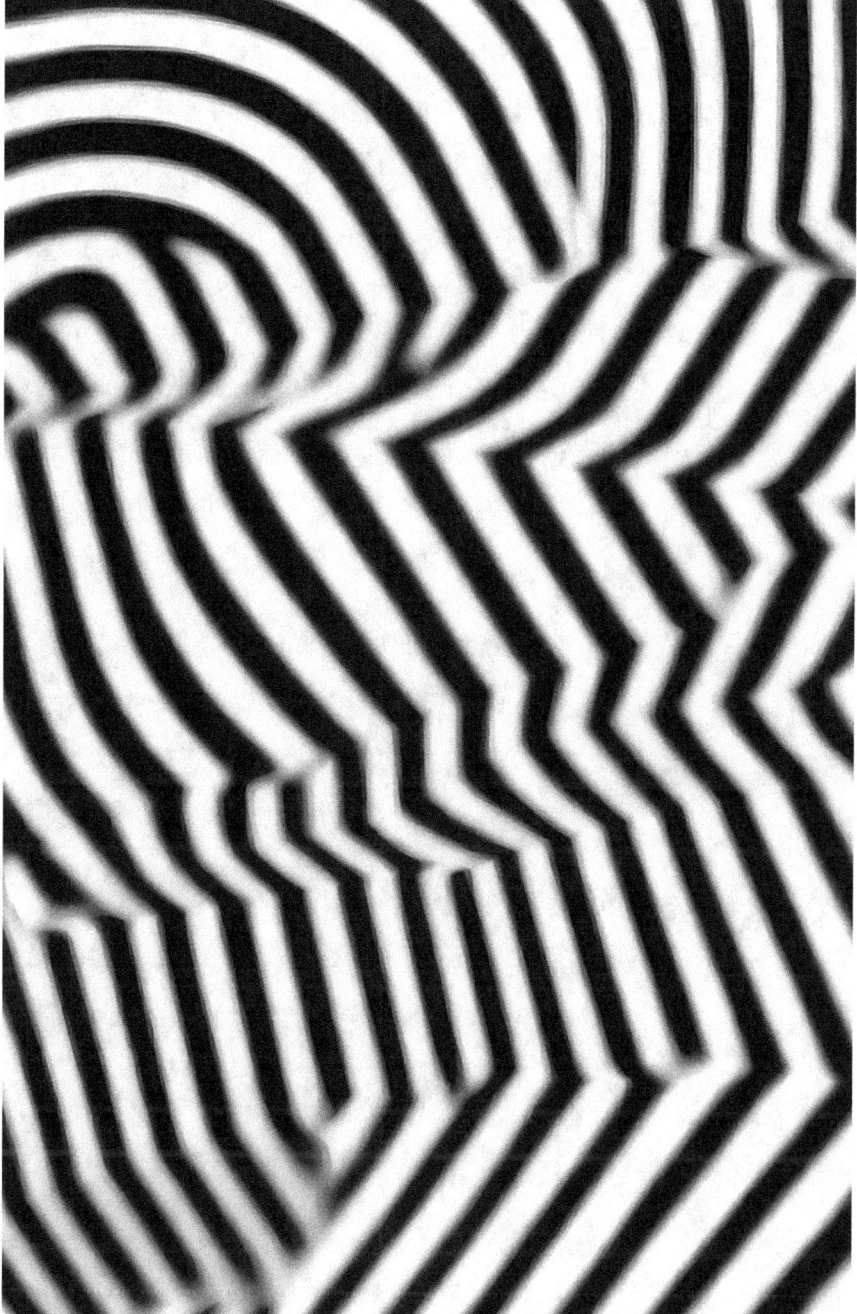

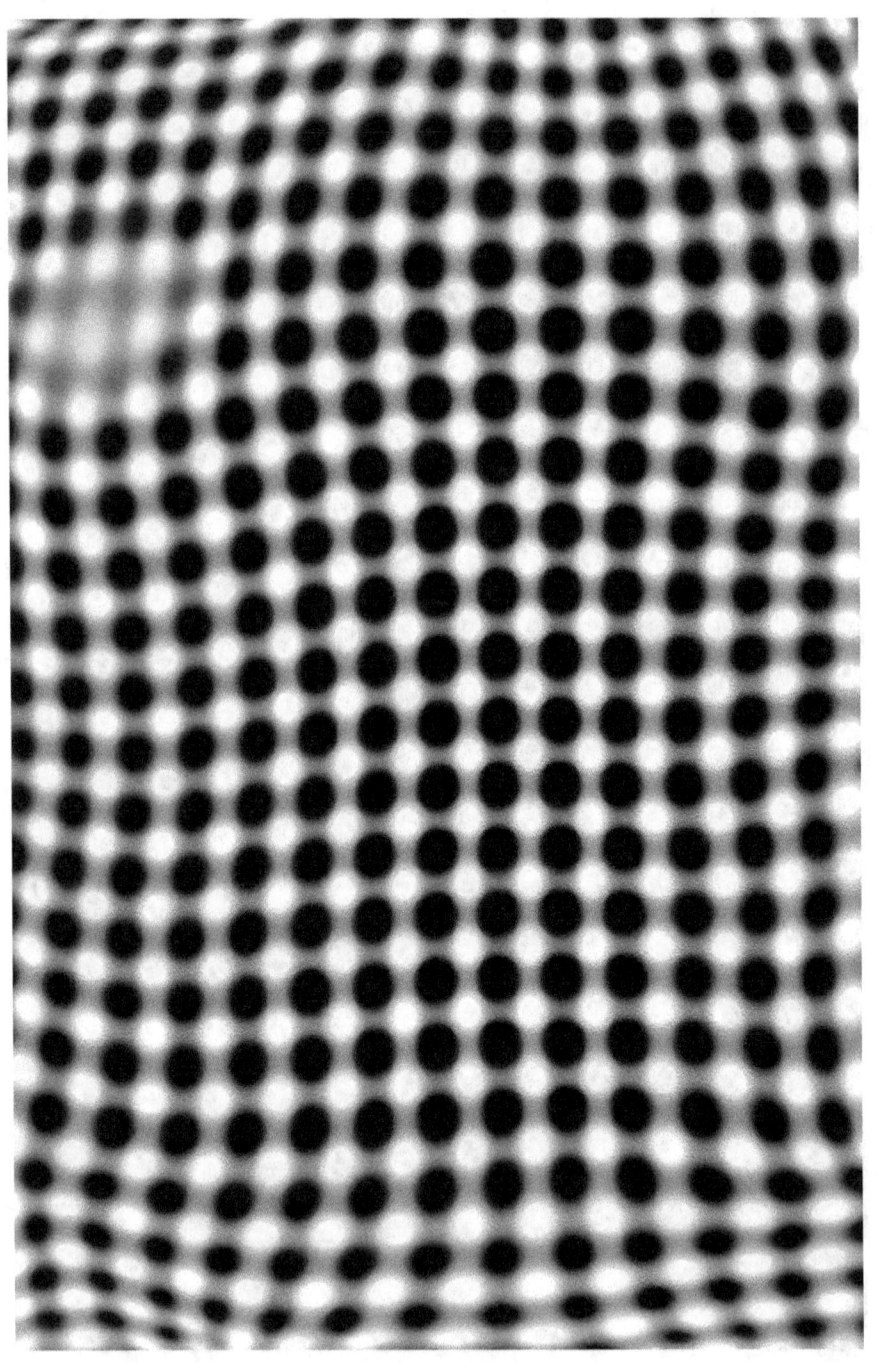

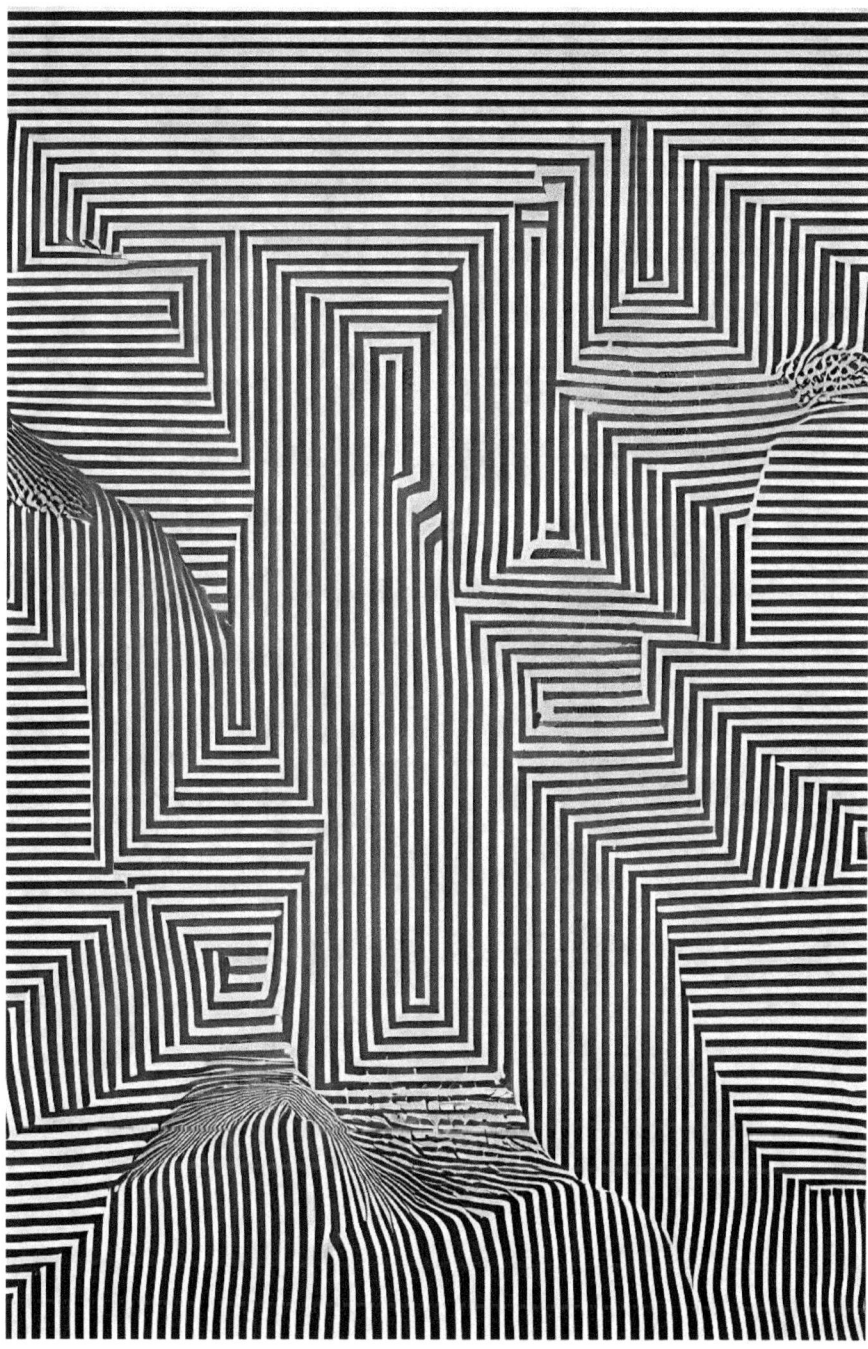

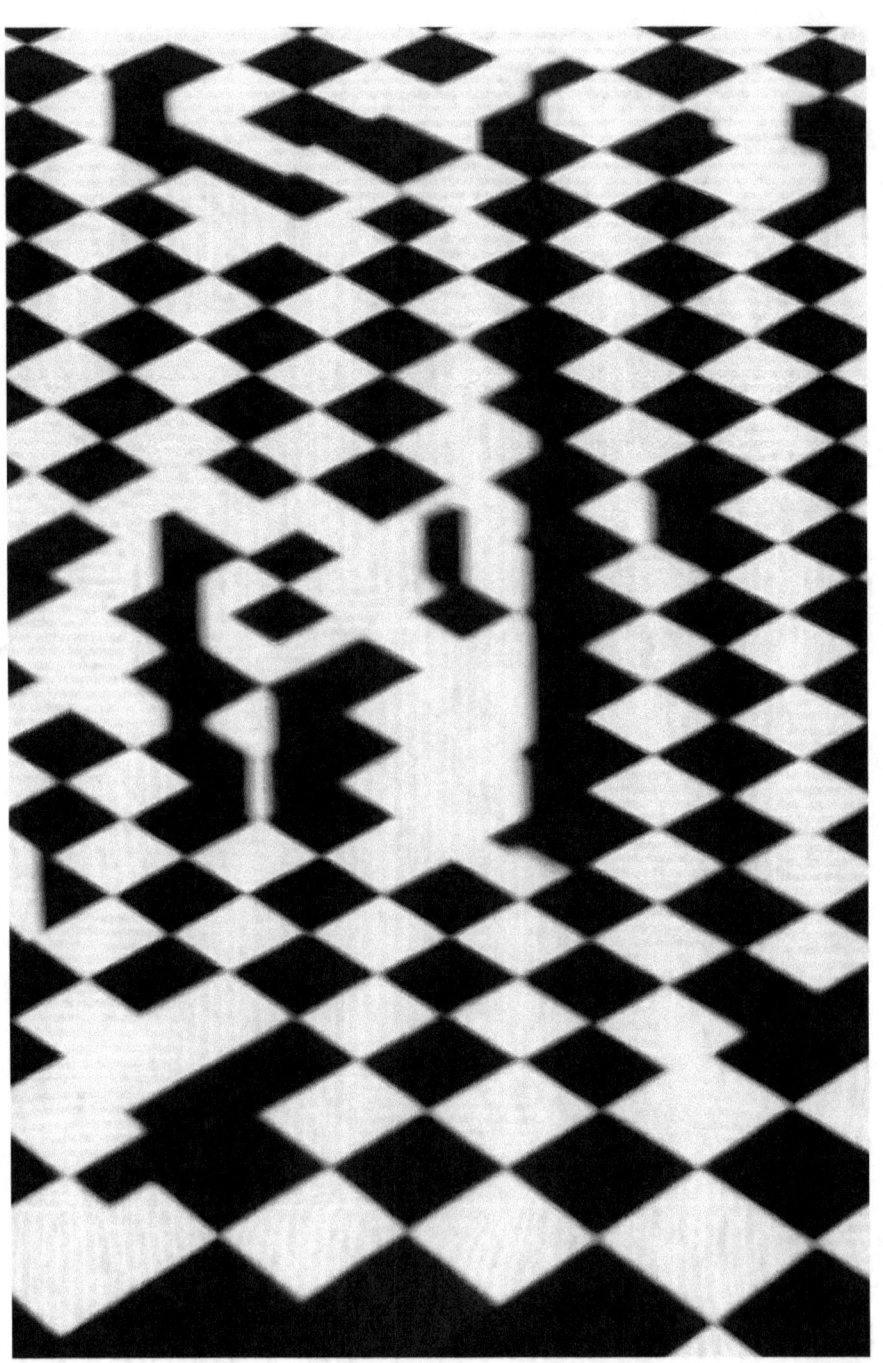

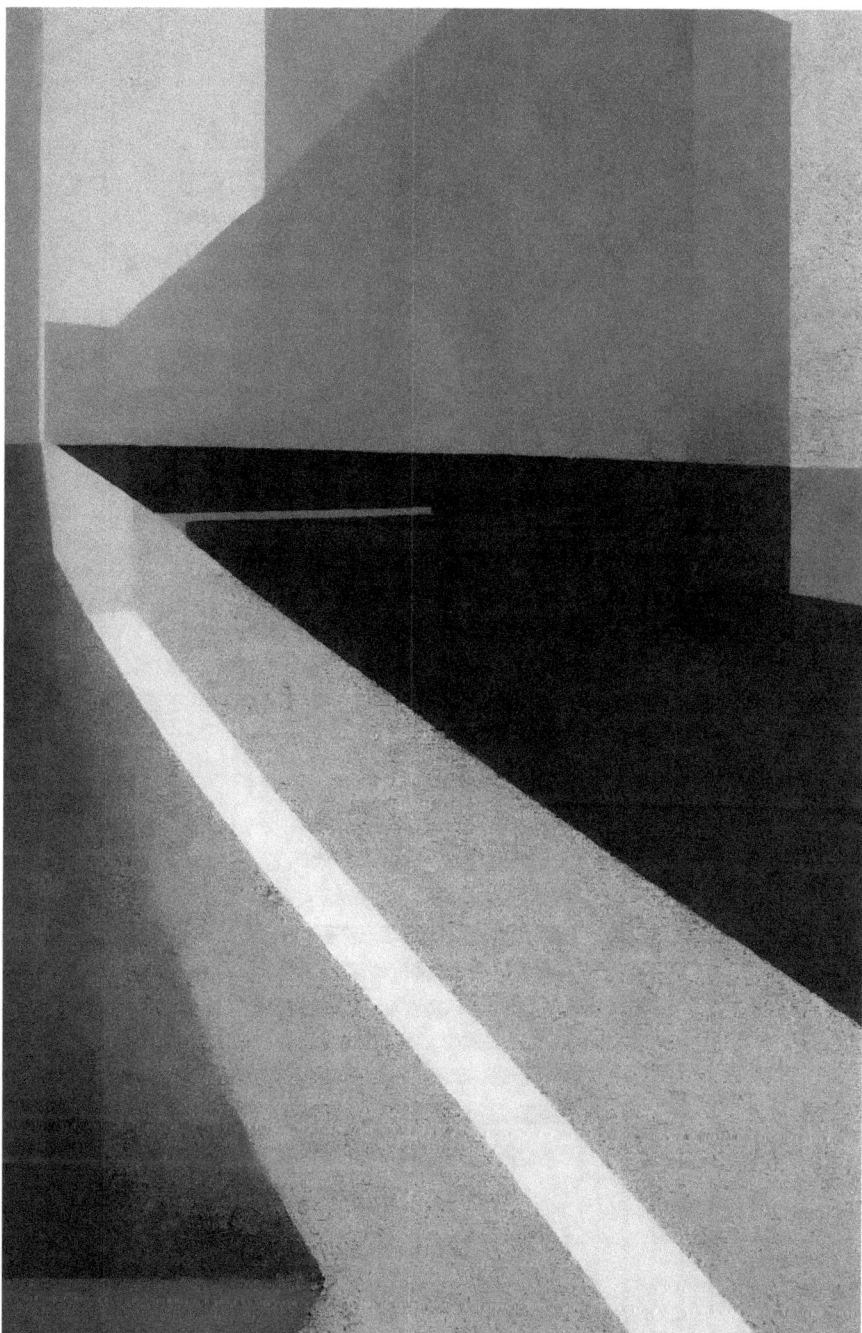

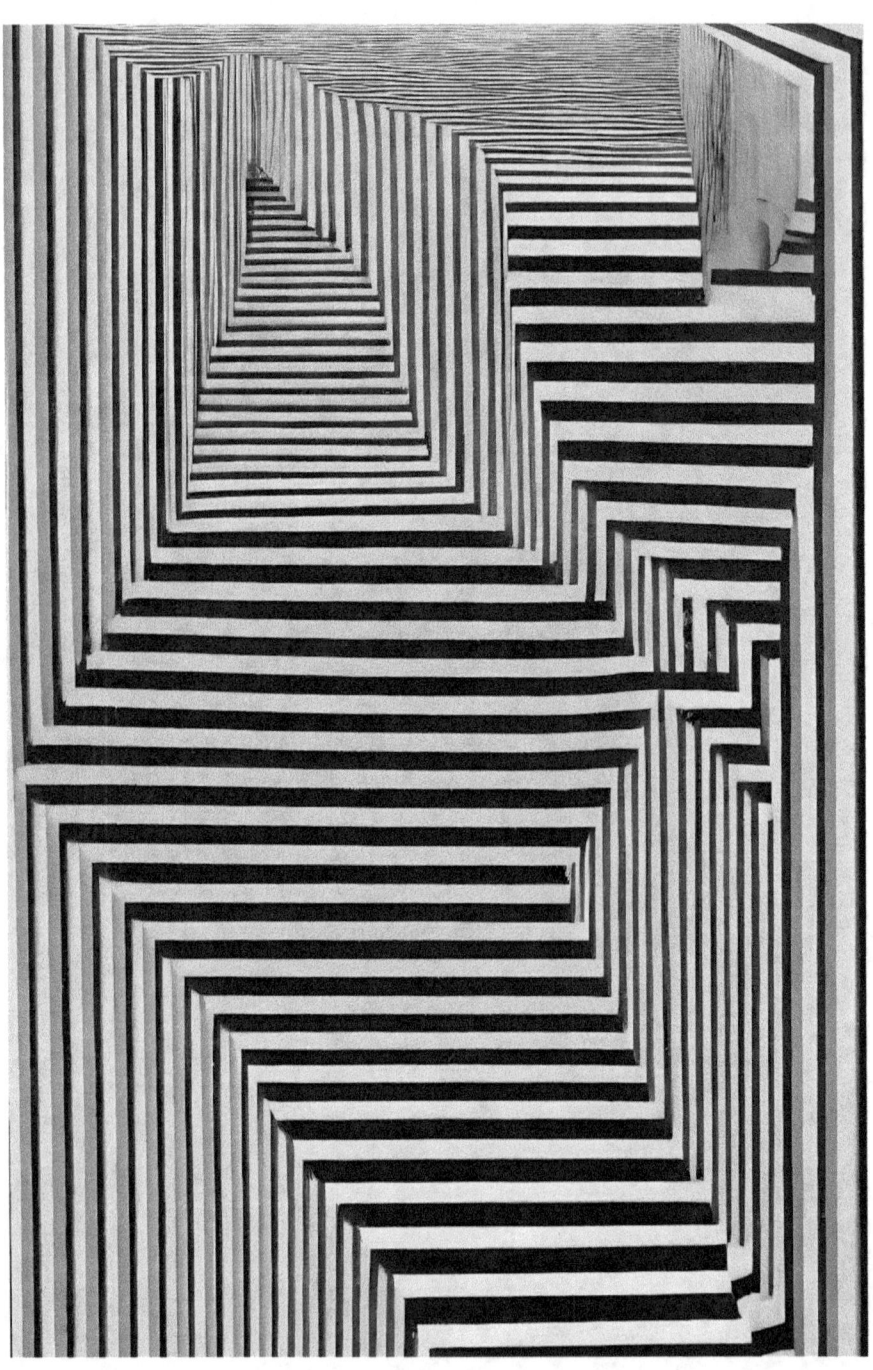

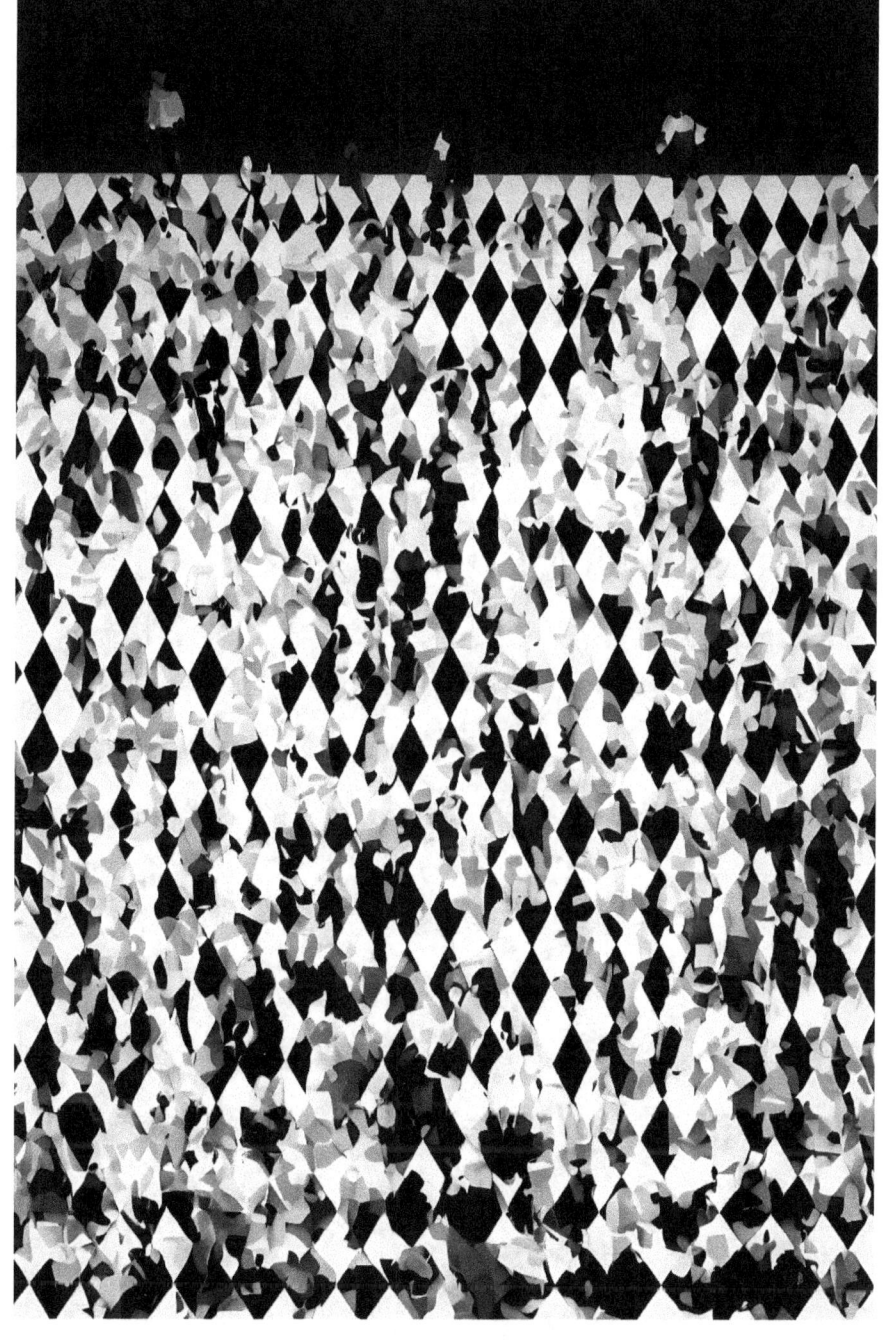

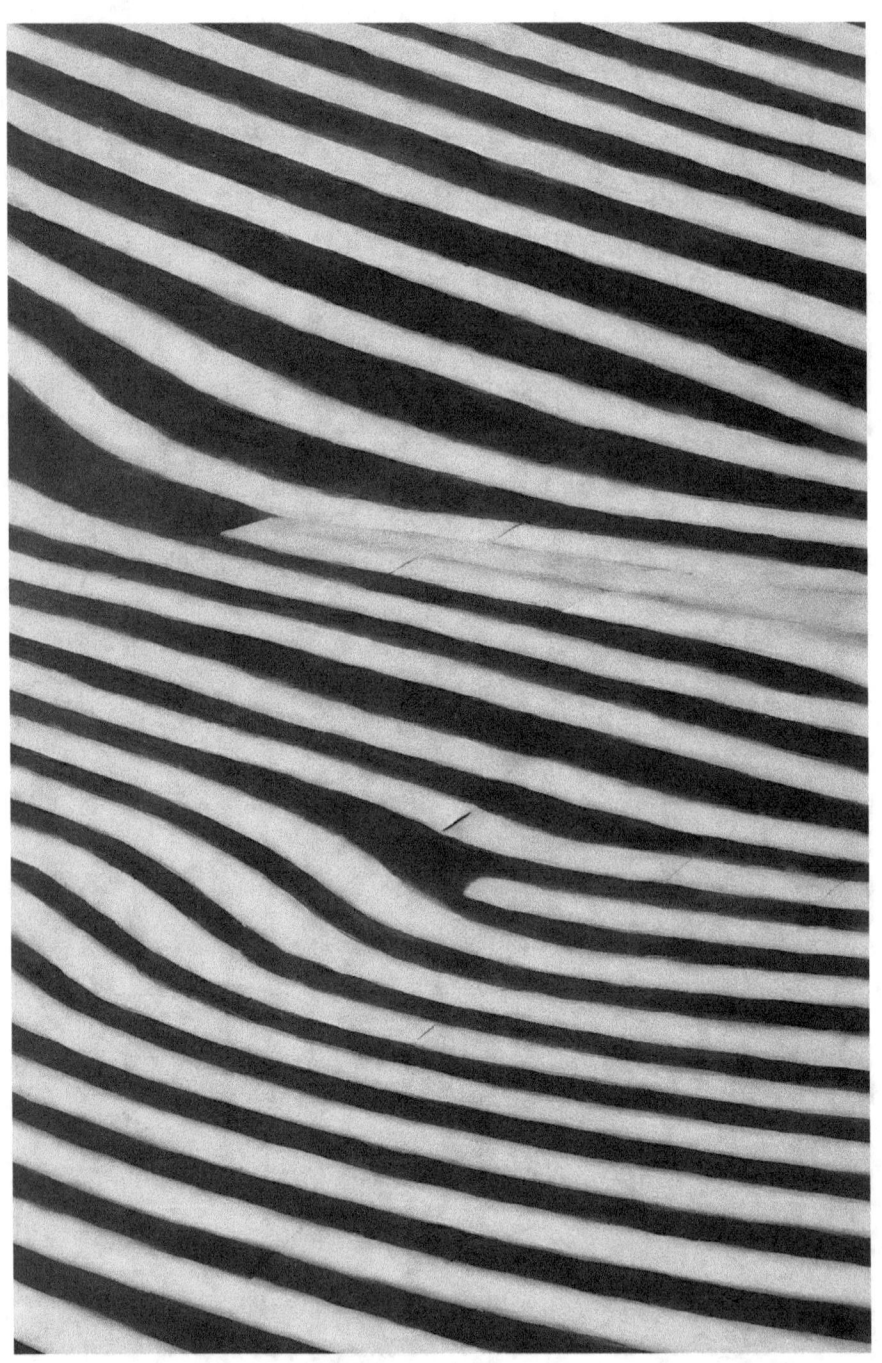

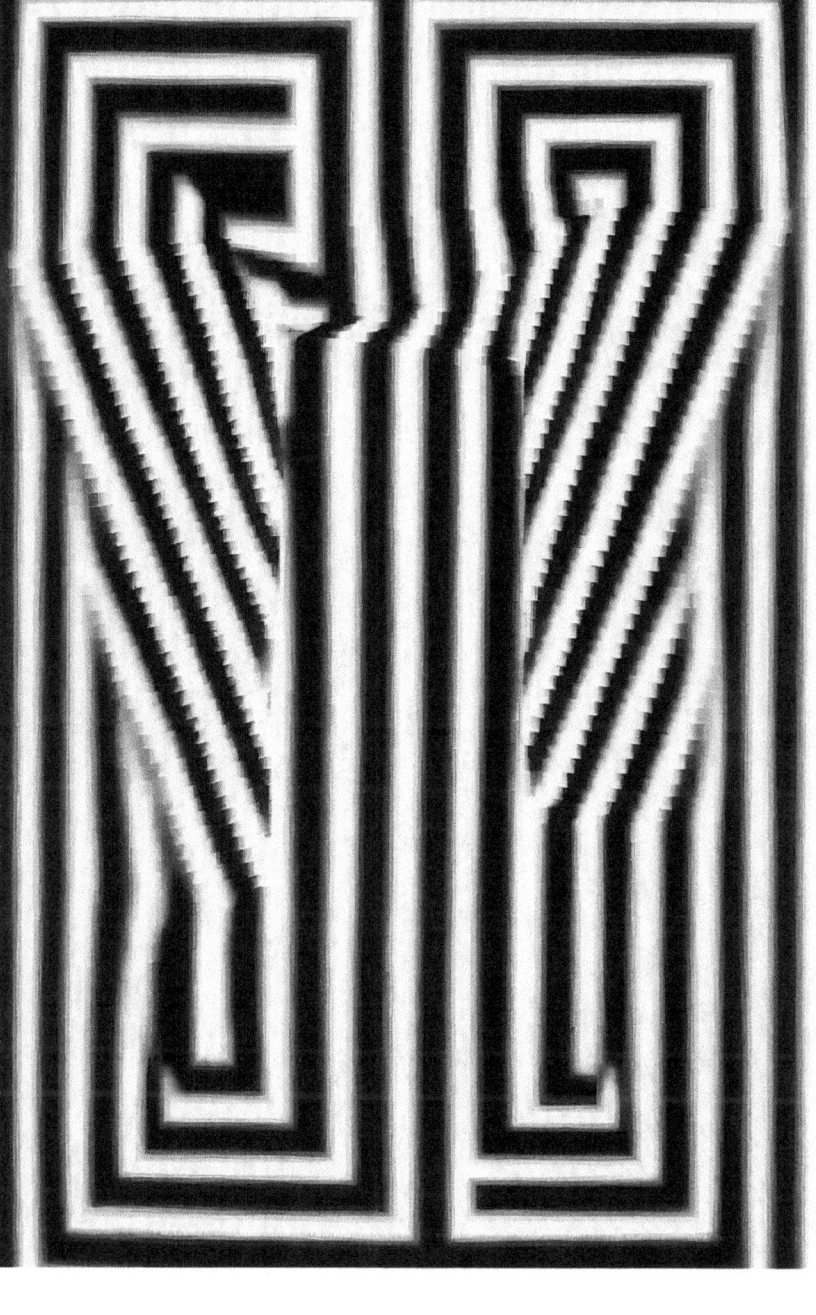

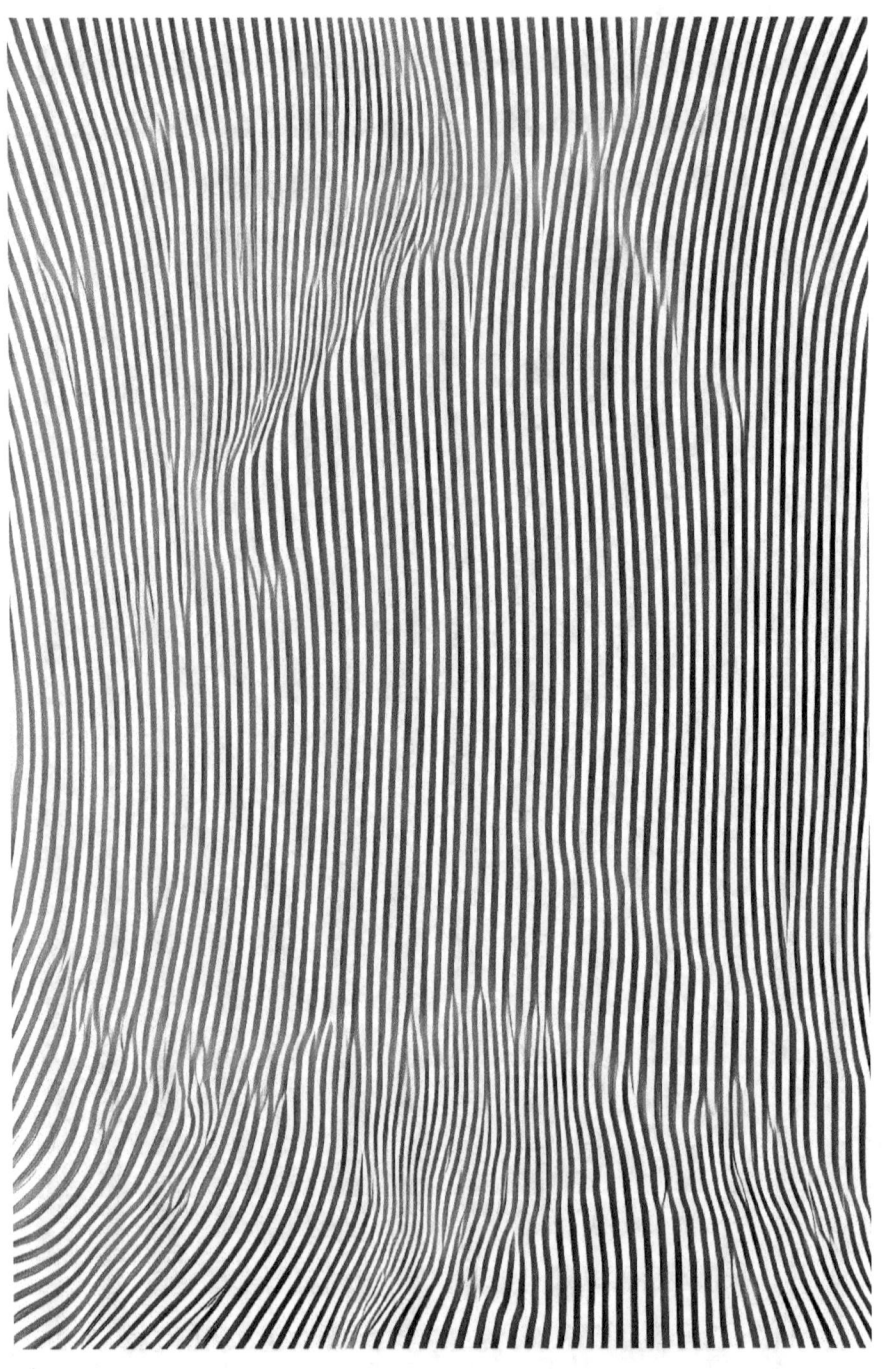

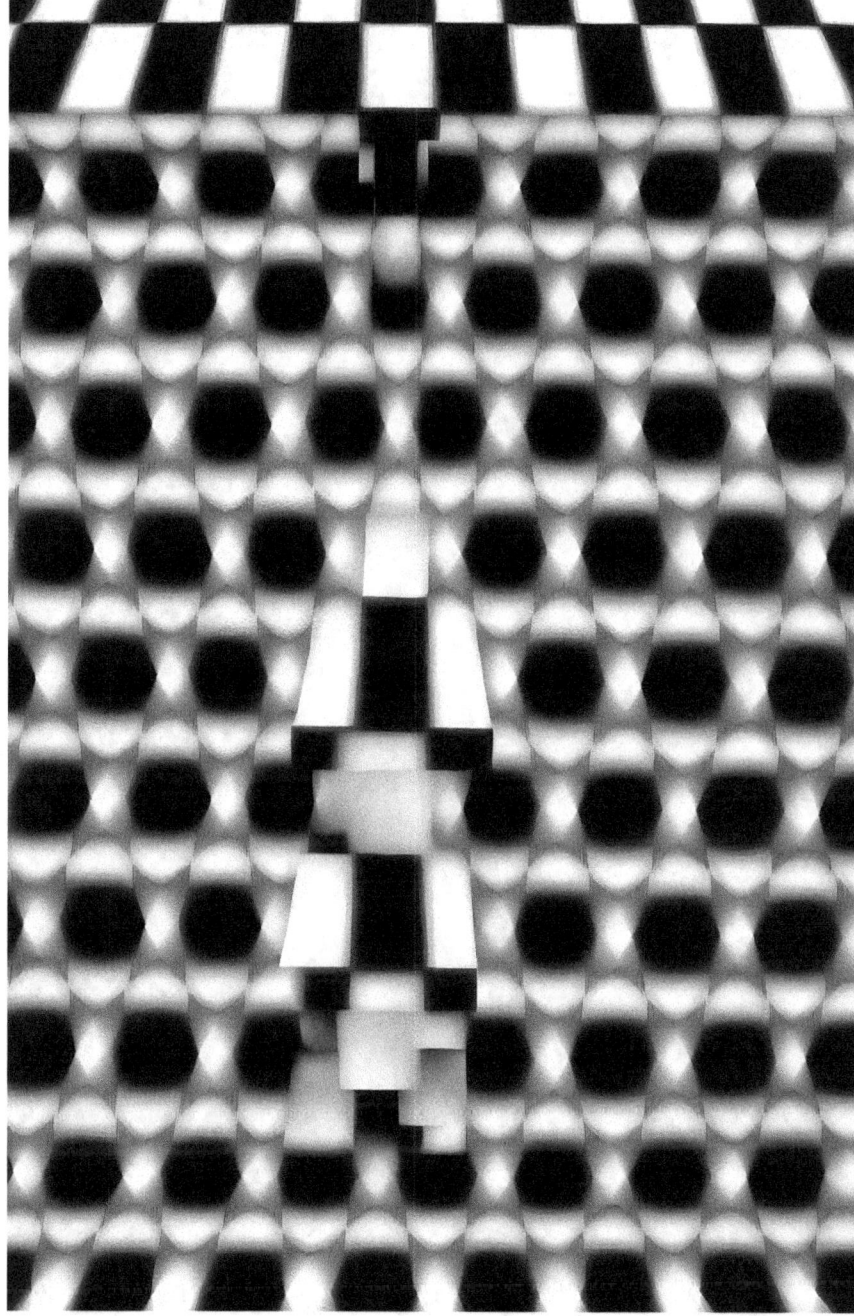

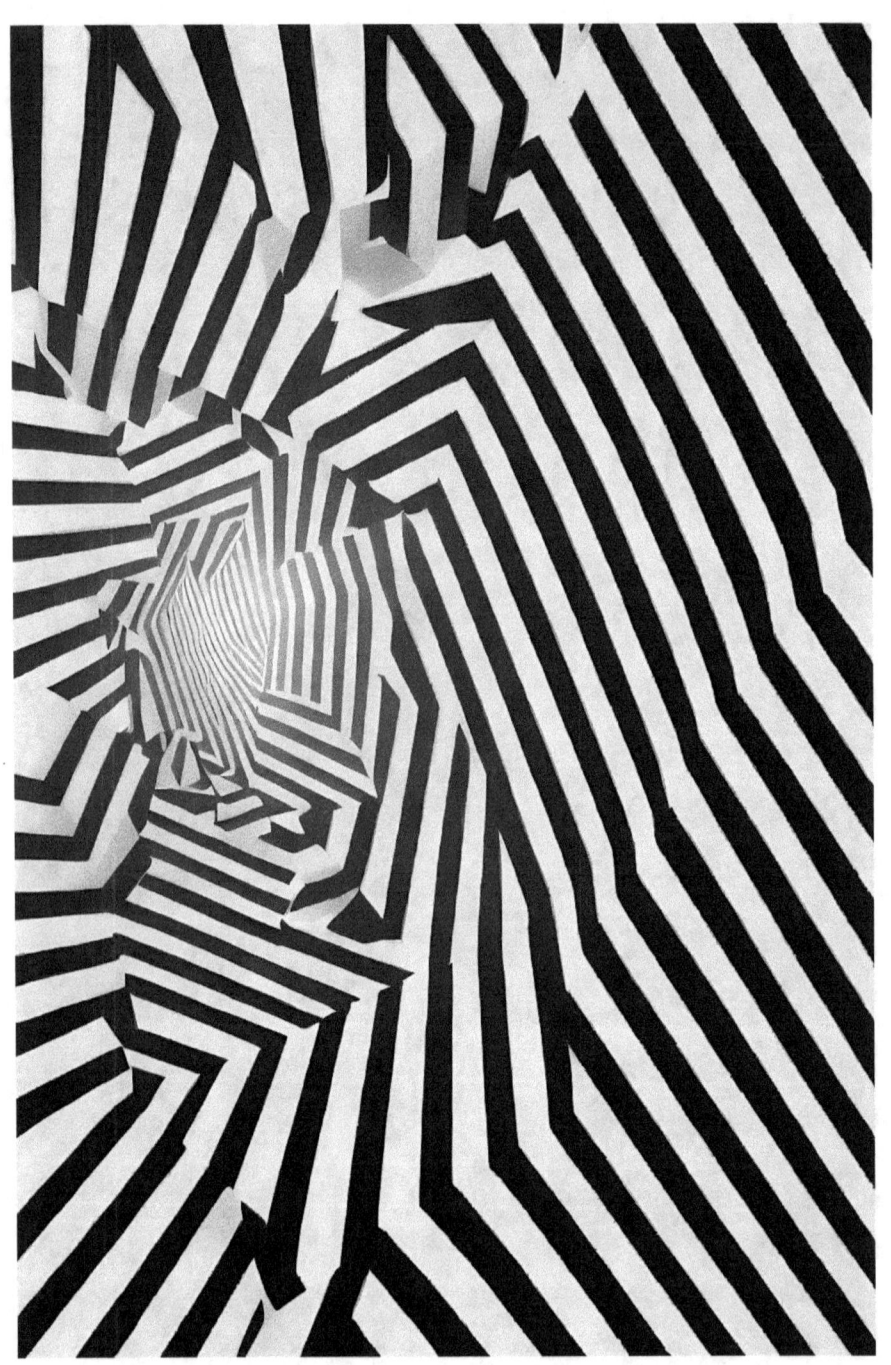

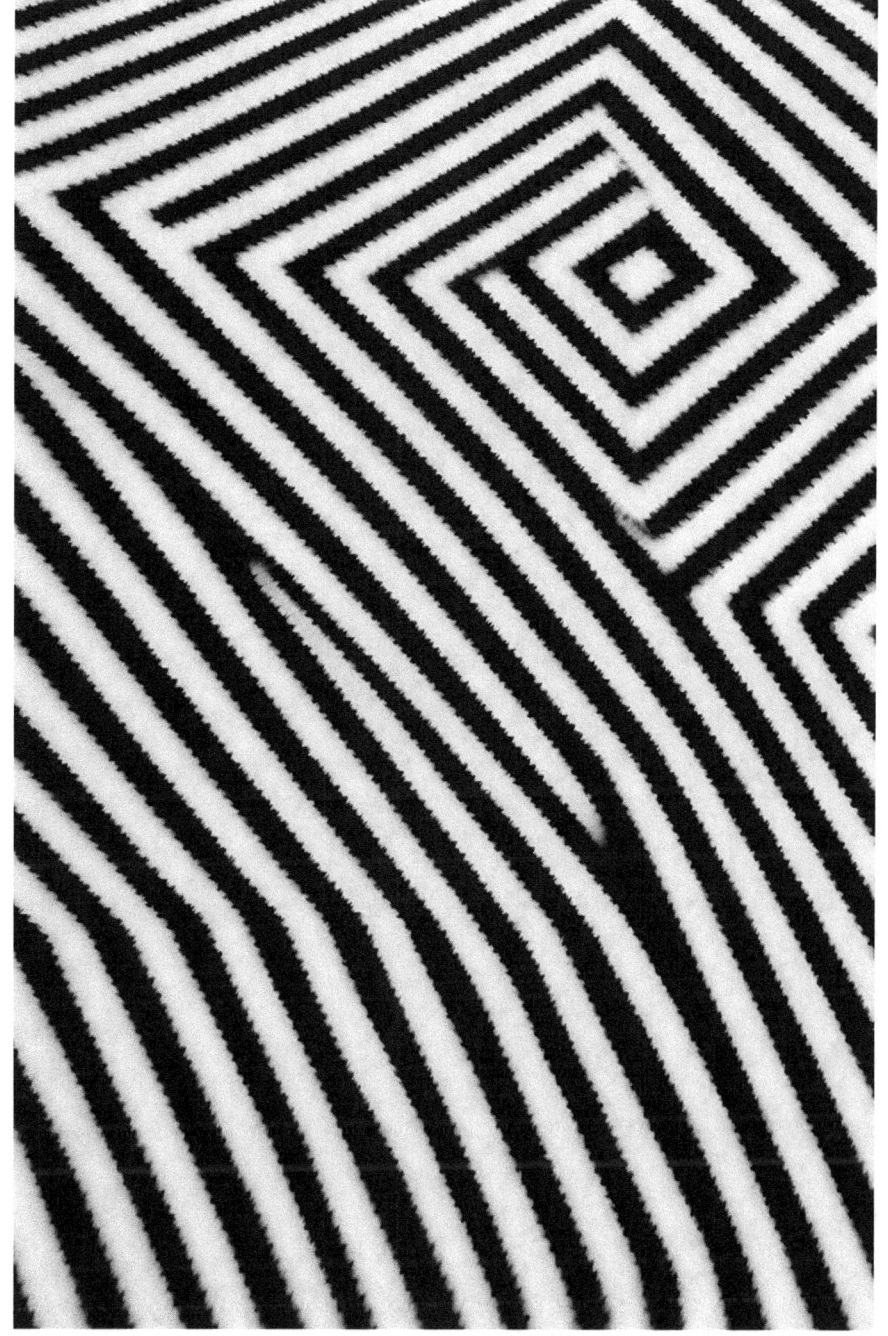

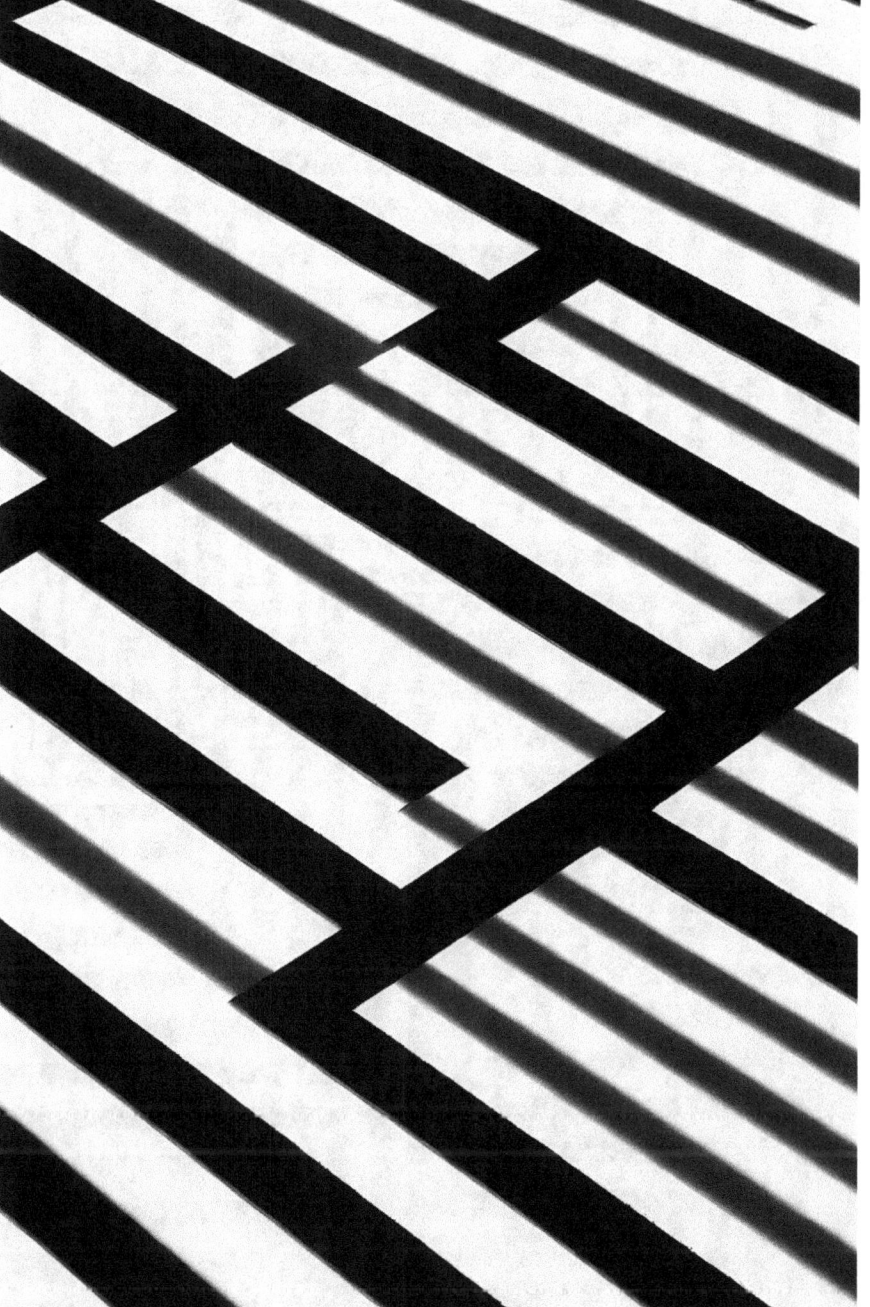

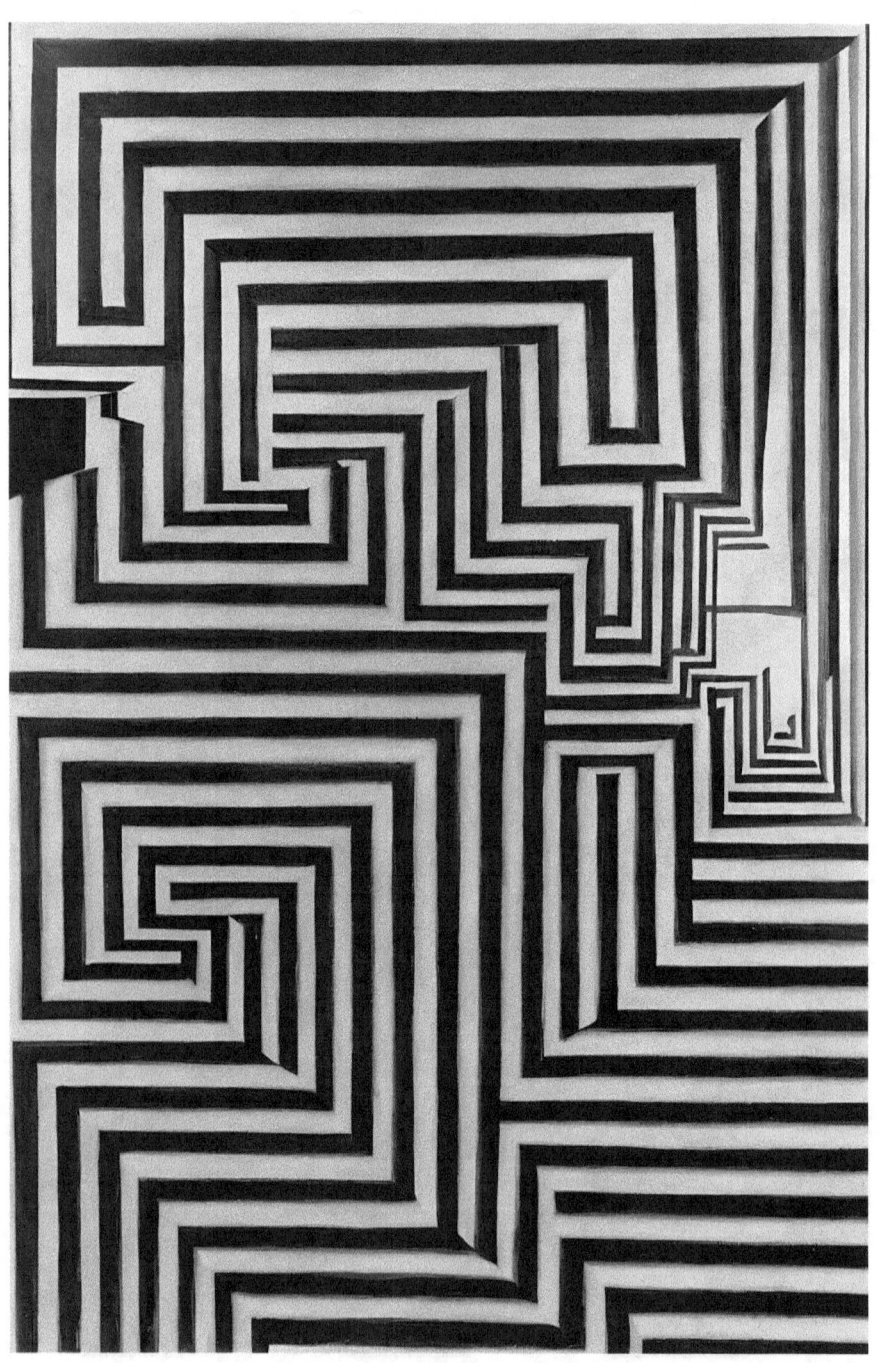

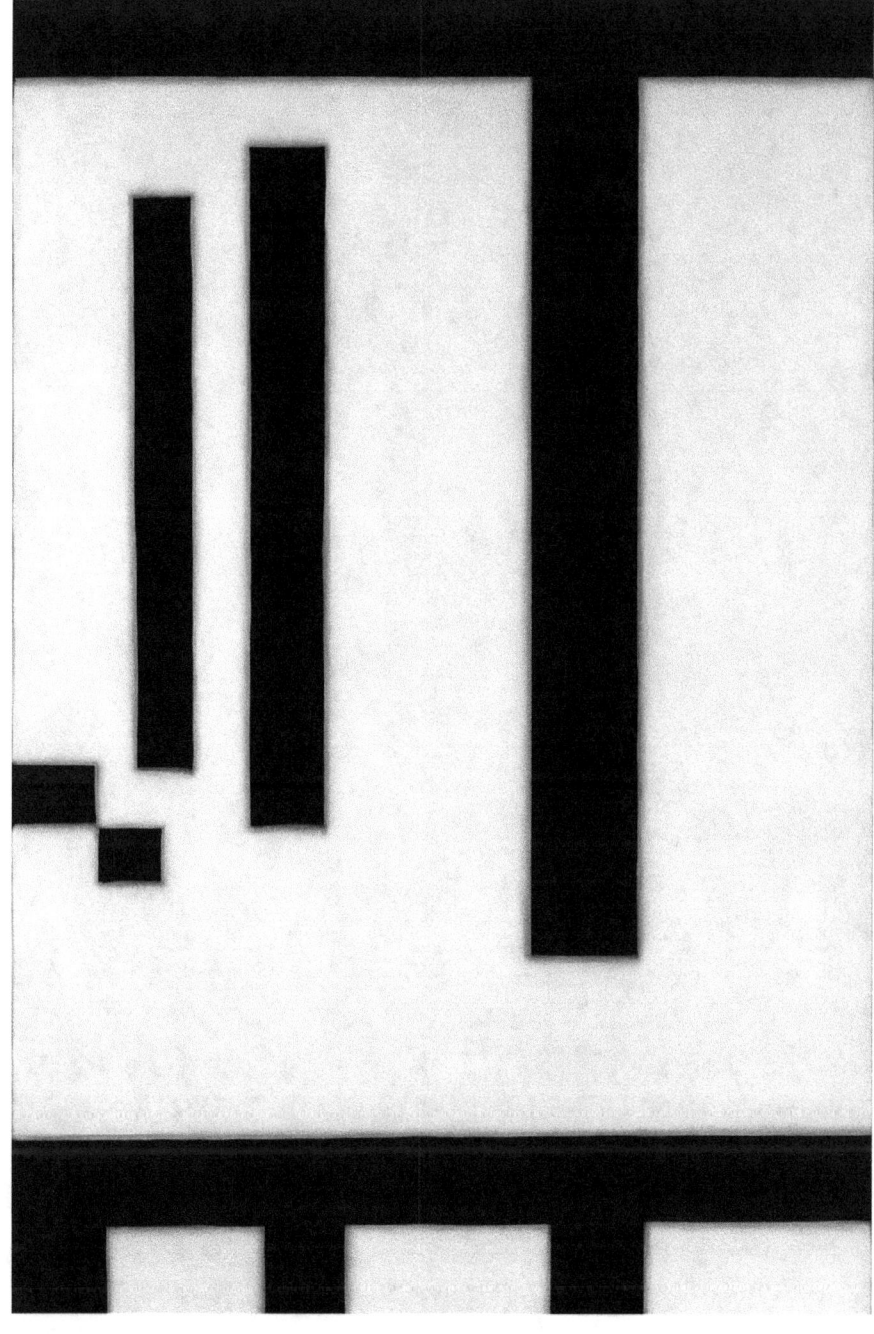

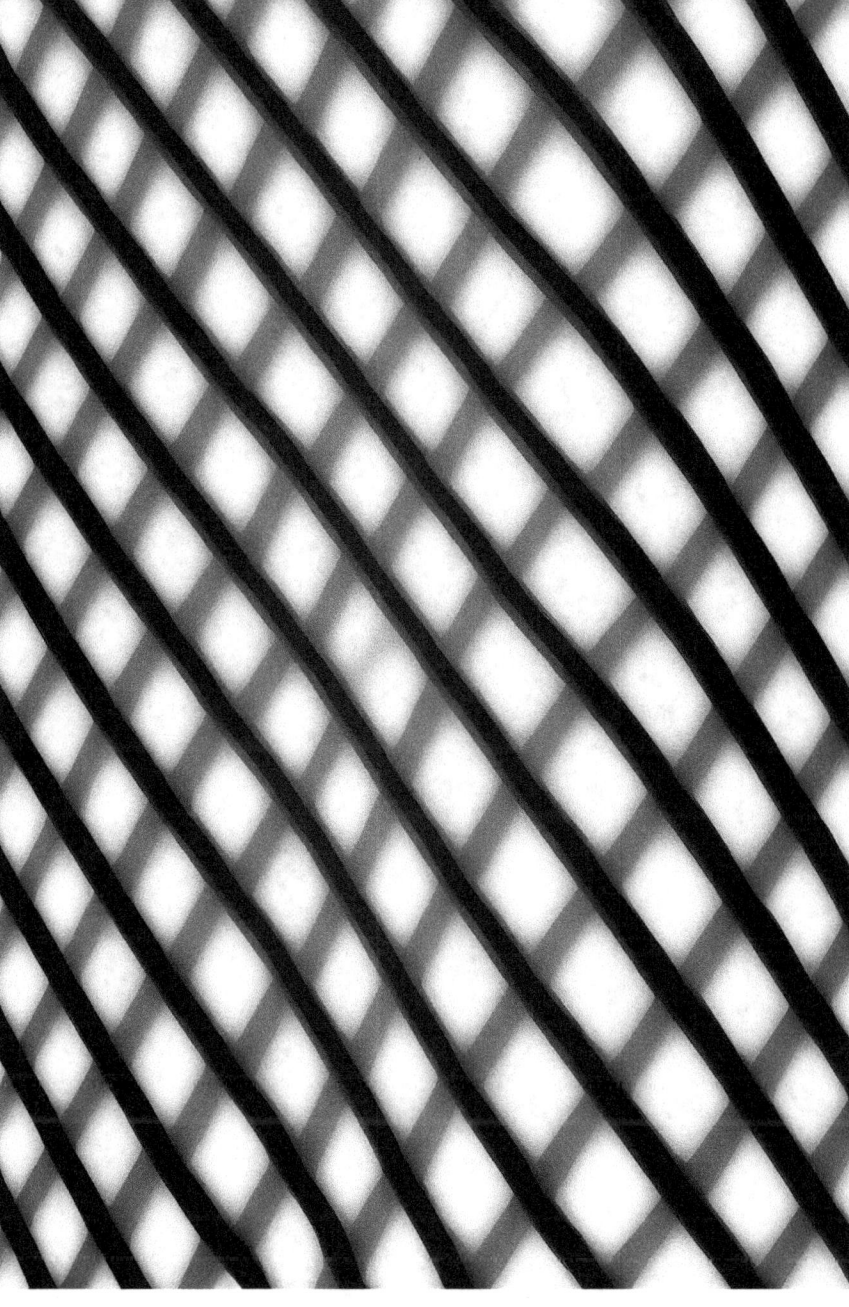

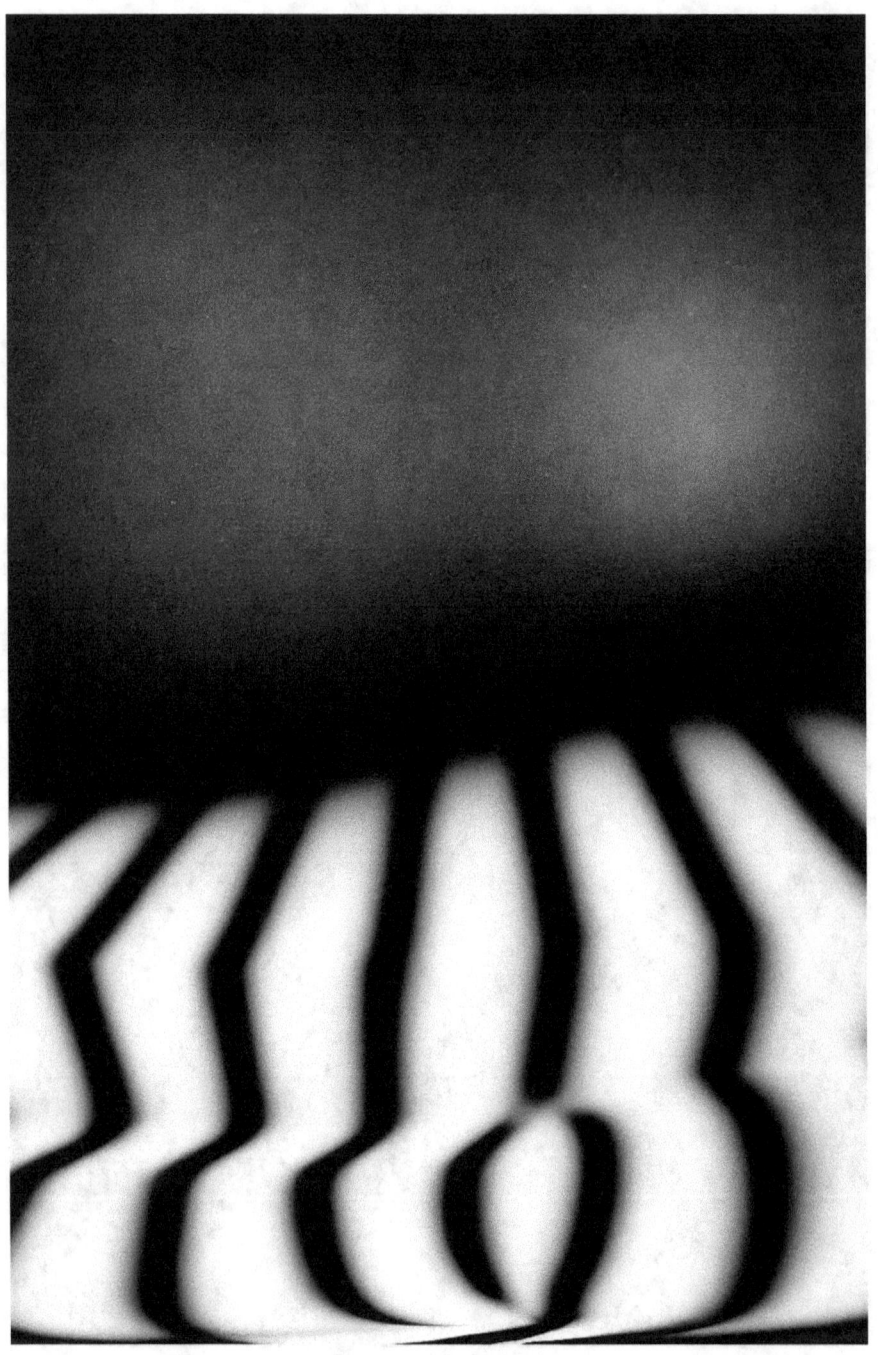

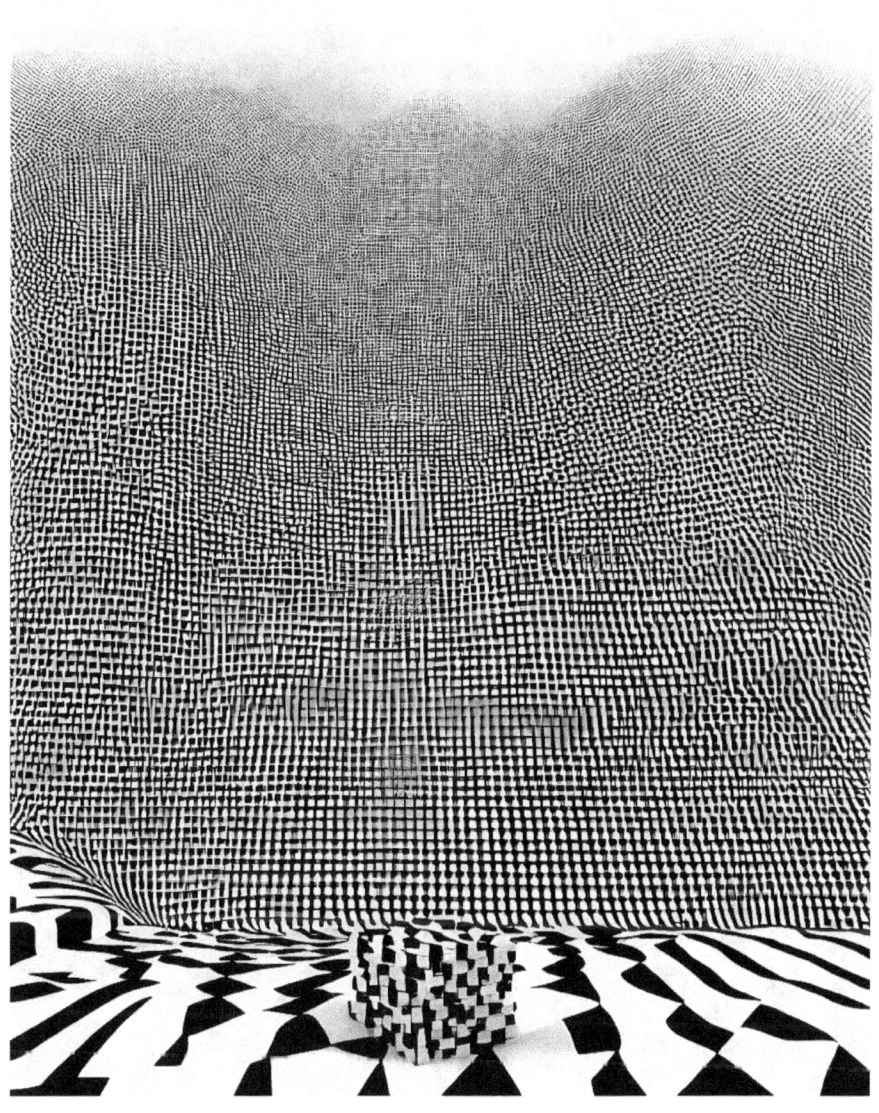

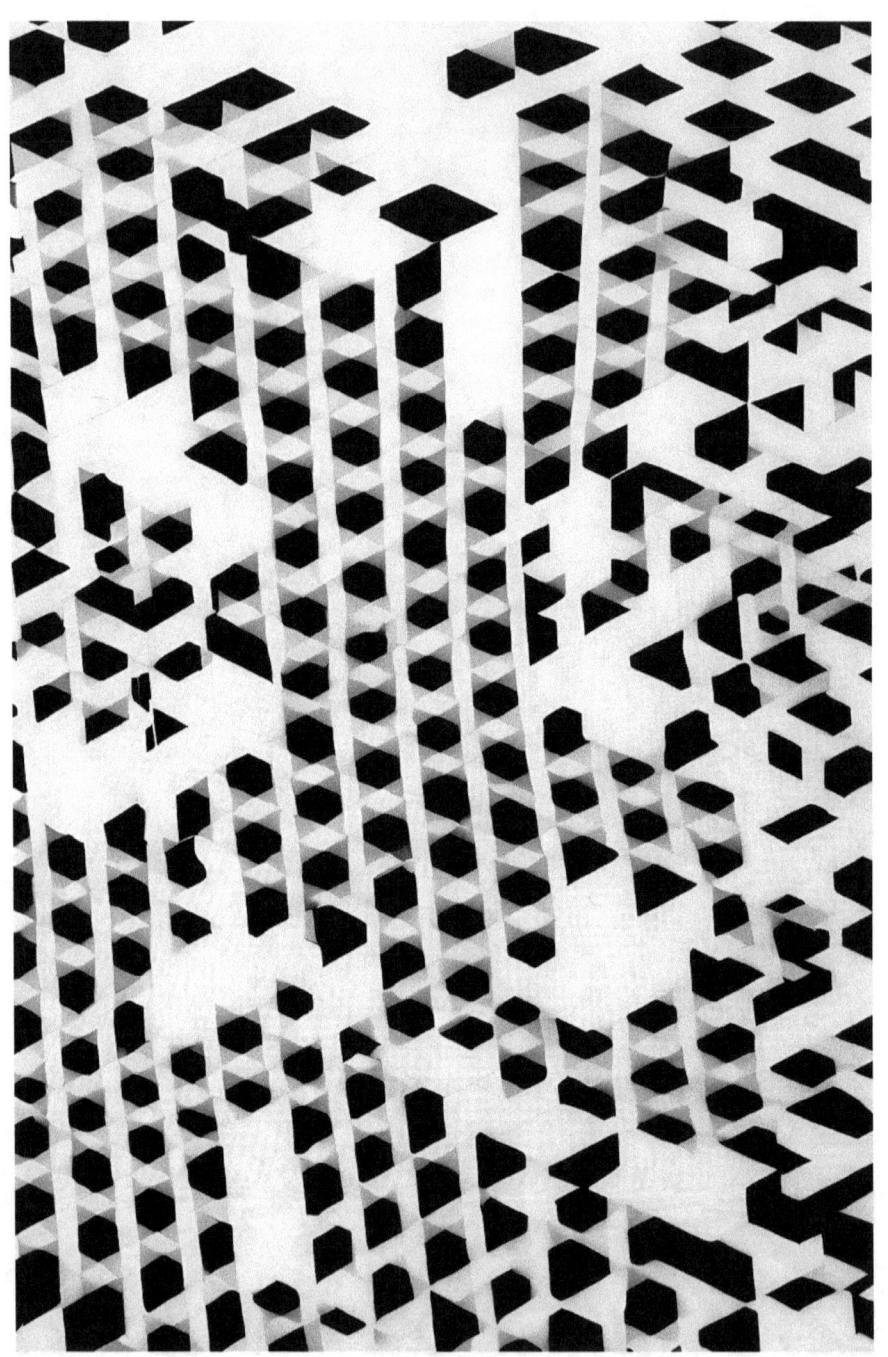

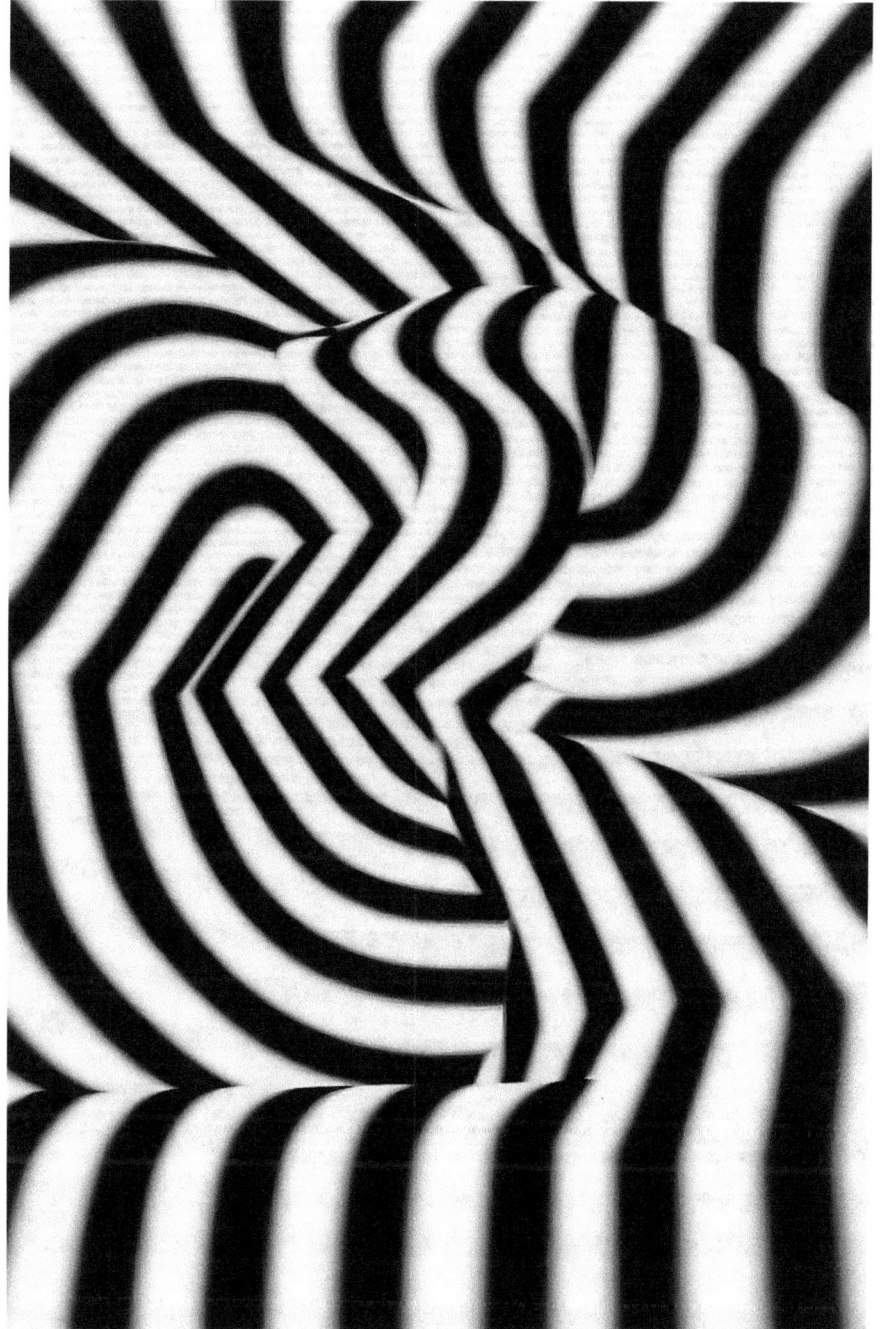

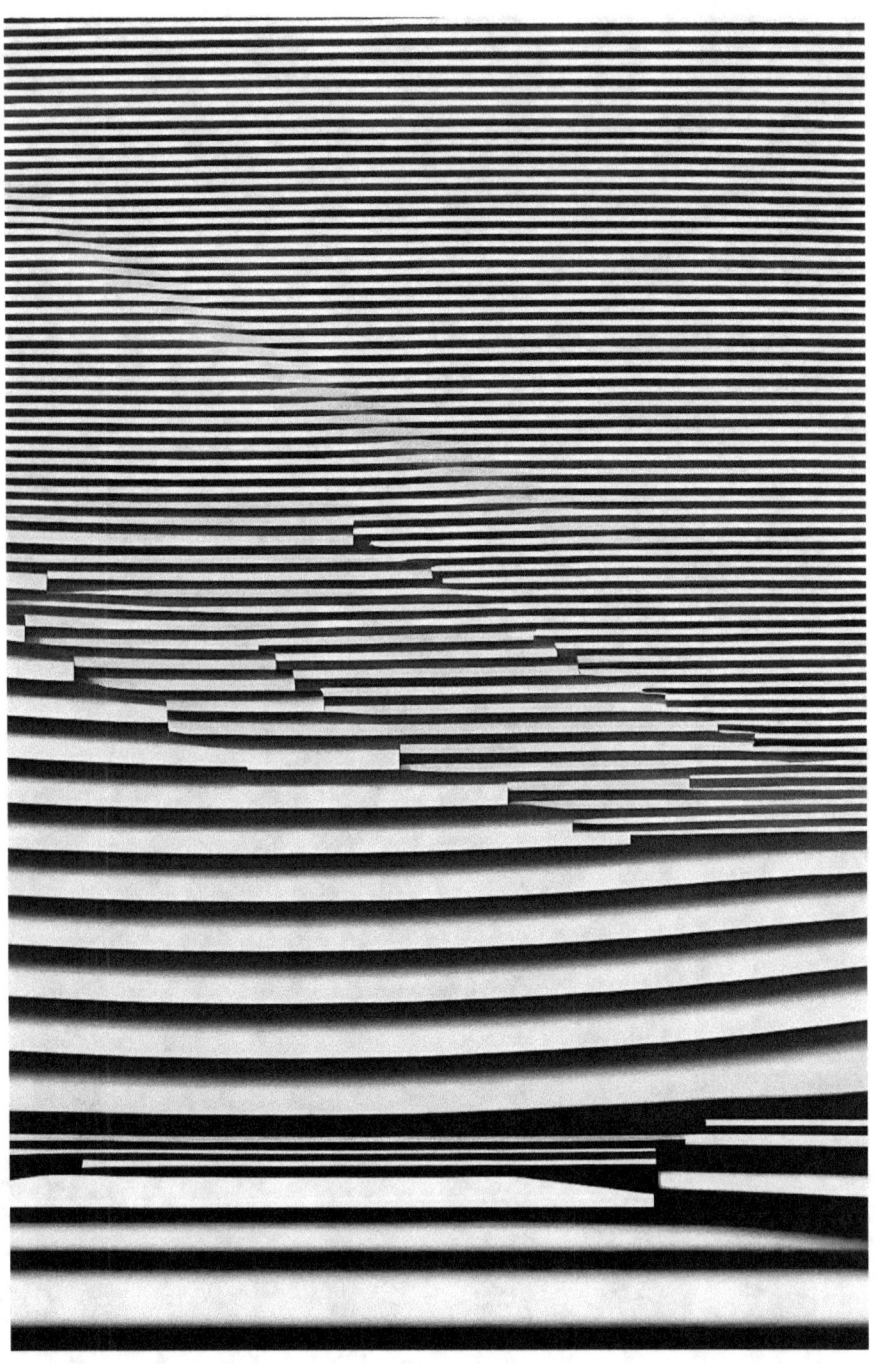

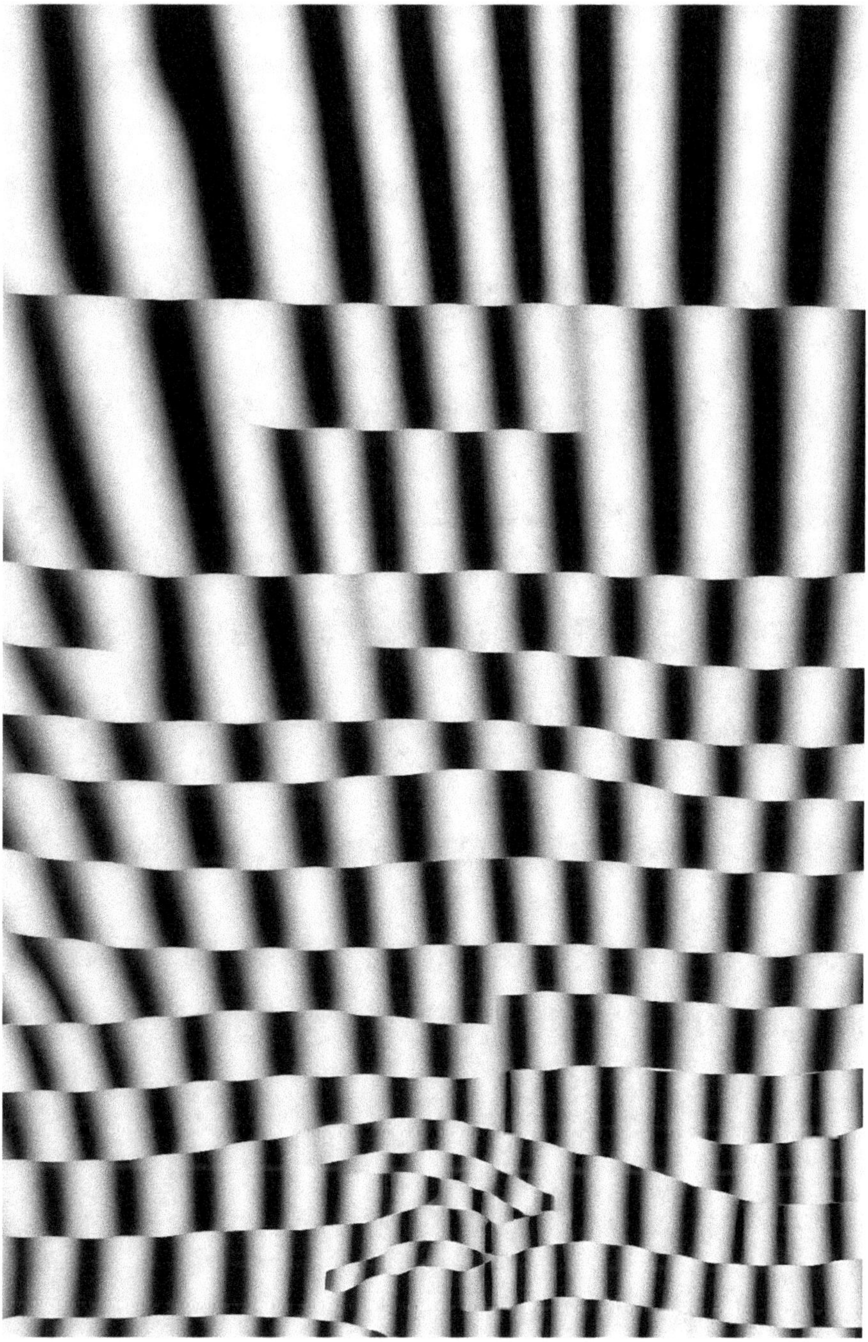

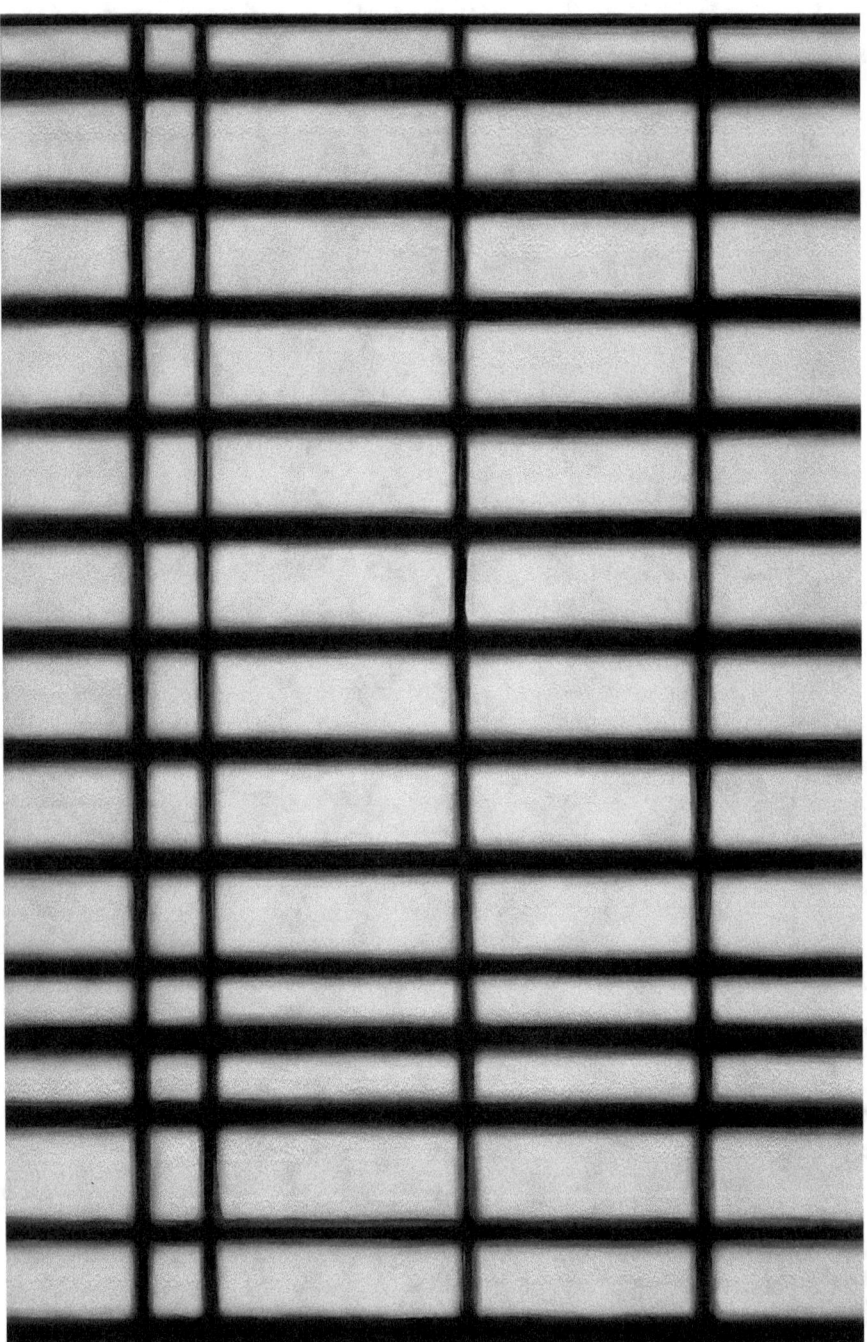

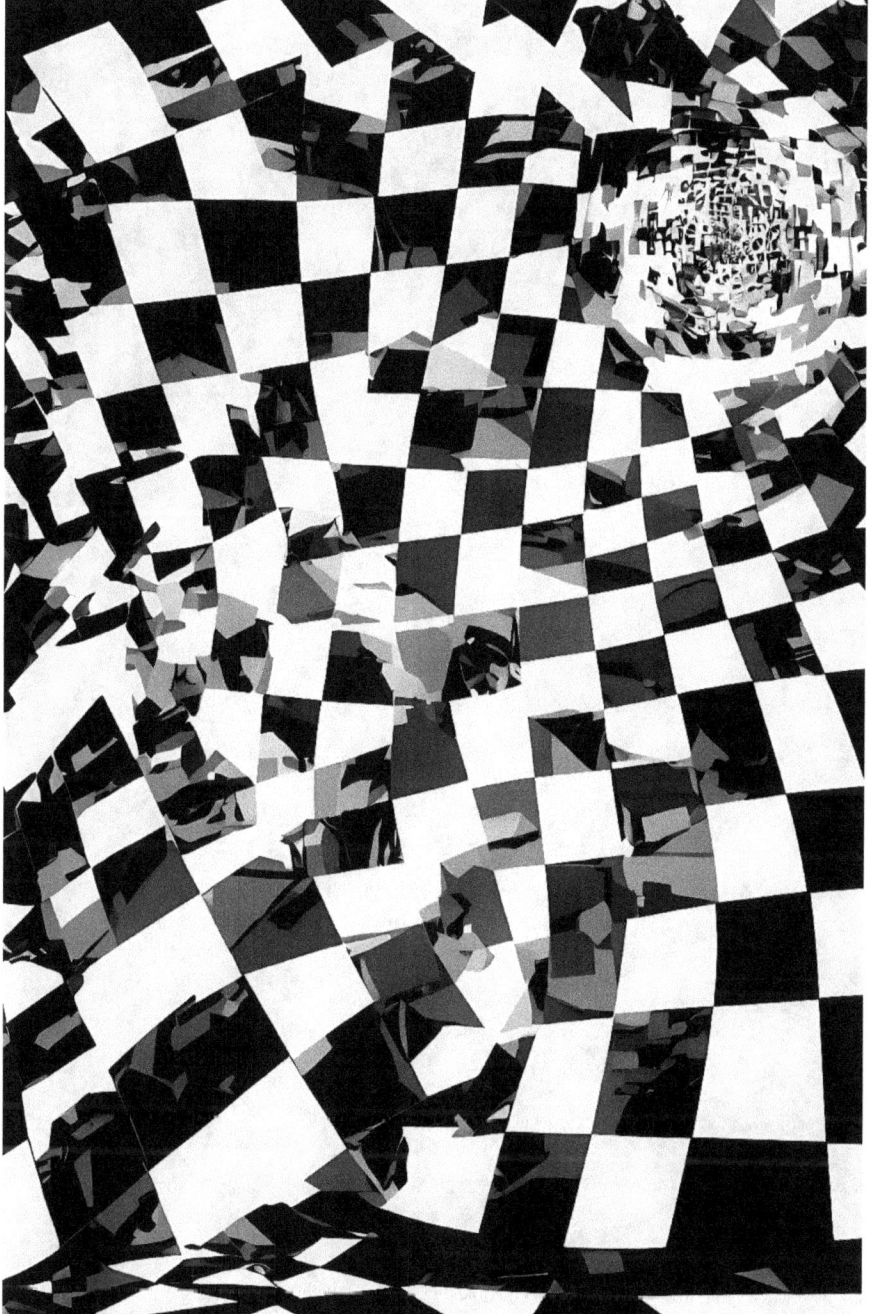

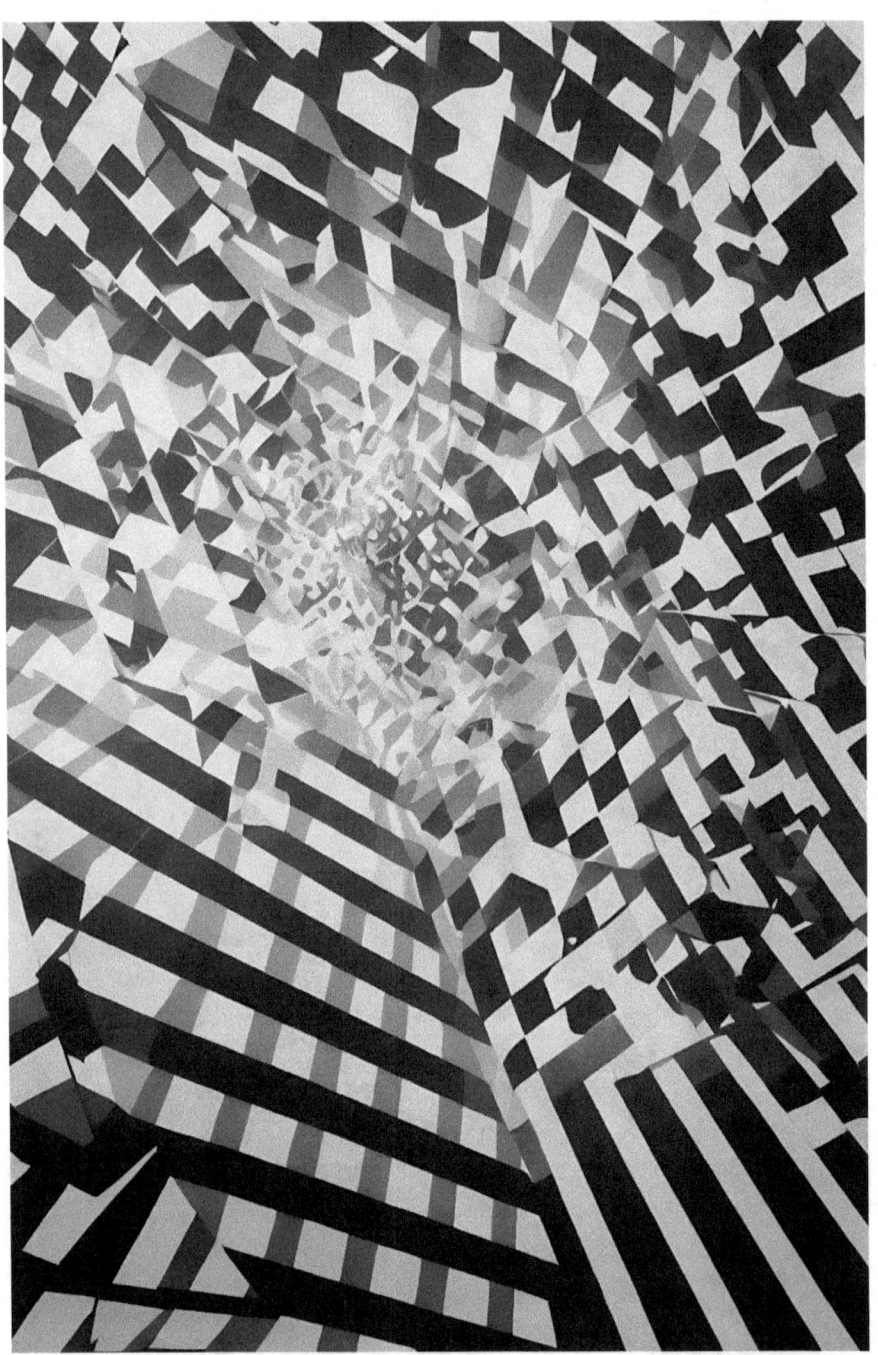

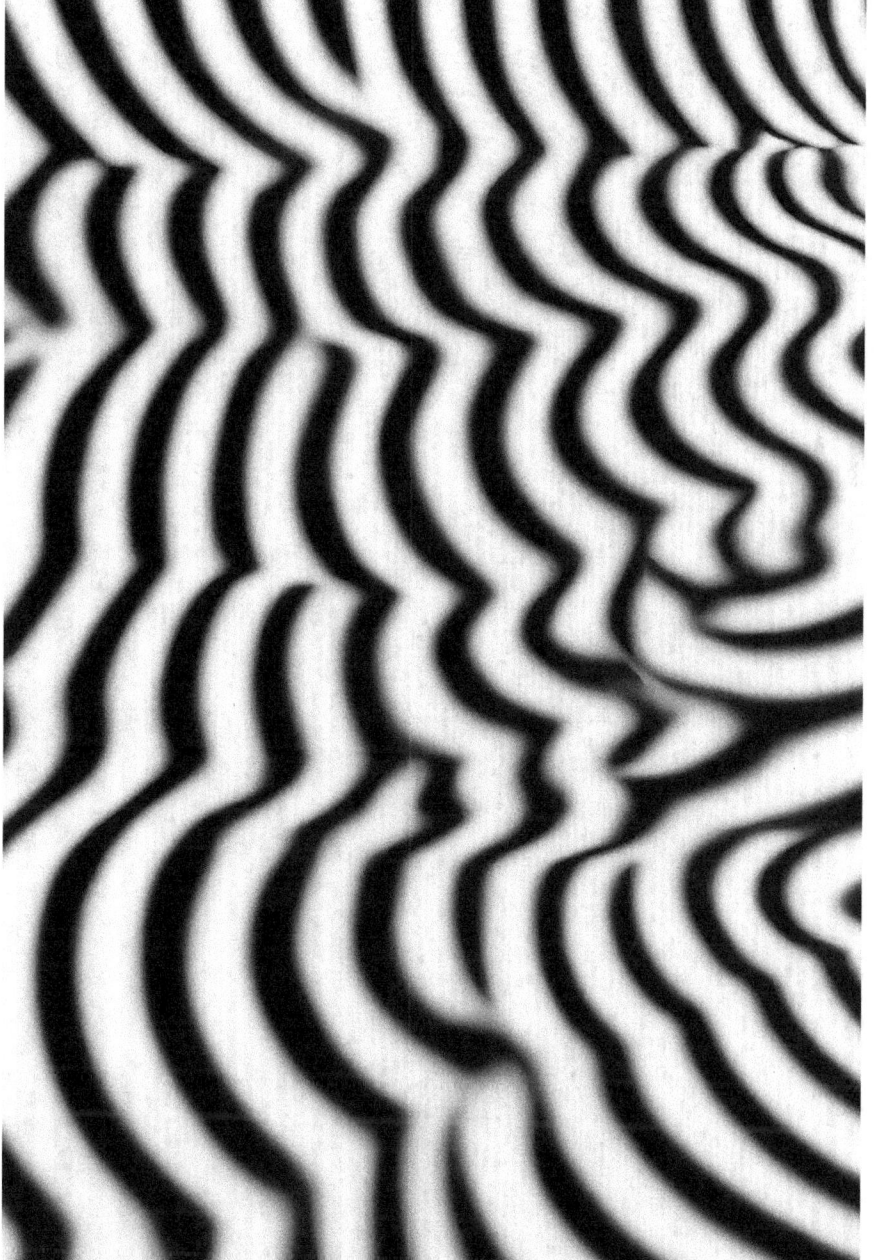

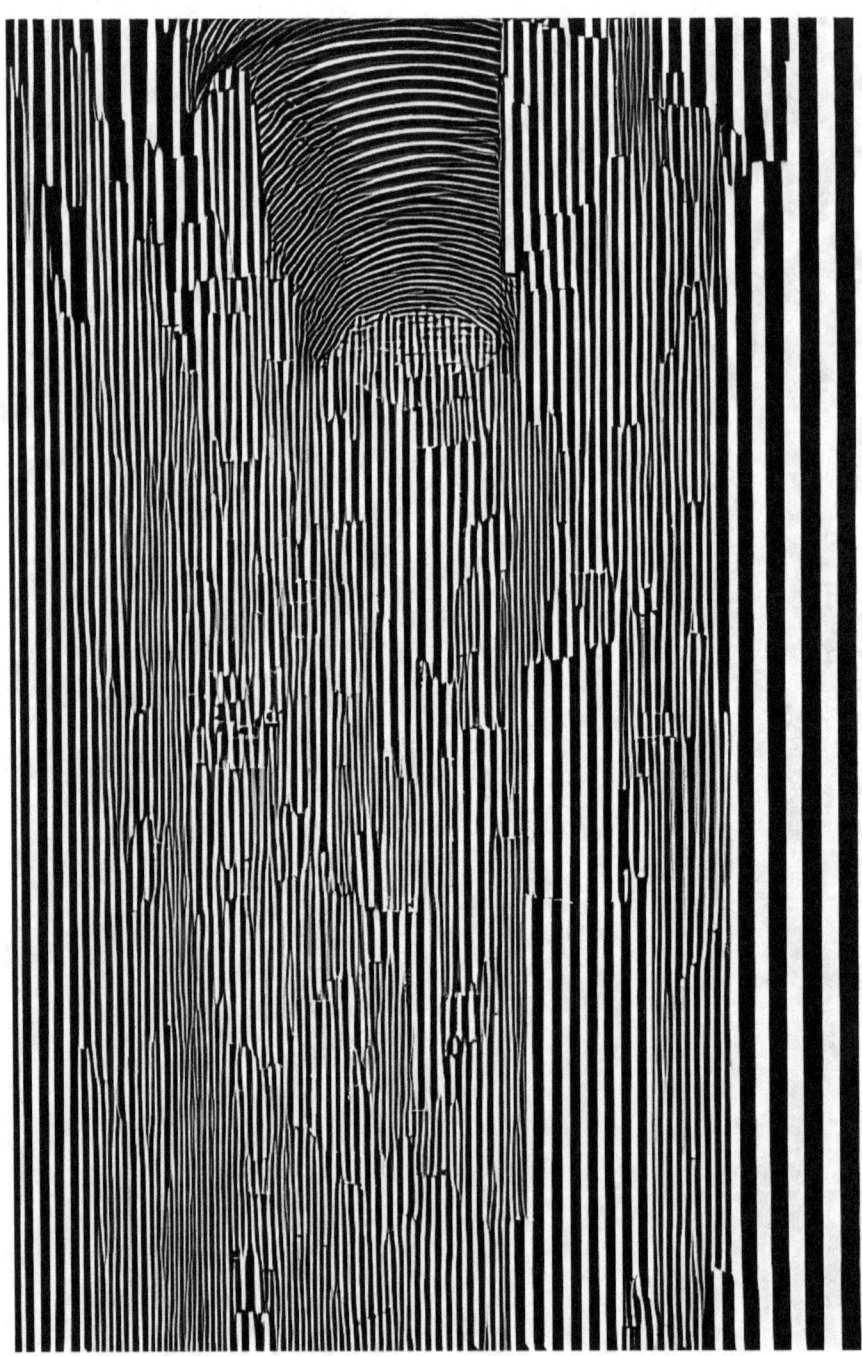

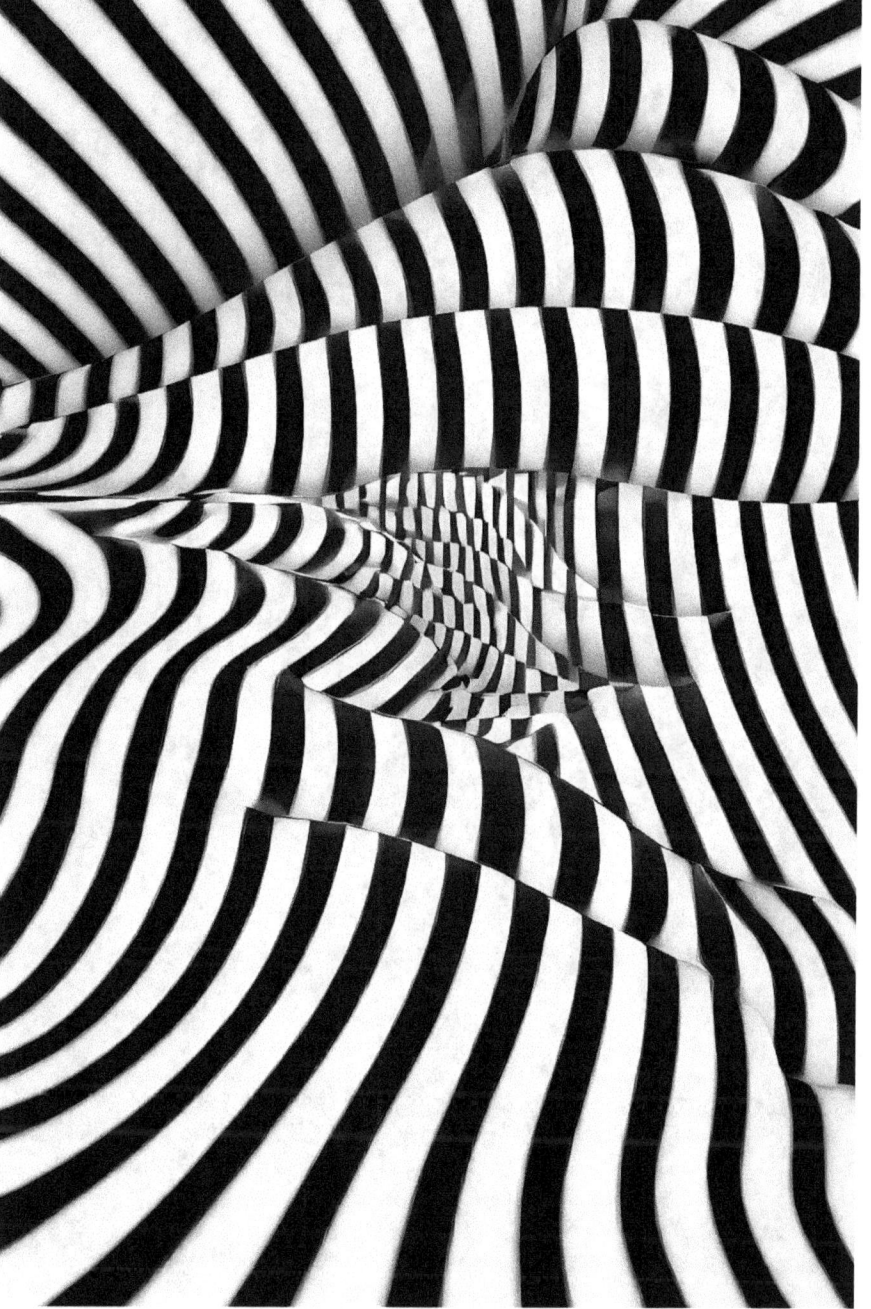

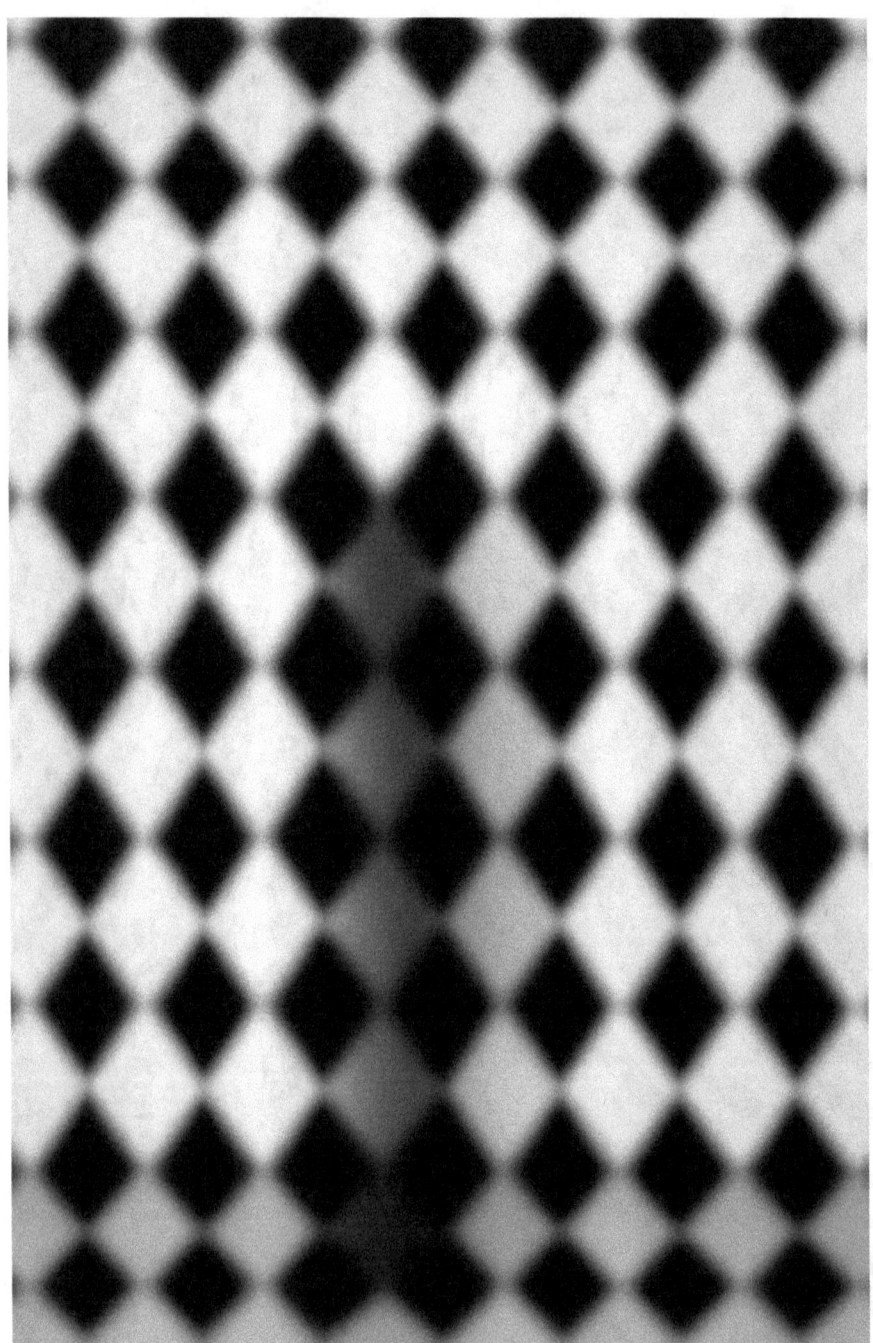

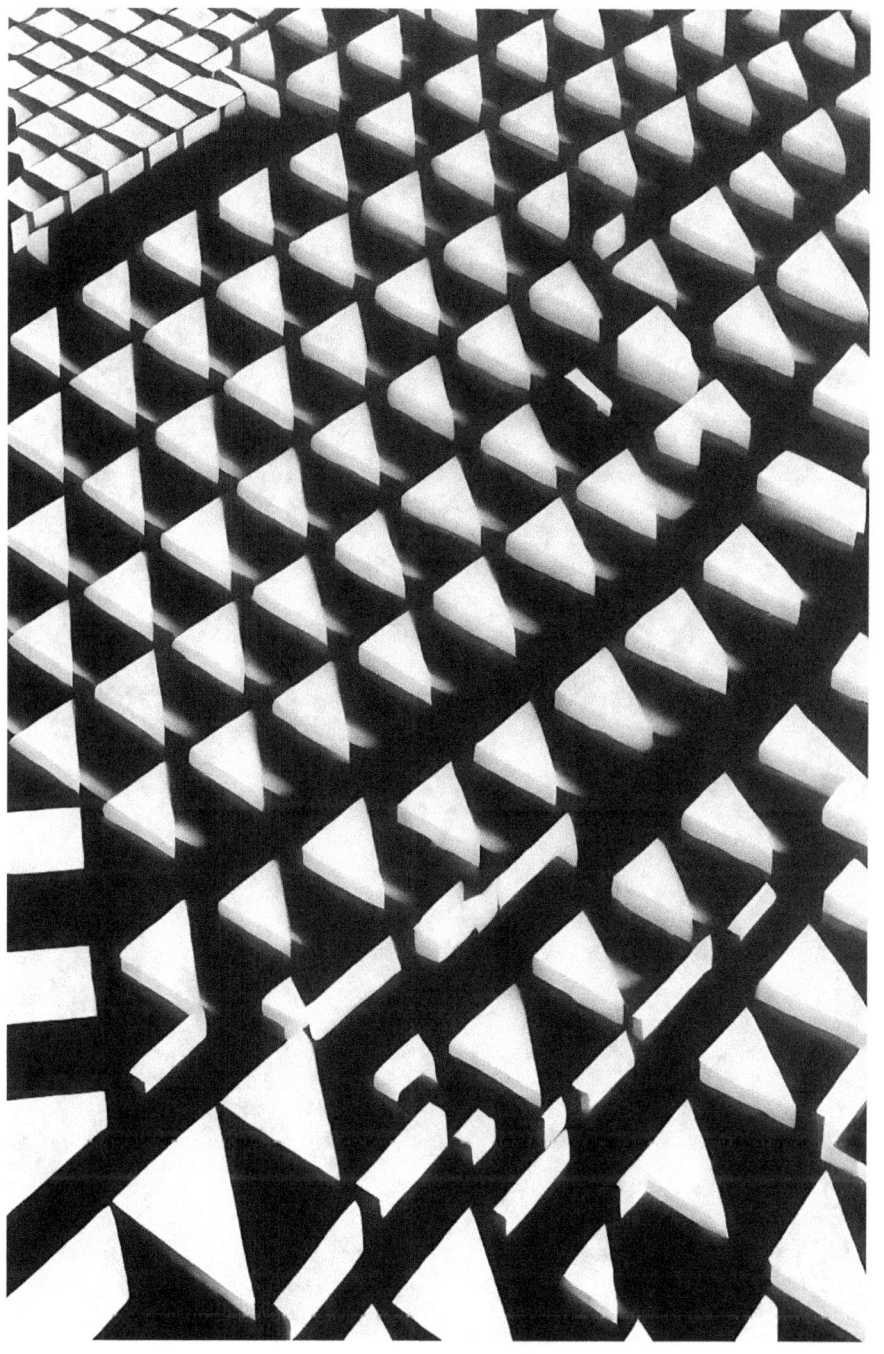

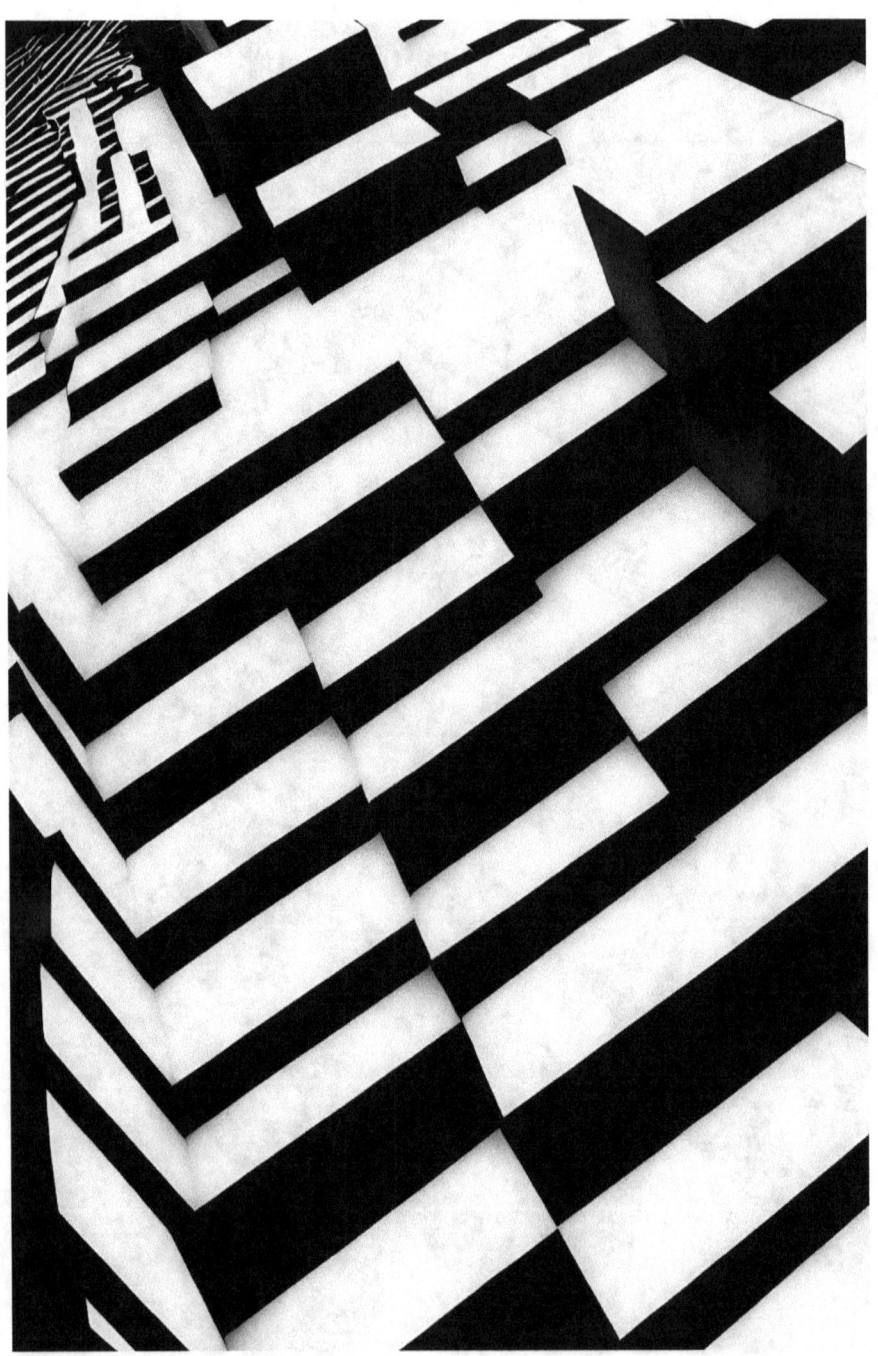

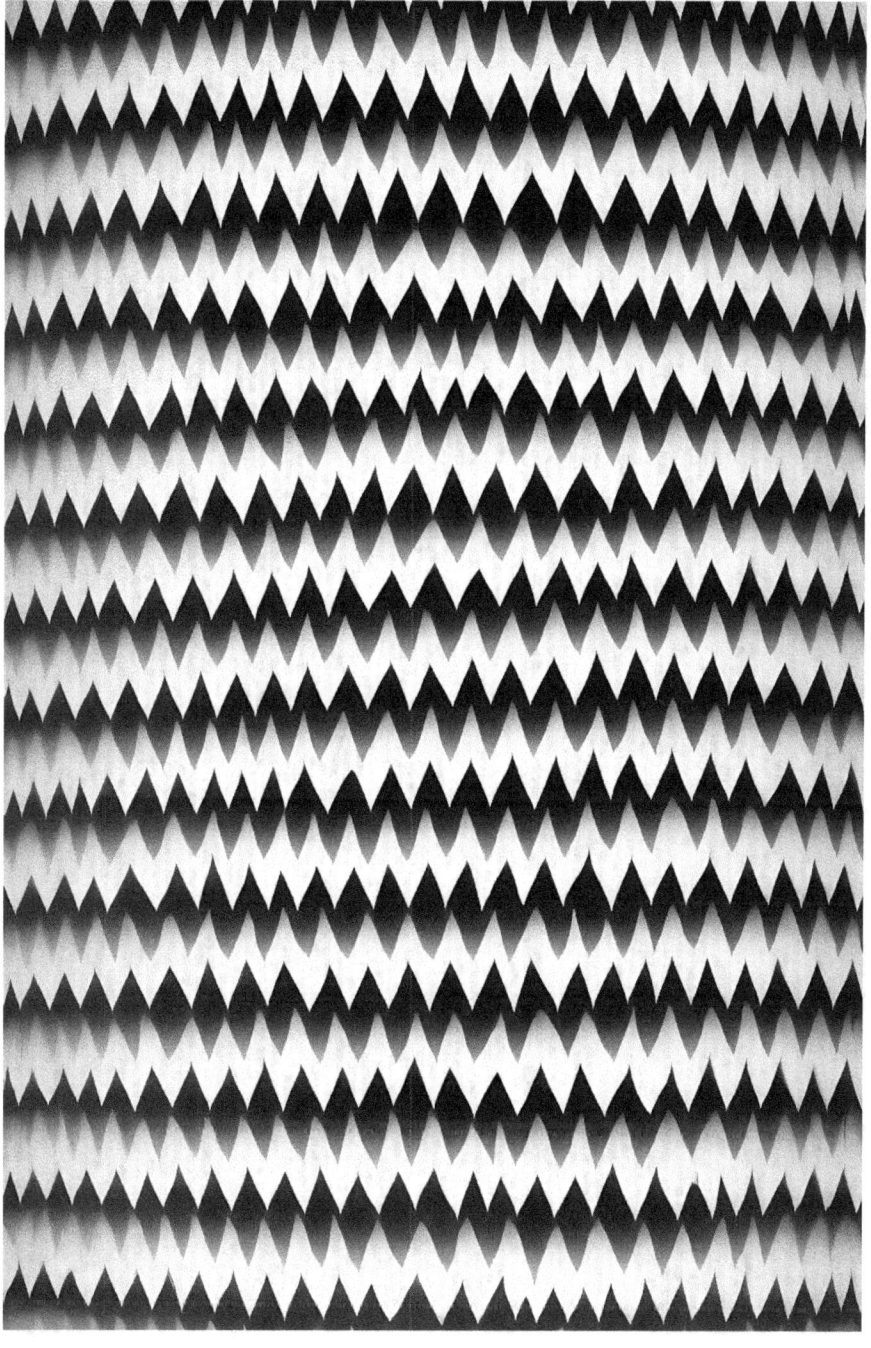

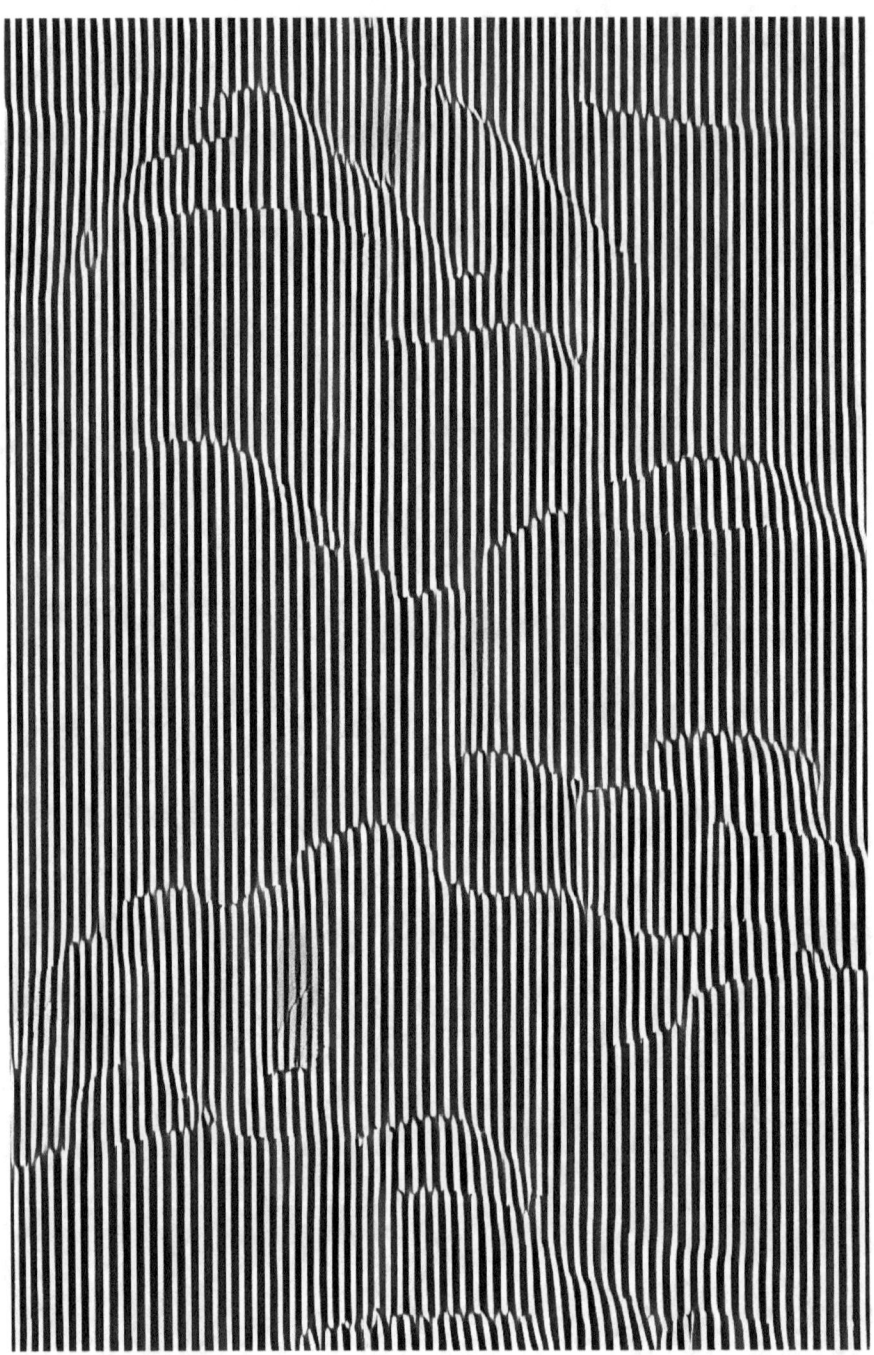

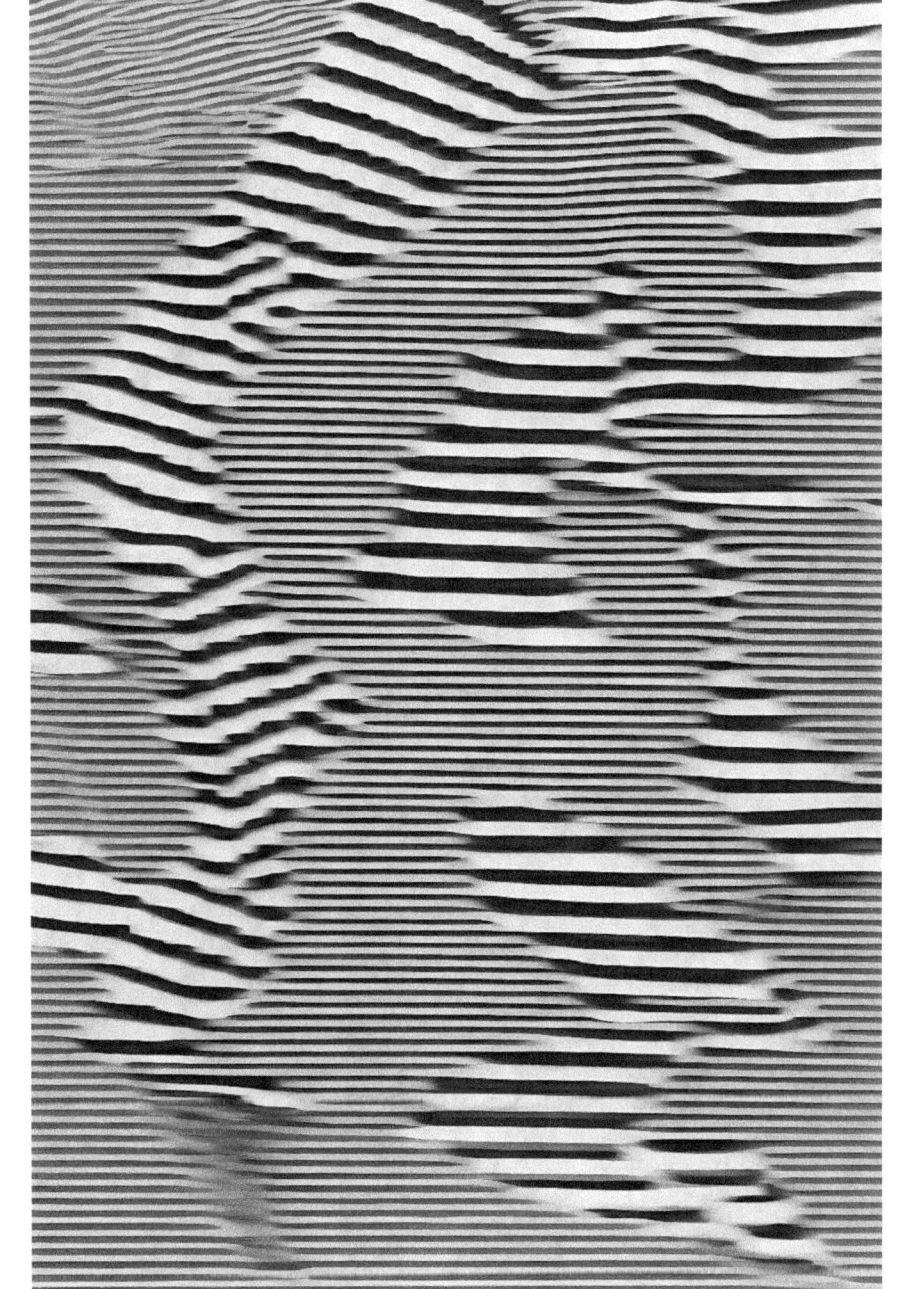

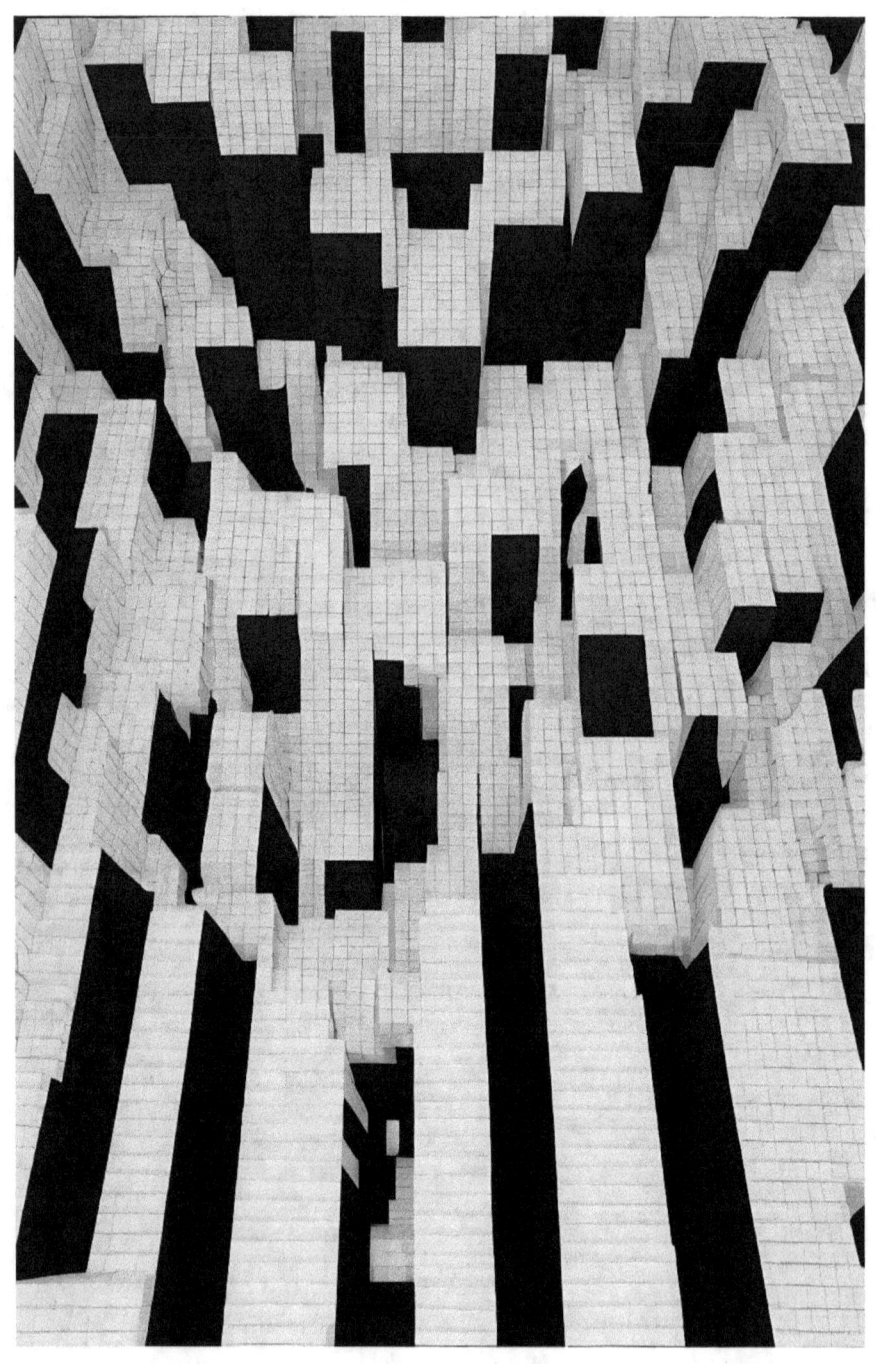

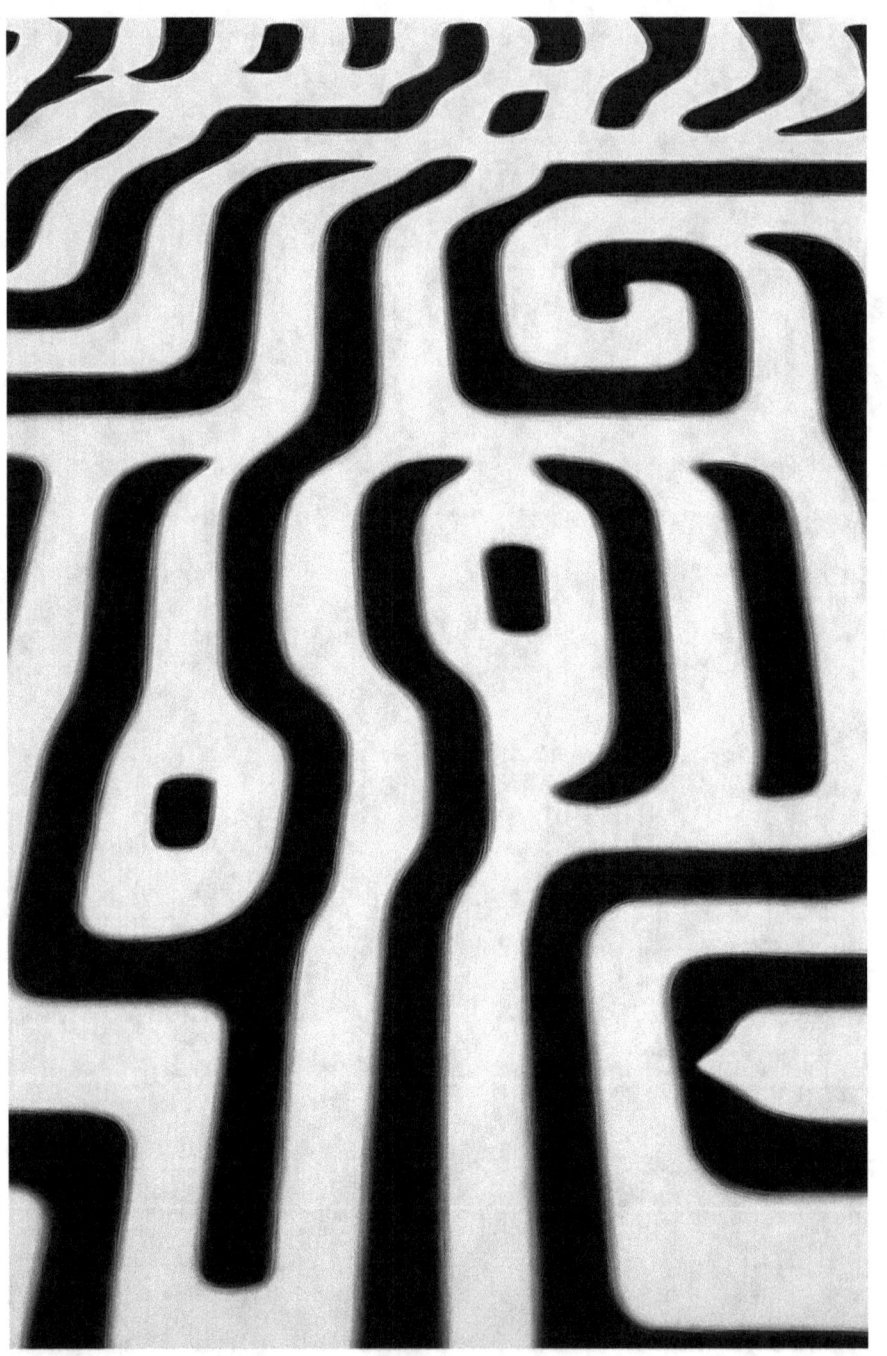

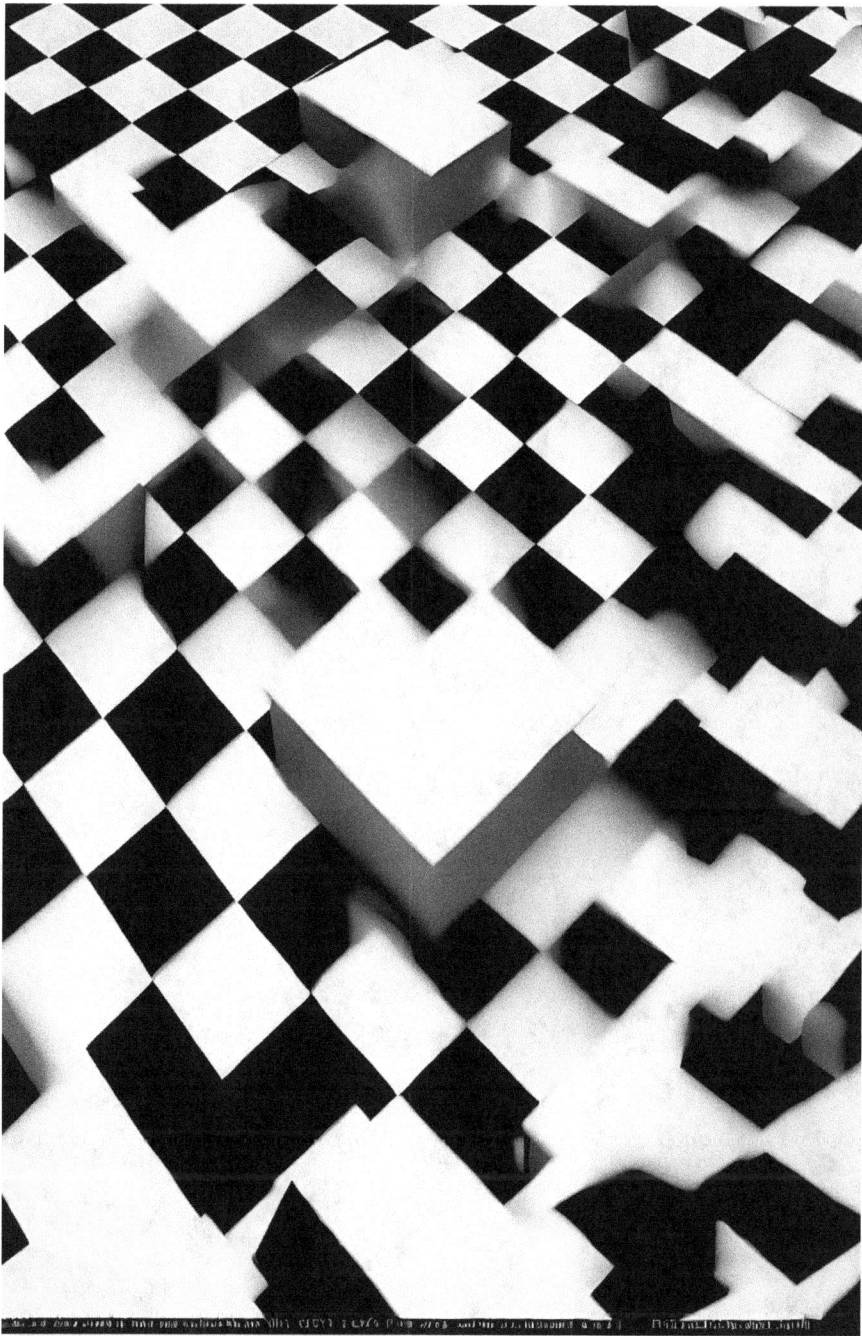

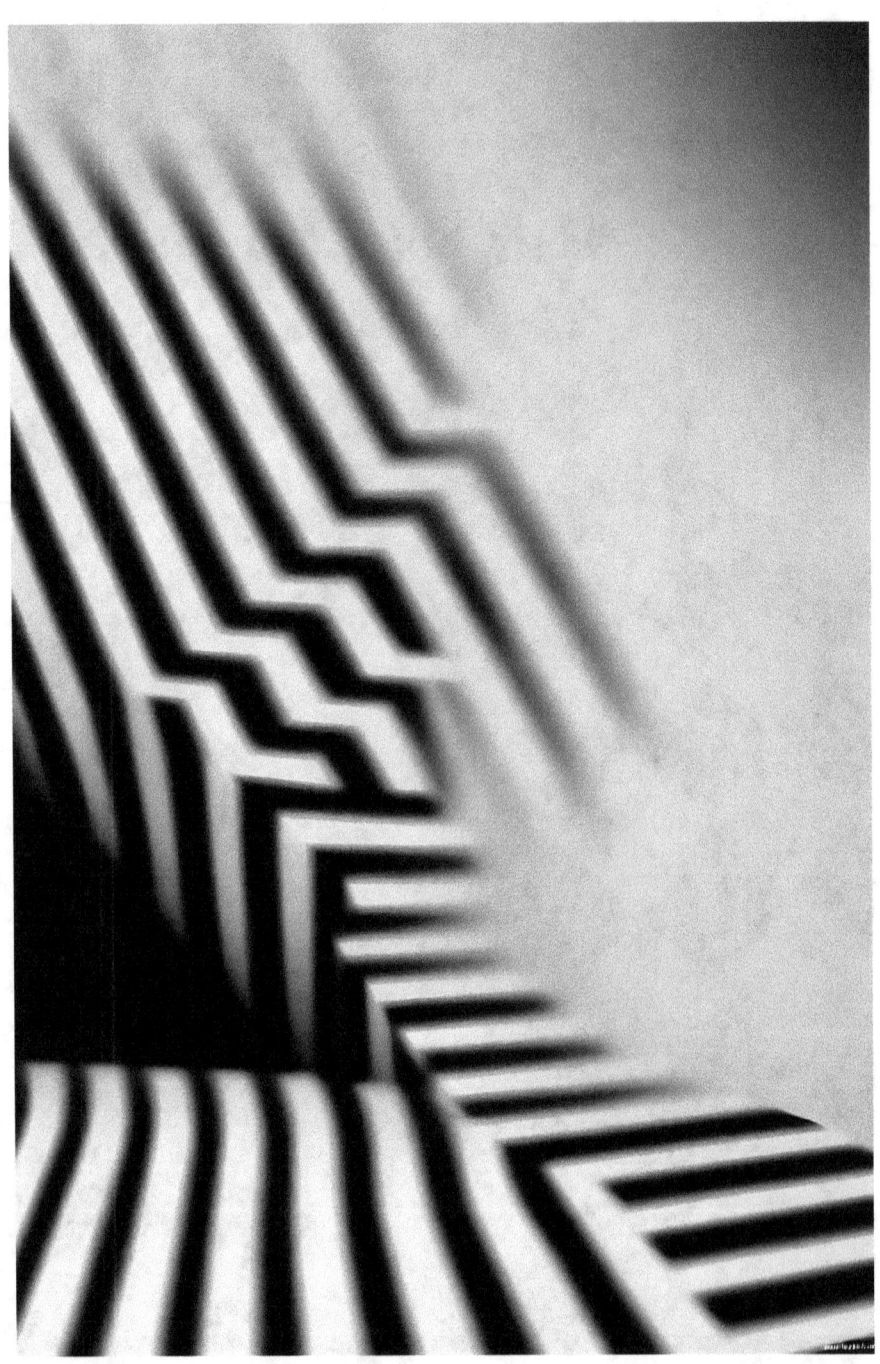

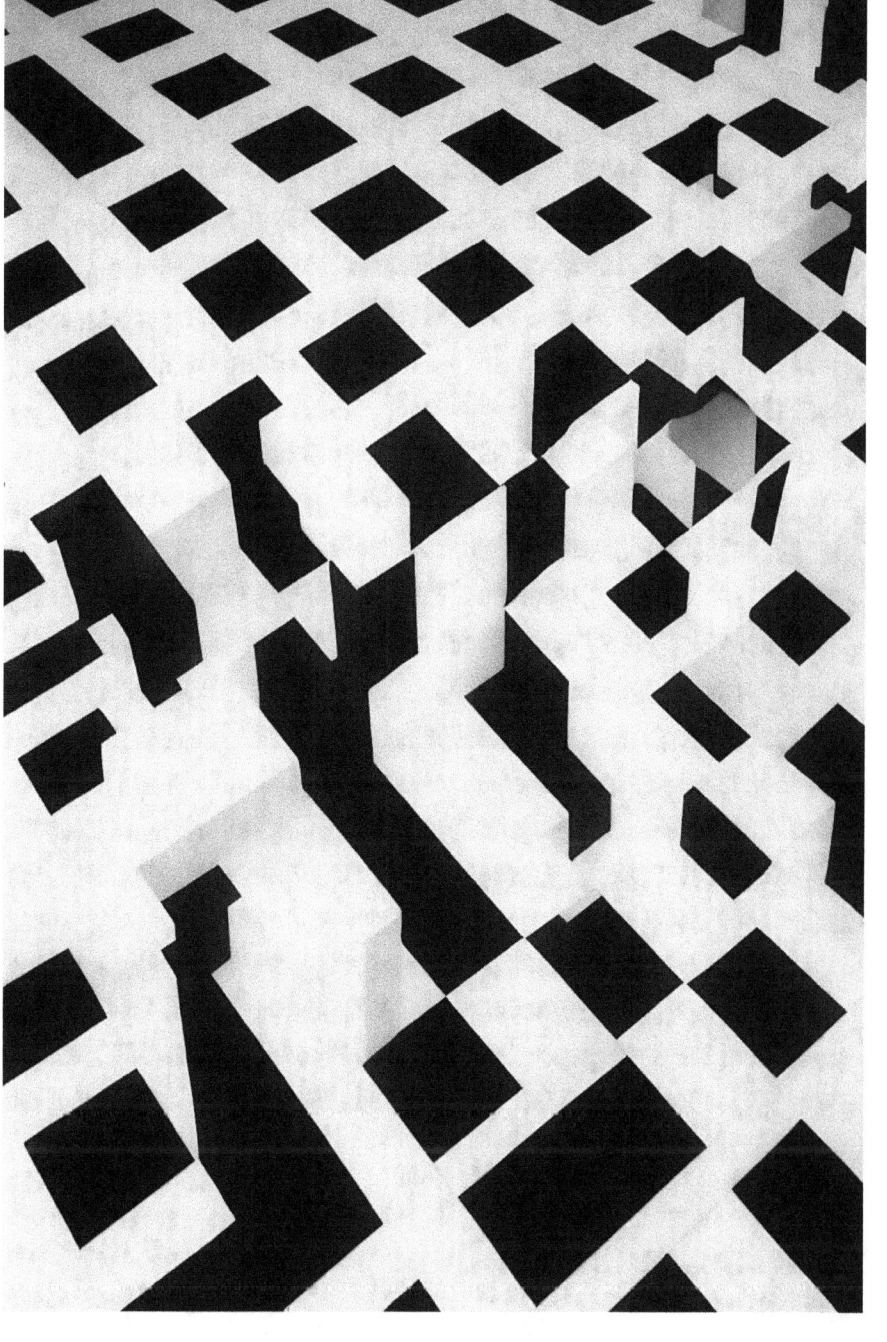

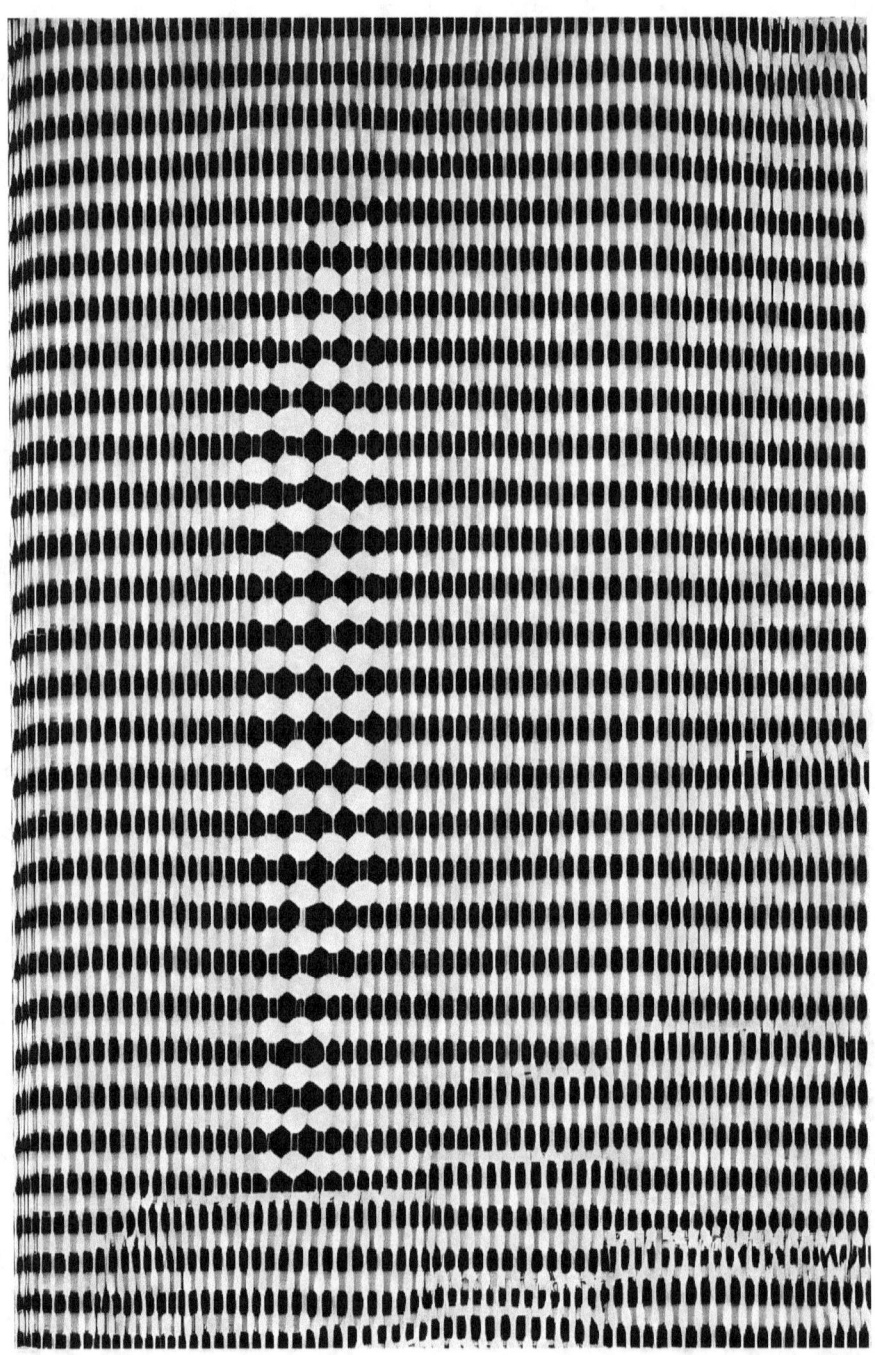

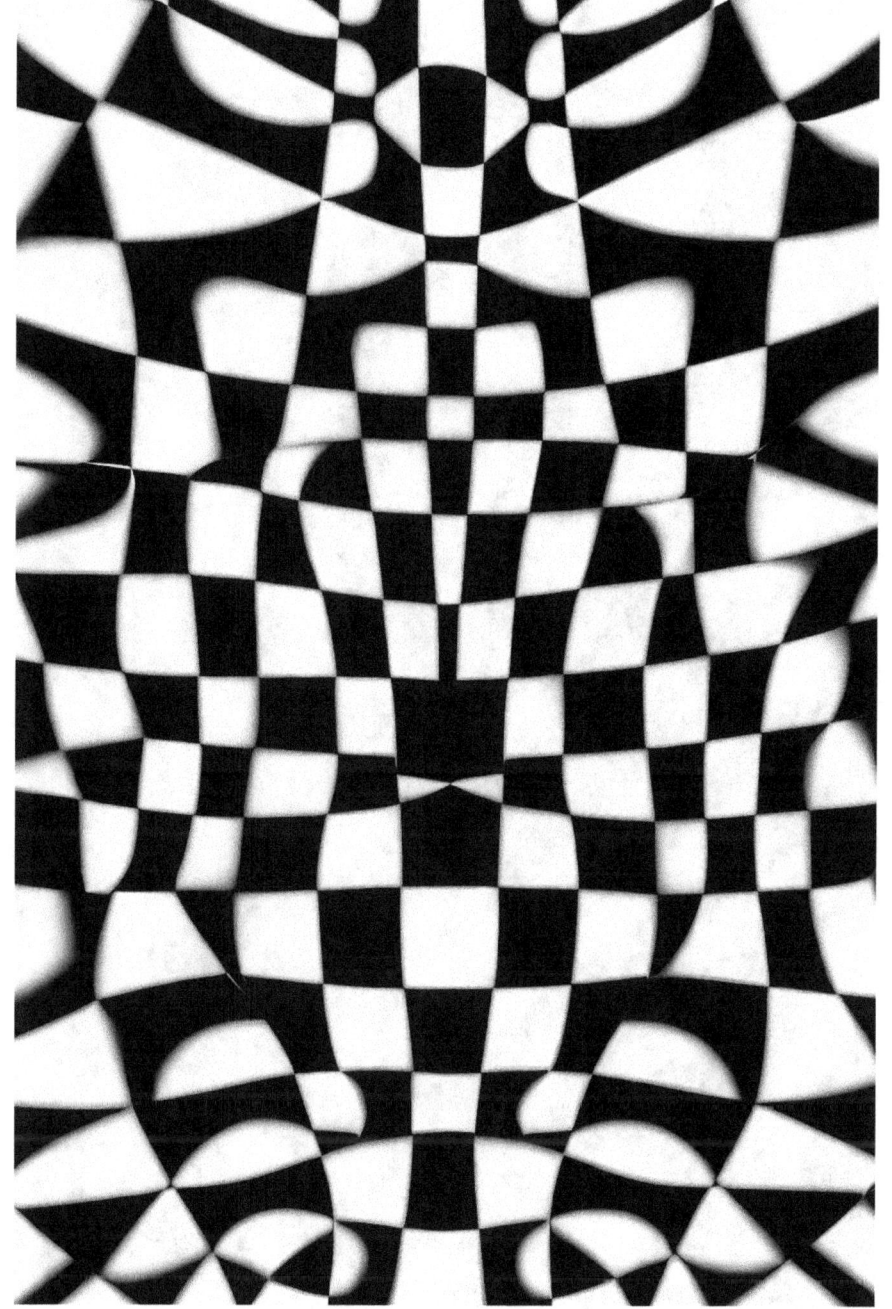

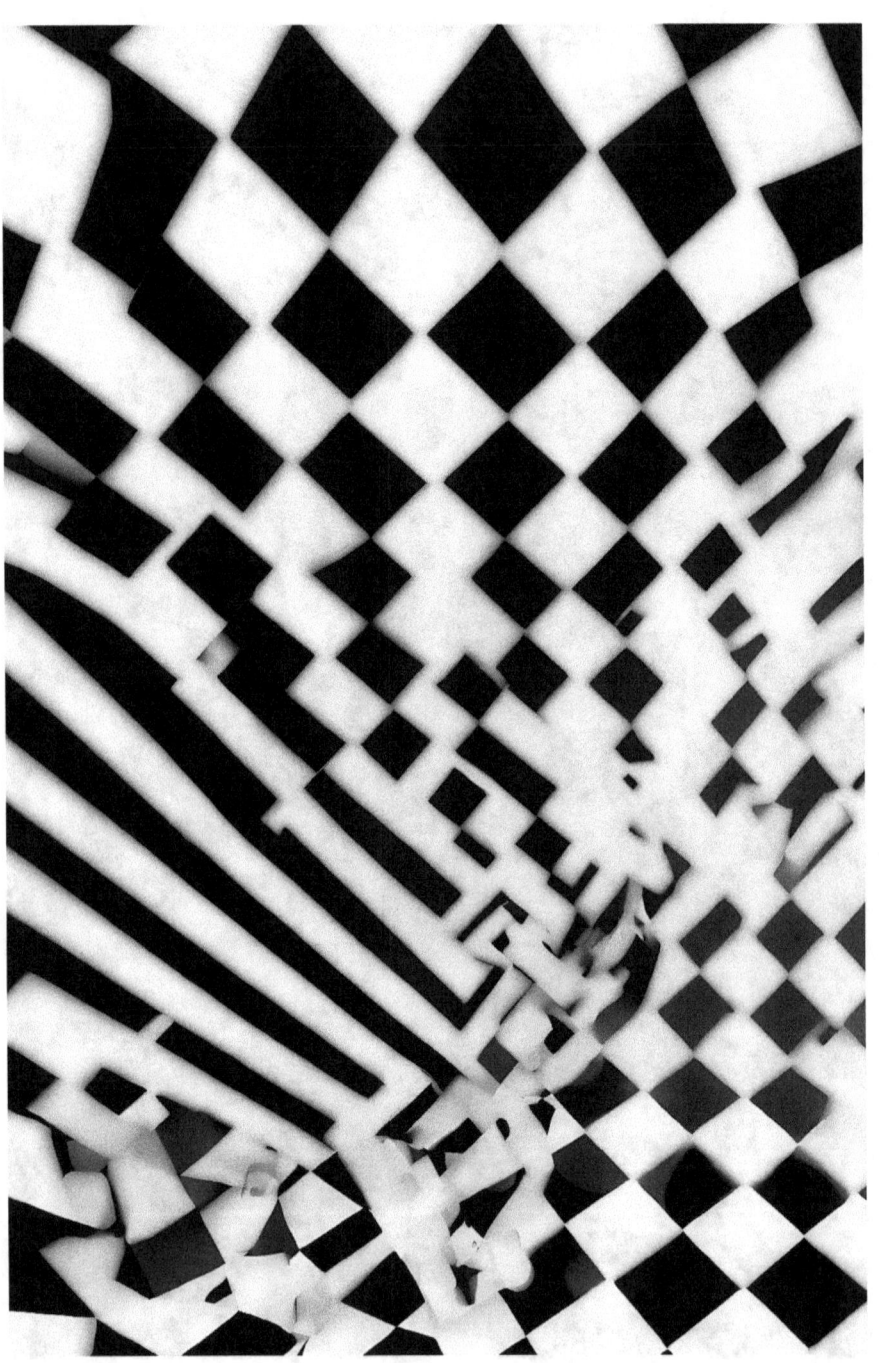

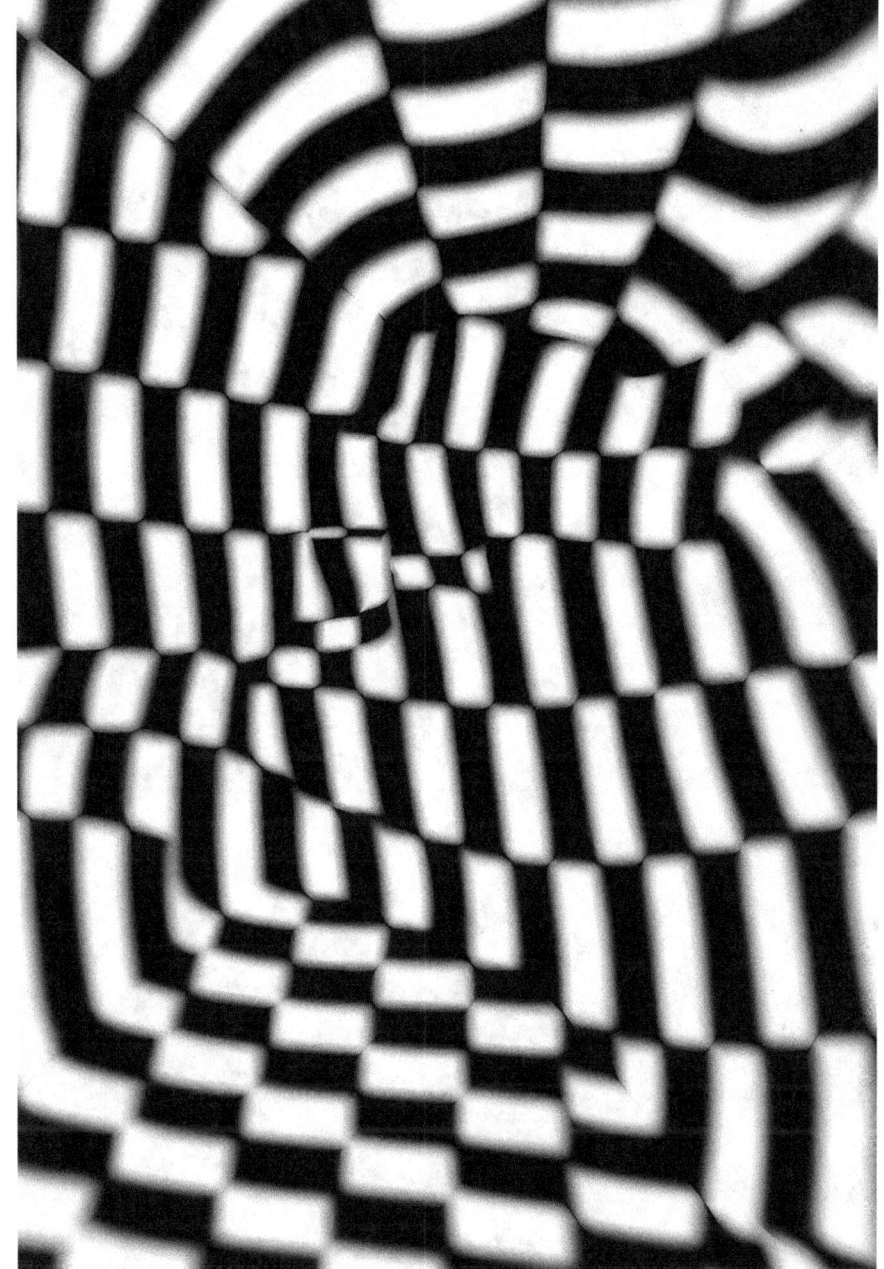

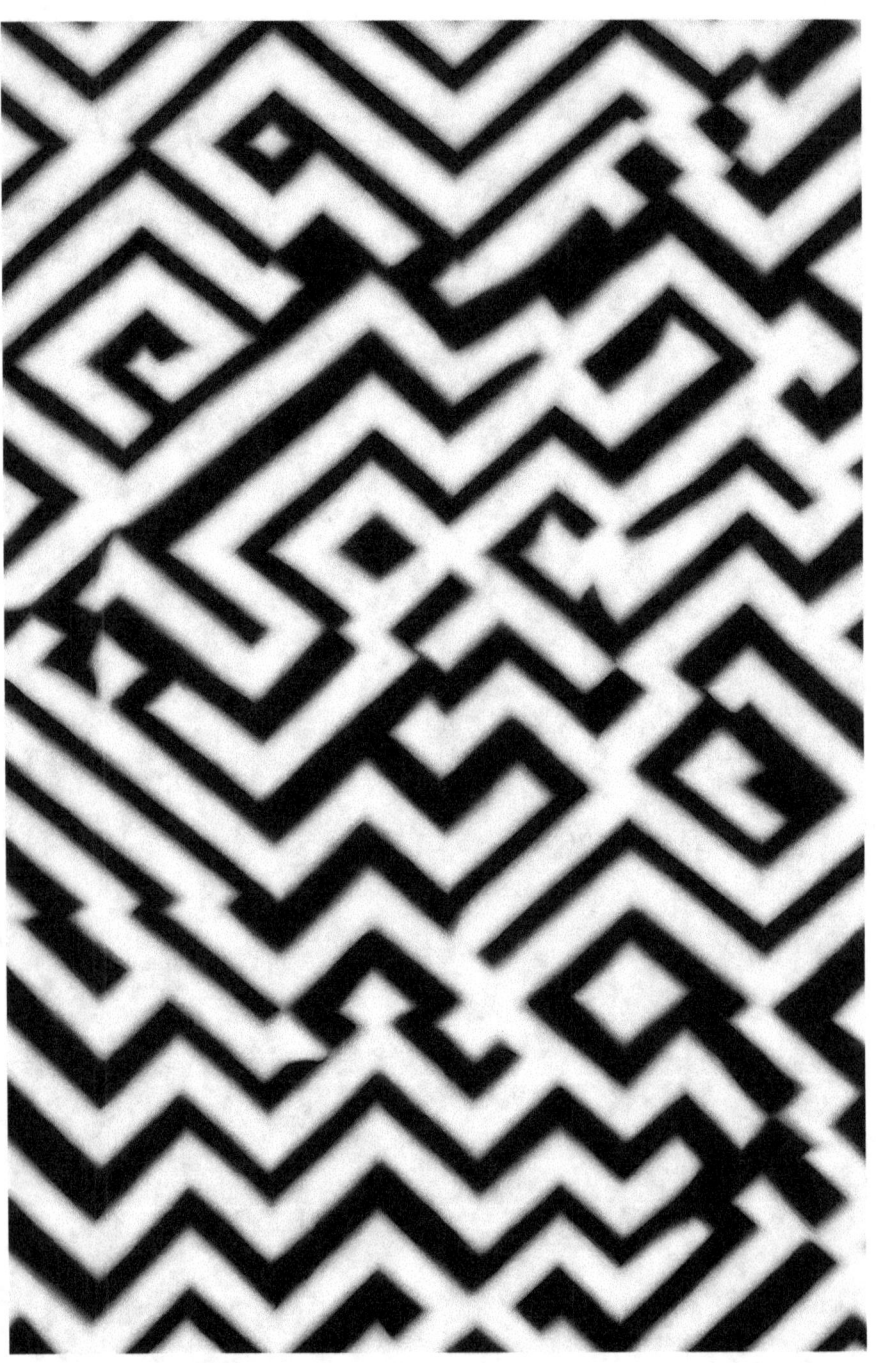

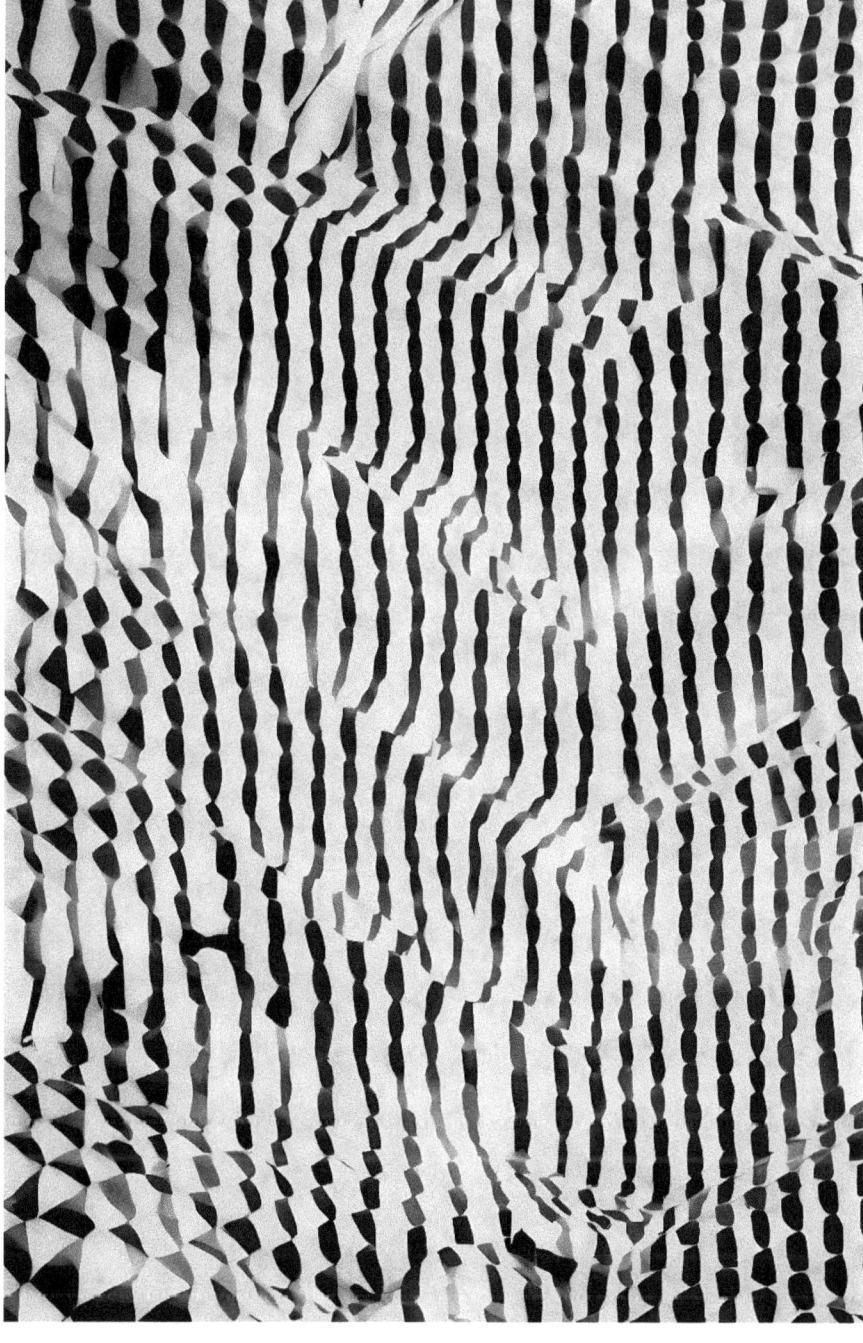

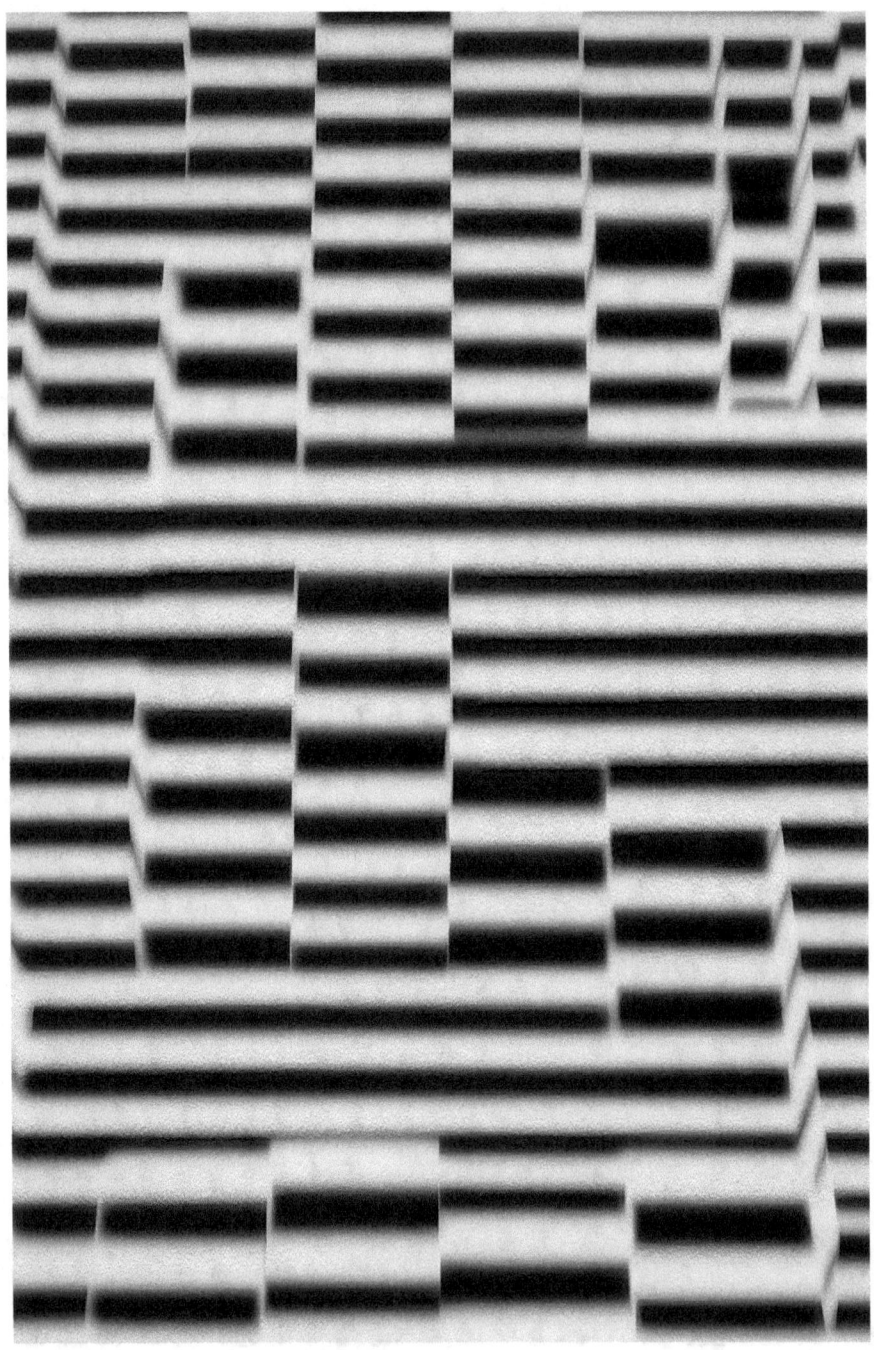

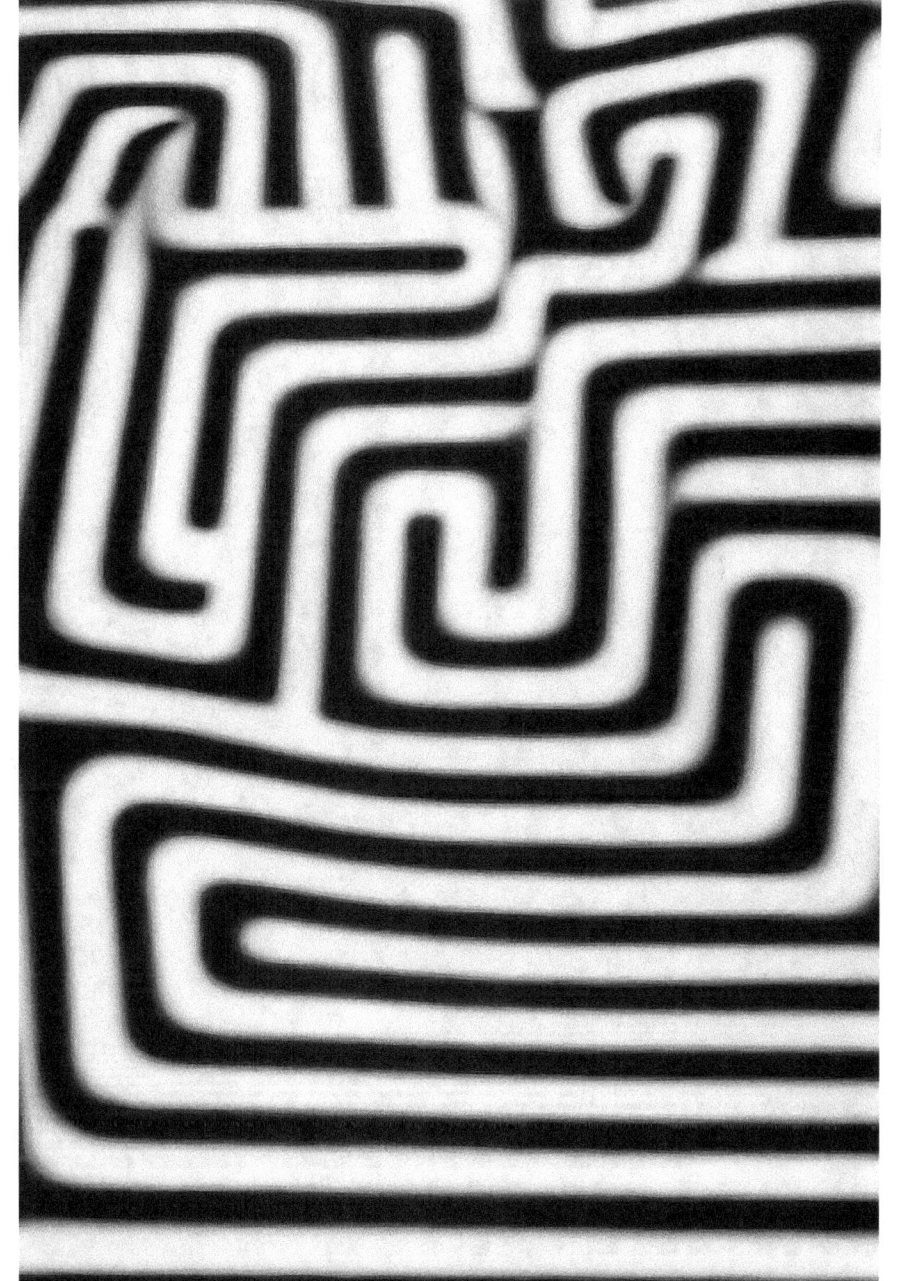

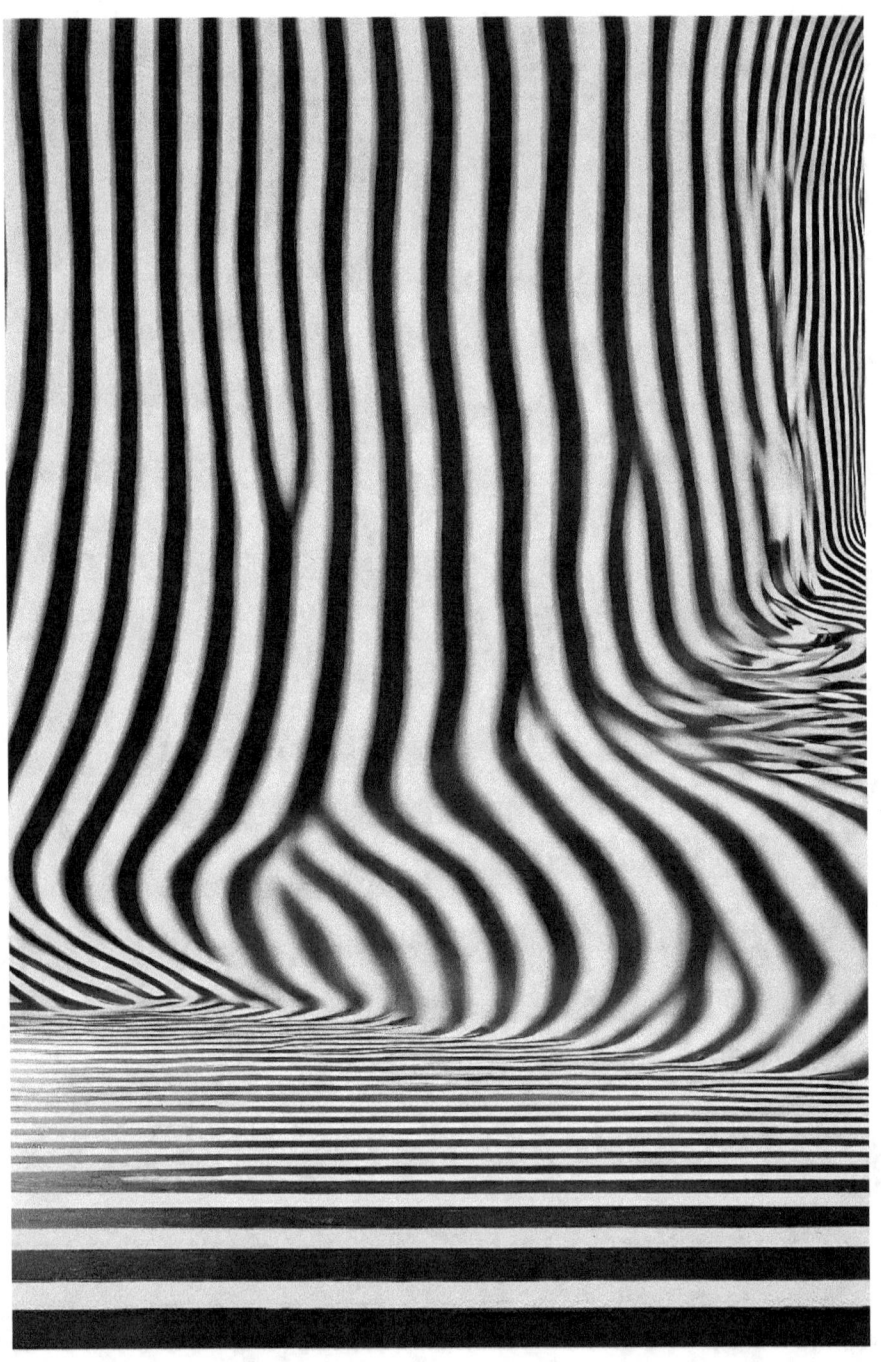

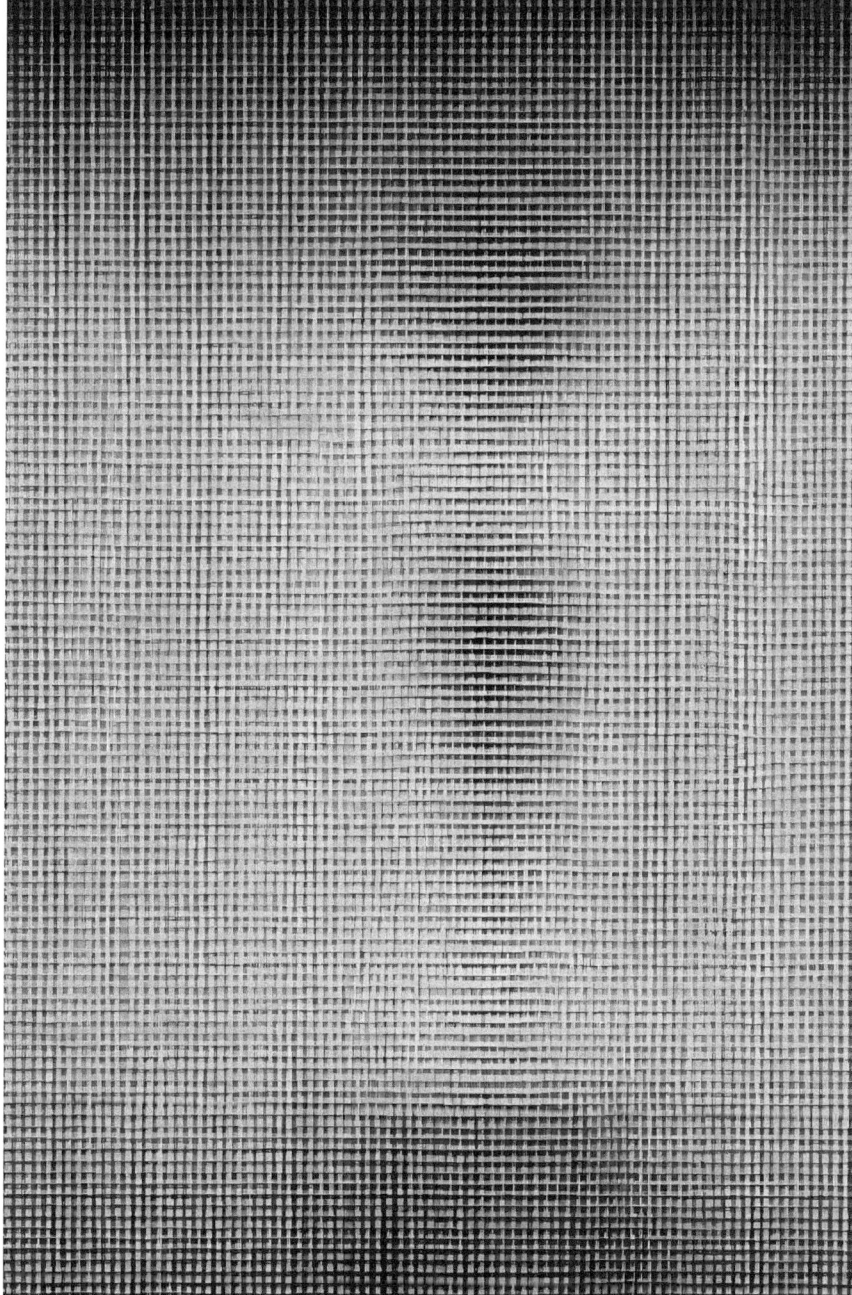

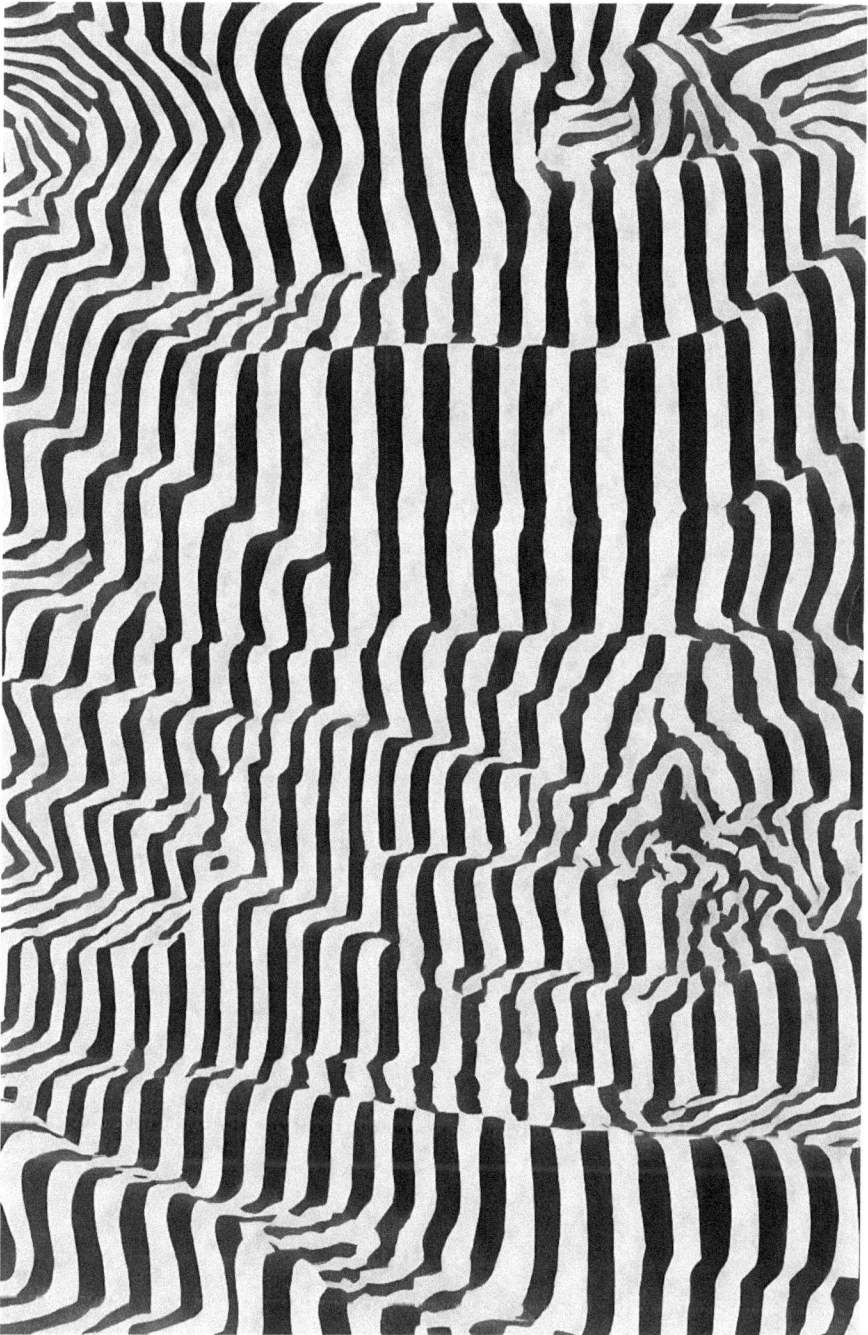

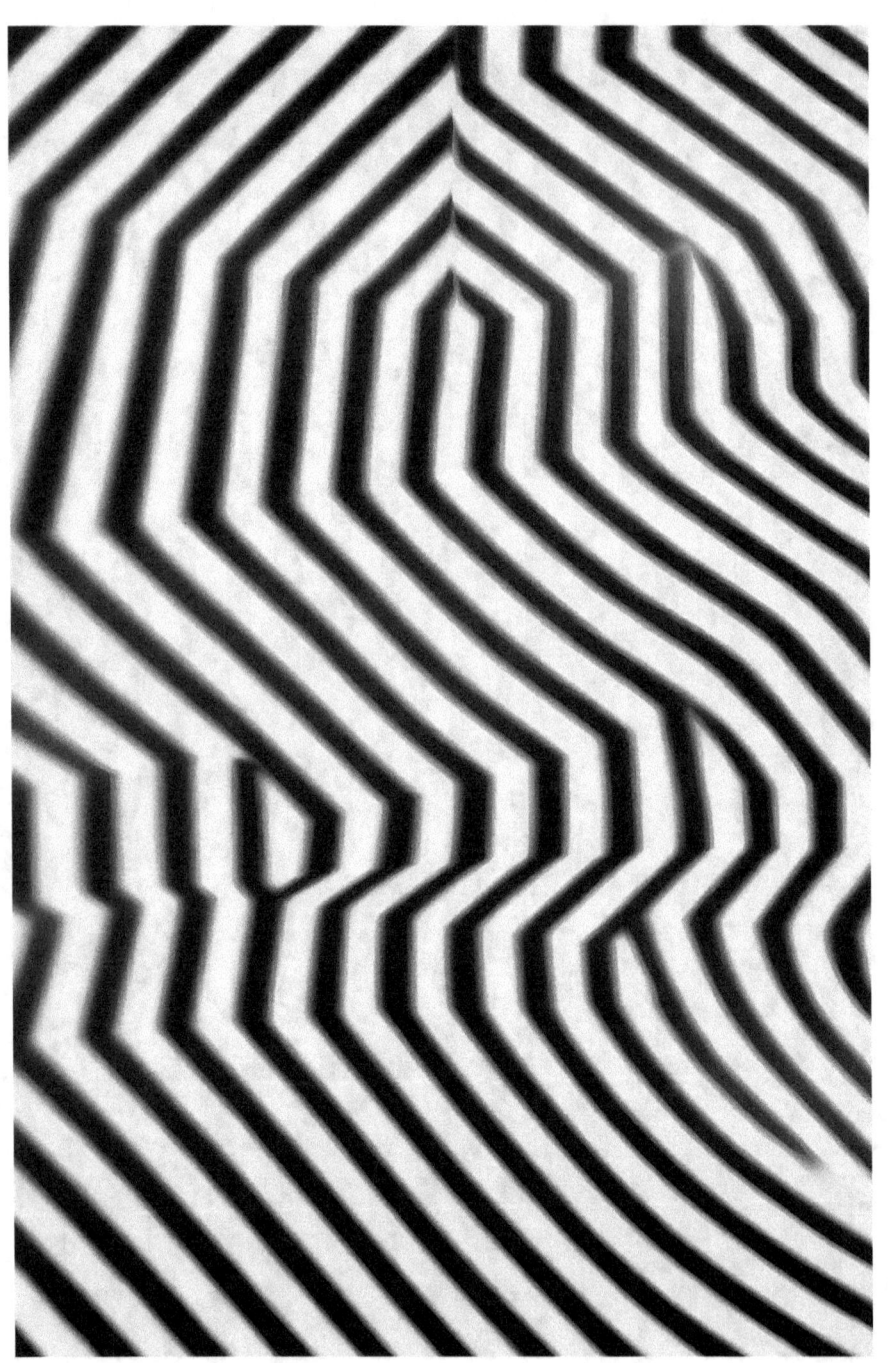

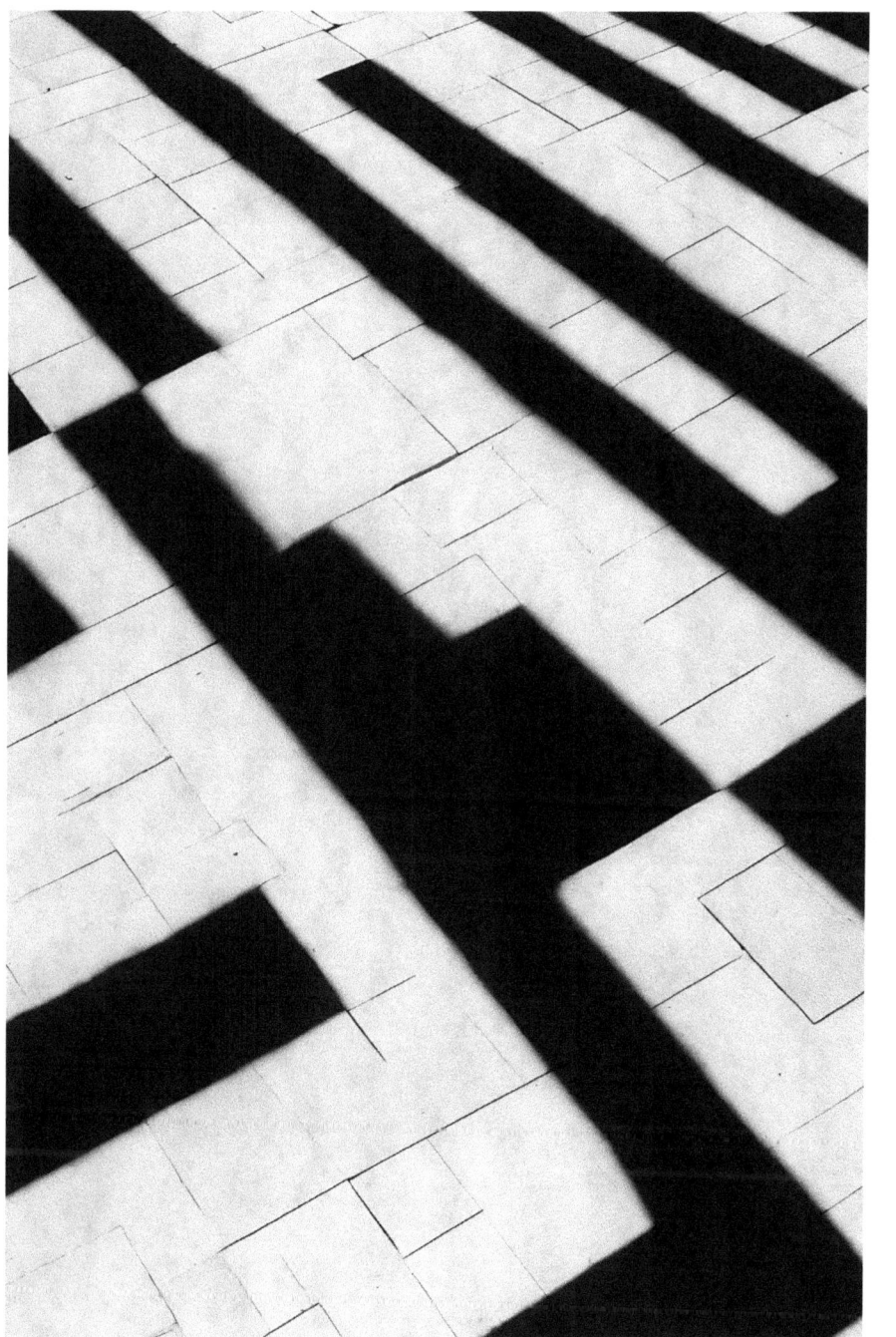

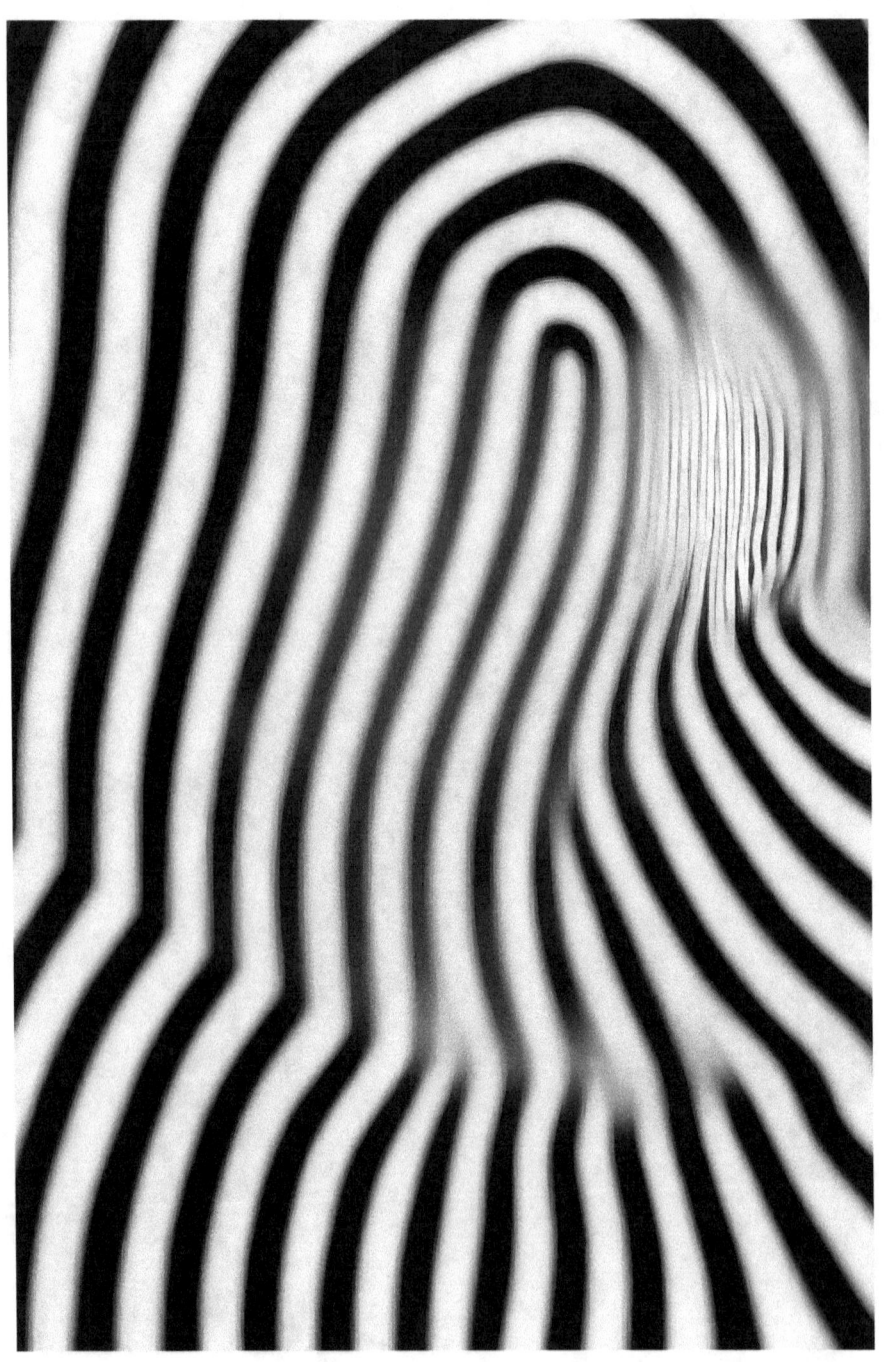

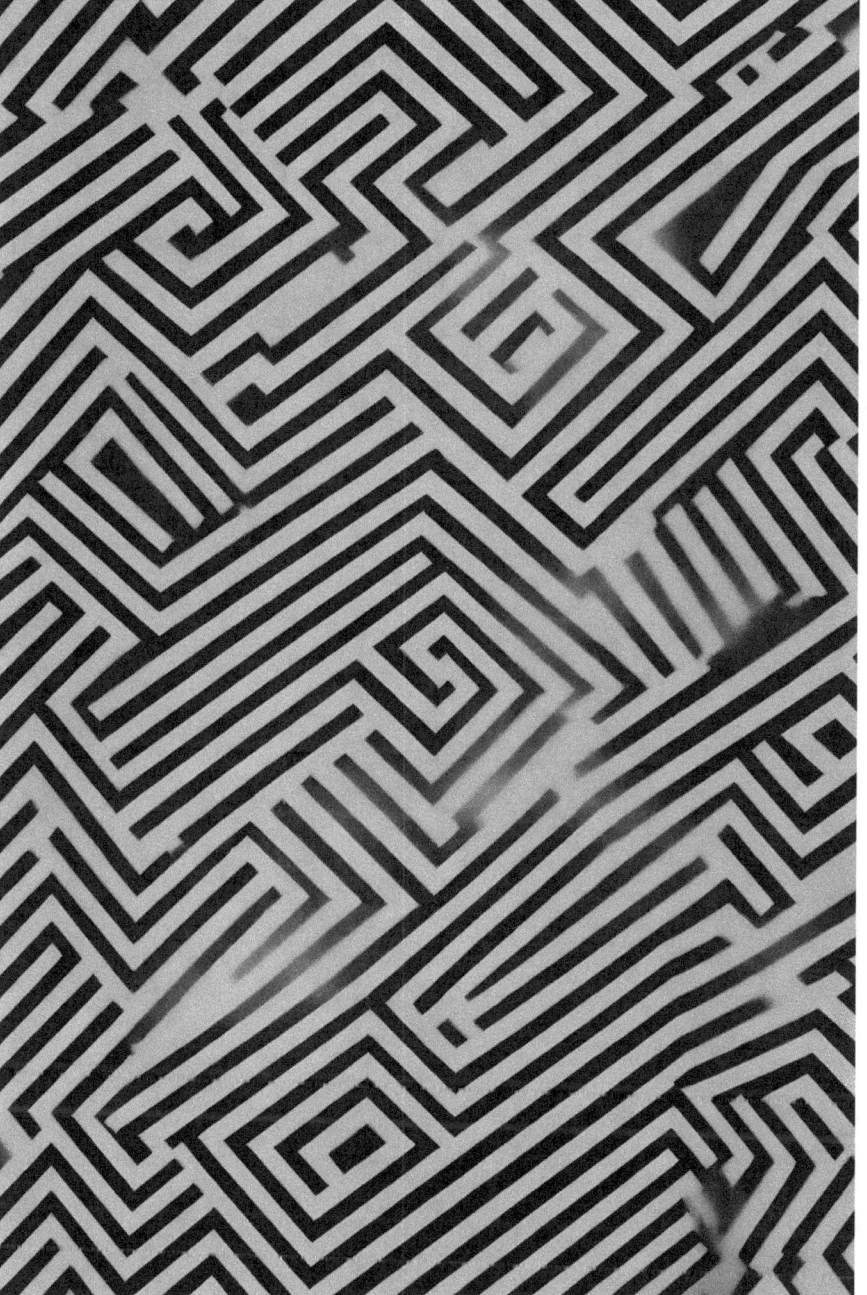

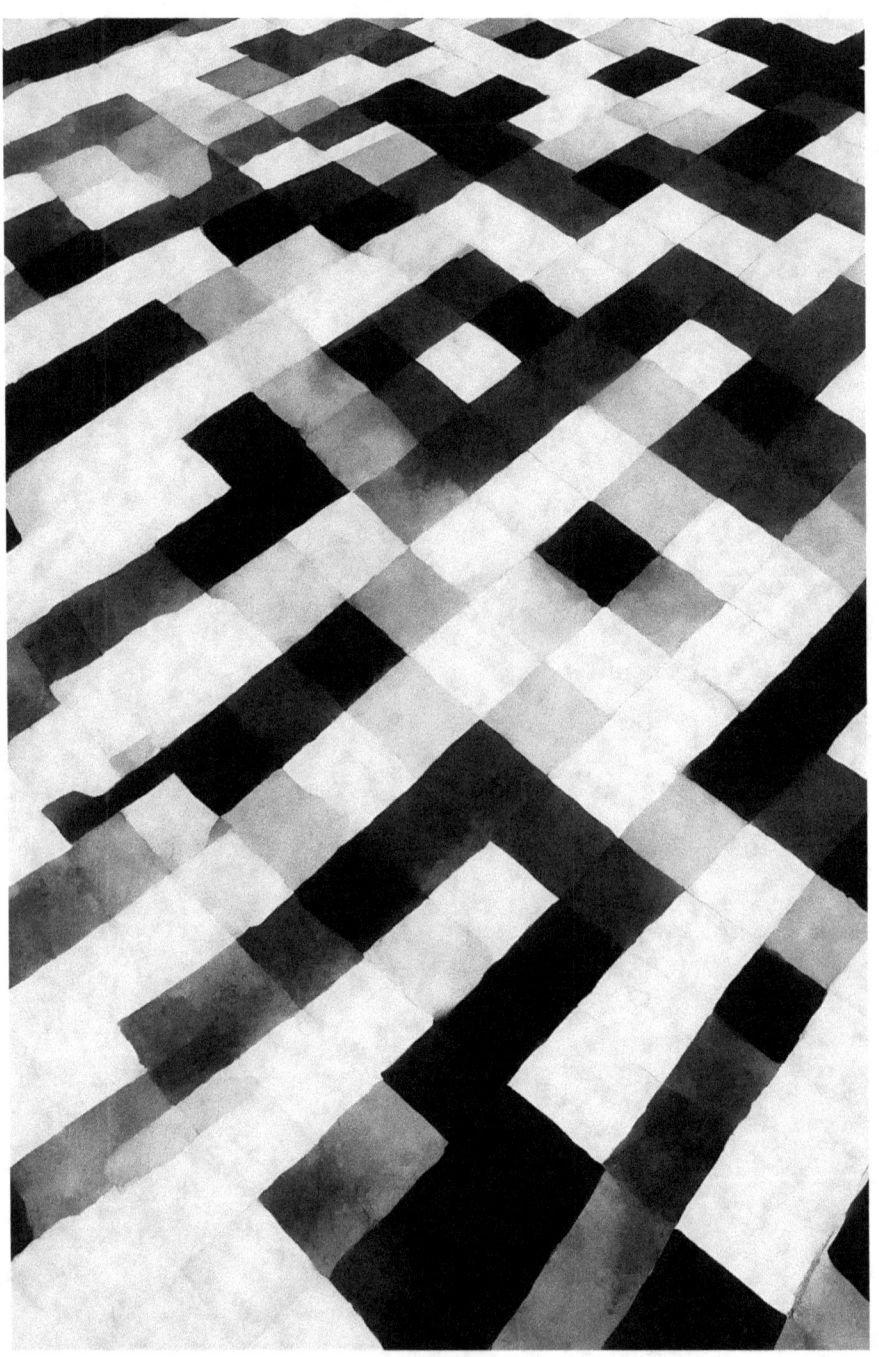

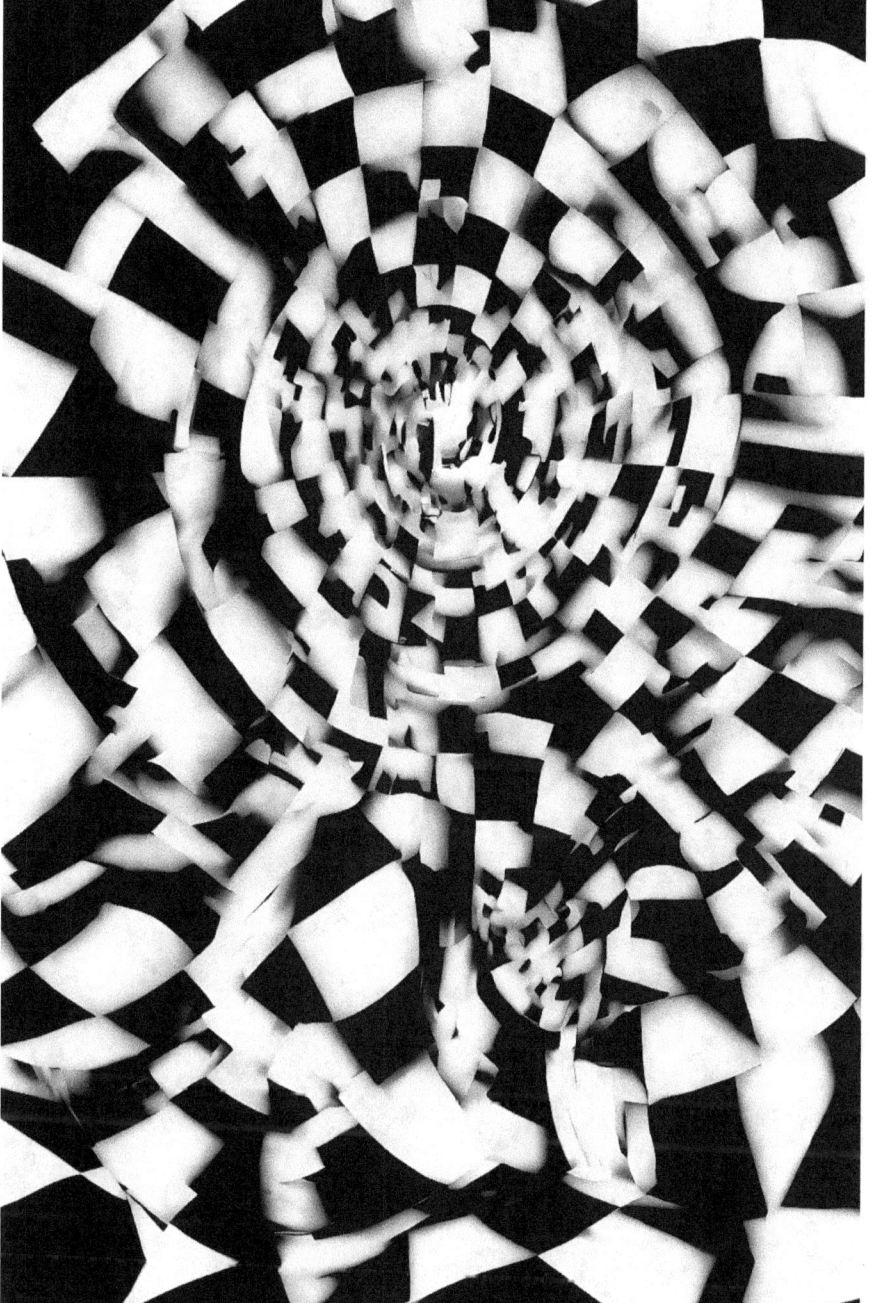

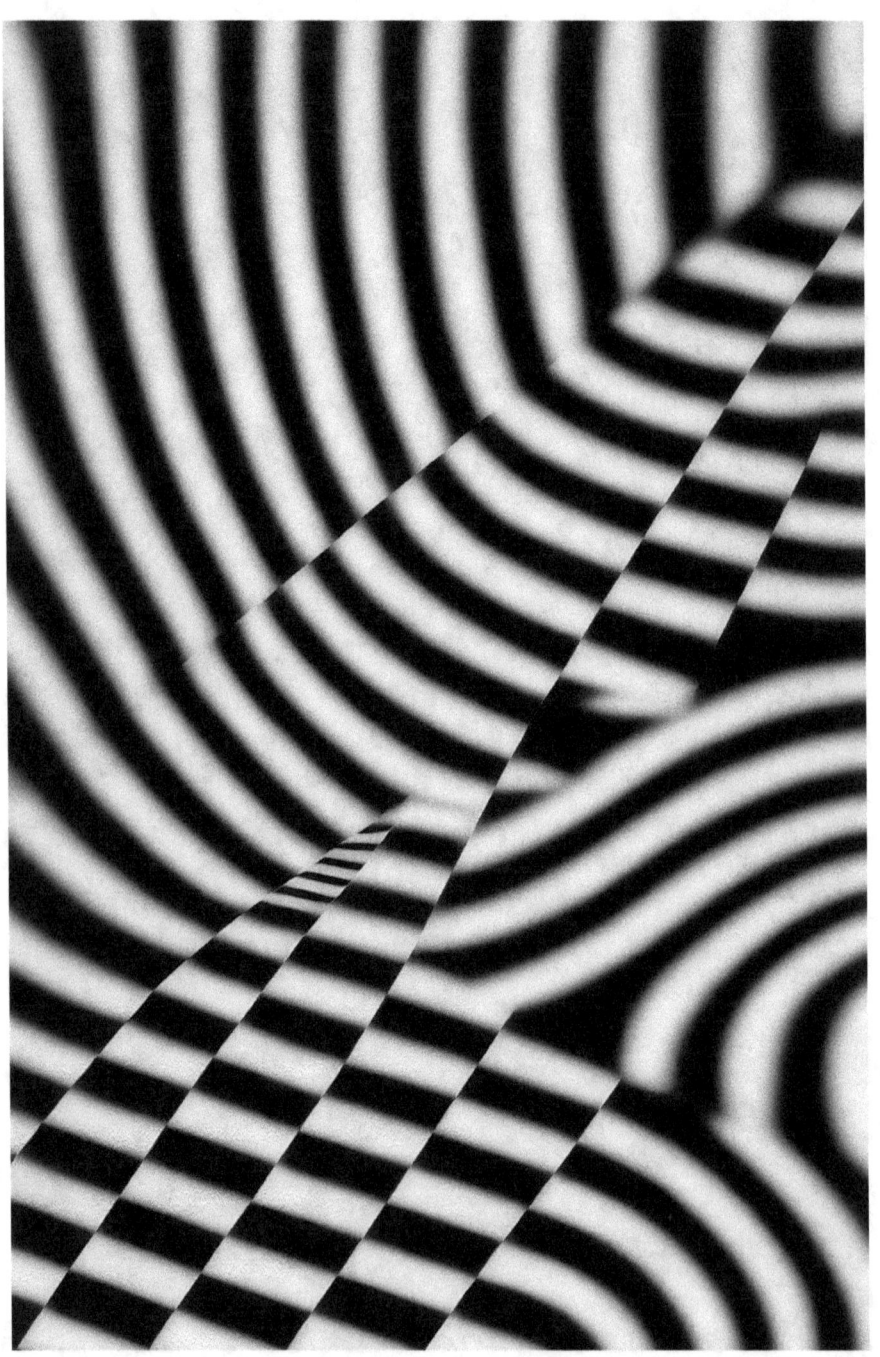

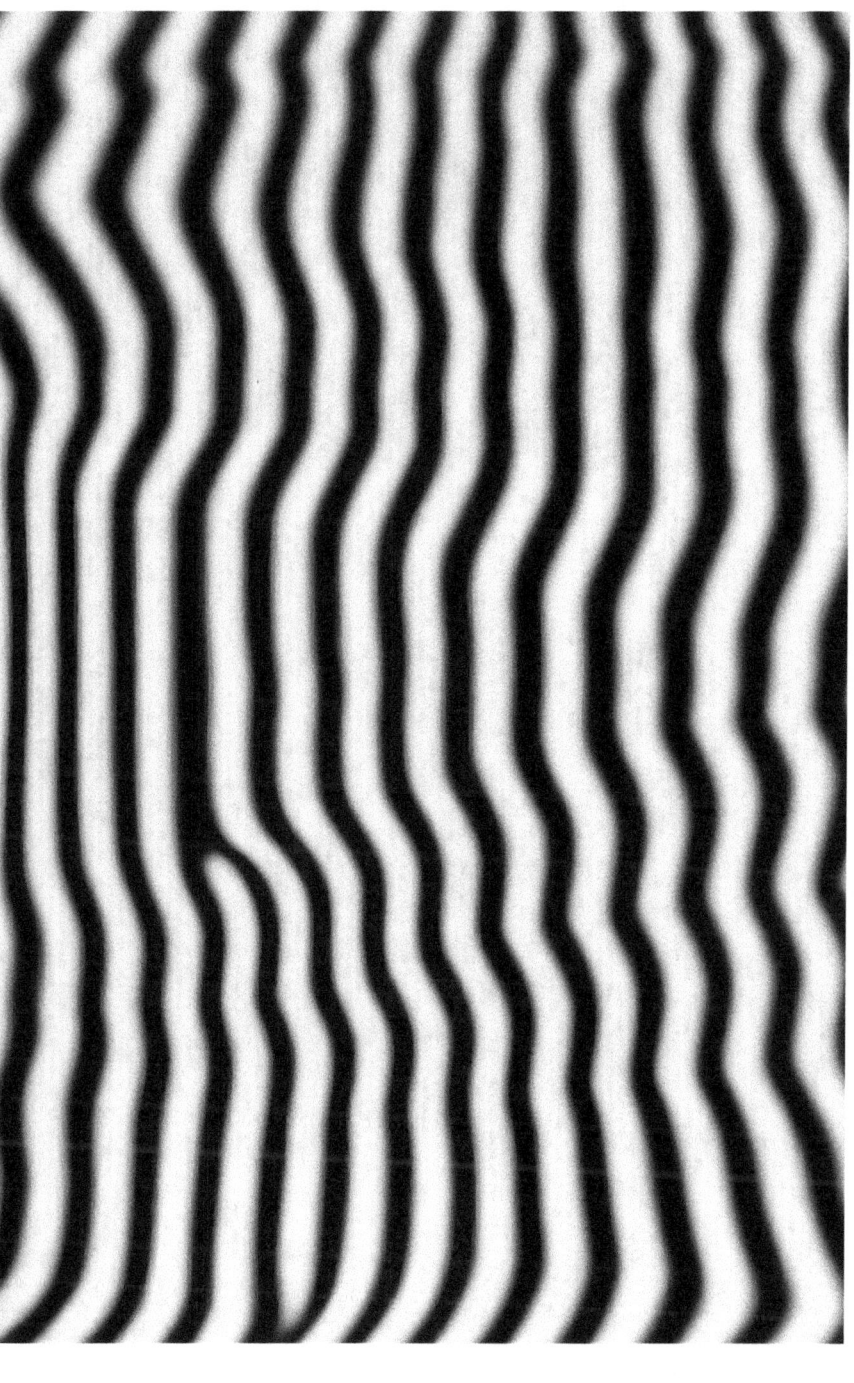

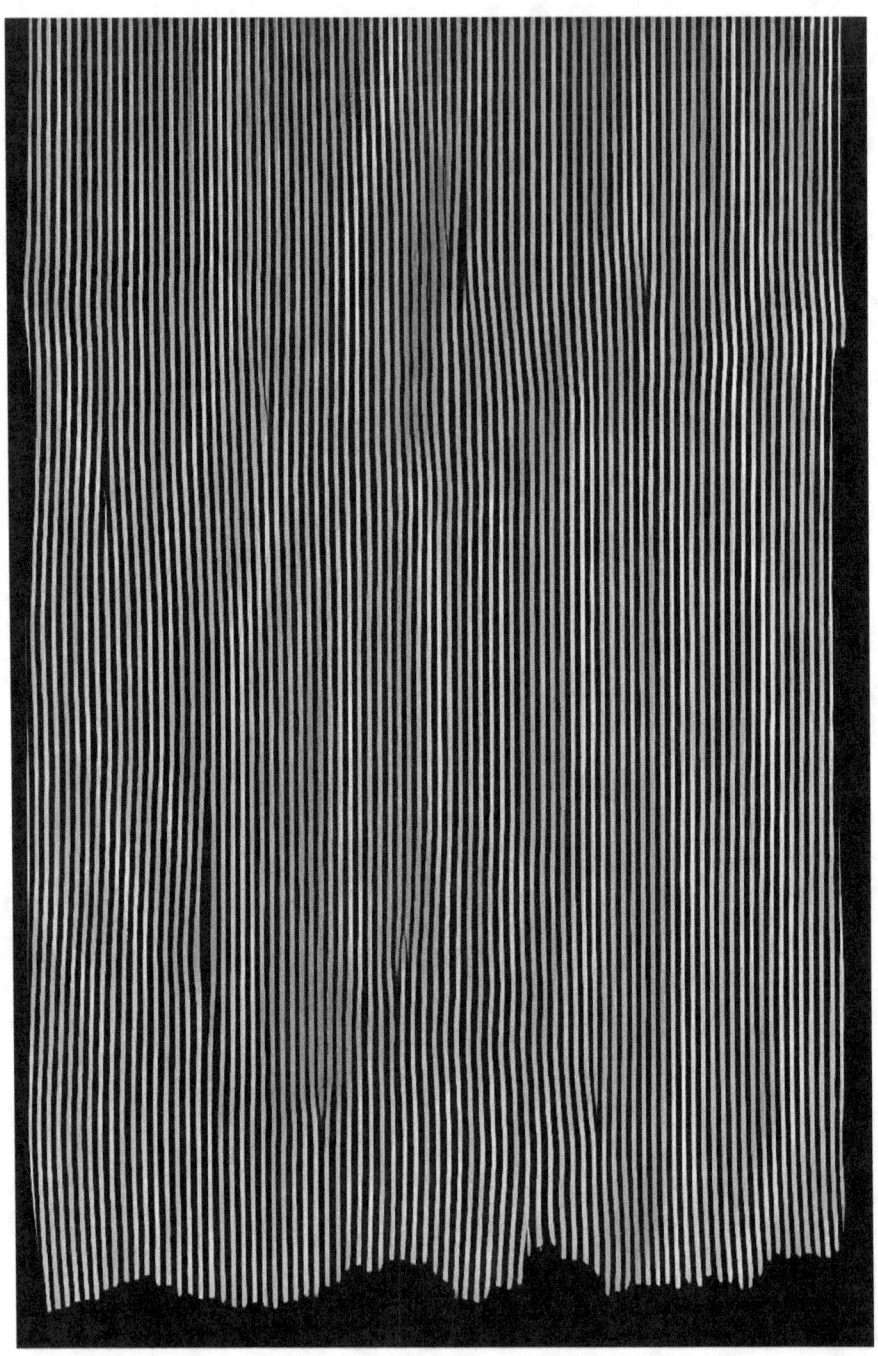

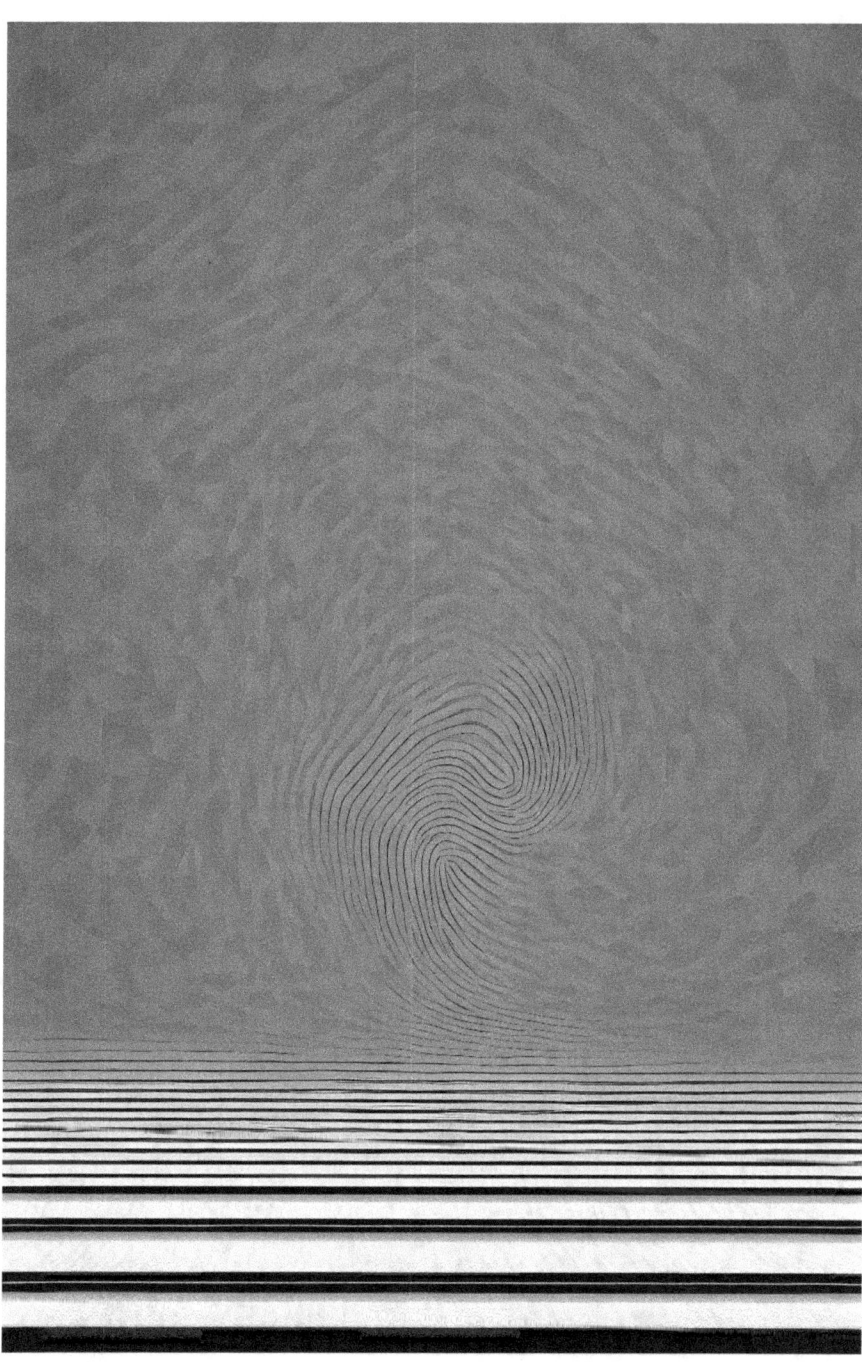

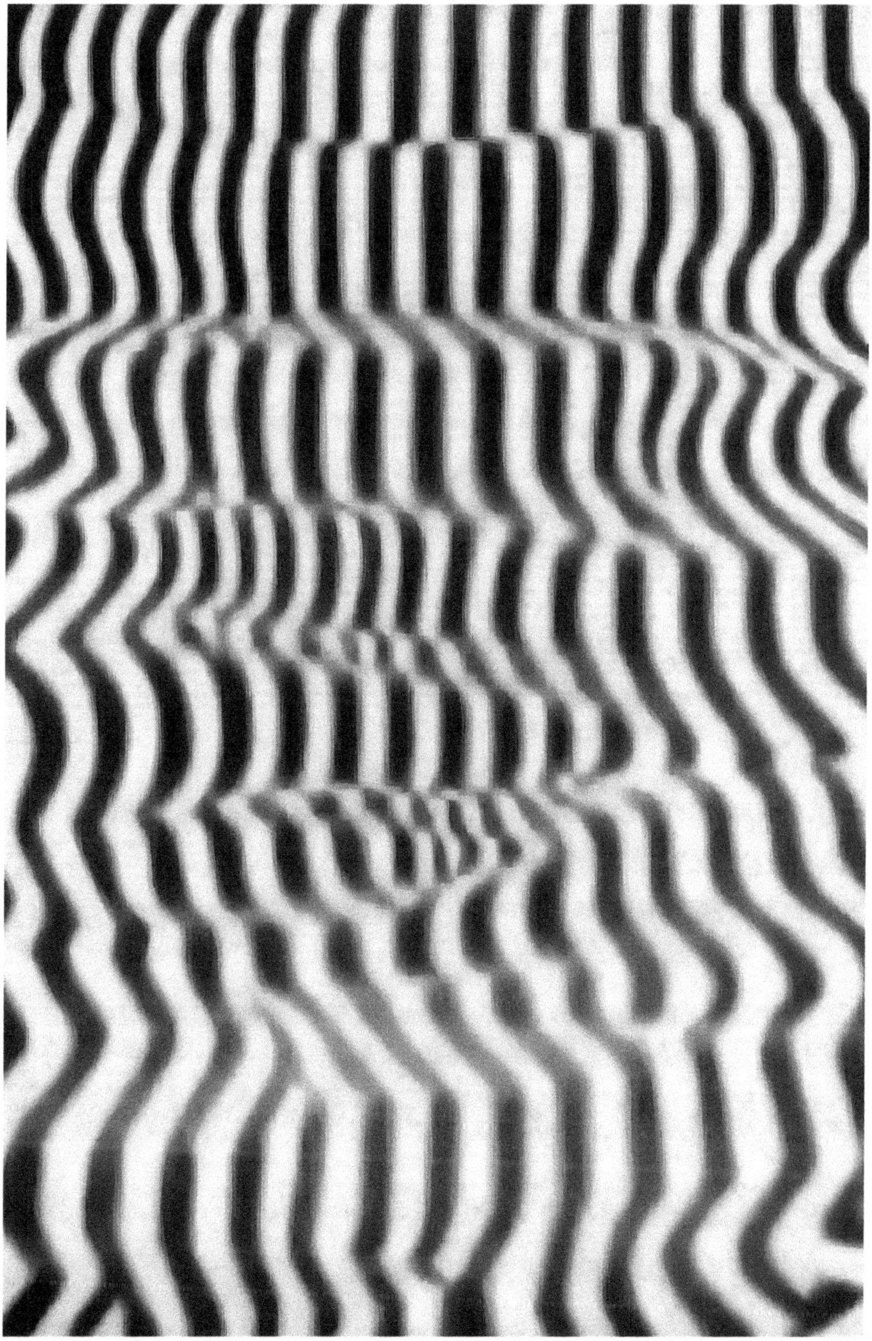

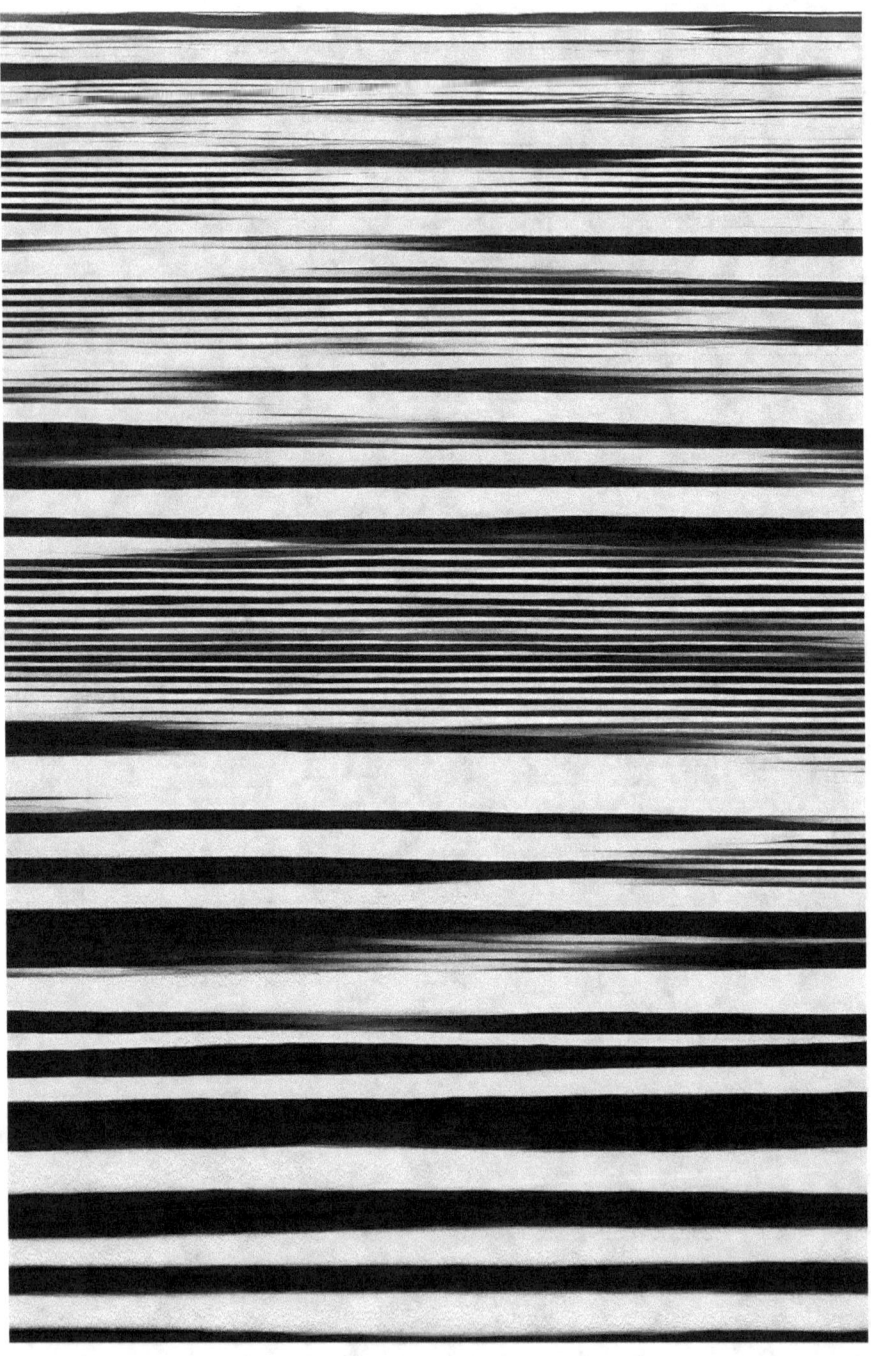